Social Critique by Israel's Eighth-Century Prophets

Social Critique by Israel's Eighth-Century Prophets

Justice and Righteousness in Context

by
Hemchand Gossai

PUBLISHERS
Eugene, Oregon

Wipf and Stock Publishers
199 W 8th Ave, Suite 3
Eugene, OR 97401

Social Critique by Israel's Eighth-Century Prophets
Justice and Righteousness in Context
By Gossai, Hemchand

Copyright©1993 by Gossai, Hemchand

ISBN: 1-59752-630-4

Publication date 5/1/2006
Previously published by Peter Lang Publishing, Inc., 1993

Acknowledgements

Ten years after its initial publication, this new paper edition allows me to thank again those who have been instrumental in giving indelible shape to this volume. I am indeed grateful for the vision and the relentless pursuit of excellence of my doctoral supervisor, Dr. J. D. Martin, and Professor William McKane whose kindness, constancy, and active interest in my work provided a necessary source of encouragement. I am also deeply appreciative of Dr. K. C. Hanson, Editor-in-chief at Wipf & Stock, who invited me to have this volume be republished.

I am indebted to my mother whose life was a living testimony to the ideals of social justice, and to whom I owe such inheritance.

Advent, 2005

For
Shannon, Nathan, Chandra and Zachary

Table of Contents

Index of Abbreviations   x

Introduction   01

Chapter I

I. Background and Meaning of צדק in the Ancient Near East   11

II. צדק in the LXX   19

III. Meaning and Use of צדק in the Old Testament   25

Chapter II

I. Background and Meaning of שפט in the Ancient Near East   91

II. Excursus on Relationship between שפט and דין   108

III. Use of שפט in the Old Testament   120

Chapter III

I. Occurrences of משפט in the Old Testament   141

II. Excursus on משפטים   176

III. משפט and the Functional Locus   178

Chapter IV

I. Salient Features of צדק, שפט, משפט 199

II. Occurrences of צדק and משפט Together in Old Testament Contexts--Exclusive of the Eighth Century Prophets 201

III. The Relationship between צדק and משפט in the Eighth Century Prophets 210

Chapter V

I. The Role and Function of the Eighth Century Prophets 221

Chapter VI

I. צדק, משפט and the Social Critique of the Eighth Century Prophets 243

II. The Intertwining of Socio-Economic and Cultic Expectations 245

III. Elements of Social Critique 251

Conclusion 309

Bibliography 313

Index of Biblical References 335

Index of Abbreviations

ABR	-Australian Biblical Review
AJSL	-American Journal of Semitic Languages
ANET	-Ancient Near Eastern Texts Relating to the Old Testament
ARM	-Archives Royales de Mari
AUSS	-Andrews University Seminary Series
ASTI	-Annual of Swedish Theological Institute
BAR	-Biblical Archaeology Review
BASOR	-Bulletin of the American Society of Oriental Research
BB	-Bible Bhashyam
BHK	-Biblia Hebraica, Ed. Kittel
BHS	-Biblia Hebraica Stuttgartensia
BhTh	-Beiträge zur Historischen Theologie
Bibl	-Biblica
BiLe	-Bibel und Leben
BKAT	-Biblischer Kommentar Altes Testament
BM	-Beth Mikra
BTF	-Bangalore Theological Forum
BTPT	-Bijdragen. Tijdschrift voor Philosophie en Theologie
BZ	-Biblische Zeitschrift
BZAW	-Beihefte zur Zeitschrift für die Alttestamentliche Wissenschaft
CAD	-The Assyrian Dictionary, Chicago
CBC	-Cambridge Bible Commentary
CBQ	-Catholic Biblical Quarterly
CIS	-Corpus Inscriptionum Semiticarum
CTM	-Currents in Theology and Mission
CuW	-Christentum und Wissenschaft
EI	-Eretz-Israel
ERT	-Evangelical Review of Theology
ET	-Evangelische Theologie

ETR	-Études Théologiques et Religieuses
HTR	-Harvard Theological Review
HUCA	-Hebrew Union College Annual
ICC	-International Critical Commentary
IDB	-Interpreters Dictionary of the Bible
Interp	-Interpretation
IOS	-Israel Oriental Society
JAAR	-Journal of the American Academy of Religion
JAOS	-Journal of the American Oriental Society
JB	-Jerusalem Bible
JBL	-Journal of Biblical Literature
JDTh	-Jahrbücher für Deutsche Theologie
JNES	-Journal of Near Eastern Studies
JR	-Journal of Religion
JSOT	-Journal for the Study of the Old Testament
JSOTS	-Journal for the Study of the Old Testament, Supplement Series
JSS	-Journal of Semitic Studies
JTS	-Journal of Theological Studies
KJV	-King James Version of the Bible
KuD	-Kerygma und Dogma
LBS	-Library of Biblical Studies
LXX	-Septuagint
MO	-Masses Ouvrière
MT	-Massoretic Text
NCBC	-New Century Bible Commentary
NEB	-New English Bible
NICOT	-New International Critical Commentary on the Old Testament
OA	-Oriens Antiquus
OTL	-Old Testament Library
OTS	-Oudtestamentische Studiën
OTWSA	-Die Ou Testamentiese Werkgemeenskap in Suid-Afrika
PEQ	-Palestine Exploration Quarterly

PRS	-Perspectives in Religious Studies
RAI	-Rencontre Assyriologique Internationale
RB	-Revue Biblique
RCB	-Revista de Cultura Biblica
RE	-Review and Expositior
NRSV	-New Revised Standard Version
SBFLA	-Studii Biblici Franciscani Liber Anuus
SBLMS	-Society of Biblical Literature, Monograph Series
SBT	-Studies in Biblical Theology
Sci Esprit	-Science et Esprit
SEÅ	-Svensk Exegetisk Årsbok
SJT	-Scottish Journal of Theology
SNTSMS	-Society for New Testament Studies, Monograph Series
SVT	-Supplements to Vetus Testamentum
SWBAS	-Social World of Biblical Antiquity Series
SWJT	-Southwestern Journal of Theology
TBT	-The Bible Today
TDNT	-The Theological Dictionary of the New Testament
TGUOS	-Transactions of Glasgow University Oriental Society
Th.Lz	-Theologische Literaturzeitung
TPR	-The Presbyterian Review
TSSI	-Textbook of Syrian Semitic Inscriptions
UF	-Ugarit-Forschungen
Ug	-Ugaritica
Vox Ev	-Vox Evangelica
VT	-Vetus Testamentum
WBC	Word Biblical Commentary
ZAW	-Zeitschrift für die Alttestamentliche Wissenschaft

Introduction

There have been few recent monographs which have studied in detail the message of the Eighth Century prophets on social justice. Moreover, there is no study which to my knowledge has systematically examined the use of צדק and משפט in the message of these prophets in relation to their social critique. This study endeavors to do just this, and in so doing, will examine the use of *ṣdq* and *špṭ* in the Ancient Near East and use this as a basis for an investigation of צדק and משפט in the Old Testament. The objective here is to establish the basic meanings and nuances of these concepts before studying their use in the context of the Eighth Century prophets. However, before outlining the manner in which this will be undertaken, it is essential to have a brief overview of the main literature written on צדק, משפט, and social justice in the Eighth Century prophets.

One of the earliest studies of the concept of צדק was done by Ludwig Diestel.[1] The primary orientation of Diestel's work is etymological, and using this method, he concludes that צדק depicts the physical image of a straight line. This idea of the "straight line" represents for Diestel the notion of an objective norm. Thus, צדק as "norm" was launched on its course. While Diestel's study set the basis for study of צדק, it is the work of Emil Kautzsch[2] which became the standard by which other studies were gauged. Even though Kautzsch adopts many of the findings of Diestel, he does not begin his examination of צדק on an etymological principle. Rather, he attempts to find the general meaning and function of צדק in the Old Testament through an exhaustive examination of its uses there. Kautzsch sees the development of צדק in three stages. He suggests that צדק is fundamentally a forensic concept out of which evolved both the ethical and the religious use. Ac-

---

[1] Ludwig Diestel, "Die Idee der Gerechtigkeit, vorzüglich im Alten Testament, biblisch-theologisch dargestellt," *JDTh* 5 (1860), 173-253.
[2] Emil Friedrich Kautzsch, *Ueber die Derivate des Stammes* צדק *Alttestamentlichen Sprachgebrauch* (Tübingen), 1881.

cording to Kautzsch, all three stages of development, and the uses implied there, conform to "norm." Thus, he concludes that צדק, regardless of its orientation (forensic, ethical or religious), is to be understood as conforming to "norm."

Two years after Kautzsch's monograph, another study of צדק was presented by Hermann Cremer.³ Cremer was the first proponent of the thesis that צדק is best understood as a concept of "relationship." Accordingly, he argues that צדק fulfills the demands and responsibilities of a relationship. Cremer further suggests that צדק, in reference to Yahweh, can only be seen in a forensic light. So while he regards "relationship" as the main orientation of צדק, he sees the forensic use as primary to Yahweh's צדק. When the individual responds to the demands of Yahweh's צדק, it is generally in the form of "trust."⁴

While Cremer's study introduced a new understanding of צדק, it was not readily accepted by all scholars. This is clearly evident in Nötscher's study of צדק in the pre-exilic prophets⁵ where he resorts to the conclusions of Kautzsch. While Nötscher adopts Kautzsch's stance regarding the general orientation of צדק as "norm," he adds a new dimension in his conclusion. Nötscher proposes that צדק in the Eighth Century prophets functions primarily as a retributive principle.⁶ This understanding leads him to conclude that צדק, when used in reference to Yahweh, is punitive.

Following Nötscher, the next major study of צדק was undertaken by Johannes Pedersen.⁷ He further develops the notion of

---

³ Hermann Cremer, *Biblisch-theologisches Wörterbuch der neutestamentlichen Gräcität* (Gotha), 1893⁸, pp. 287-295. In the third edition, Cremer had suggested that צדק and its derivatives meant conforming to a state of which God is the standard. *Biblico-theological Lexicon of New Testament Greek*, trans. D.W. Simon and William Urwick (Edinburgh: T and T Clark), 1872, p. 171.

⁴ Cremer, *Biblisch-theologisches Wörterbuch*, pp. 287ff.

⁵ F. Nötscher, *Die Gerechtigkeit Göttes bei den vorexilischen Propheten* (Münster), 1915.

⁶ Ibid., p. 27.

⁷Johannes Pedersen, *Israel: Its Life and Culture I-II* (London: Oxford University Press), 1926. About the time of Pedersen's work, there were also two other studies on צדק. The first was that of O. Procksch, "Die hebräische Wurzel der Theologie," *CuW* 2 (1926), 451-461. Procksch suggests that צדק

צדק as "relationship," but unlike Cremer, who studies צדק as a theological principle, Pedersen sees צדק as a psychological concept. For Pedersen it is a relationship between souls. He argues that, "The good man acts rightly, because he acts entirely in accordance with the nature of his soul. But the soul exists only as a link in a covenant; it maintains its nature by maintaining the covenant."[8] However, the covenant of which Pedersen speaks has little to do with Israel's ברית with Yahweh. In fact the author argues, ultimately, "It is the ability to maintain oneself which is implied by righteousness, to have a soul constructed in such a manner that it could maintain itself through all actions."[9] In other words, a relationship between individuals need not necessarily be grounded in Yahweh, but may have its source in the souls of the individuals.

What Pedersen is suggesting centers on an anthropocentric nature of צדק. True, it involves "relationship," but the ultimate source of their "relationship" is derived from the soul of the individual, and in turn, the soul is strengthened by good actions towards others in the community. It is the health of the soul which is the determining factor in the maintenance of the relationship in the community.

Perhaps it was Pedersen's daring psychological approach to צדק which prevented it from having any tangible effect on subsequent studies of צדק. This can be seen in the case of H.J. Fahlgren,[10] who overlooks Pedersen's proposals and resorts to a position which understands צדק as "relationship within a norm." Fahlgren suggests that צדק means primarily the orientation of all one's deeds to the norm which is derived from the relationship in

---

must be understood as "norm" and in so doing, he distinguishes between צדק, צדקה and צדיק. צדק, he sees as the "norm of social order;" צדקה as the "right position within the social order," and צדיק as the "one who complies with the norm of the social order." The second study was by H. Fuchs, "Das alttestamentliche Begriffsverhältnis von Gerechtigkeit (ṣedeq) und Gnade (chesed) in Profetie und Dichtung," CuW 3 (1927), 101-118. Like Procksch, Fuchs also sees צדק as "norm," but in his case, Fuchs suggests that צדק is oriented towards the conforming of the moral-order to God-order.

[8] Pedersen, Israel I-II, pp. 337-338.
[9] Ibid., p. 338.
[10] K.Hj. Fahlgren, Ṣeḏāḳā, nahestehnende und entgegengesetzte Begriffe im Alten Testament (Uppsala: Almquist and Wiksells Boktryckeri-A-B), 1932.

community, between the people and Yahweh on the one hand and between the people themselves on the other.¹¹ Even with the different positions of Kautzsch, Cremer, and Pedersen, Klaus Koch in his doctoral dissertation predicates his thesis on the belief that nothing had changed regarding the understanding of צדק in a hundred years.¹² With this in mind, Koch argues that צדק is an "entity" (*Wesen*) and not particularly associated with either "relationship" or "attribute." He links צדק with the theophany of Yahweh in the Autumn festival, and thus he sees צדק as a divine gift which comes to the fore in cultic events.

Neither of the two studies of צדק which followed Koch's incorporated his ideas. Elizabeth Achtemeier¹³ presented a study of צדק in which she combined the conclusions of Cremer and Fahlgren, without examining systematically all the occurrences of צדק in the Old Testament. The most recent comprehensive examination of צדק was done by Hans Heinrich Schmid.¹⁴ Schmid begins his study by examining the background of the root צדק, both in terms of Old Testament usage (e.g. wisdom, cult, judges, monarchy, etc.) and of the usage in the Ancient Near East, in particular comparing it with the Egyptian *Maat*. He provides a history of the Old Testament use of צדק, noting in so doing a Canaanite influence and background. Schmid argues that the noun צדק originally

---

¹¹ Ibid., p. 81.
¹² Klaus Koch, "Ṣdq im Alten Testament - Eine traditiongeschichtliche Untersuchung" (Ph.D. dissertation, University of Heidelberg), 1953, p. 3. Koch in making this assertion clearly overlooks the wide-ranging scholarship represented by scholars such as Kautzsch, Cremer and Pedersen.
¹³ Elizabeth R. Achtemeier, "The Gospel of Righteousness: A study of the meaning of *ṣdq* and its derivatives in the Old Testament" (Ph.D. dissertation, University of Columbia), 1959.
¹⁴ Hans H. Schmid, *Gerechtigkeit als Weltordnung* BHTh 40 (Tübingen: J.C.B. Mohr [Paul Siebeck]), 1968. The study by Ahuva Ho, *Sedeq and Sedeqah in the Hebrew Bible* (New York: Peter Lang Publishers), 1991, was brought to my attention too late for consideration in the body of this study. It is Ho's contention that צדק and צדקה have entirely different functions in the Hebrew Bible. In coming to this conclusion, Ho explores צדק and צדקה in biblical and extra-biblical literature. Within the biblical sources analyzed, the author concludes that every genre distinguishes between צדק and צדקה. Also, a study by Moshe Weinfeld, *Justice and Righteousness in Israel and the Nations: Equality and Freedom in Ancient Israel in Light of Social Justice in the Ancient Near East* (Jerusalem: The Magnes Press), 1985. (Hebrew)

meant cosmic world order, becoming concrete in wisdom, justice, etc. He suggests that the fundamental meaning of the root צדק is "recht, richtig, in Ordnung."[15] After a discussion of what he calls texts which are "specifically Israelite," Schmid concludes that *Weltordnung* is the central term for understanding צדק and this covers the spheres of the cult, ethics, and the natural world.

These studies of צדק indicate two important points. First, they reflect the immense importance of צדק for a proper understanding of the theological construct of the Old Testament. Second, the large number of studies with their variety of conclusions suggest a definite lack of consensus regarding the primary orientation of צדק.

With regard to the distribution and contexts of משפט, there have been few comprehensive studies undertaken. One of the earliest examinations of משפט in the Old Testament was by H.W. Hertzberg.[16] Before his examination on משפט, Hertzberg discusses briefly the root שפט and argues that its basic meaning is "rule." With this in mind, he concludes that the passing of judgment is the function of the ruler. In his examination of משפט, he emphasizes its ethical orientation, noting that one aspect of the fulfilling of Yahweh's will is the ethical obligation which it lays on his followers. However, Hertzberg does not develop this argument fully, nor does he outline the elements which are involved in ethical responsibility. He does go on to point out that the administration of justice must be developed upon the basis of an ethical standard.[17] There are two salient features of Hertzberg's investigation: the importance of the ethical factor and the primary involvement of משפט in a judicial framework.

---

[15] Schmid, *Gerechtigkeit*, p. 67. Schmid suggests moreover, that other Old Testament concepts also relate to some form of "world order." For example, אמת and אמונה refer to the elements of constancy and continuity in world order; כון refers to conformity in world order; שלם and תמם are viewed as "wholeness" in world order, and ישר, Schmid suggests, is similar to צדק in meaning in that it likewise refers to "justice" and "straightness" in world order. p. 68.
[16] H.W. Hertzberg, "Die Entwicklung des Begriffes מִשְׁפָּט im AT," *ZAW* 40 (1922), 256-287, and a second article with the same title in *ZAW* 41 (1923), 16-76.
[17] Ibid., p. 274.

Pedersen also has a brief examination of the use of משפט in the Old Testament. He views משפט as functioning in a similar fashion to צדק in the Old Testament. Not only does he conclude that "*mishpāṭ* ...virtually means the same as *ṣedhek*"[18] but, suggests that, like צדק, "*mishpāṭ* ...has its root in the very essence of the soul."[19] The primary difference between משפט and צדק, as Pedersen sees it, lies in the premise that צדק is principally rooted in one's own soul while משפט is best understood in relation to other souls. In effect, he examines משפט with a psychological slant and thereby concludes that משפט is a term which is primarily used in the context of the maintenance of souls.

As a part of his monograph *ṣᵉdākā*, Fahlgren examines משפט as a synonym for צדק.[20] Like Hertzberg, Fahlgren suggests that the background meaning of משפט is "rule" and that this is the dominant meaning in the Old Testament. Fahlgren goes on to argue from this basis that the Judges have nothing to do with the judicial office, but are exclusively rulers. Moreover, Fahlgren follows Pedersen in suggesting that משפט is used as a concept involved in the maintenance of relationships within the community. Fahlgren does not develop this position, but it appears likely that he views משפט in certain instances as a psychological term.

The most comprehensive study of משפט was undertaken by Osborne Booth.[21] Booth's examination of משפט is a semantic one. He proposes that there are eleven possible meanings associated with משפט and these may be classified in three categories: "custom," "law" and "right." According to Booth, "custom" is the earliest meaning and is followed by "law," and "right" in that order. He argues that משפט in the Prophets means "proper adminis-

---

[18] Pedersen, *Israel I-II*, p. 351.
[19] Ibid., p. 351.
[20] Fahlgren, *Ṣᵉdākā*, pp. 120-138.
[21] Booth's Ph.D. dissertation at Yale University was a semantic study of משפט in the Old Testament. By way of an article, he provides a summary of his dissertation. Osborne Booth, "The Semantic Development of the term מִשְׁפָּט in the Old Testament," *JBL* 61 (1942), 105-110.

Introduction

tration of the law by man."²² In effect, Booth regards משפט in the Prophets as being primarily forensic in overtone.

As far as I am aware these are the only major studies of משפט which have been produced. While there are more recent studies on שפט,²³ these only deal with משפט tangentially.

With regard to studies on social justice in the Prophets, there have been several articles which focus on this area, but only few which focus exclusively on the Eighth Century prophets. Most of these articles will be cited in the body of this study. There are, however, several full length studies which deserve a brief analysis here. The first is that of Riocerezo Gutierrez.²⁴ Gutierrez suggests that Yahweh, as conceived by the Eighth Century prophets, is a universal God, concerned with the totality and unity of the people. By way of an introductory section, he discusses the historical evolution of social justice, both in secular literature and in the Old Testament. He then moves his investigation specifically into the area of the Eighth Century by examining the manner by which "justice" is developed by the prophets there. He postulates that in *Amos*, the prophet is primarily sociological; in *Hosea*, the prophet is theological; in *Isaiah*, the prophet is theo-political, and in *Micah*, the prophet is interested in moral justice. Gutierrez concludes his study with a discussion of what he sees as the three main areas of social injustice in the Eighth Century, namely, the use of property, individual rights (the poor, the slave, the stranger), and abuse of institutional power.

The weaknesses of Gutierrez's work are however apparent. First, it is a very brief study, and this in itself allows for only a superficial treatment of the subject. Second, there is a conspicuous absence of secondary sources in the body of the monograph, and this hints at an overly subjective orientation in the study. Third,

---

22 Ibid., p. 107.
23 In this regard, the two most recent studies are: M.S. Rosenberg, "The stem SPṬ: An investigation of Biblical and extra-Biblical Sources" (Ph.D. dissertation, University of Pennsylvania), 1963, and H.W. McAvoy, "A study of the root špṭ with special reference to the Psalter" (Ph.D. dissertation, University of Edinburgh), 1973.
24 Riocerezo C. Gutierrez, *La justicia social en los Profetas del siglo VIII: Amos, Oseas, Isaias y Miqueas* (Fribourg), 1970.

Gutierrez overlooks key concepts, such as צדק[25] and משפט, in his discussion.

The second study, is a Ph.D. dissertation by Claudermiro Mariottini.[26] Mariottini divides his study into four main sections. In the first section, he discusses "oppressions" in the Ancient Near East, focusing in particular on Egypt and Assyria. He argues that the oppressors are the "Government" and the "Conqueror," while the oppressed are the "governed" and the "poor and disenfranchised." This is followed by a section in which he discusses the factors that characterized Israel and Judah in the Eighth Century. In this regard, he isolates "prosperity," the "Assyrian threat," and the "Monarchy." The role of the monarchy is viewed with specific reference to social oppression. The third section focuses on the Eighth Century prophets' message against social oppression, while the final section seeks to discuss the prophetic solution to the question of social oppression.

While Chapters 1 and 2 set the stage for the prophetic critique in Chapter 3, Mariottini succeeds in only providing a general overview of the prophets' message. Specific texts are not discussed nor are elements distinctive to each prophet explored and analyzed. The brevity of Chapter 3 (35 pages) perhaps accounts for this. In this concluding section, Mariottini intimates that he will discuss the prophetic solution; however, this section centers instead on "Hezekiah's reform," the "Covenant Code" and the "Book of Deuteronomy."

The third study was produced by Devadasan Premnath.[27] Premnath's investigation has to do primarily with historical and sociological questions which affected the economic state of Eighth Century Israel and Judah. The basis of the analysis that Prem-

---

[25] Gutierrez does mention צדק, by way of a summary of an article on צדק by W. Mann in *Encyclopédie de la Foi*, volume 2. Ed. Heinrich Fries (CERF), 1965.

[26] Claudemiro Francisco Mariottini, "The Problem of Social Oppression in the Eighth Century Prophets" (Ph.D. dissertation, Southern Baptist Theological Seminary), 1983.

[27] Devadasan Nithya Premnath, "The Process of Latifundialization mirrored in the Oracles pertaining to 8th Century B.C.E. in the Books of Amos, Hosea, Isaiah and Micah" (Th.D. dissertation, Graduate Theological Union), 1984.

nath undertakes is a "hypothetical reconstruction of the systemic social history of the Eighth Century Israelite and Judahite societies."28 This study is divided into three main sections. In the first section, Premnath provides a historical analysis of Israelite society, including a diachronic survey of the period preceding the Eighth Century B.C. The second section is a discussion of the passages in the Eighth Century prophets which contain both implicit and explicit references to the process of Latifundialization. The concluding section explores the implications of the discussion for modern India. As the title indicates, Premnath's dissertation focuses on the question of Latifundia economy principally, and this does not incorporate central themes such as "cult" and "Day of Yahweh" in the examination.

This brief overview of the studies which have been developed in these three areas gives a clear indication of the variety of opinions and positions held. In this book, both צדק and משפט will be examined, considering the different meanings associated with them, with a view to demonstrating the "relationship-oriented" nature of these concepts. While some studies have been written on these concepts, it can hardly be said that there is a consensus regarding their meanings. As Klaus Koch recently suggested, "Research into these two concepts...is still in a state of flux." 29

צדק as "relationship" in this study will develop the thesis which was first proposed by Hermann Cremer, in contradistinction to the notion of "relationship" as espoused by Pedersen. Cremer's interest was in providing background information for his study of δικαιοσύνη, thus his examination of צדק in the Old Testament is understandably brief. In order to provide a systematic investigation of צדק, all occurrences in the Old Testament will be pointed to, and examined depending on their particular relevance to this study. The use of a methodology such as this ensures that all contexts in which צדק occurs are considered, thus providing a more comprehensive conclusion. A similar methodology will be

---

28 Premnath, *Diss.*, p. ii.
29 Klaus Koch, *The Prophets* I, trans. Margaret Kohl (London: SCM Press), 1982, p. 58.

applied to the study of משפט. All occurrences of משפט will be highlighted with a view to showing also the "relationship-oriented" nature of this concept. In this regard, the present study will depart from the commonly held understanding of משפט as a judicial concept.

Furthermore, the occurrences of צדק and משפט when used in the *same* context will be studied with a view to determining what possible relationship there might be between the two terms in the Old Testament. This in turn, will pave the way for the more specific investigation of a possible relationship between צדק and משפט when used together in the Eighth Century prophets. As Klaus Koch suggests, "Wer aber auf ein Gebirge zuwandert, seiht zuerst das Gebirge als ganzes, ehe er einzelne Gipfel unterscheiden kann."[30] In effect, this study will begin with a general examination of צדק and משפט in order to provide a sound foundation for the discussion of צדק and משפט as integral to the social critique of the Eighth Century prophets. That is to say, it will seek to demonstrate that צדק and משפט form the basis for the social critique of these prophets. All the areas of social injustice will be shown to be connected to the absence or perversion of צדק and משפט. Moreover, these different areas will be seen to be not only inextricably connected to צדק and משפט, but integral to the whole existence of the people of Israel, both in their relationship with Yahweh and with each other.

---

[30] Koch, *Diss.*, p. 8.

Chapter I

I. Background and Meaning of צדק in the Ancient Near East

In undertaking to discuss the uses and meanings of צדק[1] in the Old Testament, we will look briefly at the background of this term. While this type of exploration is not entirely designed to provide definitive answers, and is almost always less than accurate in its conclusions, this study takes into consideration some of the common theories which have been proposed, though none of which has been able to claim the distinction of being foolproof or even going unchallenged. With the knowledge that unanimity may be impossible, we will nevertheless discuss three areas in Near Eastern Literature which will give us some idea of the background meaning of *ṣdq*. *Ṣdq* is widely found in the Semitic languages, and the meanings which are derived from its use in these contexts show a distinct similarity to the use of צדק in the Old Testament.[2]

A. Ugaritic/Akkadian

In the ancient Ugaritic epic of King Keret, there is an occurrence of the use of *ṣdq*.[3] In this occurrence *ṣdq* is used to mean

---

[1] The term צדק will be employed as the point of reference for both the roots צדק and צדקה and their derivatives unless the discussion necessitates specific allusion to a particular derivative.

[2] See, Franz Rosenthal, "Ṣedaka, Charity," *HUCA* 23 (1950-51), pp.413ff.

[3] King Keret has lost his entire family, including his progeny. In the introductory section of this epic, we are told that Keret has lost his "rightful wife;" "rightful" in this context is used for rendering *ṣdq*. See, H.L. Ginsberg, trans. "The Legend of King Keret" *ANET* ed. James B. Pritchard. (New Jersey: Princeton University Press),1969, p.143. See also, the following: Cyrus H. Gordon, *Ugaritic Literature* (Roma: Pontificum Institutum Biblicum), 1949, pp.66-83. David Hill, *Greek Words and Hebrew Meanings*, SNTSMS (Cambridge: Cambridge University Press), 1967. Hill includes in his study a brief discussion of *ṣdq* in the King Keret context, p. 82. Also, J. Swetnam, "Some Observations on the Background of צדיק in Jeremias 23.5a," *Bibl* 46 (1965), pp. 29-40. Swetnam observes that while the interpretation in the legend of Keret does not allow us to make apodictic statements,

"rightful" or "legitimate," and clearly has a legalistic overtone. It is not surprising therefore that Ginsberg translates ṣdq in this context as "lawful."[4] The root ṣdq is used similarly in the Tel el-Amarna tablets.[5] In no. 287 of these tablets, in which Abdu-Hiba pleads to the king, imploring him to believe that he is innocent, the term sa-du-uk [6] is employed. Abdu-Hiba uses this term to aid him in the explanation to the king regarding his innocence. It is possible however that sa-du-uk in this context could denote more than one idea.

Because there is no systematic punctuation in the original text, scholars and translators are faced with the task of punctuating their translations, using only the context as a guide. The original text reads: "...sa-du-uk a-na ia-a-si as-sum am el uti ka-si-wi,"[7] and as it stands, it is typically translated, "I am in the right with regard to the Kasi people." Albright translates no. 287, line 32 as an independent line and thus his rendering reads, "Behold, O King, my lord, I am right."[8] Because of the context, this must be understood as being "...I am in the right," which in effect casts a legalistic overtone upon it. Based on the story of Abdu-Hiba, sa-du-uk does have a forensic implication, for in fact Abdu-Hiba is pleading innocence with regard to his relationship with the Kasi people.[9] This forensic use, found in Semitic antiquity, is supported also by Knudtzon and Hill.[10] The *CAD* rendering of this section of

---

still the use of ṣdq in this context points clearly to a meaning of "legitimate." p. 37.

[4] Ginsberg, *ANET*, p. 143.

[5] See, *ANET*, p. 488 for a translation of no. 287 done by W.F. Albright. The authoritative work in this regard is: J. A. Knudtzon, *Die El-Amarna Tafeln* (Leipzig: J. C. HINRICHS' sche BUCHHANDLUNG), 1910.

[6] Even though sa-du-uk is in this Akkadian context, it does in fact have a western Semitic origin. See Ignace Gelb, et. al. eds. The *Assyrian Dictionary*, vol. 16 (Chicago: Oriental Institute), 1962, referred to hereafter as *CAD*.

[7] Knudtzon, *Die El-Amarna-Tafeln*, p. 846, no. 287, lines 32-33.

[8] Albright, *ANET*, p. 488.

[9] See J. Skinner, "Righteousness in the Old Testament," *A Dictionary of the Bible* IV, ed. James Hastings (Edinburgh: T & T Clark), 1900.

[10] Knudtzon's translation, "Siehe, O König, mein Herr, Recht habe ich in Bezug auf die Kasi-Leute," suggests clearly a different punctuation from Albright, and points to a forensic meaning, *Die-El-Amarna-Tafeln*, p. 365. Hill is in agreement with Knudtzon on this point. *Greek Words*, p. 82.

the Tel el-Amarna letters is: "... see my lord, I am right about the people...."[11] This is a version which in scholarly opinion, neither does justice to the word nor fits the context in which it is found.

What is important in looking at the use of ṣdq in this context is that even though scholars such as Albright and Knudtzon punctuate the passage differently,[12] still the forensic overtone is sustained. The connotations shift according to sentence structure, but the meaning of ṣdq as "right" in a forensic sense is still derived.

B. Phoenician

A second example of צדק in Ancient Near Eastern literature is found in Phoenician epigraphy.

בת זבני יחמלך מלך גבל
האת חזי כל מפלת הבתם
אל יארך בעלשממ ובעל [ת]
גבל ומפחרת אל גבל
קדשם ימת יחמלך ושנתו
על גבל כמלך צדק ומלך
ישר לפן אל גבל קדשם

The text is translated as follows: (1) The temple which Yehimelek, king of Byblus built - (2) it was he who restored the ruins of these temples. (3) May Baal - Shemem and Baal (ath) - Yebal (4) and the assembly of the holy gods of Byblus (5) prolong the days of Yehimelek and his years (6) over Byblus as a rightful king and a true (7) king before the h[oly] gods of Byblus.

---

[11] The *CAD*'s rendering of this section gives an unacceptable connotation to *sa-du-uk*. It is transformed into something of a secular term, meaning "confirmed knowledge."

[12] While Knudtzon focuses on the innocence of Abdu-Hiba regarding the Cushites, Albright uses "in the right" on behalf of Abdu-Hiba, in reference to disloyalty in the annexation of land.

This inscription of Yehimelek[13] clearly contains the root צדק.[14] This particular reference is dated in the Tenth Century B.C. by Albright[15] and if this use of צדק is deemed an authoritative reference, then it certainly would be a legitimate source for a study of its background. Because of a lack of context of the Yehimelek inscription, some scholars have argued that "the extrinsic value of authoritative interpretation is accordingly weakened."[16] However, even though there is no specific context in which the Yehimelek inscription is placed, it is nevertheless useful in determining the origin of *ṣdq* in the Ancient Near East. There is, in this inscription, indication that the verbal construction is not unique to this situation but in fact shows similarity to earlier texts. Albright notes that "it has not yet been observed that there is a striking verbal parallel between this passage, in which the abstract noun *ṣdq* and *ysr* are successively combined with *mlk*, 'king', and Keret I i:12f. :'*att sdqh l-ypq mtrht ysrh* = "Let him find his rightful wife, his true spouse."[17]

The strength of this reference as a source of confirmation for the background of צדק is further enhanced through the fact that here "there is the formalized language characteristic of western Semitic royal inscriptions."[18] Thus the parallel which is drawn between the Yehimelek and Keret references is strongly supported by the Yehamelek inscription which comes some five hundred years after the Yehimelek inscription. In lines 8-9 of the Yehamelek inscription the words כמלך צדק הא are present.

---

[13] See, W.F. Albright, "The Phoenician Inscriptions of the Tenth Century B.C. from Byblus," *JAOS* 67 (1947), p. 156.

[14] See Franz Rosenthal, "YEHIMILK of Byblos," *ANET*, p. 653. According to Rosenthal, this inscription records the dedication of a new building, possibly a temple.

[15] As in Albright, "The Phoenician Inscriptions...." pp. 156-157. Hill, *Greek Words*, p. 83, suggests a Twelfth Century date, but most scholars agree on a Tenth Century date.

[16] Swetnam, "Some Observations...." p. 32.

[17] Albright, "The Phoenician Inscriptions...." p. 157, note 36.

[18] Swetnam, "Some Observations ...." p. 33. See also, Z. Harris, *A Grammar of the Phoenician Language* (New Haven: American Oriental Series) 8, 1936, p. 140.

Chapter I

... תברך בעלת גבל אית יתומפך
מלך גבל ותחוו ותארך ימו ושנתו על גבל
כמלך צדק הא ותתן

This text is translated as: "May the mistress of Gebal bless Yehamelek king of Gebal, and grant him life and prolong his days and his years over Gebal, for he is a righteous king."[19] Not only is this reference identical to the Yehimelek's כמלך צדק, but the parallels in terminology and constructions in other sections are also striking. In the Yehimelek inscription, there is a plea for the prolonging of the king's life in the words... קדשם ימת יחמלך ושנתו,[20] a plea which resonates in the inscription regarding Yehamelek,... ותארך ימו ושנ.[21]

This kind of stylized language however, is not unique to Byblos, for it is also found in Ancient Aramaic references, as in the text of Nerab:[22]

2 ... בצדקתי קדמות
3 שמני שם טב והארך יומי

These lines are rendered in English as: (line 2) "because of my righteousness before him (3) he gave me a good name and prolonged my days."[23] What these examples serve to establish is not so much the precision with which the meaning of צדק is known, but rather to demonstrate certain traits which together give us reasonable assurance both of the use and meaning of $ṣdq$ in the Ancient Near East. In all of this, one factor distinguishes itself with some certainty, namely that the use of $ṣdq$ in these Ugaritic, Phoenician and Aramaic references are within forensic contexts.[24]

---

[19] G.A. Cooke, *A Text-Book of North Semitic Inscriptions* (Oxford: Clarendon Press), 1903, p. 18.

[20] Albright, "The Phoenician Inscriptions ...." p. 156.

[21] Cooke, *A Textbook of North Semitic Inscriptions*, p. 18.

[22] Rosenthal, *ANET*, p. 661. This document was found in 1891 in Nerab, in the vicinity of Aleppo and dates back to about the Seventh Century B.C.

[23] Translation from Rosenthal, *ANET*, p. 611.

[24] Rosenthal's translation of צדק as "righteousness" in the Nerab text does not fit this conclusion. This does not alter the forensic theory, for there is no

With respect to this forensic use, Hill makes a constructive observation. He notes that the use of צדק in the inscription of Yehimelek points to the *quality* of the rule of Yehimelek, rather than its *legitimacy*. He also believes that the Yehamelek inscription connotes the same meaning.25 It is the idea that צדק in these references alludes to "quality" rather than "legitimacy" of rule that prompts Hill to examine the association of the root צדק with divine beings.26 He notes that early references such as מלכיצדק (Gen. 14:18) and אדני-צדק (Josh. 10:1) bear an implication which is fulfilled in the use of the respective name. That is to say, the name expresses both the belief of the person who bears the name and also a confession of divine quality.27 The principal interest for Hill in proceeding with this perspective is to show that in some way the early use of צדק was associated with a deity. Regarding מלכי-צדק and צדק-אדני he notes:

> It is possible ... that the names should be construed like Jehozadak ('Yahu is righteous') to give the meaning 'My (The) Lord or King is righteous'. Likewise the Ugaritic name *Ṣdk-il* may mean '*Ṣdk* is (my) God or Il (EL) is righteous.' In either case, its use in personal names suggests the very early association of *ṣdq* with deity....28

The value of Hill's observations is twofold. First, it points to an early use of צדק in which it can possibly be rendered "righteous." Second, צדק, when rendered as "righteous," is used in the same context as

---

clear reason why Rosenthal chooses "righteousness" as an appropriate translation for צדק within this context. For a brief discussion of Rosenthal's translation see, Swetnam, "Some Observations...." p. 33, n.2.

25 Hill, *Greek Words*, p. 83.

26 Hill arrives at an erroneous association at this point. There is no indication that Yehimelek's and Yehamelek's inscriptions refer to quality of rule. The preceding discussion points to a use of צדק which is much more forensic than it is religious. In order for Hill to examine the relation between צדק and the divine, it is not necessary to have a link to "quality of rule" in the Yehimelek and Yehamelek inscriptions, *Greek Words*, p. 83.

27 Hill, *Greek Words*, p. 83.

28 Ibid., p. 83.

God. It is clear that צדק not only has a theological orientation, but other orientations as well, as will become apparent later in this chapter. It is true that in saying that צדק in these references means "righteous" would be similar to saying as Rosenthal says "sedaka means sedaka."[29] Granted, there is not a particularly concrete context from which to evaluate these references, yet צדק is used in association with אל, מלך, and אדני and that in itself is of great significance.

C. Arabic

The third example of a possible background for *ṣdq* is found in pre-Islamic Arabic. Generally, the meaning which is derived from *ṣdq* in Arabic has to do with "straightness" and that which is "right."[30] "The verb *sadaka* means to speak the truth; *saddaka*, to attribute truth to a speaker...; *saddiq*, a true or sincere friend. All these embody the ethical idea of trustworthiness or genuineness."[31] The presence of *ṣdq* in Arabic testifies to its use in the ethical sense, meaning "straightness."[32]

---

[29] Rosenthal, "Ṣedaka...." pp. 411-412.

[30] See, Rosenthal, who suggests that *ṣdq* meant "proper" in pre-Islamic Arabic and when used in a similar syntactic construction in Quranic Arabic, the meaning is the same. He opines that, "At least this meaning would make much better sense than 'truthful' or the like, in the Quranic phrase *mubawwa'a sidkin*, 'a proper place'" (Quran 10:93), "Ṣedaka...." p. 416. If in fact "proper" is rendered as the English equivalent of *ṣdq* in the Arabic, then the reference is clearly one which connotes subscription to an ethical norm. See also, Ibn Manzur, Muhammad ibn Mukarram al-Masri, *Lisan al `Arab*, vols. 11-12, Bulaq, 1303-7. In this Arabic encyclopedia we find the phrases "*rajul sadq*" meaning "righteous man."

[31] Skinner, "Righteousness...," p. 247.

[32] In this regard, Skinner believes that "straightness" could only refer to a "norm" and hence does not fit the concept of relationship, which he holds to be crucial in reference to צדק, "Righteousness...," p. 274. This view however is challenged by E.R. Achtemeier, "Righteousness in the Old Testament," *IDB*. IV, ed. George Buttrick (Nashville: Abingdon Press), 1962, who sees "straightness" as responsibility within a relationship. See also K.J. Scaria, "Social Justice in the Old Testament," *BB* 4 (1978), p. 165. The question as to whether צדק must be understood in the context of "norm" or "relationship" will be discussed later in this chapter.

The discussion in the preceding three sections invites us to take notice of certain factors. In looking at the different views and theories regarding the background of צדק, it becomes evident that unanimity is virtually impossible. Whatever information there is to be gleaned regarding צדק, comes primarily from contextual observation. What then, can be said regarding the background of צדק?

First, it is clear that צדק has some association with deity. It is noted in the inscription of Yehimelek that he is a "מלך צדק," and this legitimizes his bid to have his days prolonged. Twice in this inscription אל is used, and clearly the association of צדק with Yehimelek is vital in the sight of אל. Moreover the connection between deity and צדק is seen in the names of מלכי-צדק and אדני-צדק. Whatever might be missing from the precision of a firm context is certainly aided by the number of occurrences.

Second, it might be concluded that the occurrences of ṣdq in the Keret, Tel el-Amarna, Yehimelek, and Yehamelek texts all point to a forensic use. In this regard, it is evident that ṣdq in its oldest occurrence, is in a forensic sense; with all the differences and lack of contextual support, still the one common element in these texts is that ṣdq is employed in a forensic context. Equally noteworthy in these instances, is a recognition that ṣdq is used within a framework of "relationship." This may be seen in the case of Keret who loses his "rightful" (ṣdq), that is to say, legitimate wife. The legitimacy is established by the fact that Keret and his wife entered into a recognized relationship. In no. 287 of the Tel el-Amarna tablets, the use of ṣdq as a term of relationship is much more pronounced. That Abdu-Hiba is "in the right" with the Kasi people intimates a relationship between the two parties. The use of צדק in the Phoenician inscription of Yehimelek of Byblos is similar to its use in the Keret text, namely as a parallel to the nature of Yehimelek's relationship with Byblos. Even though these occurrences are forensic, nevertheless they are all used within contexts of relationship.

Third, the use of "straightness" as a rendering of צדק points to an ethical principle. That this has to be understood in the context of relationship intensifies the ethical responsibility of the individual within community. The צדק of the individual is thus not solely for the sake of the individual and surely is not to be understood and applied narrowly, but must have implications for and connections to the body politic.

Fourth, we are constantly reminded of the difficulty in tracing the background of צדק in the Old Testament. It is not so much finding a similar root or meaning, for these are evident, but rather to see צדק used in similar ways as in the Old Testament. That is to say, the occurrences of *ṣdq* in Ancient Near Eastern texts bring to the fore certain external similarities and points of reference for determining influence on Old Testament usage. However, what is missing from these examples is precisely that which is unique to the Old Testament, namely concepts such as "covenant" and "election" and of course the subject of Yahweh's presence in and association with Israel. To the extent that these examples have allowed us to see the variety in meanings and the way they might have been of influence on the Old Testament, then they are useful; no more than this ought to be expected, for it is only in taking the variables of Old Testament life, culture, and religion that a fair comparison of uses of צדק can be entertained. The significance of these Near Eastern examples will become evident later in this chapter when the use and meaning of צדק in the Old Testament is discussed. It will then become clear that the theological, forensic and ethical elements of צדק which are aspects of the uses in the Ancient Near Eastern texts, are all intricately tied up in the Old Testament understanding of צדק, even though terms such as "covenant" and "election" will add to the complexity.

II. צדק in the LXX

One factor which will be useful in this discussion is to study the rendering of צדק in the LXX. The LXX is a complex composition, yet the text in its final form provides some basis for exploring and analyzing the rendering of צדק. The following brief discussion recognizes the many layers involved in the composition of the LXX, and the study here is intended only to provide a survey, and not to explore nuances of the many layers. The LXX overwhelmingly employs δικαιοῦν and its cognates in rendering צדק. Out of a possible four hundred and ninety-three occurrences, δικαιοῦν and its cognates are used in this respect some four hundred and sixty times. If in fact δικαιοῦν were always used to render צדק, then the transition would be smooth and we would be assured that the translators of the LXX perceived צדק as being only δικαιοῦν. However, this is not the case, and there are at least two points with which to support this. First, δικαιοῦν is not a term which is reserved exclusively for rendering צדק; indeed it is used to render a variety of words in the Old Testament. As an example here, Isa. 57:1 uses both צדיק and חסד and these are rendered by δίκαιος and δίκαιοι, respectively, in the LXX. The following list[33] gives select examples of the vast spread of the meaning and connotation of δικαιοῦν.[34]

חסד	(Gen. 19:19; 20:13; 21:23; 32:11 [10]; Exod. 15:13; 34:7; Prov. 20:28) = δικαιοσύνη
אמת	(Gen. 24:49; Josh. 24:14; Isa. 38:19; 39:8; Dan. 8:12; 9:13) = δικαιοσύνη
מישרים	(I Chron. 29:17) = δικαιοσύνη
טובה	(Ps. 38:21 [LXX 37:21]) = δικαιοσύνη
מדון	(Prov. 17:14) = δικαιοσύνη
נקון	(Gen. 20:5) = δικαιοσύνη
פתים	(Prov. 1:22) = δικαιοσύνη

---

[33] For more examples and a longer discussion in this regard, see Gottfried Quell and Gottlob Schrenk, *Righteousness*. Trans. from Gerhard Kittel's *Theologisches Wörterbuch Zum Neuen Testament* (London: Adam and Charles Black), 1951, pp. 2-3.

[34] See C.H. Dodd, *The Bible and the Greeks* (London: Hodder and Stoughton), 1935. Dodd notes that חסד "lies outside the scope of what δικαιοσύνη meant to the Greek." p. 43.

Chapter I   21

זכו   (Dan. 6:23 [Aramaic]) = δικαιοσύνη

השכל   (Prov. 21:16) = δικαιοσύνη

ישר   (Job 1:1,8; 2:3; Prov. 3:32; 11:3; 14:9; 21:2,18) = δίκαιος

נקים   (Job 9:23; 17:8) = δίκαιος

תמים   (Prov. 28:18) = δίκαιος

ריב   (Mic. 7:9; Isa.1:17) = δικαιοῦν

שפט   (I Sam. 7:6) = δικαιοῦν

Based on the above references and their connotations, it is evident that the LXX, in translating certain concepts from the Old Testament, focuses on particular elements which constitute meanings based on contextual considerations. It is this disposition which might have prompted the translators to use δικαιοῦν not only for צדק, but also to translate all of the above terms. There is some element within each of these terms which can be used synonymously with צדק in particular contexts. From the variety of terms listed above, it is apparent that there is no automatic matching of pairs of words, but rather, the connotation, *Sitz im Leben* together with other factors are all considered. Having said this, however, it would be difficult to deliver a reasonable explanation for δικαιοσύνη being used to render השכל in Prov. 1:22. What this all points to is a problem that is built into any piece of material which undergoes translation. This is clearly a concern which we face in our attempt to find an appropriate meaning for צדק. The fact is, not only has צדק been translated into different languages, but it has also been interpreted, and as such, the rendering of צדק is not only a translation but also an interpretation. For example, the Vulgate translates צדק as *iustitia* while the German translation is *Gerechtigkeit*. There is no doubt that in themselves these translations reflect elements of צדק; however they fail to capture fully its versatility.35

Further, it has been noted that in the LXX, the word which is used overwhelmingly for צדק is δικαιοῦν and cognates, yet the richness of the concept of צדק has prompted various other terms to be used to convey the appropriate contextual meaning. Once again we are reminded by the following examples that there is no precise, all-encompassing Greek parallel for צדק. In the references which follow we see the variety of words employed, in Greek with English equivalents. This is not an exhaustive outline, but a selective one.

צדק in:	LXX	
Isa. 9:6	κρίμα	(judgment)
Isa. 11:4	κρίσις	(judgment)
Isa. 41:26	ἀληθής	(true)
Isa. 56:1	ἔλεος	(pity, compassion)
Isa. 61:10	εὐφροσύνη	(gladness)
Job 4:17	καθαρός	(pure)
Job 17:9	πιστός	(faithful)
Job 22:3	ἄμεμπτος	(blameless, faultless)
Prov. 12:12	εὐσεβής	(pious, reverent)

What seems to be evident as we study this list of references is that צדק within certain contexts connotes meanings which cannot be sustained by δικαιοῦν and cognates: "Where...δικαιοσύνη differs from צדק it is not a matter of difference in the meaning of the terms, but of different conceptions of the content of 'righteousness.'"36 However, there are still instances where contexts in which צדק is used appear to be left unconsidered when

---

35 See Gerhard von Rad, *Old Testament Theology* I, trans. D.M.G. Stalker (Edinburgh: Oliver and Boyd, Ltd.), 1965. Von Rad notes that the use of Gerechtigkeit suggests, "a man's proper conduct over against an absolute ethical norm, a legality which derives its norm from the absolute idea of justice." p. 371. Von Rad finds this view untenable in the light of the history of Ancient Israel.

36 Dodd, *The Bible and the Greeks*, p. 44.

Chapter I

δικαιοῦν is used as the appropriate term. An obvious occurrence in this regard is seen in Deutero-Isaiah, where צדק is commonly rendered "deliverance," "vindication," or "salvation," by the NRSV precisely because of contextual considerations, such as the political, social and religious atmosphere. In Isa. 46:13a צדק is used in the following context: ...קרבתי צדקתי לא תרחק.[37] These words are rendered in the LXX as: ἤγγισα τὴν δικαιοσύνεν μου.... The political context of Israel at the time of Deutero-Isaiah is certain to shape צדק in this text to mean "deliverance" or "vindication," for Israel is in bondage and Babylon its captor is about to fall. The Greek-reading person who reads this text in the LXX would certainly assume δικαιοσύνη to mean "righteousness" and not "deliverance," for the latter is not a concept which is associated with δικαιοσύνη.[38]

In addition to the variety of Greek terms employed to render צדק in the LXX, there is still another one which is used in a somewhat more specialized manner. In several instances, ἐλεημοσύνη (pity) is used to render צדק, which in itself is not entirely uncommon, particularly in view of the other Greek terms which are also employed. However, with one exception,[39] ἐλεημοσύνη[40] is used only in contexts where there is a reference to the צדק of Yahweh.[41]

---

[37] Schrey, translates צדק in this context as "righteousness." Clearly the context suggests that an English rendering of "vindication" or "deliverance" be used. See Heinz-Horst Schrey, et al., *The Biblical Doctrine of Justice and Law* (London: SCM Press, Ltd.), 1955, p. 53. For a different view to Schrey, see Dodd, *The Bible and the Greeks*, p. 54.

[38] δικαιοσύνη is also used similarly in Isa. 46:12.

[39] ἐλεημοσύνη is also used in Dan. 4:24 [LXX 4:27], where it does not refer to the צדק of Yahweh. Furthermore this is an Aramaic reference (צדקה).

[40] It is useful to note that צדק, in many of the apocryphal works of the Old Testament, is rendered by ἐλεημοσύνη. See e.g., Tob. 4:10; 7:9; Sir. 3:30; 7:10; 29:12. For more discussion on this, see von Rad, *Theol.* I, p. 383n.

[41] See Deut. 6:25; 24:13; Isa. 1:27; 59:16; Pss. 24:8; 33:5; 103:6; Dan. 9:16. All these instances use the feminine צדקה, with Isa. 59:16 and Ps. 103:6 using the plural form. There is no evidence to support a theory that צדק and צדקה are used differently in the Old Testament; in fact it is almost certain that they are used interchangeably. However, there may be patterns, and Rosenthal notes one, namely, that the translator's "purpose might have been to distinguish in his translation ṣedek from ṣedākā and he occasionally translates צדקה through ἐλεημοσύνη which is a more abstract term and denotes more of an exclusively moral quality than δικαιοσύνη." "Ṣedaka...." p. 428. See also, Alfred Jepsen, "צדק und צדקה im Alten Testament" in *Gottes Wort und*

The attempt here by the LXX to give precise meanings based on contexts occasions a critical problem. The LXX creates (perhaps unknowingly) a dichotomy between the two natures of God. On the one hand Yahweh is perceived as a merciful, charitable, kind God when ἐλεημοσύνη is associated with him, but as a God of judgment, when δικαιοσύνη is applied to him. Dodd suggests that "...the two aspects of צדק are polarized into ἐλεημοσύνη and δικαιοσύνη. In place of the comprehensive virtue of צדקה, we have justice on one hand, mercy on the other."[42]

The one unmistakable point which emerges from this is that even though there is a great degree of consistency regarding the Greek rendering of צדק, nevertheless the LXX has been unable to capture the richness and versatility of צדק with one term. Before the translators of the LXX employed δικαιοῦν for צדק, the meanings and connotations were firmly fixed on the minds of the people, and for them, the established meaning of δικαιοῦν gave shape to the understanding of צדק. Hence צדק of the Old Testament is shaped to fit δικαιοῦν, rather than vice versa. One of the grave imbalances which necessarily results from this is the picture of Yahweh as being principally a God of judgment. Whether this was thought of by the translators when they selectively employed ἐλεημοσύνη remains a mystery, but the result was the creation of a sharp dichotomy in the nature of God. It is imperative that we are aware of the LXX rendering of צדק, for it will certainly be of importance as the general meaning of צדק in the Old Testament is discussed.

Gottes Land (Göttingen: Vandenhoeck and Ruprecht), 1965. Jepsen suggests that צדק and צדקה must be distinguished. Accordingly, he notes that צדק refers to "right order" while צדקה refers to "right relation," which in turn leads to right order. p. 80. Agreeing with Jepsen on this point is Hans Heinrich Schmid, *Gerechtigkeit*, p. 67, and Ahuva Ho, *Sedeq and Sedaqah in the Hebrew Bible*. There is really no support for this theory either. See also, A.E. McGrath, "Justice and Justification: Semantic and Juristic Aspects of the Christian Doctrine of Justification," *SJT* 35 (1982), pp. 403-418. McGrath also sees a distinction between צדק and צדקה. He notes that צדק is used in contexts which refer to weights and measures, while צדקה does not. p. 408.

[42] See Dodd, *The Bible and the Greeks*, p. 56.

III. Meaning and Use of צדק in the Old Testament

The meaning of צדק in the Old Testament varies considerably depending on context, subject, time, and circumstances. In order to understand the uses, a general overview of the occurrences of צדק in the Old Testament is necessary. Such an overview will allow us to recognize the way in which צדק is dispersed, the preponderance or lack of references within a certain framework (Prophetic, Wisdom), and the meanings associated with them.

The following distribution of צדק within the books of the Old Testament is designed to serve two particular functions. First, it will introduce us, in a brief manner, to the diversity of contexts,[43] and meanings within each book, and enable us to see in perspective, a contextual and functional distribution of צדק. This is crucial as a foundation; later there will be an attempt to draw conclusions based on occurrences, use, and context. Second, this is a necessary framework out of which certain patterns of usage of צדק will be developed and analyzed. That is to say, we will observe whether the contemporary understanding of צדק in the Old Testament is predicated on the notion of צדק as developed by "J" and "E" or that used by the Prophets. Moreover, it will enable us to mark whatever distinctions there may be between usages, while noting the similarities.

---

[43] As a point of interest, when we look at the way the NRSV renders צדק, it can be seen that there are over a dozen different words that are used. The following will serve as an indication of this: honesty (Gen. 30:33), saving deeds (I Sam. 12:7), equity (II Sam. 8:15), triumphs (Judg. 5:11), uprightness (Jer. 4:2), vindication (Jer. 51:10), saving help (Ps. 40:10), truth (Ps. 52:3), righteous help (Ps. 71:24), righteousness (Job 33:26), prosperity (Prov. 8:18). What these terms demonstrate more than anything else, is the complexity and rich nature of צדק. For further Old Testament references on these English translations, see, Achtemeier, "Righteousness...." p. 80.

A. Distribution and Contexts of צדק in the Old Testament

GENESIS

There are fourteen occurrences of צדק and of this number, six (18:23, 24 [2x], 25, 26, 28) are used in the context of the Sodom and Gomorrah story. Whenever צדק is used in this story, it is employed in antithesis to רשע. In every instance it is the lack of ethical practice of showing hospitality to strangers that צדק is used. Four other occurrences (6:9; 7:1; 15:6; 18:19) refer to the righteousness of Abraham (6:9 and 7:1 simply note that Abraham is a righteous man). In the instances where צדק is used with respect to Abraham, it should be noted that it is not to Abraham's perfection that the term applies, but to the continuing trust in the relationship of promise. However in 15:6, Abraham is reckoned by Yahweh as righteous and in 18:19, צדק is used to describe Abraham doing צדק. Of the remaining four instances, one (20:4) is used in the context of Abimelech's plea to Yahweh for sparing those who are "innocent." The occurrence in 30:33 refers to the "honesty" (צדקתי) of Jacob in his dealings with Laban. The sustaining of the relationship with Laban is central here, and the honesty of Jacob alludes to the importance of honesty in any relationship. The occurrence in 38:26 involves the accusation of Tamar of being a harlot, yet the perception of her as "more righteous" than Judah. In a pointed way, the occurrence of צדק in this context introduces us to the complexity of the Old Testament concept of צדק.[44] The final occurrence in 44:16

---

[44] Hill suggests that this occurrence in its particular context has nothing to do with ethical uprightness, but rather refers to the strength of Tamar's case in terms of the levirate marriage law. *Greek Words*, p. 84. While the first half of Hill's observation may find consensus among scholars, the second part is seriously flawed. To say that the צדק of Tamar has to do with levirate marriage law is to cast a forensic connotation over צדק. In contrast to this, others have supposed that this reference is clearly in regard to Tamar's obligations to her familial relations. For agreement with Hill's view, see also Lester J. Kuyper, "Righteousness and Salvation," *SJT* 30 (1977), p. 234. Also, J.P. Justeson, "On the meaning of ṢADAQ," *AUSS* 2 (1964), pp. 53-61. Regarding this text, Justeson says, "because of the levirate marriage laws, Tamar in her deception, was more free from guilt or sin than Judah in his lust." p. 58. For a different perspective, see von Rad, *Theol.* I, p. 374.

Chapter I

is used in the hithpael (נצטדק) in reference to the clearing of oneself of guilt. As part of the brothers' reconciliation with Joseph, their confession includes the necessity to return to a state of צדק. צדק thus is perceived to be an essential element for the sustaining of a relationship.

EXODUS

There are four occurrences with at least three different meanings and connotations. The first (9:27) involves Pharaoh's admission that Yahweh is "in the right" while he is "in the wrong," a use which appears to be forensic rather than religious. However, even though this use may be forensic in overtone, it is primarily concerned about the relationship between Yahweh and Israel which is in the process of being healed. When Pharaoh confesses that Yahweh is in the right, it is not so much a matter of judicial rightness as a matter of Yahweh's acts on Israel's behalf. The other three occurrences of צדק are in 23:7,8, two of which are in v. 7, both with distinctive meanings. The first use in 23:7 ties several ideas together; it follows the emphasis in v. 6 which condemns the perversion of justice to the poor and then in v. 7 צדיק is used alongside נקי. In a sense, then, אביון, צדיק and נקי are used in the same context, not as synonyms but certainly as related terms. The second use in v.7 is employed in a legal sense meaning "to acquit," and finally in 23:8 the reference regards those who are "in the right" within the judicial system. These final references underline the fact that for proper relationships to exist within a community, the judicial system must be above reproach with the regard to the execution of justice.

LEVITICUS

All of the five occurrences of צדק are found within the "Holiness Code," and four of them are in 19:36. Included in the commands of Lev. 19 is one (19:15) that involves the pronouncement of judgment within the courts; instead of administering judgment with עול, do it rather with צדק. This occurrence of צדק

lends credence to the concept of "righteous judgment." The remaining four instances of צדק are all clustered in 19:36, all being used in the context of societal ethical standards with respect to weights and measures. The use of צדק in this context might create some degree of difficulty in interpretation.⁴⁵ It is certainly not suggestive of a religious connotation, yet this unusual occurrence cannot be overlooked, for once again we are reminded that even mundane items such as מאזנים, אבן, איפה and הין are associated with צדק, and it is precisely in these areas of life that צדק is needed to protect the victims. Moreover, a term such as צדק, often used to express the quintessential nature of God and the people of Israel, when used in a context such as 19:36, pointedly functions as a reminder of the inseparable connection between the sacred and the secular in ancient Israel.

NUMBERS

No occurrences.

DEUTERONOMY

There are sixteen occurrences of צדק with a diverse set of meanings. In 16:18-20, there are four instances of צדק, all of which are used in the context of "doing justice" to the poor and not perverting justice and taking bribes. In 9:4-6, there are three occurrences which are used in a somewhat negative sense in order to emphasize to Israel that the basis for possessing the land is not its צדק, but rather the צדק of Yahweh, the sole decision-maker.⁴⁶ Also,

---

⁴⁵ It is interesting to note that the LXX renders the occurrences of צדק in this context with cognates of δικαιοῦν. This is a suitable translation, particularly for the Greek-speaking world at the time; it corresponds with their understanding of δικαιοῦν and demonstrates the meaning of צדק in this context. Equally interesting is the fact that the RSV translates these occurrences with "just," intimating a clearly forensic overtone, while the NRSV has changed it to "honest."

⁴⁶ Even though this allusion to the צדק of Yahweh does not make explicit reference to the dynamic nature of Yahweh's צדק, nevertheless it is implied in the fact that Yahweh does something on Israel's behalf through his צדק.

צדק is used twice in 25:1, once to mean "innocent" and a second time to mean "acquit." Both of the occurrences are clearly within a forensic framework. (cf. Exod. 23:7) On two occasions צדק is used as an attribute, once in 32:4 in connection with Yahweh and again in 33:21 in association with Gad; in both of these instances it is used together with משפט. צדק is used as "righteous," describing the ordinances of Yahweh, in 1:16, while in 4:8, it is used in the context of a rhetorical question, pointing to the greatness of Yahweh's righteous ordinances. The ethical aspects of צדק come into consideration in 24:13 where it is used regarding the "restoration of pledges" to the neighbor, and in 25:15 where it is employed in association with "weights and measures."[47] Finally, in 33:19, it is used in a context describing acceptable and unacceptable sacrifices; what is desirable and expected are not sacrifices which are simply mechanical, but ones which have intrinsic connections with צדק.

JOSHUA

No occurrences.

JUDGES

There are two occurrences, both in 5:11, two of the oldest uses of צדק in the Old Testament. They are a part of the "Song of Deborah" which sings of the "triumphs" (צדקות) of Yahweh and the "triumphs" (צדקת) of his peasantry in Israel.[48] Both of these occur-

---

The צדק of Yahweh becomes explicit later as it begins to be understood in the context of "deliverance," "vindication," and "salvation."

[47] צדק used in the context of "weights" and "measures" is fairly common as we note in Deut. 25:15, Lev. 19:36, cf. also when משפט is used with weights and balances, Prov. 16:11. See also, Ezek. 45:10 which has the theme of "honest weights and balances" but which uses only צדק.

[48] It is noteworthy that צדק in this context speaks clearly of the צדק of Yahweh in a manner which suggests action. In making Israel triumph over its enemies, Yahweh demonstrates two basic elements of צדק: 1) Yahweh acts on behalf of his chosen people and brings them victory, and 2) צדק is much more than an abstract concept; for Yahweh and Israel, it is most clearly understood in tangible deeds.

rences specify that the defeat of Sisera was God's doing on behalf of the people.

I SAMUEL

Each of the three uses of צדק here has a specific context. In 12:7, Samuel reminds Israel of the "saving deeds" (צדקות) of Yahweh on its behalf[49] and in 24:18 [17] it is used in the context of David sparing Saul's life, even though the latter is undeserving of this act; this prompts Saul to remark צדיק אתה ממני.[50] Finally in 26:23, it is used as an attribute of an individual, one who is rewarded by Yahweh.

II SAMUEL

Of the seven occurrences, in three instances (8:15; 15:4; 23:3) צדק suggests something which can be administered (e.g. equity, justice) by an individual. In 8:15, it is used within the context of the king administering "justice" and "equity" (צדקה) to the people. This reference is singularly important as it points to an element in Israel's society which is often missing in its later history, namely the assertion that צדק and משפט must be a part of any king's scheme. (cf. Ps. 72:1; Isa. 9:7) In 23:3, the significance of "just rule" is underlined by the idea that it is akin to the beauty of nature. In 15:4, Absalom[51] is portrayed as one who longs to bring צדק to any-

---

[49] See, Walter Brueggemann, *First and Second Samuel* (Louisville: John Knox Press), 1990. "The term 'saving deeds' (ṣidqot) is important. 'Saving deeds' and 'righteousness' are Yahweh's characteristic acts of making things right for Israel by way of powerful intervention." p. 91

[50] Hill suggests that צדק is employed in this context, "with reference to the duty of preserving the life of the Lord's anointed." *Greek Words*, p. 85. Hill's observation gives the allusion that there is an objective standard which is established for the protection of kings and with this in mind David is "more righteous." However, it is more probable that David understands the relationship of king to community as that of Yahweh to Israel and hence acts the way he does.

[51] Regarding this particular reference, Pedersen points out that Absalom is rather reckless in his ambitions to bring צדק to all who are needing משפט. It is not so much that the ideal is wrong or unethical, but rather it is a question of the way צדק is understood by Absalom. His actions suggests that any-

has a cause.⁵² Of the remaining four occurrences, צדק is twice (22:21; 22:25) used in reference to individual righteousness and once (4:11) in antithesis to רשע. Finally in 19:29 [28] צדק is used in the sense of a "right." Mephibosheth's plea to David is one based on his inherent "right" as Saul's son, even though in this instance he is unsure as to whether this "right" is sufficient. Indeed this "right" of Mephibosheth is not enough in and of itself, and it is only David's integrity and magnanimous gesture which save Mephibosheth.

I KINGS

Three of the six occurrences are found within Solomon's dedication prayer, specifically in 8:32. In this section Solomon prays to Yahweh that he would vindicate (הצדיק) the righteous (צדיק) and reward a person according to his or her righteousness (צדקתו). These three occurrences point to a God who executes judgment: not only will the "righteous" be vindicated, but the guilty will be condemned. In this context, צדק is used in a forensic manner. In 2:32, the term "more righteous" is used again. (cf. Gen. 38:26 and I Sam. 24:18) In this instance Solomon describes Abner and Amasa as being "more righteous" than Joab. This comparative description of Joab is clearly not to be understood in a religious framework, but rather it is reckoned that Abner and Amasa were "more righteous" in terms of the execution of their commitments to the community as commanders of the armies of Israel and Judah. In essence then, Abner and Amasa were "more righteous" because they played a special role within their community and executed it well. As leaders, they were responsible for the welfare of

---

one who comes to him will be proven right - whether justly or not. *Israel I-II*, p. 346. See also, Justeson, who says that Absalom's words must be understood in a forensic sense. "On the meaning of ṢADAQ." p. 55.

⁵² NRSV renders צדק "justice" while משפט is "cause" in this context. In the MT, the suggestion from this context is that those who lack משפט seek צדק, which is what Absalom hopes to offer. This kind of relationship between צדק and משפט is not only uncommon in the Old Testament, but rather complex, and thus it is not surprising that the complexity is diluted in the NRSV by the respective use of "justice" and "cause."

the people; their success meant that this special relationship within the community continued, and in this pursuit they were killed. Indeed, being "more righteous" registers the idea that their commitment to the goodness of their cause is held in contradistinction to the intransigence of Joab. In 3:6, צדק refers to David's character to the manner in which he lived life and to the relationship he had with Yahweh. In 10:9 צדק is found within the context of the Queen of Sheba's words regarding Solomon as a king who Yahweh elected so he might execute צדק and משפט.

II KINGS

The one occurrence of צדק is in 10:9, where Jehu tells the people that they are "innocent" regarding the killing of Ahab's sons. Even though the English term rendered here for צדק is "innocent," implying a forensic direction, the sense of the context suggests an ethical one. The innocence of the people is pronounced in light of the confession of conspiracy. Having said this, this is only in reference to the immediate context. The larger context of chapter 10 suggests clearly that Jehu's involvement in the killing is intended precisely to cleanse Israel of those who would disobey Yahweh. The disobedience of Yahweh and the worship of Baal are both expressions of brokenness and the killing of those who opposed Yahweh is meant to repair this broken relationship.

ISAIAH 1-39

There are twenty-seven occurrences and of this number, four (10:22; 11:4; 26:9; 33:5) are in reference to Yahweh. The occurrences are used in contexts which point to an active sense of צדק, insofar as it is connected with Yahweh. Two of these four (10:22; 26:9) demonstrate the dynamic sense of צדק in the contexts of "judgment" and "destruction." In 11:4, it is צדק which is the basic element in shaping the Messiah's judgment. Of these four texts,

33:5 may be post-exilic.[53] In four other instances, צדק is used in a forensic manner. Three of these instances are in 5:23, while the fourth is in 29:21. The English terms used to render צדק in 5:23 are "acquit," "innocent," and "right" respectively;[54] this particular verse is part of a long series of "woe" oracles. In 29:21, צדק is associated with forensic language such as "offender," "gate" (here referring to the place of executing judgment), and "plea." There are four occurrences where צדק is used in the context of "ruling:" once (11:15), it refers to the Messianic figure who will rule with צדק, and on three occasions (9:6; 16:5; 32:1), it is used with respect to the future rulers and kings of Judah. In four other instances (3:10; 26:7 [2x], 33:15) it simply refers to "the righteous."

In the remaining eight occurrences, צדק is used in 1:21 in comparison to מרצחים, where the latter is seen to have replaced צדק and the city of Jerusalem has become consumed by מרצחים and thus instead of relationship and life, there is death. In similar fashion in 5:7, צדקה is replaced by צעקה. In 1:26, when the city of Jerusalem is restored, it will be called עיר הצדק; this restoration reflects the brokenness spoken of in Isa. 1:21. In 1:27, צדק is portrayed as intrinsic to the act of repentance. In 26:2, צדק is used to describe Judah; it is a song of victory, for Judah will become a "righteous" nation. In 26:10, it is used in antithesis to רשע and in 28:17, it is coupled with משפט as the standards by which Judah will be judged. Finally, in 32:17, the presence of צדק results in "peace" and "serenity."

---

[53] This section of Isa. 33 contains admonitions and post-exilic oracles. It has been called a "prophetic liturgy." This prophecy points to the destruction of a certain world power. Certain elements in the prophecy make it clear that the conditions which are being described are contemporary and not apocalyptic. Perhaps the most obvious point which suggests a later authorship has to do with the message of the chapter, namely, the rising fortunes of Jerusalem and the destruction of the enemy. See Otto Eissfeldt, *The Old Testament*, trans. Peter Ackroyd (Oxford: Basil Blackwell), 1965, p. 327.

[54] See Hans Wildberger, *Isaiah 1-12*. (Minneapolis: Fortress Press), 1992. Wildberger suggests that given the antithesis of צדק and רשע, the understanding of צדק cannot be "righteous one" in an absolute sense, but rather the declaration of innocence for a particular indictment. p.211

ISAIAH 40-66

There are fifty occurrences here and of this number, seventeen (41:2,10; 45:8,19,25; 46:12,13; 50:8; 51:5,6,8; 54:14,17; 61:11; 62:1,2; 63:1) are used with respect to Yahweh as a God who *does* צדק. In these contexts, צדק is used to note "deliverance," "vindication," "declaring צדק," "establishing צדק." It is in these instances that there is the greatest indication of צדק as a dynamic and potent concept, particularly with regard to Yahweh. In eight other instances (48:18; 51:7; 57:1 [2x],12; 58:8; 59:16; 60:21), צדק is used in something of a general manner to refer to "the righteous" and the righteousness of person in various circumstances of life. There are also seven occurrences (42:6,21; 45:13,21,23,24; 58:2) where צדק is used as an attribute of Yahweh and the standard by which God relates to humanity. In four instances (48:1; 58:2; 64:4[5], 5[6]) צדק is used in an active and concrete sense; typically rendered "deed" in English. Four other instances find צדק being used as a part of a metaphor: in 59:17 it is "צדק as a breastplate;" in 60:17, the phrase ונגשׂיך צדקה is used;[55] in 61:3 there are "oaks of צדק" and in 61:10 there is "robe of צדק." In both 59:17 and 61:10, the presence of צדק as part of the clothing necessary for humanity invites us to understand that צדק is an essential aspect for one's life. Of note here is that all of these metaphors have to do with care and protection. On three occasions (43:9,26; 59:4) it is used in contexts which suggest a forensic use. In two other instances (41:26; 58:2) צדק is used to refer to Yahweh in contexts where the connotations are ethical and judicial respectively. The use of צדק in 51:1 and 56:1 is related. In 51:1, it is used in the context of Yahweh speaking to those who "pursue deliverance," while in 56:1, it is within a context which finds the prophet calling for צדק and משׁפט to be done. In 59:9,14 צדק is seen as something essential, but which is absent from society. With the absence of צדק and משׁפט (which is used in both contexts), the community now has "darkness" instead of "light" and "gloom" instead

---

[55] The NRSV translates this phrase as "and righteousness as your taskmaster." This phrase while pointing to part of the intended message, creates a picture of domination and cruelty. The JB better serves the intent of the text when it translates the phrase: "and integrity as the government."

of "brightness." Finally, in 53:11, there are two occurrences, one which describes the suffering servant and the second noting the new state of those for whom this servant will suffer.

JEREMIAH

Of the eighteen occurrences, four are used in reference to Yahweh. In 12:1, it is mentioned as an attribute, and in 9:23[24], 11:20 and 51:10 it is used in an active sense; in the first context, it is noted that Yahweh practises צדק while in the second instance, Yahweh judges with צדק. In the third occurrence, Israel is vindicated (צדק) by Yahweh, a vindication which is seen in part through the punishment of Babylon. There are three occurrences in 23:5,6 all of which are in reference to the "righteous branch." This king will execute both צדק and משפט, and in fact Israel and Judah will become secure. Security, thus is borne out of the practice of that which generates kinship and relationship. This king will be the embodiment of righteousness and hence his name will be יהוה צדקנו. The words and message of 23:5,6 are repeated *verbatim* in 33:15,16. On two other occasions צדק is used in connecting themes; in 31:23 it is used within the description regarding the restoration of Israel; Yahweh says that Israel will be known as the "habitation of righteousness." In 50:7 Yahweh is described as Israel's "true habitation" (נוה צדק) and it is against Yahweh that Israel[56] has sinned. Of the remaining four occurrences, twice it is used in the context of Israel's estrangement from Yahweh. In 3:11, "faithless" Israel is seen to be less guilty than Judah, and in returning (3:12), 4:2 looks for a confession of the צדק of Yahweh. Arguably, these two occurrences are most fundamentally the ones which best reflect the relationship between Yahweh and his people. That is to say, Israel's faith is the essence for continued communion with Yahweh and when faith dwindles then only repentance (שוב) can restore

---

[56] "Israel" is here referring to the "people of Yahweh" and not to the Northern Kingdom. In 31:23 and 50:7, Israel and Judah are both mentioned - in the first place, sinning against Yahweh and then being restored.

it.⁵⁷ The final two occurrences are used in 20:12, a context which notes that Yahweh puts to the test the righteous, and in 22:3, where there is the call to do צדק and משפט. This latter occurrence is particularly important for two reasons. First, Yahweh's message is to the king, who is the person with the greatest responsibility for the executing of צדק. Not only is he the ruler but in that position, he is also Yahweh's deputy. Second, there is a certain class of people who is specified, the ones who are apt to be oppressed, the orphan, the widow, the alien. The importance of justice for these people is that it is their inherent right, but equally important, is the reality that oppression of these individuals reflects and lead to brokenness in the society, which in turn creates a rift in the covenant relationship. Thus Yahweh's message to the king, must be seen in the light of Yahweh's relationship with Israel.

EZEKIEL

Of the forty-one occurrences of צדק in this book, twenty-four are used within contexts which dwell on the elements that result in "life" or "death."⁵⁸ Seventeen of these instances (3:20[3x]; 21; 18:24[3x], 26; 33:12[4x]; 33:13[3x]; 33:18[2x]), are used in contexts which call attention to the reality that turning away from righteousness leads to "death." In effect, righteousness at one point in one's life is not a policy of assurance which guarantees sufficiency to ensure a continuation of life. Rather, righteousness is regarded (implicitly here) as something which is dynamic; it is a life long process. The parallel view is seen in nine instances (18:5[2x],⁵⁹

---

⁵⁷ The words which are in 3:11 (משבה) and in 4:1 (תשוב) are both derivatives of שוב, the term which is most often employed to refer to "repentance." It is interesting to note that משבה in 3:11 is in reference to Israel's "turning away."

⁵⁸ Von Rad, observes that "the nature of righteousness and who the righteous man is, is determined by Jahweh alone, and a man lives as he acknowledges this." *Theol.* I, p. 379.

⁵⁹ This is one of the rare instances in the Old Testament where there is an explicit listing of the elements which constitute צדק. In 18:5-9, we have items such as "lack of oppression," "restoration of dues to debtor," "no robbery," "feeding the hungry," "clothing the naked," "lending without interest," "executing justice," and "keeping the ordinances." While there is no

9,21,22,27; 33:14,16,19). In these instances, it is expressed many times that "life" comes from righteousness, even if the person in question was once "wicked." Righteousness is thus portrayed as being able to overcome and erase wickedness. In other words, one period of "wickedness" in one's life is not an invitation to be subsumed in "wickedness" for the rest of one's life. Righteousness may be embarked upon at any given point in one's life. Five other occurrences (14:14,20; 18:19,20[2x]) are used with respect to the possibility of righteousness being hereditary or transferable. In these contexts, it becomes clear that the "sins" of the parents are not inherited by the children and conversely the righteousness of some will be of no use to those who are "wicked." Four other occurrences are found in 45:9,10[3x], all of which are used in the context of doing צדק. In 45:9, the doing of צדק and משפט is seen as desirable acts, in contrast to doing חמס and שד. The three appearances of צדק in 45:10 underline a use which has already been discussed.[60] In this instance, צדק has practical implications, and has clear ethical overtones. On three occasions (21:8,9 [3,4]; 23:45), צדק is used to refer to those who are "righteous." In 23:45, "the righteous" is used in something of an ethical sense, connoting in this particular context, those who are not adulterous. In 21:8,9 [3,4] "righteous" is seen in antithesis to "wicked," even though in these particular references, the fate of the צדק and רשע are the same. The three remaining occurrences of צדק are in 16:51,52[2x], where the situation in Jerusalem is compared to such nations as Samaria and Sodom. In 16:51, it is noted that Samaria has not committed half the sins of Jerusalem, a situation which makes Samaria "appear righteous"[61] in comparison; this phrase is also repeated in 16:52. The

---

indication that this list is exhaustive, it clearly includes many of the salient elements which are scattered throughout the Old Testament.

[60] For similar occurrences of "balances" and "measures" see above, note 47.

[61] The Piel (הצדקי) form of צדק, because of the context is best translated "appear righteous." Dodd suggests that this form of the verb can never carry any connotation having to do with the "declaration of righteousness" or "making righteous." He argues that "appearing righteous" is consequently an erroneous rendering of הצדקי, rather it should be translated "in the right," *The Bible and the Greeks*, p. 47. It is arguable here, that Dodd's theory demonstrates weakness on two counts.

first of the two occurrences in 16:52 may be used in the sense of being "in the right," comparatively speaking.62 Finally in 13:22, צדק is in antithesis to רשע.

HOSEA

There are four occurrences of צדק and of this number, two are in 10:12. In this context, there is much farming imagery. Israel is living in "fallow ground" which suggests readiness for farming but absence of seeds. The prophet suggests that Israel sow צדק and in so doing, reap חסד and Yahweh will "rain" צדק. In 2:21[19] צדק is used as a part of the marriage imagery, between Yahweh and Israel. One of the qualities which Yahweh will bring into the relationship between Israel and himself, one is צדק. Finally, in 14:10 [9] it is used in the context of a request to Israel to return to Yahweh, whose ways are "right" (צדק); Yahweh's ways are "right" presumably over against those of idols.

First, "in the right" as Dodd suggests implies a forensic sense, which in turn presupposes that Israel is in a legal harangue with Sodom and Samaria. This is clearly untenable, as chapter 16 focuses on the apostasy and "harlotry" of Israel; that Sodom and Samaria among other neighboring nations are mentioned, is not to detract from the underlying theme, namely, the breakdown of the relationship between Israel and Yahweh. The significance of the contiguous nations in this regard is clearly tangential.
Second, as is noted earlier, the major point in this chapter has to do with the relationship between Israel and Yahweh. With this in mind, it is not possible that Sodom and Samaria are "in the right" with Yahweh, over against Israel. Israel and Yahweh are in a covenant relationship, Israel is Yahweh's chosen people; they alone can be "in the wrong" or "in the right" in that relationship. Sodom and Samaria are used as props in a drama which involves directly only Israel and Yahweh. As such, none of the contiguous nations mentioned in chapter 16 is in a position to vie with Israel regarding the relationship with Yahweh; only Israel can be "in the right" in this respect.
62 Hill notes that, "Samaria and Sodom" are more "in the right" at "judgement than Jerusalem, because the extent of their sinning is less great." *Greek Words*, p. 85.

Chapter I 39

JOEL

The one occurrence, which is in 2:23, is used in a context that points to the vindication of Israel by Yahweh. Israel is vindicated on several counts in this chapter-the remission of the plague, (v. 20); the restoration of the covenant, (vv. 26-27) and specifically, in the context with which this study is concerned, the return of fertility. This latter occurrence is an important one particularly because there is a clear association between the vindication of Israel and the restoration of the covenant. What is at stake here is the relationship between Yahweh and Israel.

AMOS

Of the five occurrences, three (2:6; 5:7, 12) point to the way צדק has been crushed within the community in general, and in particular against the disenfranchised. In 2:6, it is in the form of a judgment oracle. Here, there is judgment against Israel for selling and oppressing the "righteous," and in this instance a formula identical to the ones used against Judah and Moab is incorporated in the judgment oracle against Israel. In 5:7, צדק is trampled into the ground by a particular segment of the community, while in 5:12, it is in reference to those who are being afflicted, "the righteous." In this instance, "the righteous" are those persons who need the impartiality of the elected leaders; instead they discover that the very persons who have been mandated to care for them are corrupt. In 6:12, צדק has become poisonous; this occurrence forms a part of an answer to two rhetorical questions which in their respective form indicate that certain things are by their very nature impossible. According to the text one of these is surely צדק, yet Israel is able to turn צדק into wormwood. What is needed is for צדק to cascade like a waterfall (5:24), an idea that displays movement, action, dynamism-not death, but life.

OBADIAH

No occurrences.

JONAH

No occurrences.

MICAH

Both of the occurrences in this book are in reference to Yahweh, in an active sense. In 6:5, the prophet recounts for Israel, the saving acts (צדק) of Yahweh on their behalf, and proceeds to outline for Israel the many expressions of their sins against Yahweh.[63] In 7:9, צדק is used in the context of Israel's deliverance, by Yahweh.[64]

NAHUM

No occurrences.

HABAKKUK

There are three occurrences of צדק and two of these (1:13, 2:4) are used in contexts which place it in antithesis to some other concept. In 1:13 it is in opposition to "wicked" while in 2:4, it is against "the proud." Both the notions of being "wicked" and "proud" are detrimental to matters of relationship. The third occurrence is in 1:4 and in this instance צדק is employed in its most complex use of the three occurrences. The clearly recognizable use is as an antithesis to "wicked," but in this context, the "wicked" are those who pervert the law, something which directly affects the righteous. צדק here is used alongside משפט, which is used twice in this verse.

---

[63] See, Hans Walter Wolff, *Micah* (Minneapolis: Augsburg Fortress Press), 1990. "The phrase צדקות יהוה expresses, on the one hand, the concept of Yahweh's righteousness; but it dictates on the other, that such righteousness is the result of his deeds of salvation from disaster...צדקות יהוה therefore has become the particular expression in the Old Testament for, and at the same time an interpretation of Yahweh's 'saving history.'" p. 177

[64] Some have argued that Mic. 7:8-20 is a late addition and hence cannot be viewed as a legitimate expression of his preaching. For a discussion of this view, see Eissfeldt, *The Old Testament*, pp. 411-12.

Chapter I

ZEPHANIAH

Of the two occurrences, the one in 2:3 finds the prophet imploring the people to "seek righteousness," an act which may ultimately save them from the wrath of Yahweh. The occurrence in 3:5 is used in the context of describing Yahweh; this however is not a mere attribute, but one which is reflected in the acts of Yahweh, such as demonstrating justice.

HAGGAI

No occurrences.

ZECHARIAH

Of the two occurrences, the one in 8:8 is found within the context of the description of the restoration of Israel. In this instance, when Israel is restored, there will be a reciprocal relationship expressed in the formula: "they shall be my people and I will be their God," and this relationship will exist in "faithfulness" and "righteousness." צדק thus is central for the restoration of a fractured relationship. The second occurrence is in 9:9 and here it describes the "Prince of Peace" entering Jerusalem.[65] This royalty will be one who will set about destroying all that makes for war, and thereby establish peace among peoples. In this instance, צדק is not only a characteristic of the king, but moreover, the act which brings about peace.

MALACHI

There are three occurrences and each is used in a different manner. In 3:3 it is in reference to the kind of offerings which are acceptable, namely, ones which are given in צדק. In 3:18, it is used in antithesis to "wicked;" the "righteous" serve Yahweh while the

---

[65] This particular reference is used by the Gospel writers to describe Jesus as he triumphantly enters Jerusalem. See Matt. 21:5; John 12:14-15.

"wicked" do not. Finally in 3:20 [4:2] it is part of a metaphor which is associated with Yahweh.

PSALMS

There are one hundred and thirty-five occurrences here and most of these can be classified in two main categories. Fifty occurrences (1:5,6; 5:13 [12]; 7:9,10; 11:3; 14:5; 17:1,15; 18:21 [20], 25 [24]; 32:11; 31:19 [18]; 33:1; 34:16 [15], 20 [19], 22 [21]; 37:12,16,17,25, 28, 29,30,32,39; 45:5 [4]; 52:8 [6]; 55:23 [22]; 58:11 [10], 12 [11]; 64:11 [10]; 68:4 [3]; 69:29 [28]; 92:13 [12]; 94:15,21; 97:11,12; 112:6; 118:15,20; 119:121; 125:3 [2x]; 132:9; 140:14 [13]; 141:5; 142:8 [7]; 146:8) are in reference to those who are righteous and many of these are used in antithesis to terms such as רשע and שקר. Even though 132:9 is included in this category, it is not simply an attribute which is associated with the priests, but more of a requirement and expectation. (cf. Job 29:14) The second category has צדק in association with Yahweh. In this regard, there are three main sections. First, there are thirty-five occurrences (4:2 [1]; 5:9 [8]; 7:18 [17]; 11:7 [2x]; 19:10 [9]; 35:28; 36:7 [6], 11 [10]; 50:6; 71:16,19; 72:1,2; 85:12 [11], 14 [13]; 89:17 [16]; 103:17; 106:3,31; 111:3; 112:3,4,9; 116:5, 119:40,138,142 [2x],144; 129:4; 143:1,2,11; 145:7) which simply refer to the righteousness of Yahweh without any particular contextual overtone. Second, there are twenty instances (22:32 [31]; 24:5; 31:2 [1]; 35:24,27; 37:6; 40:10 [9], 11 [10]; 48:11 [10]; 51:16 [14]; 65:6 [5]; 71:2,15,24; 82:3, 88:13 [12]; 98:2; 103:6; 119:123; 145:17) in which צדק is used within the context of Yahweh's dynamic righteousness. That is, in these occurrences, there are references to Yahweh's "vindication," "salvation," "deliverance," "saving help" and "ways." Third, there are ten occurrences (7:12 [11]; 9:5 [4], 9[8]; 15:2; 51:6 [4]; 96:13; 98:9; 99:4; 119:75,137) which use צדק in the context of "righteous judgments of Yahweh." Clearly in these contexts צדק is not meant to be understood as an attribute of Yahweh, but rather to be seen in a judicial sense.

There are also six occurrences, in Psalm 119 (7,62,106,160, 164,172), which refer to the ordinances of Yahweh and in three other instances (72:3,7; 85:11 [10]), צדק is viewed as the source out of which peace and serenity come. In 33:5; 45:8 [7]; and 106:3, it is viewed as an aspect of life which is pleasing to Yahweh. In 4:6 [5] and 51:21 [19], it is used in reference to sacrifices; the only sacrifices which are acceptable are "right" (צדק) sacrifices. צדק in this context does not refer to a type or kind of sacrifice, but rather to the attitude of the presenter. The external characteristics of the sacrifice will not change, whether "right" or not, but if it is to be "right," then the one who is making the sacrifice must be צדק.[66] In 58:2 [1] and 69:28 [27], it is used in a judicial sense; while in 89:15 [14] and 97:2, it is used in the description of the throne of Yahweh - one which has its foundation in צדק and משפט. Finally, in 23:3, צדק is used in the context of Yahweh leading in the "path of righteousness," while in 118:19, it is found in still another metaphor, in the phrase "gate of righteousness."

JOB

There are thirty-four occurrences, ten of which (10:15; 17:9; 22:19; 27:6; 32:1; 34:17; 35:7,8; 36:3,7) are used in contexts of an individual attribute. In nine occurrences (9:15,20; 12:4; 27:5,17; 32:2; 33:12; 34:5; 35:2), צדק is used in reference to Job's "innocence." When used in this context, it portrays Job as one party in a trial, Yahweh being the other party. In two of these instances (27:17 and 32:2) Job pointedly declares that he, and not Yahweh is the one who is innocent. As used in this context צדק is clearly meant to be forensic. In six other occurrences (4:7; 9:2; 11:2; 15:14; 22:3; 25:4), צדק is found within the context of rhetorical questions all aiming to underline the futility of boasting of personal צדק before Yahweh. On three occasions (8:3; 37:23; 40:8) צדק is used in reference to Yahweh, pointing to the fact that he is a God of צדק and will not pervert

---

[66] See Randall T. Ruble, "A study of the root ṢDK in the Psalter." (Ph.D. dissertation, University of Edinburgh), 1964. Regarding Ps. 51:21, Ruble observes that, "the sacrifice which is acceptable to God is in the final analysis a broken spirit and a contrite heart (v. 19) and this is precisely what is demanded by Yahweh in his relation with his covenant people. A sacrifice of ṣedek is thus a sacrifice which is offered not simply in accordance with a prescribed cultic format but one which expresses the life of a man who has been obedient to Yahweh by fulfilling the demands of his covenant." p. 280.

it. In 6:29 and 13:18, Job pleads for his "vindication" (צִדְקִי). Both of the occurrences in 31:6 and 33:32 point to a forensic use; the former finds Job pleading with God to have a "just" (צֶדֶק) balance while the latter occurs in Elihu's reproval of Job. Finally in 29:14 it is used to describe Job's character while in 33:26 it is in the context of describing Yahweh's salvation (צִדְקָתוֹ) which he gives to the people.

PROVERBS

There are eighty-four occurrences of צדק and forty-five of these (10:3,6,7,11,16,20,24,25,28,32; 11:5,8,18; 12:3,5,7,10,12,21,26; 13:5,9,25; 14:19,32; 15:6,9,28,29;17:15; 18:5; 21:12,18,26; 24:15,16,24; 25:26; 28:1,12,28; 29:2,7,16,27) are used in some form as antithetical references to רשע. In this way, these occurrences outline the many benefits which come to "the righteous" and the setbacks and punishments which befall "the wicked." Used in similar fashion, are eleven other occurrences (10:21,31; 11:6,9,19,30; 12:13; 13:6; 14:34; 21:15; 29:6). These occurrences are all used antithetically, but in these instances צדק is pitted against such notions as "evil," "godless," "treacherous," "fool," "sin," and "perversity." In six instances, (9:9; 16:31; 17:26; 18:10; 20:7; 23:24) it refers to those who are "righteous." On five occasions, it is used in contexts which outline what are some of the fruits of righteousness, blessings (3:33), prosperity (8:18; 13:21) and life (12:28; 21:21). On another five occasions (8:15,16; 16:12,13; 25:5), it is used in the context of identifying kingdoms and reigns with צדק; kings and rulers are expected to execute צדק since their thrones have been established in צדק. That is, in the very foundation of vocation lodges צדק. Three other instances are found in what is often regarded to be the late editorial section of the book. These instances (1:3; 2:9; 8:20) not only point to the intent of the book, but more importantly, to the necessity for there to be צדק; in each of these occurrences, צדק is used together with משפט. In some ways, the occurrence of צדק in 21:3 is similar in use to the preceding three instances. In this specific case, there is the call to *do* צדק and משפט, particularly since this is more acceptable to Yahweh than sacrifices. On three other occasions in which

Chapter I 45

צדק is used, it is employed in contrast to "wealth" and "treasures." In these instances (10:2; 13:22; 16:8) צדק is seen as the more rewarding of the two options.67 Twice (2:20; 4:18) it is used as a part of a metaphor, "paths of righteousness," and twice (12:17; 18:17) it is used in a forensic sense. Finally, in 8:8, it is used to describe the words of Yahweh.

RUTH

No occurrences.

SONG OF SONGS

No occurrences.

ECCLESIASTES

It is not surprising that most of the ten occurrences are found bearing somewhat negative overtones. In seven instances (3:16, 7:15 [2x],16,20; 8:14; 9:2) צדק is used in contexts which underline the futility of righteousness and the generic end which comes to the "righteous" and "wicked" alike. However, there are two occasions (3:17, 9:1) when Qoheleth suggests that both the "wicked" and the "righteous" will be judged; there is a time for this also. Finally in 5:8 [7], צדק is viewed as a "right" which is often usurped from the poor; as in 3:17 and 9:1, there will also be a time for the offender to be judged.

LAMENTATIONS

There are two occurrences of צדק here. In 1:18, it is used in the form צדיק, describing Yahweh as "in the right" with regard to

---

67 That fifty-six of the eighty-four occurrences of צדק in Proverbs are used in contexts where צדק is a part of an antithesis, underlines the basic intent behind much of Proverbs, namely, instruction. When צדק is placed in opposition to רשע, then it is evident as to what is of value and what is not.

the prophet's rebellion. In 4:13, it is used to mean "righteous" in the sense of not being guilty of any wrong-doing.

ESTHER

No occurrences.

DANIEL

Five of the seven occurrences in this book are found in chapter nine. Three of these (9:7,14,16) are in reference to Yahweh, the last two being with specific reference to the acts of Yahweh on behalf of his people. In 9:18, צדק is used in a context which points to the fact that when there is forgiveness for a people (in this case Israel), it is not because of their righteousness that they receive it, but rather through the mercy of Yahweh. In 9:24, צדק will replace "transgression," "sin," "iniquity;" this is part of the angel Gabriel's message to Daniel. Another occurrence is in 12:3, which is part of Daniel's apocalyptic vision. In this context, it is told that those who bring others to righteousness will themselves be like stars for eternity.[68] Finally in 8:14, צדק is used in the context of the restoration of the temple to its "rightful" state.[69]

EZRA

The one occurrence in 9:15 is used in the context of a confession of the צדק of Yahweh.

---

[68] This occurrence introduces an element which not only presupposes "living in and doing righteousness" but also extending righteousness to others.

[69] On first appearance, this may seem to be an unimportant reference, but as Pedersen notes, "...to justify and make right is to restore to normal condition. The temple is restored - cleansed of impurity and once more turned into a sanctuary." *Israel I-II*, p. 346.

NEHEMIAH

Of the three occurrences, the one in 2:20 is in reference to an individual's "right." In this particular instance it involves those who would question Nehemiah's vision and his faith in God; they have no inherent "right," precisely because they are not of Jerusalem. The other two occurrences are in 9:8 and 9:33, both of which employ צדק in reference to Yahweh, specifically in the light of his acts.

I CHRONICLES

צדק is used once in 18:14 in the context of describing David as a king who administers צדק and משפט to his people.

II CHRONICLES

There are five occurrences of צדק and of these, three are found in 6:23. The meanings and connotations here are identical to those of I Ki. 8:32. (See the above discussion on I Ki. 8:32) In 12:6, it is in the context of Rehoboam and Judah's confession of Yahweh's righteousness,[70] while in 9:8, it is used in identical fashion to the occurrence in I Ki. 10:9.(See the above discussion)

There are several points which arise out of an analysis such as this. In a very abbreviated form, it places in context and perspective the various uses and meanings which can be derived from צדק. As we study these occurrences, it will allow us to perceive what is the motivational force behind the uses, that is to say, for what particular purpose צדק is employed in a given context, and whether the aim is focused on an individual situation or whether it forms part of a larger unit. In this respect, we will discuss the possibility of צדק referring either to a "norm" or to a "relationship," when it is

---

[70] It is noteworthy that with the prospect of being abandoned at the hands of the Egyptians, the confession is צדיק יהוה. Implicit in this confession is the fact that there could be deliverance, an element which becomes a principal aspect of Deutero-Isaiah.

viewed in its entire spectrum. It is apparent after a cursory view that many of the uses of צדק have distinctive meanings, and, when isolated, they appear to have little association with any greater idea. However as צדק is discussed, we will endeavor to illustrate through the use of a variety of examples, the fact that there is a pattern which emerges.

In addition to this, this distribution will enable us on the basis of the contexts, to determine the uses of צדק. That is, there will be some indication whether a particular occurrence is "ethical" or "religious" or "forensic" in overtone and whether there is a notable pattern which can be deciphered. Moreover, this distribution will certainly point to the subjects and objects of צדק and we will then be in a position to determine if there is a preponderance of use in any particular area.

B. צדק and the Functional Locus

1. Norm

Several scholars have proposed that in order to understand the fundamental meaning behind צדק in the Old Testament, it must be viewed within the context of "norm." When there is the call to do צדק, it means primarily the wholehearted subscription to a norm which governs a particular situation or circumstance. Living in צדק, means essentially the same thing, namely, to orient one's actions in accordance with a norm. צדק as the norm of relations within a community means that power is shared by all members and there is equity and equality. In effect, it means that it brings together the ideals of the individual with those of the community and arranges them in such an order that they become mutually acceptable and beneficial. Fahlgren illustrates this point regarding צדק as norm through the idea that the norm concurs with the acceptable status quo.[71]

---

[71] See, Fahlgren, *Ṣᵉdākā*, pp. 81-82. Also Kautzsch, צדק, and H.P. Smith, "צדק and its derivatives," *TPR* 3 (1882), pp. 165-168.

It is with צדק as norm, that Yahweh is continuously acting along with the community and as such this becomes the self evident regulator of life; everything which transpires is measured by this norm. As long as this kind of foundation exists, then the norm which is set up will function, and doing צדק will automatically follow. In other words, there are certain variables, such as God, community, king, and the norm which is established purportedly combines and involves the expectations of all parties. However, if the community forfeits its position in the framework, then the norm malfunctions. Or, if a despotic ruler usurps the position of Yahweh and imposes a foreign "norm" and this is an opportunistic act only for the ruler's benefit, then it is no longer a norm but an alien law. Under ideal conditions, the community responds to the norm willingly; however, if a norm is imposed, then it creates coercion and infringes on the concept of norm. Accordingly, when a standard is unilaterally inflicted, it cannot be a norm. What Fahlgren is attempting to do here is to underline the premise that צדק as norm can be a legitimate theory, but it is imperative that all of its variables are present and participating as a unit.[72]

It must be pointed out here that צדק as conforming to a norm is not merely a theory, which has arisen in recent scholarship. Some scholars[73] have directed our attention to its use in Arabic, a use which they claim signifies conformity to a norm. This particular citation is meant to demonstrate the historical background for the use of the concept of norm, and by implication a concept which must find legitimacy in Old Testament usage. It is this belief which prompts Jacob to conclude, "righteousness is therefore conformity to a norm; in origin it is neither punitive, nor distributive, nor justificatory, but in a general way fidelity to a state or to a way of acting or thinking."[74]

---

[72] Fahlgren, $S^e d\bar{a}k\bar{a}$, p. 83.

[73] See, e.g. Edmond Jacob, *Theology of the Old Testament*. trans. Arthur W. Heathcote and Philip J. Allcock (New York: Harper and Brothers, Publishers), 1958. Jacob notes that, "when in Arabic, a date is called *tsdq* that can neither refer to its form nor to its taste but can simply mean that it conforms to what it should normally be." p. 94.

[74] Ibid., p. 94.

This norm however, is not an absolute generic norm under whose umbrella every circumstance fits, but rather "the norm is furnished by the objective standard of the thing itself: and in cases where the term is applied to persons, the rightness or righteousness of conduct depends on the fulfilling of obligations arising from a particular situation or set of circumstances."75 As such, there is a norm for each situation and when the standards are met for each situation, then there is evidence of צדק. Selective examples will at this point be helpful. There are at least three instances76 in which we find צדק used in the same context as "weights," "balances," "measures," and the argument which is proposed here adverts the need for conformity to proper standards. This example is rather apposite in that "balances," "measures," and "weights" do in fact conform to some kind of standard, and so this becomes an obvious choice which is used to sanction צדק as conforming to a norm. Hence it is not surprising that proponents of this view all discuss the significance of this example.77

---

75 Hill, *Greek Words*, pp. 84-85. See also, Th. Vriezen, *An Outline of Old Testament Theology* (Oxford: Basil Blackwell), 1966. Vriezen notes, "*Ṣaddiq* is somebody or something that is as he or it should be; the meaning of the word is '*real*,' 'pure,' 'true,' that which agrees with the end to which it has been created, that which inwardly, fundamentally corresponds to its external appearance, and therefore actually fulfills the function for which (he) it exists." p. 327. See also, Norman Snaith, *The Distinctive Ideas of the Old Testament* (London: The Epsworth Press), 1944. Snaith notes that "*Tsedeq*, with its kindred words, signifies that standard which God maintains in this world. It is the norm by which all must be judged." p. 77.

76 See above, note 47

77 Fahlgren observes that Lev. 19:36, says nothing which indicates explicitly what the "righteousness" of measuring entails, but the context leaves no doubt. He notes that עול in 19:35 is a Hebrew expression which points to injustice. כמשפט in this context should not be viewed as referring to jurisdiction in the courts, but rather to daily communication in trade and life. With this as a backdrop for v. 36, the meaning which is elicited refers to the fact that what is needed is the conforming to the norm which is laid down and which is turn will extend communication in trade and life. *Ṣᵉdākā*, pp. 85-86. Also, Jacob points out that, "objects which conform to a type are called *tsdq*: just balances, just weights, just measures are objects in conformity with what they ought to be." *Theol.*, p. 95. Hill further notes that this example "clearly connotes conformity to proper standards. The balances, etc. are to be 'as they should be,' 'correct,' or 'right.'" *Greek Words*, p. 84.

78 Jacob, *Theol.*, p. 95.

Chapter I 51

Moreover, conformity to a norm is not only subjected to external objective, measurable items, but it is also applicable to the inward dispositions of people and the manner in which they conduct themselves.[78] In this regard, the description in Ezek. 16:52 is cited as a source of verification for this point. In this text, appearance of righteousness is granted to Samaria and Sodom when they are compared with Israel, and this is based upon the comparative number of sins which have been committed by the countries. In effect, what this view illustrates is that צדק is an objective norm and the declaration of righteousness is given to the party which comes closest to the standard of the norm.[79] In addition to this, the incident between Judah and Tamar is cited as another example which underlines צדק as conforming to a norm. This story in Gen. 38:1-26 is viewed as a situation which is corrupted by Judah, specifically with respect to the obligatory marital standard which is violated.[80]

One further example will suffice at this point. In Joel 2:23, צדק is used in the context of "rain" and "fertility of crops," and in some ways it is an awkward occurrence of צדק to explain. However, when perceived as conforming to a norm, Fahlgren finds an explanation not so difficult. He notes that it is possible that לצדקה should be rendered as "right time," as is the case in the Swedish Bible. This would mean that it corresponds with the norm of the community, that in the expected time of harvest the rain will come; that is to say, the rain will come at the right time.[81] The implication in all of this is that the rain will arrive at the right time and in the right amount and in the right manner so that the people may be rescued from famine and death.

---

[79] Ibid., p. 95.

[80] Hill suggests that the accepted standard which is abused by Judah is the levirate marriage laws, which are respected by Tamar even though she is accused of harlotry, *Greek Words*, p. 84. Also regarding this incident, Jacob, *Theol.*, concludes that Tamar is "more righteous" precisely because she understands the circumstances and is obeying the rules of prostitution, while Judah is not; hence she is "more righteous." p. 95. Snaith notes that "Tamar, in spite of having played the harlot and thereby coming to be with child, has conformed more closely to the accepted standards than Judah himself." *The Distinctive Ideas of the Old Testament*, p. 73

[81] See Fahlgren, Ṣᵉdāḳā, pp. 88-89.

The discussion thus far regarding conformity to a norm suggests that the basis for the determination of צדק is principally the subscribing to a norm. However, even though Jacob has said, "righteousness is therefore conformity to a norm,"[82] he has also said that, "righteousness is always a concept of relationship, fashioned upon the everyday dealings between two people."[83] How do we reconcile these two statements? The proponents of the view, (צדק as norm) suggest that Yahweh has set a variety of standards depending on the situations, and these must be met in order for צדק to be present. In other words, righteousness is attributed to a person because of his or her actions: "a person is righteous because he acts justly; he does not act justly because he is righteous."[84] The ultimate norm to which an individual must subscribe is seen in the Being of Yahweh. In essence then, subscription to norms is only significant when seen in the light of family units and the covenantal relationship. Hill underlines this well when he says:

> While custom and duty may thus provide the norm by which the "righteousness" of an action is judged, these were related to a much wider and more basic criterion of behavior. The Israelite, like the member of other tribal societies, possessed a deep consciousness of the family, tribal and later national unit and regarded himself as under obligation to fulfill the demands and laws which made for the well-being and good-ordering of that unit....But in Israelite thinking, one relationship is supremely important, the covenant relation between Yahweh and his people, and this has great significance for the understanding of personal and community righteousness in Israel and of the righteousness of Yahweh. [85]

---

[82] Jacob, *Theol.*, p. 94.
[83] Ibid., p. 95.
[84] Ibid., p. 95.
[85] Hill, *Greek Words*, pp. 85-86. See also Kuyper, who suggests that "...norm, however, is not to be construed as some universal ideal which serves as a yardstick to determine the righteousness of a person or thing.

A few observations are essential at this point.[86] We cannot simply transpose certain meanings which have been used in ancient times into biblical concepts and argue for agreement in concepts. That is to say, we cannot agree with Jacob that צדק means conformity to a norm, on the basis of a similar view in Arabic; in fact there is no indication that such a view in Arabic is even verifiable. Furthermore, to create norms for everything which exists, and ultimately to use the Being of Yahweh as a norm is to miss the uniqueness of Yahweh as God and the relationship which he has with Israel. Yahweh is not a static God who has certain objective standards which have to be met, with no interference on his part. But rather, with Yahweh there are always expectations and demands and the opportunity to repent. As long as this final element is involved in a situation, it, by its nature, eschews conforming to a norm.

If Yahweh were to establish rigid, static norms by which the world would function, then in effect Yahweh could easily be transformed into a *deus ex machina*, but it is well known that the God of Israel is one who is involved in the affairs of his people. For Yahweh, there is clearly no norm which is prescribed. As early as the Song of Deborah (Judg. 5:11) we hear of צדקות יהוה. The righteousness of Yahweh is not expressed in the fulfilling of a norm but in his acts of salvation and deliverance. Yahweh cares for his people in a manner which is expressed in mercy and kindness even when this might be undeserving. Another example of this apparent undeserving state is seen in Abraham's request of Yahweh to save the city of Sodom if only there were fifty, forty, thirty, etc., righteous persons, and Yahweh is willing. "God's $ṣ^e dāqā$ or $ṣedeq$ is his keeping of the law in accordance with the terms of the covenant. But once this point has been made, it is necessary to go on at once to warn the reader against thinking simply of a kind of

---

...The norm, therefore, is determined by what the relationship demands." "Righteousness and Salvation," pp. 233-234.

[86] The observations and critique given here are general. At the beginning of the discussion on "צדק as relationship," certain specific critiques will be provided. The development of the "relationship" concept will by necessity entail a pointed critique of "norm."

iustitia distributiva....In Hebrew thinking there is no such thing as an abstract formal concept which might be classified according to an objective standard, thus presupposing a universal idea of righteousness."[87] Clearly, subscribing to a norm erases any opportunity for repentance.

One of the reasons why the idea of norm has become so prevalent has to do with contemporary translations, words which in themselves have certain connotations; one such term is *Gerechtigkeit* which, distorts the true meaning of צדק. Von Rad observes that, "ancient Israel did not in fact measure a line of conduct or an act by an ideal norm, but by the specific relationship in which the partner had at the time to prove himself true."[88] Once a person finds himself or herself as a part of a unit, familial, communal or covenantal, it takes more than merely conforming to a norm to fulfill the demands and expectations of that unit. In situations such as these, elements of kindness, faithfulness, mercy, always become engaged, depending on circumstances.[89] These brief observations indicate that in order to have a firm grasp of the biblical view of צדק, "conformity to a norm" is at best questionable and at worst undesirable as a viable option. A more suitable alternative has to be sought.

2. Relationship

צדק is a concept which has its most profound meaning when seen within the context of relationship. There is, inherent in the concept of צדק, elements such as expectation, responsibility, demand, characteristics which are expressed in the relationship amongst individuals and, more importantly, in the relationship between Yahweh and his people. It is on the basis of the relationship between Yahweh and his people that צדק is done and exists amongst individuals. Von Rad, who believes צדק should be understood in the context of communal relationship, remarks:

---

[87] Walther Eichrodt, *Theology of the Old Testament*. I. OTL. trans. J.A. Baker (London: SCM Press, Ltd), 1961, p. 240.
[88] Von Rad, *Theol.* I, p. 371.
[89] Ibid., p. 371.

This communal relationship may be a civil or social one but more often in the Old Testament refers to that relationship with Israel, which Yahweh has enshrined in his covenant. When Yahweh is said to be "righteous" it means that he is faithful to this covenant relationship which he has condescended to establish. Israel is "righteous" in so far as the nation assents to this covenant relationship and submits to its cultic and legal ordinances. [90]

In other words, in order for an individual to be צדיק, it means that of necessity he or she must exist and live in a manner which allows him or her to respond correctly to the values of the relationship; this may mean strict adherence to the customs, laws, moral code, of the community. "As long as he remains within the fellowship of covenant and cult, and has done nothing to exclude himself from this fellowship, he is ṣaddîq and belongs to the ṣaddîqîm."[91] As such when we see צדק used in antithesis to רשע, it is not that the latter has broken an existing objective ethical code of conduct, but rather, the רשע is the one who has failed in the corresponding responsibilities and demands of the covenant. Achtemeier notes that "the רשע is he who exercises force and falsehood, who ignores the duties which kinship and covenant lay upon him, who tramples the rights of others under foot. His sin is not murder, theft, falsehood, evil in itself, but evil which is committed against one with whom he stands in relationship."[92]

Moreover, in discussing צדק within the context of relationship, one particular point must be noted. Each individual is established in a variety of relationships, and each relationship has its

---

[90] Gerhard von Rad, "'Righteousness' and 'Life' in the Cultic Language of the Psalms" in *The Problem of the Hexateuch and Other Essays* (Edinburgh: Oliver and Boyd), 1966, p. 249. Von Rad's view here while largely acceptable, does not limit the responsibilities and expectations of the people by his category of "cultic and legal ordinances." Surely there are social and economic demands also.

[91] Sigmund Mowinckel, *The Psalms in Israel's Worship*. trans. D.R. AP-Thomas (Oxford: Basil Blackwell), 1962, p. 209.

[92] Achtemeier, "Righteousness...." p. 81.

unique demands and responsibilities. An individual may be simultaneously a spouse, worker, parent, friend,[93] and in each of these capacities his or her relation to the other party may entail a particular set of rules to which he or she must subscribe. For example, the uniqueness of relationship may be illustrated in the following association: "king with people, judge with complainants, priests with worshippers, common man with family, tribesman with community, community with resident alien and poor, all with God."[94] In essence then צדק is not simply an objective norm which is present within the society, and which must be kept, but rather it is a concept which derives its meaning from the relationship in which it finds itself. So we are able to say that "right judging, right governing, right worshipping and gracious activity are all covenantal and righteous, despite their diversity."[95]

This then would be ideally the nature of a relationship: the realization of the significance of the other individual and his or her importance in the covenant - between God and others. The evidence of צדק is present and seen when there is the mutual caring for each other. This care is best manifested not only in rituals but in action on the other person's behalf.[96] This however does not always happen and one of the primary parties who is frequently responsible for its collapse is the king. The king is a natural link between Yahweh and the people and vice versa. As the elect of Yahweh, the king is crucial in his responsibility to establish and execute צדק and משפט in his community. The nation, as a single and unified force finds its focus in the king. The nation and, indirectly, the local communities depend on the king for their "right-ordering and well being, for it is his concern to see that the life of the total society and all relations within it are 'as they should be,' that is, are such as to maintain and promote national unity and prosperity. This state of affairs constitutes the צְדָקָה of the society: in bringing it about,

---

[93] See von Rad, *Theol.* I, p. 371.
[94] Achtemeier, "Righteousness...." p. 80.
[95] J.A. Ziesler, *The Meaning of Righteousness in Paul* (Cambridge: Cambridge University Press), 1972, p. 42.
[96] See Pedersen, who allows for this idea, but sees it entirely within the framework of the maintenance of souls. *Israel I-II*, p. 345.

the king is himself צַדִּיק both in the manner of his performing his functions, as well as in his personal character."[97] It is principally the sustaining of this understanding of the role of king that allows for the presence of צדק in the society. When the king, through weakness, corruption or poor guidance does not practice צדק in the society, then invariably the society is divided into two sections: those who are powerful and wield their power and those who are oppressed, the poor, the widow, the orphan. When this chasm in society occurs, inevitably it is the latter group which finds itself with little redress.[98]

The problem of the corruption and occasional absence of צדק in Israelite society is a problem which, because of its nature, is regularly overlooked by the people of Israel. Israel is obviously aware of the covenant relationship with Yahweh, a covenant which has as one of its main pillars, an element which involves Yahweh's deliverance of Israel, in the event that its existence is threatened or endangered. However, it is precisely this matter of protection that allows Israel to overlook the gravity of its internal problems, particularly the presence of injustice and the absence of righteousness. It is now a question of whether Yahweh will continue with a relationship which has gone against the main grain of the covenant. But, it is exactly this point which brings to the fore the unmistakable distinctiveness of the covenant.

It must be understood that one of the most important aspects of the covenant is that the relationship does not hinge for its existence on the righteousness of Israel. Righteousness, it is to be remembered "is neither a virtue nor a sum of virtues, it is activity which befits the covenant....Everything (including inward disposition) which fits the requirements of the covenant in a given situation is then...'righteous.'"[99] As long as Israel is within this understanding then the relationship is valid. When Israel apostasizes and drifts into wickedness, already there is the signal that respon-

---

[97] Hill, *Greek Words*, p. 87. See also Pedersen, *Israel I-II*, p. 344.
[98] When we read Ps. 72, a royal psalm, the importance of צדק for the king is stated explicitly. The plea in this psalm implies that the king is to reflect the צדק of Yahweh and hence defend the poor and needy.
[99] Ziesler, *The Meaning of Righteousness in Paul*, p. 40.

sibilities and expectations are overlooked. However, it must be noted that with all of this, Israel is not making the covenant null and void; the covenant relationship cannot be dissolved by Israel, even though corruption, perversion and the choice to be unrighteous could damage it. If in fact the covenant were to come to an end, then it would be Yahweh who would do so, though not arbitrarily, but on the basis on some justification. What Israel does in terms of keeping the laws and ordinances is important but not conditional for the validity of the covenant. For before there were the laws and ordinances, there was the covenant.

> He [Yahweh] was Lord of the Covenant, its initiator, its defender, its preserver. He and he alone upheld it. Only he could break it. Israel could reject her God and thereby bring his wrath upon her, but she could not escape her relationship with God. The relationship might be one of wrath, which led to Israel's destruction, but nevertheless it was a relationship. God initiated the covenant. He alone could nullify it. [100]

The "righteousness of Yahweh" remains constant and this is reflected in his role in the covenant. The statements "Yahweh is righteous"[101] and the "righteousness of Yahweh" are found throughout the Old Testament and in fact there is no biblical reference to the lack of righteousness on the part of Yahweh. Certainly if there were a situation which might have warranted and justi-

---

[100] Achtemeier, "Righteousness...." p. 82. By way of substantiating this view, the author cites Ps. 89:28-37. Achtemeier's view in this regard is one which is surely correct, but it is one which is in contrast to Hill's position. Hill says, "If Yahweh was to be faithful to this relationship and declare Israel 'in the right' (with all that meant to her in terms of success and well being) then Israel must be 'in the right,' she must *have* a 'righteous' cause, she must *possess* 'righteousness' that would reflect the character of Yahweh's righteousness." *Greek Words*, p. 93. The difference in the views of Achtemeier and Hill is best seen in the fact that Hill suggests that the covenant relationship is conditional in Israel being "in the right." Achtemeier says that regardless of Israel's position, the covenant is not nullified, precisely because it is not Israel who is the main architect.

[101] Later in this chapter, we shall examine in detail צדק with specific reference to Yahweh.

fied such a statement, it would have been in the mouth of the suffering Job, but even there it is absent. The expression of the righteousness of Yahweh within the context of the covenant is not contingent on the assumption or even knowledge that Israel would live up to expectations. The righteousness of Yahweh has to fit neither norm nor condition outside of himself. "Yahweh's righteousness is in his fulfillment of the demands of the relationship which exists between him and his people Israel, his fulfillment of the covenant which he has made with his chosen nation."[102]

Finally, at this point, we examine the examples which have been cited in the preceding section and demonstrate that צדק in all instances must be seen and understood in the context of "relationship." Some scholars have suggested that צדק in "weights," "balances," and "measures" must be understood as conforming to a norm. However, to hold such a view is to miss the point that צדק in that context is not an objective standard to which each citizen must subscribe. The expectation is different. That there must be צדק in this aspect of life simply underlines an element of צדק which is integral and indispensable in the relationship among individuals. In this context what is at stake is the survival and sustenance of the individual. To say that צדק with regard to mundane items such as "weights" is a detached objective norm, is to detract from a most crucial factor, namely the individuals who suffer as a result of the injustice in these areas. It is clearly not merely the credibility of a norm that is lost, but the life of an individual. When an individual is cheated out of everyday necessities of life, not only does the individual suffer, but it gnaws away at the very fiber of the covenant community. As such, it is more than not simply subscribing to a norm, it is as Pedersen perceives, the abolishing of "the natural equilibrium between himself and his neighbour, and thus he loses his righteousness, which is the very maintenance of the will of the covenant. Justice demands that equilibrium shall be re-established between the wronged and him who committed the breach, for thereby the covenant is healed. To re-

---

[102] Achtemeier, "Righteousness ...." p. 82

establish this relation is to *justify* a man. To justify a man means to obtain for him the place due to him within the covenant."[103]

In addition to this example, there is the one which is cited from Ezek. 16:51-52. In this instance, צדק cannot be viewed as conforming to a norm, particularly if we were to base our arguments on the context out of which it comes. The primary consideration in Ezek. 16 is in reference to the fractured relationship between Yahweh and Israel. When Sodom and Samaria "appear righteous" it is not an objective standard which is being used for measuring, but rather "appearance of righteousness" is entirely contingent on the relationship between Yahweh and Israel.[104]

Another occurrence which would be helpful in this discussion, is found in Gen. 30:33. צדק in this context has traditionally been rendered "honesty."[105] The צדק of Jacob in Gen. 30:33 is one of the major elements in this narrative.[106] The crucial factor which must be considered here, is the motivation for Jacob's צדק. On a peripheral and secondary level, it is true that it is Jacob's honesty which is in question, in addition to the fact that the agreement must be maintained. However, even more fundamental than these factors, is the question of Jacob's relationship with Laban. Jacob is asked by Laban to remain with him, and afterwards Jacob convinces Laban that he should have as his wages, all of the speckled and spotted sheep and goats from the flock. Jacob remarks that his צדק will indicate to Laban that he has sustained the agreement. This, however, is not merely an objective, detached agreement but rather, Jacob's remark is meant to verify his relationship with Laban. That is to say, Jacob's צדק is to suggest that he is planning to keep intact his relationship with Laban.

---

[103] Pedersen, *Israel I-II*, p. 345.
[104] See a detailed discussion of this point above in note 61.
[105] See, e.g., the NRSV, where צדק is rendered "honesty." In doing so, the NRSV points to a specific characteristic of Jacob, rather than involve the entire gamut of characteristics which צדק gives.
[106] Ruble is correct in his observation that it is not Jacob's honesty which is at stake. However, his conclusion that צדק in v. 33, simply means that Jacob will live up to his agreement with Laban, sorely misses the crucial point in the text. See, Ruble, *Diss.*, p. 43.

After Jacob decides to cheat Laban in return, it is certainly not merely an agreement which is broken; Jacob's honesty is not the fundamental issue, but rather, the larger issue of his relationship with Laban. Several elements underline this view. The rift in the relationship between Jacob and Laban and his family, is evident in the words of Laban's sons, namely, that Jacob has cheated their father. Moreover, Jacob's own perception indicates the brokenness in the relationship; he notices that Laban does not look upon him with favor as before. The finality in this relationship is seen in Jacob's departure and the ensuing quarrel with Laban.

Still another instance which exemplifies the use of צדק in the context of relationship is the occurrence in Jer. 51:10. Contextually, "vindication," is perhaps the most suitable rendering of צדק in this verse, however "vindication" cannot be overlooked without posing the question as to the motivation for vindication. There is no suggestion, and thus no reason to believe, that punishment is the primary motivation. Clearly, as one studies Jer. 51, it is evident that the evil of Babylon alone, warrants this kind of judgment from Yahweh. However, this cannot be taken to be the primary reason for the destruction of Babylon; it has to be placed in perspective and understood in the light of the relationship between Israel and Yahweh. Yahweh has always been the protector and redeemer of Israel. Thus, when Israel is in bondage and is oppressed, the relationship between Israel and Yahweh is strained. The fact that Yahweh brings forth Israel's vindication, not so much reflects the merits of Israel, as it points to Yahweh's desire to sustain and restore the covenantal relationship.

A further example of צדק as "relationship" which may not be immediately apparent is in Dan. 8:14. This is a part of the vision of Daniel in which he is told of the restoration of the sanctuary to "its rightful (צדק) place."[107] The restoration of the sanctuary as spoken

---

[107] There seems to be some uncertainty among scholars regarding the use of צדק in this context. See, e.g., Louis F. Hartman and Alexander A. Di Lella, *The Book of Daniel*. AB (New York: Doubleday and Co.), 1978. Hartman questions the legitimacy of צדק in this text and suggests instead that צדק is a corruption of the Aramaic ידכי, and thus he emends the text to read "...the sanctuary will be purified." p. 227. However, for the retention of צדק as a proper part of the text, see, Maurice Delcor, *Le livre de Daniel* (Paris:

of here, refers to its re-establishment to its intended function. The sanctuary serves as an essential constituent for the communion between Yahweh and his people and the corruption of this under Belshazzar, removed the sanctuary from "its rightful place." Clearly, it is not merely a matter of re-opening the sanctuary for its original function, but moreso, the relationship between Yahweh and Israel, of which theサnctuary is an integral part, is also renewed.

Finally, in some ways, the illustration of the story of Tamar and Judah (Gen. 38:26) gives the most profound argument for the understanding of צדק in terms of relationship. Because of this, it is important that we describe the incident once again. Tamar dresses as a בזה קדשה and seduces her father-in-law, and this results in her pregnancy. When Judah hears of Tamar's "harlotry," he immediately sentences her to death, only to discover that he is the one who impregnates her. With this scenario, it would be possible for us to raise a multitude of ethical questions, including the fact that Judah participates in the act, and then has the audacity to sentence Tamar to death and of course the fact that Tamar knowingly seduces her father-in-law. However, for our purposes here we will focus primarily on Tamar's reasons for her action rather than the act itself. It is in this aspect of the narrative that the importance of Tamar's צדק is seen. When Judah remarks that Tamar is "more righteous" than he is, he is certainly not referring to her legal rights nor is he referring to her conforming to a particular ethical code. Tamar seduces Judah with the sole intention of having an offspring. Since her husband was killed, and Onan his brother fared likewise, Tamar sees the seduction of Judah as an opportunity to sustain her loyalty to the family, by having a child. As such, Judah's words regarding the צדק of Tamar must be viewed in reference to her relationship with her family. As ironic as it may be, it is only in seducing Judah that Tamar is faithful to her familial re-

---

Libraire Lecoffre), 1971. Delcor suggests, "La fin du verset précise qu'á la fin de cette période la sanctuaire sera rétabli dans son droit (וְנִצְדַּק). Le TM est a préférer à la LXX, a Théodotion et à la Vulgate qui traduisent 'sera purifié.'" p. 177. See also, James A. Montgomery, *The Book of Daniel*. ICC (Edinburgh: T and T Clark), 1927, who says that this is a "perfectly proper use of צדק." p. 343.

lationship. Tamar's צדק allows her to sacrifice a present relationship for a future and the responsibility which she bears.

It can be said, based on the above discussion that the Old Testament concept of צדק is best understood when seen in the context of relationship. In this way, it is not stifled into being a detached objective norm, but rather, we are able to appreciate and understand its distinctive features. Furthermore it places in focus the reasons behind the salvific acts of Yahweh on behalf of Israel. In no way would "norm" encompass and define the inexplicable acts of Yahweh for a people who are invariably undeserving; only a special relationship would begin to explain and account for such acts.

C. Meanings in Contexts

In arriving at this point, we have seen the complexity in nature of צדק and have observed that it is best understood when seen from the point of view of relationship. It is possible that the use of צדק can be classified in three categories: (1) religious, (2) forensic, (3) ethical. One observation which emerges instantly is the realization that there is certain to be overlapping with such a categorization. This notwithstanding, it will nevertheless allow us to see the development and presence of צדק in certain situations which are not identical.

1. Religious

This is the area about which more has been said than about any of the other two categories. Often, when the idea of righteousness as a religious term is proposed, it is done so at the expense of the ethical and forensic aspects.[108] There is not doubt that the צדק

---

[108] Eichrodt suggests, "the righteousness of God remains *an essentially religious conception*, which resists any attempt to water it down into ethical ideas." *Theol.* I, p. 250. This view of Eichrodt is too narrow in its summation and detracts from the richness which the concept of צדק does have. It is important to note that not every use of צדק has a religious basis Achtemeier observes that "an act on the social plane is not righteous, because it at the same time satisfies a demand of the law, though this of course often hap-

of Yahweh was first of all understood as a religious term.[109] When this aspect of Yahweh is expressed, it is generally in response to the covenantal demands, on behalf of Israel or the individual. An example of a purely religious use occurs in Gen. 15:6, where because of his faithfulness, Abraham is reckoned as righteous. The concept of holiness is still another area in which צדק as a religious principle is found. In contemporary religious vocabulary, holiness is often viewed as an abstract quality or attribute of Yahweh, or something narrowly skewed to reflect one's personal association with the church. There is however, nothing abstract about the holiness of Yahweh. In this respect, the transcendence of Yahweh must not be confused with abstraction. Rather, the holiness of Yahweh is concretely manifested both in his actions within history and the subsequent expectations of the recipients of such actions. This finds its biblical support in references such as the one in Isa. 5:16. Yahweh, and Yahweh alone, is seen in holiness, and hence the preaching and preservation of monotheism became avenues in which this might be expressed. Some scholars in fact argue that the focus of the preaching of the pre-exilic prophets is to re-establish the monotheistic principle in Israel. Snaith notes that, "with the establishment of a true monotheism among the Hebrews, it came to stand pre-eminently for the nature of Jehovah."[110] The fact is, צדק as a religious principle can be found or perceived in many areas, but with few exceptions, it cannot be neatly divorced from the ethi-

---

pened. It is righteous because it fulfills the demands of a social relationship. The relationship is always the determinative factor." "Righteousness ...." p. 82.

[109] In fact, with reference to צדק in the pre-exilic prophets, Snaith supposes that the root of their teaching is religious. "Primarily they were religious prophets; only secondarily were they ethical teachers." *The Distinctive Ideas*, p. 59. See, also, Martin Buber, *The Prophetic Faith* (New York: Harper and Row, Publishers), 1949. Buber notes that what Yahweh demands is "the combination of righteousness and justice, right judgment and right action, this basic concept is not ethical nor social, but religious." p. 101. For a view which is the opposite of Snaith's (in respect to the pre-exilic prophets) see Skinner, "Righteousness...." p. 274.

[110] Snaith, *The Distinctive Ideas*, p. 51. That perhaps the element of monotheism evolves as a factor in this period is clearly an arguable point, but this is not the place for such an argument. Suffice it to say however, that צדק in respect to monotheism is a religious principle.

cal and forensic aspects. In fact, the principal area in which the religious principle of צדק is witnessed at work is in the concrete acts of Yahweh, acts such as deliverance, vindication, salvation. This area will become clearer as we develop later צדק with reference to Yahweh and Israel.

2. Forensic

When we look at the distribution of צדק in the Old Testament and examine its usage it becomes immediately evident that צדק does not occur in any large numbers in the earliest sources of the Pentateuch, "J" and "E."[111] In and of itself this observation may not be important, but it is significant to note that the most prominent use of צדק in these occurrences is a forensic one. Skinner explains this phenomenon when he says, "What is meant is that questions of right and wrong were habitually regarded from a legal point of view as matters to be settled by a judge."[112] The description of Yahweh as judge does give a superficial indication of a forensic role. In fact, some scholars hold the view that the צדק of Yahweh cannot be separated from the figure of God the judge.[113] However, it will be pointed out in the following discussion, that the forensic aspect of צדק goes beyond use in the context of the "judge." In fact there are those who believe that the forensic aspect of צדק is the basic Old Testament usage.[114] While such a generalization

---

[111] In fact, of the some four hundred and sixty occurrences of צדק only thirty-five are found in the Pentateuch and most of these are used in a forensic sense.
[112] See Skinner, "Righteousness...." p. 273.
[113] Jacob, *Theol.*, pp. 96-97.
[114] See C.H. Dodd, *The Bible and the Greeks*, pp. 46-47. Dodd argues that the verb צדק has as its primary meaning "to be in the right" rather than "to be righteous." He proposes that when the hiphil (הצדיק) is used, the causative element of this form of the verb means "to put someone in the right." What in fact Dodd is saying is that צדק in any form cannot mean "to declare righteous" or "to make righteous." This is too general a view and others (e.g. von Rad) have suggested that declaration of righteousness is in fact possible. See von Rad, *Theol.* I, p. 380. Also, O. Palmer Robertson. *The Books of Nahum, Habakkuk and Zephaniah*. NICOT (Grand Rapids, Michigan: Eerdmans), 1990. "The concept of righteousness (Heb. ṣ^{e}daqâ) in

might be untenable, nevertheless the widespread use of צדק in a forensic sense will be shown.

There are primarily two aspects of צדק where the sense is a forensic one. First, צדק in many instances refers to a person or party being "in the right," in a particular situation. When a case is brought to the court for the judge to decide, the one who is found to be innocent is deemed to be צדק while the guilty one is the רשע. One passage which illustrates this point and includes many of the above mentioned elements is Deut. 25:1.

כי יהוה ריב בין אנשים ונגשו אל המשפט
ושפטום והצדיקו את הצדיק והרשיעו את הרשע

In this example, the two parties come to המשפט in order to settle their dispute. Not only is the "court" understood as the place where lawsuits are heard, but the use of המשפט in this context suggests more than a mere hearing; it indicates that the two parties have come with the expectation that justice will be executed. It is clear that, after the innocent party is declared צדיק and the guilty on רשע, that in fact צדק in this context is used to designate innocence in a legal sense, while simultaneously being antithetical to רשע.[115]

However, in order to be "in the right," a case need not be taken to a court. For example, if an individual is *falsely* accused of a crime he or she is regarded as צדיק, regardless of whether or not there is a court hearing, as is the situation in II Ki. 10:9. And in another instance, in Exod. 9:27, there is a description of Pharaoh confessing that he and his people are "in the wrong" (הרשעים) while Yahweh is "in the right" (הצדיק). Clearly in these instances, no judge is needed to determine the innocence and guilt of the parties, nor is this determination contingent on the presence of a judge. Skinner notes that "in these cases righteousness is an inherent quality, not depending on the decision of the judge, but at the most demanding recognition by him."[116] From the preceding discussion

---

the OT develops a distinct flavor in that is bound inseparably to the idea of judicial standing." p. 175

[115] For examples of this, see Exod. 23:7,8; Isa. 5:23; 29:21; Prov. 18:5-7.

[116] Skinner, "Righteousness...." p. 273.

on the forensic use, it is apparent that the most common and certainly the most obvious way of showing the forensic aspect is to focus on the use of judges and tribunals. However while this may be the area most often referred to, it is clearly not the only one.

Second, צדק is expected of those who are placed in a position to execute justice. In the example of Deut. 25:1, discussed earlier, the innocent is "in the right" while the one "in the wrong" is deemed guilty. In some ways this result is the most important part of the judicial procedure, for it brings to the fore "the end" of the case. However, we must not overlook the quality of the instrument which is used as the "means;" that is to say, the judge. It is important in this regard that in order to have "innocence" and "guilt" pronounced on the appropriate parties, the one executing such a judgment must be righteous. One of the most important parties in the sphere of executing justice, is of course the judge. The righteousness of the judge is crucial and, in a very pointed way, the righteousness of the judge is most clearly manifested when he or she vindicates the powerless: the orphan, the widow, the poor, the oppressed and the sojourner. We note that Isaiah pronounces "woe" on those who corrupt the area of justice by taking bribes and thus distort "innocence" and "guilt."[117] One of the major obstacles in the path of executing judgment in righteousness is the real potential for bribery. The judge is expected to rise above such corruption and execute judgment with "impeccable impartiality," but this unfortunately does not preponderate in the daily judgments. Perhaps though, *the* most important person in the community who has the power to execute judgment is the king; this importance is underlined throughout the Old Testament.

It is expected that all kings and rulers will have צדק as a guideline in their administration of justice. In this sense the king or ruler is not playing the role of one who is keeping the "law," but rather they are doing that which is an inherent aspect of their position. Vriezen suggests:

---

[117] For a specific example, see Isa. 5:23. The importance for judges to have צדק can be seen in references such as Lev.19:15; Deut. 16:18; Isa. 11:4-5.

> The word-stems denoting justice, both ṣdq and šfṭ though they are both used most frequently in juridical and political life do not have a theoretical or exclusively forensic, juridical meaning, starting from a given law, but denote the task of the king and the judge who have to restore justice....[T]hey cause justice to prevail; thus each man gets the share to which he has a right....[118]

The prophet Isaiah notes that the Messiah will judge with צדק and in fact it will be his constant companion. In an ideal way, the Messiah will incorporate those characteristics which are integral to a covenantal relationship, but צדק and its practice in communal relations, particularly in the matter of executing justice, is not reserved for the ideal king; every ruler is expected to have it.[119] In the event that the king or ruler is unrighteous or unjust, then he becomes an abomination. (cf. Prov. 16:12)

One final point with respect to the forensic use of צדק needs to be noted here. As long as the difficulties which Israel faces are external, specifically from contiguous nations, then the distinction between the people of Yahweh and those of other religious persuasions is clear. However, when problems of apostasy, oppression, perversion of justice, syncretism, bribery begin to be recognized as elements common to Israelite society, then the צדק of Yahweh is directed within Israel, delivering judgments on behalf of one particular group. Yahweh intervenes on behalf of the oppressed and declares them to be "righteous." This however does not mean that the quality of righteousness is bestowed on whomever is oppressed, but rather the declaration of righteousness has a forensic overtone. That is to say, the person who is oppressed is *ipso facto* "in the right" against those who are the oppressors.[120]

---

[118] Vriezen, *An Outline of Old Testament Theology*, p. 327.
[119] Cf. e.g. II Sam. 15:4; I Ki. 10:9; II Chron. 9:8.
[120] A lengthier discussion of צדיק in parallelism to concepts such as דל and אביון will be discussed later in this chapter.

3. Ethical

As was noted earlier, the primary concern of the covenant relationship between Yahweh and his people is to maintain צדק as its foundation. With this in mind, one of the principal expectations is an ethical and moral conduct which is a direct correlate of צדק. Thus, when there are specific expectations of a relationship, and elements such as bribery, corruption and oppression, begin to dominate society, then what is necessary to counteract these elements is a hitherto unused aspect of צדק. In order to restore Israel "in the right" before Yahweh, what is necessary is "quite clearly ethical and moral reform of such a kind as would produce the principles of right community order (justice, equality, sincerity, etc.), and to ensure the maintenance of the covenant."[121] This is obviously an important area of the covenant and any approach which seeks to dilute it, results in the shaping of צדק as a limited and narrow concept.[122]

It is perhaps in the pre-exilic prophets in general and the Eighth Century prophets in particular that the use of צדק develops this ethical overtone.[123] While there is some indication that the forensic aspect of צדק has religious overtones, the use of צדק in Eighth Century prophecy leaves no doubt as to its connection with Yahweh. What is true is that "social righteousness is the necessary and inexorable demand of J's [Yahweh's] moral character,"[124] and

---

[121] Hill, *Greek Words*, p. 94.

[122] In this regard, see Eichrodt, *Theol.* I, who, in his quest to make צדק a "purely religious" concept, arrives at an inadequate conclusion. He says "the essence of the original biblical concept of God's righteousness lie neither in the ethical postulate of a moral world-order nor in an ideal of impartial retribution imposed by some inner necessity nor in the personification of the ethical in God." p. 249.

[123] Having said this, there are clear instances with ethical implications which are found in several areas of the Old Testament. For example the concern over injustice in "weights and measures" is seen in Amos 8:5 but is also found in Lev. 19:36, in Deut. 25:15 and in Ezek. 45:10. It can be said that the ethical expectation is not limited to one period, but while this may be true, it is apparent that its greatest development is in Eighth Century prophecy.

[124] Skinner, "Righteousness...." p. 274. See also James Muilenburg, *The Way of Israel* (London: Routledge and Kegan Paul), 1961. Muilenburg sug-

this is the primary element behind the preaching of the prophets. They are preaching to a people who are party to a covenant with Yahweh where the doing of "justice and righteousness" is an integral component with regard to its proper existence. There are clearly ethical expectations, and the fact that their message has an ethical inclination reflects the nature of the problem in Israel, that there is a breakdown in the ethical fiber of the covenant. However, it would not be entirely accurate to suggest that the prophets are ethicists,[125] for once the *Sitz im Leben* of the prophets' message is established, it is evident that the ethical undergirding is necessary for the restoration of the covenantal relationship. That is to say, the ethical aspect is used in order to restore the religious orientation of the covenant. Having indicated the importance of the need for a sense of morality in human behavior, it should be noted that this moral sense and ethical behavior are reflective of the character of Yahweh, which is consummately expressed in his covenant with Israel.

What then, are some of the areas in which there is necessity for use in an ethical sense? It would appear that the administration of justice by those who are placed in a position to do so, is the sphere of life in which the well-being of the people most depends. There is a need for "justice in the gate," "justice in weights and measures," "justice in the rulers," "justice in daily transactions." This may appear at first glance a description of the use of צדק in a forensic sense, but in fact it goes beyond that in the prophetic application. For example, in Amos 2:6-7 צדיק is used in a context where דל and אביון are employed synonymously, the poor are regarded as being "in the right." In fact this is not a forensic reference, but rather a description of one who continues to be in good relations with Yah-

---

gests, "the ethical foundations of the prophetic proclamation may be stated in another way. One God and only one God is Lord over history and wills to make himself known in history. This one God manifests his holiness in justice and righteousness, but is also compassionate and faithful." p. 75.

[125] That is to say, the prophets do not preach a generic message, based on their experience as ethicists. "They speak to the time to which God has sent them and their words are directed to the conditions of that time." Muilenburg, *The Way of Israel*, p. 77. The role of the prophets will be discussed in Chapter 5.

weh; this individual is a צדיק. In view of this, the powerful and affluent who, according to the prophets, have deprived the poor and powerless to arrive at their own wealth and power, have become "the unrighteous."[126] Yet, in a fundamental way, צדק is more than the mere outward expression of "justice," it is something which is absent from the very being of the person. Skinner is correct when he perceives that what the prophets are pointing to in their message is "the instinctive perception of what is due to others, the recognition of the inherent rights of human personality. The idea is far broader than what we usually mean by right and justice; it includes a large hearted construction of the claims of humanity; it is, as has been said, the humanitarian virtue *par excellence*."[127]

An area frequently elaborated on, focuses on the need for the judges to execute justice and hence decide in favor of the "poor" and "innocent." Given this, most scholars[128] have argued that more than mere impartial justice is needed; rather the judge is obligated to decide on the side of the poor. At a glance, this may appear to be an attractive proposition, but in fact there are some serious problems with this position. It is presupposed that impartiality is not an issue about which a judge needs to worry, but rather satisfying the claims of one party within the relationship. It is true that the person who is executing justice has to be aware of the relationship and act accordingly, however for the judge not to be impartial would be to defeat the purpose of the judicial procedure. If in fact a particular party is "in the right" then impartiality will indeed ensure that this party is vindicated. Not to have impartial judgment would in effect be creating an evil in order to erase an evil. Having said this, it is important to note that even though the one who exe-

---

[126] See, Amos 5:7, 15, 24; 6:12; Isa. 1:17,21; 3:14ff; 5:7,23; 10:1ff; Mic. 2:1ff; 2:8ff; 3:1-3; 3:9ff; Hos. 10:12. This applies to references in Jeremiah as well. See, 22:3,13,15; 23:1ff.
[127] Skinner, "Righteousness...." p. 274. See also Robert Davidson, *The Old Testament* (London: Hodder and Stoughton, 1964. Davidson notes, "The demand for 'justice' and 'righteousness' within the community is a call for a single-hearted loyalty to Yahweh which will express itself in a society whose life is ordered in the light of Yahweh's law." p. 79.
[128] See Skinner, "Righteousness...." Eichrodt, *Theol.* I, and A. Heschel, *The Prophets* I (New York: Harper and Row), 1962, among others.

cutes justice is called upon to do so impartially, he or she is nevertheless not doing so in a vacuum, oblivious of the parties involved. But rather, ingrained within this person is the importance of the concept of relationship and of judging impartially, always conscious of this framework.

Moreover, the idea of showing partiality to the poor is biblically untenable.[129] It is clear that the prophets are calling for the protection of the poor, the defending (שפט) or the orphan, but they are also calling for the judges to be impartial in their execution of justice. As long as the judge is impartial, "justice and righteousness" will be administered, precisely because the poor will be judged to be "in the right." To show partiality to the poor is to commit a crime on the side of the poor. It is clear that impartial execution of justice is proposed not so much to give the oppressed and oppressor equal opportunity of "victory" in court, but rather to eliminate perversion and corruption. In theory then, if perversion and corruption are eliminated, the judge will be righteous and justice will be executed. To be of help to the poor is not to overlook their faults and sins, but rather to ensure their well-being.

Finally, a word about categorization is necessary in order to place the forensic, ethical and religious aspects of צדק in perspective. From the preceding discussion, it is apparent that the three categories overlap, for while there is distinctiveness about each, there are also common elements. The most noteworthy element in this regard is the relation to Yahweh, even in areas where the ethical and forensic aspects are predominant, they nevertheless have religious overtones. This appears to be the singularly most significant factor which unites all the different aspects. However, there does seem to be a chronological pattern which has developed. The pre-exilic prophets form a bridge between the use of צדק in Ancient Israel and the later view of Deutero-Isaiah. In Ancient Israel, it appears that צדק as it relates to Yahweh is a concept which is expressed principally in terms of defending Israel from foreign na-

---

[129] See Lev. 19:15. Muilenburg suggests, "God shows no partiality, so Israel must not 'recognize faces,' but must act impartially, without regard to rich or poor, patrician or peasant, great or small." *The Way of Israel*, p. 71. See also Snaith, *The Distinctive Ideas of the Old Testament*, p. 69.

tions. This must be the fundamental understanding of צדק during this period, for the shout of צדקות יהוה means that Yahweh has acted on Israel's behalf, an action which results in victory and vindication for Israel. It is therefore no surprise that the use of צדק in Ancient Israel then is predominantly forensic, namely, judging Israel "in the right" and providing vindication. This situation alters later during the pre-exilic period, for then there are elements both outside and inside Israel which threaten the relationship with Yahweh and with the citizens. The use of צדק in these latter times do not have a forensic overtone but rather alludes to ethical principles. While, in Ancient Israel, it is the nation which is the focus of צדק, in pre-exilic Israel, the focus is on both the nation and the individual. In this period, the ethical fiber of the covenant becomes loose and hence the expectations and preaching are shaped in this direction. The period of the exile brings to life the idea of "deliverance" and "salvation," concepts which may be termed religious, in part because they are specifically in reference to the acts of Yahweh. As we now direct our attention to the next section, we will examine subjects which were mentioned in passing in the earlier sections of the chapter.

D. צדק and Its References

In order that our discussion on צדק might be complete we will, in the next few pages, observe the use of צדק in relation to its three main subjects in the Old Testament, namely Yahweh, Israel and the individual. Each section will allow us to grasp the function of צדק with a particular focus and also enable us to examine the contexts in which it predominates.

1. צדק and Yahweh

The use of צדק as an attribute of Yahweh is a well established notion in the life and religion of Israel. From the time of Moses onwards Yahweh has always been regarded as righteous, and even in the Eighth Century prophets[130] where the concept of righteousness with respect to Yahweh is not explicit, it is nevertheless the underlying factor in the preaching of the prophets. The interest of the prophets is not in establishing the righteousness of Yahweh, but rather using it as a basis for their pronouncements. While it is true that "righteousness of Yahweh" is often found in the context of judgment,[131] a feature which has prompted scholars to conclude that צדק with respect to Yahweh is most often used in the forensic sense, nevertheless, it is in fact contexts which find Yahweh acting on behalf of Israel, which are predominant. "Yahweh's righteous judgments[132] are saving judgments (Ps.

---

[130] With regard to a possible reason for the absence of צדק with respect to Yahweh in the Eighth Century prophets, see J. Lindblom, *Prophecy in Ancient Israel* (Oxford: Basil Blackwell), 1963. Lindblom suggests, "The idea of 'righteousness' ṣᵉdākāh, is in these prophets not often used as an attribute of Yahweh. The reason for this is that, as we have seen, they avoid the idea of bᵉrît." p. 338. This view of Lindblom's perhaps explains the absence of צדק in relation to Yahweh, but it is clearly only an explanation which is deduced from common external factors; it misses the deeper theological sense of continuity. Even though ברית is not found in pre-exilic prophecy prior to Jeremiah in reference to Yahweh's covenant (with the exception of Hos. 6:7 and 8:1) nevertheless the preaching of משפט and צדק by the Eighth Century prophets must be understood in the light of the covenant. In this regard we are reminded of two elements. First, the Eighth Century prophets knew of the Mosaic age (e.g. Amos 5:25) and hence of the covenant and second, the fact that the prophets' message is focused in an ethical direction must not be viewed as being estranged from covenantal ties. See also, Ruble, who notes that ברית is found in the Psalms only twenty times and in twelve of these, it is associated with צדק. *Diss.*, p. 76.

[131] See for example, Isa. 5:16; Jer. 11:20; Pss. 9:4; 50:6; 96:13; 99:4.

[132] Having a forensic overtone does not exclude the fact that even in these contexts Yahweh is acting on behalf of Israel. Judgment is not synonymous with punishment and if there is a semblance of the latter, it must be understood in the context of the covenant. In essence, there is never punishment which is wantonly distributed simply for its own sake. As von Rad notes, this kind of "punitive aspect of צדק would be a '*contradictio in adiecto.*'" *Theol.* I, p. 377. The occasions in which there is evidence of punitive action (such as the woe oracle in First Isaiah and in the numerical formula of Amos 1-2) are in fact directed against neighboring nations. Once again though, these nations are not arbitrarily punished, but instead punishment is meted out precisely because there are ethical values which are expected of all peoples. There is, if you will, an international code, the very essence of which testifies to the importance of all nations being in proper relationship with each other. See Hendrik van Oyen, *Ethik des Alten Testaments* (G'esambherstellung: Claussen and Bosse, Leck), 1967. Van Oyen argues

36:6) and Deutero-Isaiah can therefore speak of Yahweh as a 'righteous God and a Savior.'"¹³³ The implicit references of the Eighth Century prophets become very explicit at the hands of the editor of Deutero-Isaiah. In Isa. 45:19-21, Yahweh is described as "the one who declares what is right;" "the only God and there is no other God beside him;" "a righteous God and a Savior." Yahweh is God of all, and in essence that means that all redemption, deliverance and salvation must be secured through him.¹³⁴ Deutero-Isaiah is in reality the principal source in which צדק is regarded as synonymous with "deliverance" and "salvation." In some ways, Deutero-Isaiah establishes a principle of צדק with respect to Yahweh which declares the magnitude of the latter's acts for Israel. In describing the use of צדק in Deutero-Isaiah, Jacob observes that, "righteousness is not only for him the deliverance of the oppressed and the restoration of their normal state, but the gift of a new reality superior to what previously existed."¹³⁵ In addition to Deutero-Isaiah, there are in fact other sources which exemplify Yahweh's righteousness in his preservation of Israel. The exile is certainly a classic example of a period when Israel needed deliverance, but there are many such times throughout the life of Israel. When, for example, trouble (Ps. 143:11) appears, Yahweh's righteousness is demonstrated as he intervenes on Israel's behalf. The righteousness of Yahweh is not a static characteristic or attribute, but rather it is alive and dynamic and is expressed pointedly through its action on behalf of Israel.

In addition to the "salvation" and "deliverance" contexts, there are also other uses for which the צדק of Yahweh is employed. Occasionally, Yahweh is seen as one of two parties involved in a lawsuit (Isa. 43:26), a situation which inevitably places Yahweh "in the right." Also, it is used in the context of describing the צדק of

---

that von Rad's theory of Yahweh's punitive actions is unfounded, particularly when seen in the light of Ps. 7:12 [11]. However, van Oyen's argument seems unconvincing, as he regards "righteous judgment" as punitive, an idea which in fact is introducing a foreign element into "righteous judgment...." pp. 51-52.
¹³³ Achtemeier, "Righteousness...." p. 83.
¹³⁴ See references such as Isa. 41:10; 42:6; 45:13.
¹³⁵ Jacob, *Theol.*, p. 101.

Yahweh in reference to nature,[136] as in Ps. 72:3 or also often in a manner which may be termed as a "material use,"[137] such as Ps. 89:15 [14]; Isa. 11:5; Hos. 10:1. But even more frequent than these is the context in which Yahweh is presented as the ideal judge, the one who executes justice for all of creation. (Jer. 11:20) Clearly when צדק is used in this context, it has a judicial overtone, but in describing Yahweh as the ideal judge it implies that he is the epitome of one who bears such a title and in fact "steadfast love," "impartiality," "faithfulness," all belong to the character of Yahweh. These preceding points enable us to see the vastness of צדק when used in reference to Yahweh, for it is certainly all encompassing in its orientation, whether in a religious, forensic, or ethical sense.

2. צדק and Israel

The area of the "righteousness of Israel" provides us with an inherent problem, namely that Israel is not chosen by Yahweh because of its righteousness, nor does the validity of the covenant depend on the righteousness of Israel. As we study the writings of the Eighth Century prophets, it is apparent that the notion of Israel's righteousness does not find a place here, but the focus is on the lack of righteousness on the part of Israel. One incident which clarifies this point involves the inversion by the prophet Amos on Israel's expectations from the "Day of Yahweh." In this section of Amos it is obvious that Israel has neither righteousness nor the right to expect that which had traditionally been associated with the "Day of

---

[136] Von Rad regards this usage as having "spatial" overtone, *Theol.* I, p. 376. This designation by von Rad bears a rather static connotation, which does not correspond with our discussion regarding the dynamic nature of צדק. We are led to agree with van Oyen in this regard; he says that even in instances where nature is used together with צדק, we must not lose sight of the personal and ontological framework which is heavily used in the definition of most Old Testament categories. *Ethik*, p. 51.

[137] Von Rad, *Theol.* I, p. 376. Von Rad allows for a metaphorical interpretation of such references, but does not dismiss the possibility that they may be literal.

Yahweh."[138] The nature of the situation in Israel during the Eighth Century does not warrant the preaching of Israel's righteousness, for it is principally the social, economic, and political atmosphere which influenced the themes on which the prophets spoke. If in fact, there is any time when one can point to צדק in particular relationship to Israel, it would be in the exilic period.[139] Two hundred years after the Eighth Century prophets preached, Israel is in exile; the pronouncements of the pre-exilic prophets are largely fulfilled and Israel finds itself in captivity in Babylon. It is this situation in particular which prompts the exilic prophets to employ צדק in the sense of "deliverance" and "salvation."

In this regard, it is once again Deutero-Isaiah who is the chief proponent. The writer of Isa. 40-55 includes in his writing several crucial elements which aid us in our study of the righteousness of Israel. It is not so much the outstanding righteous nature of Israel in exile which prompts the writer to speak of Yahweh's salvation, but rather that Israel has endured enough punishment. However, by no means does the exile perfect Israel. The "deliverance" of Israel is certainly not contingent on its perfection or absolute righteousness. There is no doubt that despite the favor which Yahweh has shown to Israel, this people will continue to be "in the wrong" against Yahweh. There is an immensely powerful section in Isa. 49 which places this tension in perspective. Beginning from v. 8, the writer points to the many ways in which Yahweh helps the people of Israel; he keeps the covenant with them and gives them the land; he quenches their thirst; he comforts and has compassion on the afflicted, and yet Israel replies that it has been forgotten and forsaken by Yahweh. The writer describes the love of Yahweh for Israel as a mother's love for her child; how could Yahweh forget Israel when there is such a love.

---

[138] See Amos 5:18ff. A more detailed examination of the "Day of Yahweh" with regard to the social critique of the Eighth Century prophets is developed in Chapter VI of this study.

[139] It can be argued that the influence on the exilic prophets might have been derived from the Deuteronomic reformation which contains an element that hints at the righteousness of Israel. (Deut. 6:25) There are also scattered references in pre-exilic prophets, such as Habakkuk, who incorporate this Deuteronomic concept in their preaching. (See, Hab. 1:4,13)

Even if a mother would forget her child, still Yahweh would never forsake Israel; such is nature of this extraordinary love. Yet with all of Israel's unbelief and rejection of Yahweh, Yahweh has still forgiven the sins, "...her iniquity is pardoned." (Isa. 40:2) Yahweh brings salvation to Israel,[140] not because of what the latter has done but despite it and wholly through the צדק of Yahweh.

With this knowledge, how is it that Israel can be seen as righteous by the writer of Deutero-Isaiah? There are two points which are germane here. First, there is an inherent right (צדק) within Israel which is the element that dominates its cause before Yahweh. It is a righteousness which comes to Israel exclusively because of the covenant relationship with Yahweh, a covenant which is initiated by Yahweh and the validity of which is sustained by Yahweh. This covenant, because it is fundamentally a relationship between Yahweh and Israel, bequeaths to Israel an inherent right. On a more specific level, the incident between David and Mephibosheth, the son of Saul, is illustrative of this "inherent right." Mephibosheth's plea to David is one based on his inherent right as Saul's son, even though in this particular instance he is unsure as to whether that right is sufficient.[141] That David overlooks the wrong of Mephibosheth is based solely on relationship and the "right" inherent in it and not on the latter's righteousness. It is important in this regard to note that inasmuch as Israel has apostasized against Yahweh, nevertheless Israel remains Yahweh's elect.[142] In fact, while in exile, Israel becomes the witness of the true God as opposed to the god of Babylon, (Isa. 43:10) and this is precisely why Israel has such a "right."

Second, it is the one who is "in the right" that is justified. In this sense, "justification" is used synonymously with "deliverance" and "salvation;" thus when Israel is delivered from exile in Babylon, this is an act by Yahweh which signifies that Israel is justified. Yahweh's divine intervention on Israel's behalf underlines not only the covenantal relationship but also the fact that Israel is "in

---

[140] See, e.g. Isa. 46:13; 51:5; 52:10.

[141] See, II Sam. 19:29 [28].

[142] Israel must have been aware of this when it boasts of Yahweh's vindication and deliverance. See Isa. 49:4; 50:8.

the right" precisely because of the Babylonian captivity. The "righteousness of Israel" is dependent on the righteousness of Yahweh.

3. צדק and the Individual

The idea of individual righteousness is a concept not entirely unknown in Ancient Israel, even though it cannot be regarded as having overarching influence. There are references such as I Sam. 26:23 which point to individual righteousness, but it is perhaps in Proverbs and to some extent in Psalms that a pattern of individual righteousness develops. More than half of the ninety-four occurrences of צדק in Proverbs are in relation to the individual, and this is explained in part by the system of instruction which was in vogue during this period. The instruction in both clans and royal courts is to individuals, teaching them how to live. One of the most common antithetical statements in Proverbs pits "righteous" against "wicked," the implications of being in either category are well understood, and with the presence of this kind of distinction, the doctrine of retribution is also established. In this context, there is no particular eschatological reference, for both "the righteous" and "the wicked" will face the fruit of their actions on earth.

In the case of Psalms, it is somewhat more difficult to decipher whether some of the occurrences of צדק are used in the context of the individual or of Israel. Like Proverbs, there are a large number of antithetical references, most of which involve צדק and רשע, but unlike Proverbs, whether these are in reference to the individual or to Israel is much more difficult to ascertain. There are of course instances in which the individual is clearly the one on whom the focus is directed, as in Pss. 1 and 73. The "righteous" in the Psalms are those who trust in Yahweh (16:1; 22:9; 26:1) and believe that Yahweh's presence is on the earth (58:11) and, with this knowledge, act in accordance with the demands and claims of the relationship.[143]

---

[143] In this regard, Lindblom observes that, "Yahweh's claim on His people was first that they should remain faithful to their God and secondly that they should obey Yahweh's moral commands as expressed in law and tra-

However, the uncertainty which is found in the Psalms is absent from the other later sources in which individual righteousness establishes its dominance. This dominance in Israelite thought does not come until the time of Ezekiel. Even though there is a clear indication in Jeremiah of the advancement of the concept of individual righteousness, it is not firmly established. In Jeremiah, there are several elements, including individual laments to Yahweh and questions regarding the state of the individual in relationship to Yahweh. Jer. 12:1ff is a classic example of the prophet's torment, and, as righteousness becomes personalized, there is no longer the community righteousness behind which the individual may hide. Individual righteousness, however, does not erase or exclude community righteousness. Even with these examples of individual righteousness in Jeremiah, there are still hints of community righteousness, and one way in which this is seen is the transfer of sin from one generation to the next, from one person to the next. In effect, the actions of the individual are still inexorably tied to the community. The fact that "the parents have eaten sour grapes, and the children's teeth are set on edge" (Jer. 31:29)[144] indicates that precise individualism with respect to righteousness is not yet in vogue. The Deuteronomistic theology underlines this view in the description of Yahweh's determination to punish Judah because of the sins of Manasseh.[145]

This focus on the transfer of sin shifts in Ezekiel, where the precision of individual righteousness becomes the norm. Before we look at this dominance in Ezekiel, it is necessary to discuss the reasons which might have been responsible for the movement from the righteousness of the community to that of the individual. In this regard, Skinner[146] suggests that two elements are of importance in identifying the conditions which might have prompted the

---

dition." *Prophecy in Ancient Israel*, pp. 312-313. See also von Rad, *Theol.* I, p. 381 and van Oyen, *Ethik*, p. 54.
[144] While this might have reflected the situation in Jeremiah's time, the context is one in which the prophet prophesies that this would no longer be the case when Israel is restored.
[145] See II Ki. 21:10ff.
[146] Skinner, "Righteousness...." p. 276.

birth of this concept, namely, the dissolution of the nation of Israel and the introduction of the written code of law.

First, because of the Babylonian captivity, the nation of Israel is in effect dissolved and with it the suspension of the concept of collective retribution with regard to Israel. This is certainly not a suggestion that Yahweh is unconcerned about affairs of Israel as a nation, for there is every indication that Yahweh *is* concerned, and Israel's deliverance from Babylon attests this. However, now for the first time while in captivity, there is evidence which suggests that each individual is accountable to Yahweh, on a personal basis. The description in Ezek. 18:20 verifies this thesis. In this instance the prophet says, "A child shall not suffer for the iniquity of a parent, nor a parent suffer for the iniquity of a child; the righteousness of the righteous shall be his own, and the wickedness of the wicked shall be his own."[147]

The second element which is instrumental in establishing the concept of individual righteousness is the introduction of written law as the basis of the practice of religion. The primary aim of the Deuteronomic code is to transform Israel into a divinely oriented nation, through the subscription to a Divine code. This appeal however, in the first instance is to the individual, and it is this aspect which is incorporated and developed in the preaching of Ezekiel in particular. Of the thirty-nine occurrences of צדק in Ezekiel, only on seven occasions (16:51,52; 23:45; 45:9,10 [3x]) is it used with reference to anything other than the individual. In every other instance it is employed in reference to the individual, whether with respect to the religious condition (as in 3:20ff; 13:22) or with respect to good deeds which may be integral to the makeup of a righteous person. (See, 18:24) The overtone of individual righteousness is predominantly legal and ethical, primarily because it entails obedience to a code which, at its roots, has ethical implications. One of the far-reaching effects of the concept of righteousness is the theory of individual retribution; the righteous will live and the wicked will die. It is particularly this theory which is put to the test in the story of

---

[147] On this theme, see also Ezek. 14:14,20; 18:19.

Job. To conclude the discussion on individual righteousness, we take a brief look at the book of Job.

As long as the theory of retribution is in reference to judgment by Yahweh (as Ezekiel intends it), then the difficulties and practical implications are limited. However once this focus is shifted from the eschatological to the present, then there evolves a new set of issues, and it is in Job that these are most profoundly present. The retribution theory was very well known by the time of Job, and consequently, when his suffering commences, there is little doubt in the minds of Eliphaz, Bildad and Zophar that Job must have done something sinful, for it was known that the righteous would live and the wicked would die and Job in this view clearly falls in the latter category. The dramatic irony of the story of Job allows the reader to know the truth behind Job's suffering, but Job who does not enjoy such a vantage point, must face the reality of being in opposition to Yahweh. Job's charge to Yahweh as the ideal judge is that the latter is "in the wrong" while Job is "in the right." In essence, Job is challenging the belief that Yahweh's judgment is both impeccable and unimpeachable. But for the three counselors, who are obviously knowledgeable about the theory of retribution, an idea such as Job's is not only inconceivable, but in their minds underline the guilt of Job.[148] Ultimately it is Job who has to face the reality of being pronounced guilty, even though he has continued to plead his innocence (צדק).[149] The element which relentlessly pains Job, ironically is not his physical decay, but the belief that Yahweh has become inaccessible. That Job insists on his own righteousness sounds offensive and it is not surprising that this view of Job's has led to many misunderstandings. But in the arguments which are produced by Job, neither sanctimony nor "justification by works" is a basic presupposition.[150]

As we reflect on the suffering of Job and the concept of individual righteousness, many questions arise, most of which we have to bypass here. However, we must point to what is perhaps the

---

[148] See, Job 8:3; 34:17; 36:3; 37:23; 40:8.
[149] See, Job 9:20ff; 13:18; 34:5.
[150] Van Oyen, *Ethik*, pp. 55-56.

most crucial question that involves individual righteousness, namely, can a person be righteous before God, and if so what are the elements which would constitute such a righteousness? With their sometimes textbook reflection, the counselors direct our attention to elements such as: piety, worship, faithfulness to Yahweh and the covenantal expectations, morality, uprightness and integrity. The greatest irony is the fact that Job is the epitome of a righteous person, but yet is "in the wrong" before Yahweh, a situation which prompts us to conclude that it is perhaps not the suffering of Job with which we may ultimately have to concern ourselves, but rather the question of integrity with regard to the covenant relationship.

In conclusion, several observations may be drawn from our discussion of צדק in the Old Testament. Even with the description of the use of the root *ṣdq* in the Ancient Near East, still the meanings derived and the contents of these early uses, do not reflect the vastness and versatility of צדק in the Old Testament. What in fact this brief etymological study does is to demonstrate the resemblance in the Near Eastern and Old Testament uses; what it does not do is suggest or verify a wholesale transition of *ṣdq* from Near Eastern to Hebrew thought. It is therefore not surprising that the translation of the Old Testament into Greek involves the use of some ten different Greek terms in order to render with close proximity the meaning and connotation of צדק, and this in turn enables us to observe once again the wide-ranging reference of צדק.

The distribution of צדק in the Old Testament facilitates the categorization of its different uses and in so doing aids us in our discussion regarding the basic concept out of which צדק must be understood, namely relationship. This foundation is reflected in all aspects of life, "spiritual" as well as "secular," and between different parties. This is a crucial point, particularly since צדק is often labeled a "religious" term and regarded therefore as applying only to spiritual matters. Not only is צדק found in reference to "piety," "faithfulness," but also in temporal matters such as "weights and measures." In some ways, the relationship motif finds its greatest strength and support in the temporal situations, where the claims of relationship are not as apparent as a situation which involves

Yahweh's deliverance of Israel. Furthermore, there are no norms (in reference to צדק) to which an individual must subscribe, but rather it is the claims and responsibilities of the relationship, the validity of which must be sustained. The fulfilling of the expectations of צדק are intricately connected with the particular relationship in which individuals and Yahweh are involved. That is to say, the practice of צדק cannot be understood outside relationship, and as a result, it involves each individual within his or her station in life. Thus, the king has his obligations to his subjects and vice versa, and the subjects each in his or her particular area has responsibilities to each other, and therefore responsibilities cannot be executed by a "deputy."

Moreover, in our discussion it is evident that even though צדק is ultimately associated with Yahweh, and its greatest manifestation is in the form of a covenant, nevertheless its use is not entirely religious. All uses though, whether ethical or forensic, or whether in reference to Israel, Yahweh or the individual, finally have a religious foundation, precisely because the originator and sustainer of the covenant is Yahweh.

E. צדיק in the Old Testament

The importance of צדיק is seen in the fact that it is the form of the root צדק which is accountable for half its occurrences in the Old Testament. צדיק occurs two hundred times, and the majority of them (115 times) occur in the Psalms and Proverbs. The remaining occurrences are scattered throughout the Old Testament. There are three subjects which are principally associated with צדיק: Yahweh, Israel and the individual. These three subjects are found primarily in three categories namely, religious, forensic and economic. While these categories accommodate most of the occurrences, there are nevertheless isolated occurrences which do not fit into any of these.[151]

---

[151] See, e.g., Gen. 20:4 and I Sam. 24:18 [17] where צדיק is used in a context of morality.

Chapter I 85

1. צדיק as a Religious Term

In the Psalms, whenever an individual or Israel is called צדיק, Yahweh is typically the one who brings about this righteousness.[152] The title צדיק is not granted through self-righteousness, but through obedience to Yahweh and living within an acceptable relationship with other members of the created order. This foundation in Yahweh may be seen for example in Pss. 14:5; 34:16 [15]; 55:23 [22], for the צדיק is in turn protected by Yahweh. Obedience to Yahweh and the subsequent title of צדיק transpire primarily through religious observances, that is to say, participation in the cult and the keeping of the commandments. (e.g. Ps. 26:1-7) These are the areas in which Israel is involved and through which is invited back into the fold of the צדיקים.[153] In addition to this use, צדיק is also used as an attribute of Yahweh (e.g. Ps. 11:7) and in describing the actions of Yahweh. (e.g. Ps. 7:12 [11])[154] These are the main ways in which צדיק is used in the Psalms.[155]

In Proverbs, fifty-three of the sixty-five occurrences of צדיק[ים] are in antithesis to terms such as רשע, חטאים and פעליאון. The positive nature of the צדיק in these occurrences can be traced to its source in Yahweh. Even though the instruction in Proverbs may

---

[152] See, Mowinckel, who suggests that Psalms such as 1, 37 and 73 may be regarded as setting in opposition the individual צדיק and the individual רשע. However, he sees the majority of the occurrences of צדיק[ים] and רשע[ים] as Israel and the enemies of Israel respectively. Using Ps. 58 as an example, he concludes that, "There can be no doubt whatsoever that 'the righteous' in this case indicate Israel as a nation -- rĕšaʾîm in the Psalms does not signify any single group of men, but all those who act as the enemies of the worshipper." *Psalms*, p. 208.

[153] See, von Rad, who suggests that the people "had been taught by the cult that Yahweh alone could bestow this title, and that he assigned it to those who clung to him. It is not the least surprising, therefore, that the men designate themselves as *the* צדיקים, since anyone who participated vocally in the cult in any kind of way was צדיק ...." *Theol.* I, p. 381.

[154] See, e.g., Deut. 32:4; Isa. 24:16; 45:21; Jer. 12:1; Zeph. 3:5; Dan. 9:4; Ez. 9:15; Neh. 9:8.

[155] Against this view, see Arvid S. Kapelrud, "New Ideas in Amos," *SVT* 15 (1966), pp. 193-206. Kapelrud suggests that both the psalms of lamentation and psalms of thanksgiving focus on the economic suffering of the צדיק and these psalms seek to restore the צדיק to a more successful state. p. 202. There is no indication however, of such a development in the Psalms.

be regarded as secular in its tone, there are several references in which Yahweh and צדיק are closely connected.[156] In these instances, the צדיק is seen to be in close relationship with Yahweh, while the various antagonists are not. This relationship with Yahweh appears to be religious in its primary orientation. With the exception of 10:3, which says, "...The LORD does not let the צדיק go hungry...," all the other occurrences suggest nothing but a religious orientation in the relationship. This view of צדיק is also dominant in Qoheleth, who perceives that the fate of the צדיק is the same as that of the רשע and, Yahweh is the one who determines both.[157] Two other examples will suffice here. First, in Gen. 18:23ff, where Abraham intercedes on Sodom's behalf, צדיק is used as a religious concept. In this instance, it is clear that the צדיקים are meant to be those who live in accord with the expectations of Yahweh, and specifically on this occasion they were to demonstrate hospitality to the outsiders. The fact that no צדיקים can be found indicates that the people of Sodom have departed from the code of conduct essential for a proper relationship. Second, thirteen of the fifteen occurrences of צדיק in Ezekiel are used with regard to the individual's relationship to Yahweh, and appear often in antithesis to רשע.

These various examples give some indication of the presence of צדיק as a religious term.

2. צדיק as a Forensic Term

צדיק as a forensic term occurs several times in the Old Testament, particularly within a judicial context. In these instances, the צדיק is considered as the one who is not guilty in a particular situation. In this regard it is important that צדיק be distinguished from נקי. Exod. 23:7 is one instance in which both צדיק and נקי are used together,[158] and 23:8 suggests that they are used together within a judicial framework. However, in this instance, it would seem that these terms are not meant to be understood as syn-

---

[156] See, e.g., 3:33; 10:3; 15:29; 17:15; 18:10.
[157] See, e.g., 7:14; 8:14; [2x]; 9:1,2.
[158] For two other occurrences of צדיק and נקי together, see, Job 22:19; 27:17. In these instances, however, צדיק is not used in a forensic context.

onyms. It is evident that a monetary transaction is involved when שחד is used with either צדיק or נקי, but the circumstances of these two cases are entirely different. When שחד occurs with נקי, the נקי, is an individual who is not associated in any way with a lawsuit or trial or with any form of judicial procedure. Thus, when Deut. 27:25 and Ps. 15:5 refer to an "innocent" person, they are in fact referring to an individual who has not committed a crime and is not guilty of any offense. Hence, when someone is "paid" to kill such a person (Deut. 27:25), or to perform some action which is to his or her disadvantage (Ps. 15:5), there is every reason to believe that such an action has no connection with legal proceedings.

On the other hand, when שחד is used together with צדיק, it is a legal proceeding which forms the background for the words. The צדיק is seen not as an "innocent" person in the sense in which נקי is used, but the situation refers rather to the legal status of the individual. Exod. 23:8 states, "...you shall take no שחד, for a שחד blinds the officials and subverts the cause of those who are צדיקים." Here the context is clearly a forensic one. Both נקי and צדיק have the sense of "innocent," but the contexts in which נקי occurs alongside שחד are non-forensic, while צדיק with שחד occurs in a forensic context.[159] Also, in Isa. 5:23, where the root צדק is used three times, שחד is also used, and here the context is also clearly forensic, and the "innocent" are the צדיקים in the legal sense. A final example will suffice here. In Deut. 25:1, צדיק is used in antithesis to רשע, and in an instance such as this, if there is a dispute to be settled in court, the צדיק will be acquitted (declared to be in the right) while the רשע will be condemned.[160]

3. צדיק as an Economic Term

צדיק as an economic term appears only twice in the Old Testament, and both occurrences are in Amos (2:6; 5:12). In Amos's time, the צדיקים were those who saw themselves as firmly within Yahweh's design for his people. The צדיק considered himself or her-

---

[159] For an almost identical use of שחד and צדיק together, see, Deut. 16:19.
[160] For other occurrences of צדיק as a judicial term, see, I Ki. 8:32; Isa. 29:21.

self blessed and understood their successful state as a reflection of the relationship with Yahweh. According to Kapelrud, "the condition of the suffering was not a normal one, he had to be brought back to a more successful state if he should be considered as a real צדיק. This view was commonly accepted, yea, more than that, it was part and parcel of daily life in ancient Israel. Poverty and suffering were indications that a man was, in one way or another, outside the ranks of the צדיקים in ancient Israel."[161] This is a particularly important observation, for it testifies to the belief that success and well-being were elements which were representative of the צדיקים. This belief implies that the poor and powerless were lacking that which was necessary to attain the state of the צדיק. In this way, the concept of צדיק was linked to the socio-economic status of the people. This position, moreover, became a shield with which these so-called צדיקים might protect themselves and simultaneously disregard and neglect those who were not also צדיקים. This was the situation which Amos faced. The so-called צדיקים were now oppressing the poor and powerless in order to build and preserve their own positions in society. The consequence was that the poor and powerless were unable to achieve the state of the צדיק as the term was normally understood.

Amos takes this situation as he did that of the "Day of Yahweh" and inverted the expectations. In 2:6, Amos uses צדיק as a parallel to אביון. The אביון has become the צדיק, and this parallelism is repeated in 5:12. Both occurrences point to the socio-economic ills of the צדיקים; in 2:6 the צדיק is sold into slavery because of debts,[162]

---

[161] Kapelrud, "New Ideas...." p. 202.
[162] See, G. Johannes Botterweck, "אביון" in *TDOT* ed. G. Johannes Botterweck and Helmer Ringgren. Trans. John T. Willis. (Michigan: Eerdmans Publishing Company), 1974, pp. 27-41. Regarding Amos 2:6 and 5:12, Botterweck notes that, "Of particular significance is the parallelism of *'ebhyon* and *tsaddiq*....' The parallelism of *tsaddiq* and *'ebhyon* here [2:6] is rooted in the unjustified selling of the poor into slavery as a payment for debts." pp. 31-32. Also, regarding the use of צדי in Amos 2:6, see, H.-J. Fabry, "דּל" in *TDOT*, ed. G. Johannes Botterweck and Helmer Ringgren. Trans. John T. Willis, Geoffrey W. Bromiley and David E. Green. (Michigan: Eerdmans Publishing company), 1978, pp. 208-230. Fabry suggests that, "*tsaddiq* in 2:6 does not mean a 'righteous' person, but one who is innocent of an accusation...." p. 223.

Chapter I   89

while the צדיק in 5:12 suffers injustice at the local judiciary. While 2:6 and 5:12 are the only two instances in which צדיק is used in an economic sense, there is one other instance in Amos which is relevant here. In 8:6, the message is strikingly similar to that of 2:6b, except that in 8:6, צדיק is absent. However, in 8:6 דל replaces צדיק, in parallelism to אביון. The economic overtone in 8:6 is self-evident.[163]

This brief discussion of צדיק in the Old Testament indicates clearly that the use of צדיק is a varied one. It is safe to say that the two categories which predominate are the "religious" and the "forensic." However, Amos's use of צדיק as an economic term is an important element in his overall message.

---

[163] See, Botterweck "אביון," p. 32 and Fabry, "דּל," p. 223, both of whom agree that in 8:6, דל replaces צדיק.

Chapter II

I. Background and Meaning of שפט in the Ancient Near East

In order to determine the different uses and shades of meaning of משפט in the Old Testament, it is necessary that the root שפט be examined both in the biblical and extra-biblical material. In this examination an attempt will be made to trace the meanings of משפט in the Bible and ascertain whether there is an evolution of meanings or whether the original meaning(s) are maintained. This brief study will come to bear on the larger investigation of משפט in the Eighth Century prophets.

It has become acceptable in recent years in biblical scholarship to proceed on the assumption that the societies of the Ancient Near Eastern countries have been influential on Israel. It is true that there are certain elements which are unique to Israel (e.g. covenant relations with Yahweh) but there are also many instances in which aspects of Israelite life have been influenced, if not shaped, by its neighbors. In the following study it is the aim to determine the way in which שפט is used in the Ancient Near East and then to consider whether these uses could have, and did influence the use and meaning of שפט in the Old Testament.

A. Mari

The oldest Western Semitic texts which use the root *špṭ* were found at Mari, and these have provided a particular pattern of usage of *špṭ*. There are in fact enough references for there to be a consistent traceable meaning. Moreover, the presence of various derivatives will allow us in this study to form a conclusion, based not only on one particular derivative but on all those which are found. The following terms are found in the Mari texts: *šipṭum* (noun), *šapāṭum* (verb), *šāpiṭum* (participle), *šāpiṭūtum* (noun). The different contexts in which these terms occur will be examined, and then a conclusion based on this examination will be formed.

The term *šipṭum* occurs in several different contexts and involves a variety of characters. The first instance is found in I 6:6-19,[1] where *šipṭum* describes a royal order to draft soldiers for a military expedition. This *šipṭum* is given by King Samsi-Adad to his son Jasmah-Adad. In this section of the letter, both *ši-pí iṭ-ka-a-ma* and *ši-ip-ṭa-am* are used, and both, in this context, mean "order."[2] Another occurrence of *šipṭum* is found in I 13:24-30[3] and once again it is used twice. *Ši-ip-ṭa-am*[4] is found in lines 24 and 30, and as in the first example, they are used to mean "order," once more coming from the king to his son, to be related to the leaders. Not every occurrence of *šipṭum* involves the king; even though the concept of "authority" and "rule" is most readily manifested in the king, *šipṭum* is also employed in the context of other authoritative figures. In another situation,[5] Samadahum (a high-ranking official) sends a *šipṭum* to other members of the military, one which constitutes the admonition to refrain from securing unlawful shares of booty. This particular instance of the use of *šipṭum* is significant precisely because of its subject. That is to say, this occurrence of *šipṭum* underlines the thesis that in fact a *šipṭum* is

---

[1] Georges Dossin, *Archives Royales de Mari* I (Paris: Imprimerie Nationale), 1950. All references to the volumes of these Mari texts will henceforth be referred to as *ARM*.

[2] Dossin translates both these words as "*décision*," thereby casting a particular connotation on the words. This translation for Dossin does not include the idea of "order" in the sense in which it is used in the text. The text suggests that Samsi-Adad faces a military matter and sends out an "order." To use "*décision*" as the translation for *ši-pí iṭ-ka-a-ma* indicates that Jasmah-Adad is in charge and it is his decision which he is himself relaying. Dossin's translation is clearly untenable in view of the circumstances on which the text focuses. See, *ARM* I, p. 33.

[3] Dossin, *ARM* I, p. 47.

[4] Once again, Dossin translates this term as "*décision*." However, in this instance, the context suggests that the king made a decision regarding a complaint and is now in the process of relaying that decision via his son. As a royal directive, it has the nature of an order and so conceivably can be either "order" or "decision." However, if in the event "*décision*" were employed to mean "a precise decision," it would clearly not have any judicial overtone, even though *décision* in French could have a judicial overtone. In this case however, the king's *décision* is not based on a lawsuit, but is simply a reflection of his wisdom, his authority. See, *ARM* I, p. 47.

[5] Charles F. Jean, *Archives Royales de Mari* II (Paris: Imprimerie Nationale), 1950, 13:25-30, 35-36.

something which comes from an authoritative source. It is true that most of the examples of the use of šipṭum are associated with the king, but the occurrence in II 13:25-30 confirms the belief that šipṭum is associated with authority in general.[6]

While šipṭum is the noun which means "order," šapāṭum is the act of giving a šipṭum. Marzal suggests that šapāṭum means "to give an order which carries all the implications that we have seen in the term šipṭum."[7] In II 92:5-7 and 23-24[8] Kibri-Dagan is engaged in situations which involve the receiving and giving of a šipṭum. The šipṭum which Kibri-Dagan sends out, is one which he receives from the king and then he delivers it to the tribal leaders. It is in announcing this royal order that Kibri-Dagan uses aš-pu-uṭ [9] and the context suggests clearly that it is the act of giving an order or command.[10] Once again this verbal form of špṭ is associated with authority and is tied to the object šipṭum.

A third cognate of špṭ found in the Mari texts is the term šāpiṭum. Arguably, this is the most important use of špṭ in the Mari texts, as far as this study is concerned. This is perhaps the term which comes closest to being a parallel to the Hebrew שפט. Some scholars have argued that the parallel which is drawn between the שפט and the šāpiṭum is one which is based entirely on the functional similarities. Two of the principal proponents of this view are Marzal and Malamat, both of whom conclude that the šāpiṭum is a provincial governor and argue by implication that the שפטים[11] are

---

[6] For other instances in which šipṭum is used with a similar meaning, see ARM I 83:27; II 13:24, 33; II 92:6; III 12:22; III 30:25; IV 16:12; VI 64:7.

[7] A. Marzal, "The Provincial Governor of Mari: His title and appointment," JNES 30 (1971), p. 193.

[8] Jean, ARM II, p. 166.

[9] This term (aš-pu-uṭ) is in fact used on three different occasions: II 92:13, 20, and 24.

[10] Jean's translation of aš-pu-uṭ as "réprimande(s)" on every occasion points to a manner of rebuking which is negative and moreover, does not fit the context. He also translates šipṭum as "la réprimande" and in so doing implies that the message is not a cautionary one, but one of rebuke. Perhaps this strong language is meant to underline the serious nature of the šipṭum (coming from both governor and king), and the consequences of disobedience (death). Even if this were the case, still réprimande connotes punishment after a particular action, and this text clearly points to a warning.

[11] The role of the שפטים will be examined later in this chapter.

similar in their functions, though the political framework is different.[12] There are in fact, several occurrences of šāpiṭum in the Mari texts and there is a noticeable pattern in the meanings. We will look briefly at the occurrences in the earlier volumes of the *Archives Royales de Mari*. In one occurrence,[13] Tarim-Sakim together with Jasmah-Adad make a recommendation for the position of the new šāpiṭum[14] in Tuttul. The position is clearly one of leadership and authority and the šāpiṭum is meant to be the ruler of Tuttul. While this context indicates that the šāpiṭum is primarily a ruler, still it must be noted that "governing" is not the only function; in fact being a šāpiṭum involves much more. One of these functions is developed quite succinctly in VIII 84.[15] This particular piece is under the section entitled "*Procédure et Documents Judíciares*," and to some extent this is indicative of the nature of VIII 84. Sumu-hadu is the šāpiṭum and he conducts a trial between two individuals (Dada and Naramtum) who have a dispute regarding their goods. This reference is of particular interest precisely because it is something of an exception and also because it is used alongside *da-ia-nu-um*. In VIII 83:4 and VIII 87:1 *da-ia-nu-um*[16] is the term which is used to describe the official who litigates in disputes and judicial matters. In VIII 83:4 the *da-ia-nu-um* de-

---

[12] See A. Malamat, "Aspects of Tribal Societies in Mari and Israel," *RAI*, 15 (1966), pp. 129-138. See specifically p. 133. Also A. Marzal, "The Provincial Governor...." p. 197. For other sources with this view, see A. Malamat "The Period of the Judges," *The World History of the Jewish People* volume III, ed. Benjamin Mazar (London: W.H. Allen), 1971, pp. 129-163. See particularly p. 131. See also, Georges Dossin, "L'Inscription de Fondation de Iaḫdun-Lim Roi de Mari," *Syria* 32 (1955), p. 25. Dossin suggests that "dans la titulature administrative de Mari, le terme šāpiṭum 'juge' désigne le préfet qui peut gouverneur soit un palais, comme Baḫ di-Lim, soit une province...." p. 25 Dossin in this instance attempts to coalesce the meanings of "*juge*" and "*gouverneur*" and perhaps is successful to some extent. However his continued use of "juge" for šāpiṭum as we shall see, casts a particular connotation on šāpiṭum.

[13] Dossin, *ARM* I 73:52, p. 138.

[14] The context clearly suggests that the role of the new šāpiṭum is to rule. However Dossin translates šāpiṭum as "*juge*" and in so doing imparts a judicial connotation, which is certainly not the principal meaning here. *ARM* I 73:52, p. 139.

[15] Georges Boyer, *Archives Royales de Mari*, VIII (Paris: Imprimerie Nationale), 1958, p. 126.

[16] In VIII 87:1, the plural form *da-ia-nu* is used.

cides in a dispute over an ox while in VIII 87:1, the decision centers around a property. In essence, what has transpired is a situation which indicates that in this particular case, both the šāpiṭum and the da-ia-nu-um perform similar functions.[17] It is evident through these references that the office of judge, (a judicial functionary) was conventional at the time. As such, both the da-ia-nu-um and the šāpiṭum function concurrently. Marzal notes that, "while in VIII 83 and 87 we have 'judges' (professional or functional) who in this capacity pronounced a verdict, in VIII 84, we have a high administrative official of the king, a šāpiṭum, who can act as judge and administer justice in his own territory."[18]

In addition to these occurrences of šāpiṭum perhaps it is in the most recent volume of the Mari Texts, which details the letters of Yaqqim-Addu, that the meaning of šāpiṭum is confirmed.[19] The letters of Yaqqim-Addu bring us to a point where it becomes certain that špṭ in XIV 81, does in fact mean "rule," "govern." There are two occurrences of špṭ in XIV 81 which exemplify and verify this view. In this letter Yaqqim-Addu has expropriated land for himself and in the process has aroused the anger of the queen. Realizing that the queen is angry, Yaqqim-Addu pleads his cause, noting that his predecessors enjoyed sixty acres of land and that he is thus entitled to the same. Yaqqim-Addu describes his predecessors in direct relationship to their positions, namely, they both held the principal office in the šāpiṭūtum, or "governorship." While Yaqqim-Addu does not describe himself directly as a šāpiṭum, he nevertheless does so by implication, when he refers to his predecessor as a šāpiṭum.[20] It is fairly certain that Yaqqim-Addu holds an important leadership position, perhaps in what would be a local precinct or county. The importance of the position is underlined by

---

[17] It is regrettable that in each instance Boyer uses "juge(s)" as the French translation. It is evident that in the case of da-ia-nu-um, this would be an appropriate rendering, but clearly the juxtaposition of da-ia-nu-um and šāpiṭum should have indicated to Boyer that the later cannot be a "juge," even though of course, in this particular instance he functions as one.

[18] Marzal, "The Provincial Governor...." p. 205.

[19] Maurice Birot, *Archives Royales de Mari*, XIV (Paris: Libraire Orientaliste Paul Geuthner, S.A.), 1974.

[20] Birot, *ARM*, XIV 81:40.

the fact that Yaqqim-Addu enters into direct correspondence with the queen, an act which is not prompted by the gravity of the situation, but rather, because of the position he holds. Unlike earlier translations by Dossin and Jean,[21] who render *šāpiṭum* as *"juge,"* it is now evident that the judicial overtone is removed, for Birot renders *ša-pí-ṭú-tam* as *"gouvernement"* and *ša-pí-ṭú-um* as *"gouverneur."*[22] Safren notes that *"ARM* XIV 81 now provides us with conclusive evidence that the term *šāpiṭum* refers to a provincial governor or administrator and that *ša-pí-ṭú-um* describes the office of governorship."[23] It is clear that the occurrences of the various derivatives of *špṭ* in the Mari texts[24] point to a meaning which is not judicial in its basic connotation. As Ishida concludes, *špṭ* is to be translated as "to give order, to rule, to govern, to administer, or the like."[25]

B. Ugaritic

In many ways, the presence of *tpṭ* in Ugaritic literature is the closest parallel, both conceptually and functionally, to שפט in Hebrew. Literature from this era is dated about 14th Century B.C.[26] and since it thus precedes all of the Hebrew Bible and because of Ugarit's proximity to Israel, the prospects of similarity in language and meaning are considerable. There are several occurrences of *tpṭ* in Ugaritic, particularly in the text of Aqhat and in the epic of King Keret. A representative sampling of these texts

---

[21] Dossin, *ARM* I and Jean, *ARM* II.

[22] Birot, *ARM* XIV 81.

[23] Jonathan D. Safren, "New Evidence for the Title of the Provincial Governor at Mari," *HUCA* 50 (1979), p. 5. Safren also provides an English translation of the text of XIV 81.

[24] In addition to the examples examined, other occurrences of *šāpiṭum* are found in *ARM* II 32:16; II 98:12, 13; VII 214:6; VIII 6:17; X 160:16 and XIV 98:11; 112:5ff.

[25] T. Ishida, "The Leaders of the Tribal League 'Israel' in the Pre-Monarchic Period," *RB* 80 (1973), p. 518.

[26] See H.L. Ginsberg, *ANET*, p. 149.

will be examined. In 2 Aqhat V:6-8,[27] there are two occurrences of
ṯpṭ.

> yṯšu. yṯb. bap ṯġr. tḥt
> adrm. dbgrn. ydn.
> dn. almnt. yṯpṭ. ṯpṭ. ytm

Lines 6-8 refer to Dan'el and note that he "is upright, sitting before the gate, beneath a mighty tree on the threshing floor, judging the cause of the widow, adjudicating the case of the fatherless."[28] Dan'el's role involves in general the care and protection of the disenfranchised, and in this case particularly the widows and orphans.

There are two points regarding this text which must be noted here. First, ṯġr in Ugaritic means "gate," and in this context, it clearly refers to the place where justice is executed. In the Hebrew text, the word which is generally employed to mean gate is שער. This term may refer simply to "gate" as an entrance to a city or court (e.g. Gen. 23:10; 34:20; Exod. 35:17; 40:8) or may also be used to mean a place where the elders or city leaders meet to execute justice.[29] In this latter sense it is the equivalent of the Ugaritic ṯġr.[30] Based on the context, this meaning of ṯġr is appropriate when identified with the action of Dan'el. Dan'el, as a king who is particularly committed to the execution of justice, would in his own interest, wish to sit at the gate, the principal location for the administration of justice. Second, the idea of the "threshing floor" is also commonly associated with the execution of justice. In I Ki. 22:10, Ahab, King of Israel, and Jehoshaphat, King of Judah,

---

[27] See Cyrus H. Gordon, *Ugaritic Textbook* (Roma: Pontificum Institutum Biblicum), 1965, Column I, p. 248.

[28] This translation is Ginsberg's in *ANET*, p. 151. For a similar rendering of this text, see John Gibson, *Canaanite Myths and Legends* (Edinburgh: T and T Clark), 1977, pp. 107 ff.

[29] See, e.g., Amos 5:10,12,14; Prov. 22:22; Ruth 4:11.

[30] Gordon translates ṯġr as "door," which simply does not correspond to, or suit the context in question. While in contemporary society "door" and "gate" may have common functional elements, they are conceptually different in these Near Eastern and Biblical texts. *Ugaritic Literature*, p. 88.

are together with a host of prophets sitting at the threshing floor by the שער. As is noted above, the Ugaritic word corresponding to שער is *tǵr* while the Ugaritic and Hebrew words for "threshing-floor" are identical.³¹ גרן³² in the Ancient Near East and the Old Testament is generally regarded as a place where important rituals, such as funerals and weddings are staged.³³ The fact that Ahab and Jehoshaphat are seeking a decision underlines the role of the שער and the גרן. Even though this context does not suggest a court scene, nevertheless it is a judicial action which is the focus. The important point to note in this text is that *tpt* is associated with the rulers and that there are not professional members of the judiciary connected with *tpt*. However, it is to be noted that an element of the king's rule is to administer justice.³⁴

A second example of the use of *tpt* in Ugaritic literature which is germane to this study is in the context of 2 Keret VI:33ff.

ltdn. dn. 'almnt.
lttpt tpt. qsr npš³⁵

---

³¹ In the present context, *dbgrn* is used in Ugaritic, while in I Ki. 22:10, *bgrn* is used.

³² The commonly held view regarding גרן is challenged by John Gray in his article "The *Goren* at the City Gate: Justice and the Royal Office in the Ugaritic Text 'Aqht," *PEQ*, (1953). Gray believes that the primary meaning of גרן is not "threshing-floor" but rather a derivation from the Arabic "to rub," though he concedes that a secondary meaning is "threshing-floor." See p. 121. For a different view see Gibson, *Canaanite Myths and Legends*, p. 107, note 5 and C.H. Gordon, "The Poetic Literature of Ugarit," *Orientalia* 12, (1943), p. 65, note 1.

³³ See e.g., II Sam. 6:6.

³⁴ See S. Smith, "On the Meaning of *GOREN*," *PEQ* (1952-53), pp. 42-45. Smith argues that even though *tpt* is associated with Dan'el, it is not entirely true to presuppose that he was a king who dispensed justice. Rather, "he examined the case of the widow and judged the judgement for possibly, the orphan....As lengthy studies of the meaning of *mišpāṭ* in the Old Testament have shown to judge judgement for the poor and helpless is to give them succour such as the case merits." p. 43. There are two points to note here. First, Smith's distinction between Dan'el being a king who dispenses justice and one who judges on behalf of the poor, is not clear. Second, if by suggesting through his use of "succour such as the case merits" a sense of partiality to the oppressed, then his position needs further development. Indeed, Liberation theologians regularly speak of God's preferential option for the poor.

³⁵ See Gibson, *Canaanite Myths and Legends*, p. 101.

In this context King Keret is being repudiated for not "judging the case of the widow" nor "adjudicating the cause of the importunate."[36] This accusation of Keret is extended in 2 Keret VI: 46:50:

> dn. 'almnt lṯpṭ
> ṯpṭ qṣr npš ltdy
> ṭšm. 'el. dl lpnk
> ltšlhm. ytm bed
> kslk. 'almnt km

"You do not judge the cause of the widow, you do not try the case of the importunate. You do not banish the extortioners of the poor, you do not feed the orphan before your face (nor) the widow behind your back."[37] In these six lines, *ṯpṭ* occurs only twice, but it is the context and subject of discussion which is crucial. In this section and in 2 Keret VI: 33ff, it is evident that there is some degree of irresponsibility on the part of Keret regarding the execution of justice to those who are most in need. Twice in this last section is the "widow" mentioned, together with the "poor," the "orphan" and the "importunate." It is noteworthy that when Keret's son Ysb points to his father's shortcomings and reminds him of his responsibility, the central focus of Ysb's complaint is the lack of care of the oppressed. It is unclear as to whether Ysb's request for his father's abdication, is based on this deficiency, but it must be assumed from the context that Ysb knows of the responsibility of the king to the underprivileged, hence his request.[38] The use of *ṯpṭ* in this context once again points to a use which is associated with the king. In this instance it has become clear that it is an indispensable element in the king's rule. However, when *ṯpṭ* is used, it is not meant to be understood in a judicial sense; certainly not in its

---

[36] Translation taken from Gibson, *Canaanite Myths and Legends*, p. 101. See also, Gordon, *Ugaritic Literature*, p. 82.

[37] Gibson, *Canaanite Myths and Legends*, p. 102.

[38] The discussion here is not concerned with Ysb's motives for wanting Keret's abdication, but the factors which are noted by him are ones which also appear in other literature, specifically in the Old Testament. See Deut. 10:18; Isa. 1:17; 10:2; Ps. 82:2-4; Job 22:7-9; 29:12-13; 31:16-17. See also the *Code of Hammurabi*, ANET, p. 178.

primary sense. The stress in this section on the needs of the disenfranchised and the corresponding responsibility on the part of the king have led some scholars to conclude that it is more than simply an *ad hoc* aspect of a kingship. Hammershaimb notes that these statements are as good as law, "either positively prescribing care to be taken of widows and fatherless or negatively prohibiting any infringement of their rights."[39]

However the use of *tpṭ* in Ugaritic is not exhausted with its reference to Keret and Aqhat. In the Keret and Aqhat texts, it is clear that an essential element in their reigns is the care of the oppressed. This might involve judicial acts, but not necessarily. In these instances, it is evident that *tpṭ* means more than simply "judge." However, there are other occurrences of *tpṭ* where the contexts leave no doubt as to the meaning and in the following discussion this will emerge. The idea that *tpṭ* is a concept which connotes more than simply "judge" is substantiated by the many instances in which *tpṭ* is used in the same context as *mlk*. Most of the references have Baal as king and judge in the same context:

... mlkn aliy [n] b'l
ṭpṭn win d'lnh [40]

This confession that "Mighty Baal is our King, our judge and there is none who is over him,"[41] indicates an intrinsic relationship between judge and king. There is no reason to believe that the idea of king does not encompass judicial activity. Contextually this occurrence of *tpṭ* ought to be translated "ruler," bringing it into har-

---

[39] E. Hammershaimb, "On the Ethics of the Old Testament Prophets," *SVT* 7 (1959), p. 80. Hammershaimb, in studying the texts of Aqhat and Keret has concluded that there is in fact a close concord between the Old Testament prophets and these texts. He observes that the Ugaritic 'almnt and ytm are identical with 'lmnh and ytm in Hebrew, even though he makes an erroneous assertion when he notes that ytm is mentioned only in the Aqhat and not in the Keret text. In fact ytm is mentioned in 2 Keret VI:49. Nevertheless his point regarding the similarities is sound and helps to place these Canaanite texts in perspective.

[40] See Gordon, *Ugaritic Textbook*, Text 51 IV 43-44, p. 171.

[41] English translation taken from Gibson, *Canaanite Myths and Legends*, from the section "The Palace of Baal" 4 IX, lines 43-44.

Chapter II

mony with the accepted role of the king. This parallel between *tpt* and *mlk* occurs several times,[42] a factor which leads us to surmise that *tpt* as "rule" is not an exception, but the prevailing convention.

This idea that *tpt* is associated with "kingship" and "rule" is further enhanced through the occurrences of *tpt nhr* in the same context as *zbl ym*. In the text of "Baal and Yam," Judge Nahar and Prince Yam are consistently mentioned together.[43] In several of these occurrences, the contexts suggest that *tpt* is used more to connote "ruler" than "judge." Prince Yam supposedly dwells in a palace, while Judge Nahar dwells in a mansion; this is mentioned at least twice.[44] In addition to the many times *tpt nhr* is mentioned with *zbl ym*,[45] there are also instances in which there are descriptions which point clearly to elements associated with rulers. On four occasions, Judge Nahar is said to have an embassy, and in each instance it is found in the same context as the phrase "the messengers of Prince Yam."[46] Also in two instances Yam and Nahar are spoken of in connection with their throne and dominion respectively,[47] elements which clearly suggest positions of leadership and rule. Certainly in the case of Nahar, dominion would not be associated with him in so close a manner if he were only a judicial functionary. In these two references Nahar and Yam are objects of displeasure, and they are being deposed from their positions.

This examination of the occurrences of *tpt* in parallelism with *mlk* and *zbl ym* lead to the conclusion that *tpt* should be understood as "rule(r)" rather than "judge." There is no evidence to support the meaning "decide" or "bring about justice," but rather it

---

[42] See also, Gordon, *Ugaritic Textbook*, 'nt V 40; text 49 VI p. 28f.

[43] See Gibson, *Canaanite Myths and Legends*, pp. 34-45. Also Gordon, *Ugaritic Textbook*, text 68, p. 180.

[44] Gibson, *Canaanite Myths and Legends*, "Baal and Yam," 2, iii, lines 8-9, 21, pp. 37-38.

[45] See, for example, Gibson, *ibid.*, 2 iii line 16, 21, 23; 2 i line 17, 26, 28, 30, 33, 36, 46; 2 iv line 14, 22, 24, 27.

[46] *Ibid.*, 2 i lines 19, 26, 28, 30, 44, pp. 41-42.

[47] *Ibid.*, 2 iv lines 12-13, 20. See also Ginsberg, *ANET*, p. 131, for a similar English rendering.

corresponds to the German *Herrschaft*, as Schmidt observes.[48] The conclusion here therefore concurs with Gray's; "the Ras Shamra data...clearly demonstrates that the word had a wider connotation 'ruler' of which 'judgement' was but one function. The order imposed or upheld by the *tpṭ* or ruler was *mtpṭ*...which is just as wide in its connotation." [49]

C. Phoenician

The examination of שפט in Phoenician is particularly important for this study precisely because of the similarities which exist between Phoenician and Hebrew and the frequent connections between the corresponding nations in the monarchical period. The root שפט occurs frequently in Phoenician in a variety of contexts; the important ones will be examined briefly. Perhaps the most significant occurrence of שפט in Phoenician is found in the Ahiram inscription.

ואל מלך במלכם וסכן בס (כ)נם ותמא
מחנת עלי גבל ויגלארן זן תחתסף
חטר משפטה תהתפך כסא מלכה
ונחת תברח על גבל והא

Gibson translates this inscription as follows: "Now if a king among kings or a governor among governors or a commander of an army should come up against Byblos and uncover this coffin, may the scepter of his rule be torn away, may the throne of his kingdom be overturned, and may peace flee from Byblos!"[50] This is the oldest piece of material of this nature which uses שפט, and the meaning which is deduced here, will have a dual effect: to have a glimpse of

---

[48] Werner Schmidt, *Das Königtum der Götter in Ugarit und Israel*. BZAW 80 (Berlin: Verlag Alfred Topelmann), 1961, p. 28.

[49] John Gray, *The Legacy of Canaan*. SVT 5 (1965), p. 167.

[50] John Gibson, *Textbook of Syrian Semitic Inscriptions* III (Oxford: Clarendon Press), 1982, p. 14. This inscription which was discovered in 1923 is dated in the vicinity of the Twelfth Century B.C.

the use of שפט during that period, and to shed some light on its use in pre-monarchical Israel.

There are two sentences in this inscription, and it is the second one which is germane to this discussion. The context involves the son of Ahiram placing the coffin of his father in a sepulchre and threatens destruction to anyone who would tamper with it. The son specifies governors, king or commanders as being possible or even likely perpetrators, and it is in this setting that the following words are found: חטר משפטה. There are generally two translations which are proposed as being logical and plausible interpretations of both the words and context. Rosenthal translates it as "judicial staff," which empowers the subjects to pronounce sentences in judgment. In effect, the kings, governors and commanders, in addition to their primary vocation will also have a judicial function.[51] The second translation which is associated with משפטה חטר is "scepter of his rule."[52] "Judicial staff" is the rendering which has traditionally been accepted as the correct translation, but even a cursory examination of "scepter of his rule" indicates that it contains an element which is absent from the other. Each of the categories mentioned, namely "kings," "governors," "commanders" are *ipso facto* rulers, and thus it would be a logical translation to render משפטה "rule" rather than "judicial staff." The latter can certainly be an element of the overall responsibility of these personalities, but it cannot be assumed to be the functional equivalent of "rule." Soggin observes that, "the expression $ḥṭr$ $mšpṭh$ can certainly be translated 'the scepter of his judgment,' but it is clear that 'the scepter of his rule' or 'of his kingdom' is a more obvious rendering and is a better parallel to 'his royal throne.'"[53] There is no doubt that some form of authority is being referred to here, and the context intimates that it is "royal" rather than "judicial" authority.

---

[51] See Rosenthal, *ANET*, p. 661. Cf, Keith W. Whitelam, *The Just King*. *JSOTS* 12 (Sheffield: JSOT Press), 1979, p. 57.

[52] See Gibson, *TSSI*, p. 14. See also J. Alberto Soggin, *Judges*. OTL (London: SCM Press), 1981, p. 2.

[53] Soggin, *Judges*, p. 2. See also Ishida, "The Leaders of the Tribal League 'Israel' in the Pre-Monarchic Period." p. 518.

Two other occurrences of שפט in Phoenician, though not as old as the Ahiram inscription will aid in deciphering the meaning of שפט. The first example from Kition,[54] describes Abd-eshmun as a "judge."[55] Unfortunately there is not much background data from which to determine the function of the שפט in this reference, but some scholars have suggested that "judge" in this context refers to a person who, for all practical purposes, functions as a king, in place of a king.[56] However, the evidence which is available to scholars is rather slight and circumstantial. What is known is the fact that there is no reason to believe that שפט in this context is primarily concerned with the judiciary. A safer conclusion would be a concurrence with Cooke's hypothesis, namely the connection of שפט with kingship in Tyre.[57] The other occurrence is from Piraeus[58] and once again it is used as the title "judge" for a person. The dating (about Third-Second Century B.C.) and place of this inscription suggest that שפט in this occurrence corresponds more to a "consul" rather than a member of the judiciary. While this text translates שפט as "judge," the title is clearly not indicative of the function.[59] The "judge" in this period is more akin to the idea of "consul" which suggests "rule" rather than "giving judgment."

---

[54] *Corpus Inscriptionium Semiticarum.* Tomus I (Parisiis: E Reipublicae Typographeo), 1881, i 47.

[55] Cooke, justifies the translation of שפט as "judge" by suggesting that as a title it is only found in Phoenicia and corresponds with the system of government which was in effect at the time, p. 44, note 3. It is helpful to note also that *CIS* renders שפט as "suffetis" and the later Punic references in *CIS* i 165 are translated using the same word. *A Text-book of North-Semitic Inscriptions*, pp. 236-237.

[56] See Cooke, *A Text-book of North-Semitic Inscriptions*, p. 44. Also Charles F. Jean and Jacob Hoftijzer, *Dictionnaire des Inscriptions Sémitiques De L'Ouest* (Leiden: E.J. Brill), 1965. Jean-Hoftijzer note that this designation is of an office whose exact meaning is unknown. p. 316.

[57] Cooke says, "At an early date, in the time of Nebuchadnezzar, we hear of a succession of *judges* at Tyre, who took the place of the king...." *A Text-book of North-Semitic Inscriptions*, p. 44.

[58] *CIS*, i 118.

[59] See Cooke, *A Text-book of North-Semitic Inscriptions*, p. 100.

Chapter II

D. Punic

The occurrences of שפט in Punic[60] are essential to this study particularly because there is sufficient extant material, enabling us to determine a likely meaning. שפט in Punic is found in several and varied contexts, in different areas such as Carthage, Marseilles and Malta.[61] In order to arrive at a possible pattern in meaning of שפט and the connotation which emerges, several examples from each of the three contexts will be examined. The first example is from Carthage and in this particular instance, שפט occurs twice.[62] It is a dedicatory inscription which is rendered in English as "your servant Melekjaton the judge, son of Mahar-baalis the judge, dedicated...." Unfortunately, this inscription dated in the Fourth-Third Century B.C. does not have any elaborate context from which it might be understood. However, it is known that it is from Carthage and the designation of someone as a "suffete" means that this person officiated at the highest magisterial level;[63] hence this meaning is somewhat different from that of early Phoenician.[64]

A second example is from an inscription which was found at Marseilles.[65] This text, dated in the Fourth Century B.C., is particularly useful because of its length and the common elements which it shares with other inscriptions. In this context, שפט occurs

---

[60] These occurrences are all relatively late, ranging from Fourth-Second Century B.C. However the careful transmission of language from Phoenician to Punic enables us to derive a fairly accurate meaning of שפט. If nothing else, it will allow us to see the evolution in meanings.

[61] For a list of references in which שפט occurs in Punic, see Jean-Hoftijzer, *Dictionnaire des Inscriptions Sémitiques De L'Ouest*, p. 316.

[62] *CIS*, i 176.

[63] See Jean-Hoftijzer, *Dictionnaire des Inscriptions Sémitiques De L'Ouest*, p. 316.

[64] In both the Carthaginian and early Phoenician inscriptions, the suggested Latin translation of שפט is *suffetis*. See e.g. in *CIS*, i 47, 165, 176. The fact that *suffetis* is used in these contexts would indicate, at least superficially, that there are obviously no differences in functions between the שפט of early Phoenician and the שפט of Carthage. Such a conclusion however would be imprecise and inaccurate, for while the title שפט was clearly in use during these periods, the functions of the שפט were certainly not identical.

[65] *CIS*, i 165.

twice and in both instances, it refers to the individuals who were *suffetes* at the time. Even though this stone was found at Marseilles, the style and nature of the inscription suggest that it is Carthaginian in orientation and essence.[66] The connection is further enhanced by Cooke's suggestion that the geological formations on this stone suggest that it originated in Carthage.[67]

While there is still no definite word which can be said about שפט in this period, there are certainly elements which lead in a particular direction. It is generally accepted among scholars that, in this period, there was no monarchy, certainly not in Carthage nor in the Carthaginian colonies.[68] Whether or not it is a "republican form of government" as Whitelam attests,[69] is uncertain, but it is known that there are individuals who are appointed as *suffetes*, those being the equivalent of magistrates. These magistrates are the principal rulers in both Carthage and the colonies, even though power and responsibilities varied between mother-state and colony. In each situation, there appears to have been two *suffetes* ruling at any given time.[70] While שפט then, in these contexts is used to designate the person who rules, it does not have any explicit reference to the primacy of judicial responsibility.

The third example is an inscription which is from Malta[71] and is dated in the vicinity of Third-Second Century B.C.

בעתר אדר ערכת ארש בן יאל ...
שפט בן זי בקם בן עבד אשמן בן יא (ל ...

This is rendered in English as: (4) in the time of our lord of noble worth, Arish, son of Ya'el...(5) judge son of Zibaqam, son of Abd-

---

[66] See, e.g. *CIS* i 170, which is a text from Carthage. When the Marseilles text is compared with this, the similarities become evident.

[67] See Cooke, *A Text-book of North-Semitic Inscriptions*, p. 115.

[68] Ibid., p. 115. See also, Whitelam, *The Just King*, p. 58.

[69] Whitelam, *The Just King*, p. 58.

[70] See e.g. *CIS* i 165, lines 1-2, 18-19; *CIS* i 175, line 1. Also Cooke, *A Text-book of North-Semitic Inscriptions*, p. 127, no. 45, lines 5-6. For a discussion of this, see Cooke, pp. 115-116.

[71] See *CIS*, i 132.

eshmun, son of Ya'e[l].⁷² Line 5 of this inscription begins with שפט but because of the missing ending to line 4 it is difficult to give a definitive interpretation of שפט in this context. However, there are two observations which might be helpful.

First, שפט could refer to the function of the father of Arish. The fact that Arish is of noble worth might indicate something of his functional status, rather than his birthright. If indeed Ya'el the father is a *suffete*,⁷³ then his station in life would elevate the societal worthiness of his family also. However, there is no indication that Arish is a *suffete*, and this is further strengthened by the fact that historically during the period when the *suffetes* ruled, the position was magisterial, which by its nature presupposes that it cannot be hierarchical. Moreover, two *suffetes* are not mentioned as is generally the case in other Carthaginian inscriptions, such as *CIS* i 143 and i 165. Nevertheless, this does not detract from the theory that Ya'el could have been a *suffete*, but the focus in this inscription is clearly on Arish, not on Ya'el. Since there is no indication that Arish is involved in judicial responsibilities, the use of שפט in this context may be similar to Carthaginian inscriptions.

Second, after the first three lines of this dedicatory inscription, the genealogical background of Arish is given. The missing word(s) from the end of line 4 could have been...בן, in which case it would mean that שפט was part of a person's name, rather than a title.

Finally, what can be said about these inscriptions? It is arguable that in every example discussed שפט is used as the designation of an office, specifically one which suggests the power to rule. It can therefore be concluded that in these contexts, the primary meaning of שפט is "rule" even though this position includes a judicial element.

The use of *špṭ* in the Ancient Near Eastern texts discussed, indicate that *špṭ* can be used as a judicial term, but it is clearly not its primary use. Different examples, such as *špṭ's* association

---

⁷² Cooke, *A Text-book of North-Semitic Inscriptions*, p. 105.
⁷³ There is no logical nor contextual reason for translating שפט in this inscription as "judge." Ibid., p. 105.

with "king," "government," "order," "reign" all suggest that *špṭ* in a significant way refers to "rule" in general.

II. Excursus on Relationship between שפט and דין

This section focuses principally on the content and message of שפט and דין in certain types of literature, and from this examination a particular pattern of relationship between the two terms will evolve. It will become evident that while *špṭ* is virtually nonexistent in Mesopotamian literature, nevertheless the theme of "justice" with specific reference to the ruler is germane and essential for this study.

A. *Din* in Ugaritic

In all the examples which were cited from Ugaritic literature, *din* is used alongside *tpṭ*.[74] It appears that *tpṭ* is used occasionally as a synonym for *din*, particularly in the dispensing of justice to the widows and orphans. Of the hero Dan'el, it is said that he judges with judgment (*ydn dn*) the widow; he does justice (*yṭpṭ ṭpṭ*) to the orphan.[75] Certainly from this example it appears that *ṭpṭ* and *din* are interchangeable. They are both in reference to the ruler Dan'el,[76] and both are used in a context which involves "doing of justice" to the disenfranchised.[77]

---

[74] See above, the discussion of *ṭpṭ* in Ugaritic literature.

[75] See I Aqhat 23-25 in Gordon's *Ugaritic Textbook*, p. 245, cf. Gibson, *Canaanite, Myths and Legends*, p. 107.

[76] See H.L. Ginsberg, "The North-Canaanite Myth of Anath and Aqhat," *BASOR* 97 (Feb. 1945), pp. 3-10. Ginsberg notes that both names Dn'il and Dnty are connected with the judicial function. p. 4. It is true that both names contain the root דין but "judicial function" ought not be so readily associated with them, for then it limits the meaning.

[77] For other similar occurrences of *ṭpṭ* and *din*, see Gordon, *Ugaritic Textbook*, Text 127, lines 33-34, 46-47. See also the glossary, p. 384, for more examples of occurrences of *din*.

B. Din in Mari

In addition to these occurrences in Ugaritic, there are also instances of *din* in Mari texts. In *ARM* viii 83:4, *da-ia-nu-um* occurs in the sense of a "judge" who litigates in a dispute regarding ownership of an ox. In this instance, the *da-ia-nu-um* is clearly an individual who is a member of the judiciary. Likewise, in *ARM* viii, 87:1, the *da-ia-nu* preside in a case and give a decision regarding a property. The *da-ia-nu* here function similarly to the *da-ia-nu-um* in 83:4. It can be argued that in these instances that the *da-ia-nu* are professional judges. When these are examined in isolation, nothing unusual is observed. However, in *ARM* viii 84:4, there is a reference to a *šāpiṭum* (Sumu-Hadu, a ruler) who conducts a trial involving two individuals regarding their goods. It is obvious that no firm conclusions can be drawn from this, except that it compounds the argument that there are elements which are common to both *špṭ* and *din*. It is true, as Marzal observes, that the *šāpiṭum* is a high official while the *da-ia-nu-um* is an ordinary "judge" and therefore the offices cannot be identical.[78] However, while their professional status is clearly different, their functions do coincide on occasion.

C. Din in the *Code of Hammurabi*

So far, *din* and *špṭ* have been examined briefly in Ugaritic and Mari texts, but the main focus of this section will be on the *Code of Hammurabi* and the *Hymn to Šamaš*. It is important to note that root *špṭ* is found only once in the *Code of Hammurabi* and is absent from the *Hymn to Šamaš*. However, the one text in which *špṭ* is used, it is associated with *Šamaš*. The section which contains *špṭ* reads:

> A-na (il) Šamaš šar Ša-me-e ù er-ṣe-ti-im ša pí-it ili
> ù-a-wì-lu-tim ša me-ša-ru-um i-si-ik-šu-ma[79]

---

[78] Marzal, "The Provincial Governor...." p. 204.

[79] Dossin, *Syria*, p. 12. For another occurrence of *špṭ* in this text, see v. 12, p. 17.

"To Šamaš, king of heaven and earth, [judge] of God and of men, he administers a result which is just." There are two points to note in this inscription. First, Šamaš is regarded as one who is king over both heaven and earth, and his powers cover this entire territory.[80] This description enhances the estimation of Šamaš's portfolio, since it testifies to the fact that Šamaš as the god of justice is not limited to a localized governance. Second, and perhaps more importantly for the purpose here, Šamaš is characterized as a ša-pi-iṭ. In and of itself, this may not be strikingly significant, however its importance is noted when it is realized that even though it is *špṭ* which is used here in regard to Šamaš, throughout the *Code of Hammurabi* and the *Hymn to Šamaš*, it is *din* which is used. The fact that throughout these texts Šamaš is referred to as the "god of justice" and *din* is used, leads to the conclusion that there is a connection between *špṭ* and *din*, if only thematically. In addition to this occurrence of *špṭ*, it also occurs once in the epilogue of the *Code of Hammurabi*. In this instance *ši-ip-ṭi-im* is used to mean "judgment" and is the context of Ninlil asking Enlil to pronounce judgment on anyone who would erase the laws on the stone.[81] Even though the obvious rendering of *ši-ip-ṭi-im* in this context is "judgment," it would be an error to conclude that the main thrust of the context is forensic. This occurrence must be understood in the larger context of the entire column. In the opening section of column 35:1-38, it is clear that the intent of the laws is to "set the heart at ease" and help the oppressed. In other words, the primary orientation is for the restoration of various forms of broken relationship.

In the following discussion, the intention is to underline this connection, and perhaps the clearest way in which this might be achieved is to compare message, text and context. As we look at the *Code of Hammurabi*, there are definitive words which are spo-

---

[80] This interpretation of the inscription is based on Dossin's French translation, *ARM* I p. 12.
[81] G.R. Driver and John C. Miles, *The Babylonian Laws* (Oxford: Clarendon Press), 1955, pp. 100-101. For another translation of the *Code of Hammurabi*, see, Theophile J. Meek, *ANET*, pp. 163-180. See also J.C. Fensham, "The Judges and Ancient Israelite Jurisprudence," *OTWSA*, 1959. Fensham suggests that *špṭ* in this context can only mean "judgment" in a forensic sense.

Chapter II

ken regarding the administration of justice, the care and protection of those who are not affluent or powerful and those who are not in a position to command justice and exert influence. Throughout the Code, in the prologue, the laws themselves, and the epilogue, the words of the king resound clearly: the strong may not oppress the weak, and justice must be meted out to the widow and orphan; the lack of either carries grave consequences. It is within a message such as this, that the use of *din* is found.

In this discussion, three different examples will be examined. In law no. 3, *din* is used three times.

> šum-ma a-wi-lum i-na di-nim- a-na
> šu-bu-ut sà-ar-ra-tim ù-si-a-am-ma
> a-wa-at iq-bu-u la uk-ti-in šum-ma di-nu-um
> šu-ú di-in-na-pí-iš-tim a-wi-lum
> šu-ú id-da-ak[82]

According to this text, "If a man has come forward in a case to bear witness to a felony and then has not proved the statement that he has made, if that case (is) a capital one, that man shall be put to death."[83] On every occasion in this text, *din* refers to "case," as in a lawsuit. However, the focus is not so much on the judicial aspect of a "case," as it is on the integrity of the accuser. In this instance, it is not the accused individual that is being spoken to, but rather the one who brings the "case." It is true that this context involves something of a forensic situation, but this is merely a superficial view. In reality, the context focuses on the integrity of the individual and perhaps even more importantly, on the relationship between the individuals. The fact that the consequence of deception on the part of the accused, is death, underlines the crucial nature of the faithful relationship.

The second example is from law no. 5, where *din* in different forms is used twelve times, in the conventional sense of "judge"

---

[82] Driver and Miles, *The Babylonian Laws*, p. 14.
[83] Ibid., p. 15.

and "judgment." Because of the length of this law,[84] only the English rendering will be noted. "If a judge has tried a suit, given a decision, caused a sealed tablet to be executed, (and) thereafter varies his judgment, they shall convict that judge of varying (his) judgment and he shall pay twelve-fold the claim in that suit; then they shall remove him from his place on the bench of judges in the assembly, and he shall not (again) sit in judgment with the judges."[85] The various legal terms which are used here are all expressed by *din*, and its derivatives. While the immediate focus of this law is clearly with regard to a "judge," it is the underlying theme which is crucial. The fact that a judge will be severely reprimanded for a change of decision is not so much an insult to the judge's ability as a reminder of the significance of the one being judged. That is to say, it is essential that the parties involved in the lawsuit be the main focus at all times and then an impartial and well-thought decision can be rendered. Once again, what is at stake is the integrity of the relationship between individuals. The importance of this is reflected in the consequences of an incorrect decision by the judge. This text, together with the one prior to this (no. 3) must be understood in the context of the closing words of the Prologue to the *Code of Hammurabi*, "when Marduk commanded me to give justice to the people of the land and to let (them) have (good) governance, I set forth truth and justice throughout the land (and) prospered the people."[86] The concern therefore is for the individual, ensuring that he or she is sustained within the community. False accusation and partiality or incorrect judgments will carry grave consequences.

The third example is from the epilogue, and once again Hammurabi relates his major concern. "In order that the strong might not oppress the weak, that justice might be dealt the orphan (and) the widow...I wrote my precious words on my stela[87]

---

[84] Ibid., p. 14.
[85] Ibid., p. 15. For a similar translation, see Meek, *ANET*, p. 166.
[86] Driver and Miles, *The Babylonian Laws*, p. 13.
[87] See F.C. Fensham, "Widow, Orphan and the Poor in Ancient Near Eastern Legal and Wisdom Literature," *JNES* 21 (1962), pp. 129-139. Fensham notes the important connection between king and deity, pointing to the fact

Chapter II 113

and in the presence of the statue of me, the king of justice."[88] Hammurabi is concerned about the welfare of his people; he is intent on keeping intact the community. Hammurabi's frequent reference to Šamaš clearly indicates the association between ruler and deity, and underlines the idea that it is Šamaš who is particularly interested in justice for everyone.

D. *Dīn* in the *Hymn to Šamaš* [89]

The *Hymn to Šamaš* [90] is a significant piece of Babylonian literature, when studied with the intention of determining possible influence on Old Testament thought. The discussion here will be limited to the use of *dīn* in the *Hymn to Šamaš*. There are at least seven occurrences of some form of *dīn* in this text, and each will be examined briefly. In the first instance in which *dīn* is used,[91] Šamaš is perceived as the one who executes judgment on anyone who lives and acts contrary to the established laws of the society. On this occasion, *di-in-šu-u(n)* is used to mean "judgments" and in the following five lines, *dīn* is used twice in similar fashion; once as *di-na* meaning "lawsuit" and then *di-in* as "just verdict."[92] In these three occurrences, Šamaš is seen as the one who is undeviatingly involved in the resolution of any cases and lawsuits, and his decisions are always just.

The next three occurrences are all used to mean "judge" but each is employed to illustrate a particular point. In the occurrence

---

that Hammurabi is pictured with Šamaš on the stela on which the laws are inscribed. p. 132.

[88] Meek, *ANET*, p. 178. See also Driver and Miles, *The Babylonian Laws*, p. 97.

[89] See W.G. Lambert, *Babylonian Wisdom Literature* (Oxford: Clarendon Press), 1960, pp. 126-138.

[90] As the title suggests, this hymn is in praise of Šamaš. Šamaš occupies an important place in Babylonian thought as the god of justice, and, even though he is a god of secondary status in comparison to Marduk and Ninurta, nevertheless the portfolio which is assigned to him makes him significant. As is evidenced by the *Hymn to Šamaš*, "god of justice" is not merely an honorary title, but one of substance.

[91] Lambert, *Babylonian*, line 58, pp. 128-129.

[92] Ibid., lines 62-63, pp. 128-129.

in line 93,[93] *daiani* is used to mean a member of the judiciary. In this instance, in order to uphold justice, even the siblings of the accused will not be allowed to support his case against the judge's decision. In line 97[94] *da-a-a-na* is once again used to mean "judge," but on this occasion it is employed within a context which describes the consequences of being an unscrupulous judge. The circumspect and just judge is described in line 101,[95] and he too faces the consequences of his actions, except that in his case they are positive. Finally, in line 127, *di-in-šu*[96] is used to mean "lawsuit." It is important to note that in this instance, even though "lawsuit" does have a forensic overtone, it is found within a section which lauds Šamaš as one who acts on behalf of those who are wronged. In lines 132-133 the category of the "wronged" becomes explicit when the "feeble," "humble," "weak," "afflicted," and "poor" are mentioned. It is clear that whatever actions are taken, whether in a lawsuit or not, they are meant to sustain those who are powerless.

If indeed there is a pattern which is identifiable in these examples, it is the use of *din* in every instance to refer to a judicial matter. It is true that "justice" as the product of the judge's decision is not rendered by *din*, but is nevertheless connected. For example, in line 98, "justice"[97] is the English term used, but *din* is not the Babylonian term. However, line 98 is clearly associated with the theme of the preceding line, where *din* is used to refer to the one who ought to execute "justice." In these examples, Šamaš is the subject, and this is particularly significant for two reasons. First, it indicates clearly the importance of justice to him and establishes the deity's role in the procuring of justice for the oppressed, in order to maintain the equilibrium of the society. Second, while *din* is used in connection with Šamaš, it is clear that Šamaš is not a judicial functionary. As such, one cannot argue that *din* is reserved for the professional members of the judiciary.

---

[93] Ibid., p. 130.
[94] Ibid., p. 132.
[95] Ibid., p. 132.
[96] Ibid., p. 134.
[97] Ibid., p. 133.

Chapter II   115

Rather as is seen here, the procuring of justice for the oppressed involves the use of the term *din*. Also it must be noted that once again, the execution of justice is associated with a ruler; on this occasion it is a deity.

In this brief excursus on *din*, the similarity of its use in the Ugaritic, Mari, and Babylonian texts is evident, for it is found in contexts which focus on the need for justice on behalf of the oppressed.

In order to complete this discussion, it is important to look briefly at the way דין and its cognates are used in the Old Testament, particularly with reference to שפט. There are one hundred and thirteen occurrences of דין in the Old Testament and of this number, fifty-six are used in the books of Esther (30) and Proverbs (26). Even though there are occurrences of דין in these contexts which refer to justice to the oppressed, the overwhelming number is used in the sense of "contention" and "strife" in Proverbs, and "province" in Esther.[98] However, when דין is used in a context seeking justice for the oppressed, then it becomes quite similar in connotation to שפט. Prov. 31:9 states:

פתח פיך שפט-צדק ודין עני ואביון

In this particular context, דין is not used in isolation from the general theme of justice to the oppressed, but is connected with צדק, משפט, עני, and אביון, thus making its use very pointed in relation to justice for the oppressed.

Another example which underlines this thesis is the use of דין in Isa. 3:13.

נצב לריב יהוה ועמד לדין עמים

---

[98] See, for example, occurrences of דין and its derivatives in Prov. 10:12; 18:19; 21:19; 23:29; 26:21; Esth. 1:1; 1:22; 9:2 and 9:28. It is interesting to note that virtually all of the occurrences of דין (mostly the derivative מדינה) are used to mean "province." This alerts us to an important parallel to the use of שפט in the Ancient Near East, where the latter is used frequently in such senses as "rule," "order," "governor." See also דין in I Sam. 2:10 and Zech. 3:7, where in both instances, it is used to mean "rule."

The writer uses דין in this context to mean "judge." The judicial nature of the context is emphasized by the use of ריב, and they are both employed in reference to Yahweh. What makes this occurrence of דין significant is the fact that it is the only instance in which it is used in Isaiah, and in this context it is used alongside משפט. (v. 14) משפט of course is the term which is overwhelmingly used to express such concepts as "judge," "justice" and "judgment." The other noteworthy element in this context is the portrayal of Yahweh as prosecutor, a concept which is similar to the one found in the *Hymn to Šamaš*.[99]

Moreover, by way of demonstrating this affinity in connotation between דין and שפט, we shall look briefly at the way some uses of דין in the Old Testament are rendered in the LXX.[100]

Reference	Old Testament	LXX
Gen. 30:6	דנני	ἔκρινεν
Deut. 32:36	ידין	κρινεῖ
I Sam. 24:16 [15]	לדין	κριτήν [101]
Isa. 3:13	לדין	κρίσιν [102]
Jer. 22:16	דן	ἔκριναν
Jer. 22:16	דין	κρίσιν

---

[99] See discussion above.
[100] The following is only a representative of the occurrences of דין and it is not meant to be exhaustive; rather it is simply indicative of a possible functional parallel with שפט in the specific contexts.
[101] In this important example the context includes דין, ריב and שפט (2x) and they are all used together to give a judicial connotation.
[102] It is noteworthy that κρίσις which is used to render דין in this instance, is used not only to render דין in Isa. 3:13, but also משפט in Isa. 3:14 and in both of these instances, the identical form is used. See Rosenberg, who observes that, "mišpaṭ occurs frequently in parallelism to *din* and the two terms are often treated synonymously as 'judgement.' There is, however, a real difference between them. Mišpaṭ is much more encompassing then *din*. Mišpaṭ is an abstract concept expressing that which is normative and right in the total societal experience. *Din* does not possess this abstract quality, it is much narrower and concrete, referring to a judgement that is handed down by a judge." *Diss.*, p. 245. Rosenberg's conclusion is somewhat limited for clearly the examples in this outline and the following outline (which compares Old Testament and Targumic uses of משפט) do not substantiate his view.

Chapter II

Ps. 7:9 [8]   ידין   κρινεῖ 103

What this short comparative outline intimates is the overlapping in translation within the LXX. שפט and משפט are overwhelmingly rendered by κρίσις, κρίμα and κρίνω in the LXX, and, as is indicated in the outline, two of these terms are used to render דין in the LXX. Even though the external evidence in terms of numbers does not verify דין as a synonym for שפט, nevertheless, these examples do suggest that דין is used on several occasions in contexts which espouse a message similar to, if not identical with the ones in which שפט is used. It is also interesting to note the manner in which the root שפט is rendered in some instances in the Targum. The following examples give an indication of these uses.

Reference	Old Testament		Targum
Exod. 23:6	משפט	(justice)	דין
Num. 27:21	במשפט	(judgment)	בדין
Deut. 1:17	במשפט	(judgment)	דינא
Deut. 17:9	המשפט	(decision)	דדינא
Deut. 17:11	המשפט	(decision)	דינא
Hos. 6:5	ומשפטיך	(judgment)	ודיני

Some observations are necessary at this point. Both the *Code of Hammurabi* and the *Hymn to Šamaš* indicate quite strongly that justice to the poor, the widow and the orphan is both vertical and horizontal. "The vertical protection comes from the god Shamash, which therefore falls in the religious sphere, while the horizontal protection comes from the king, the substitute of the Sun-god, which falls in the social sphere."[104] This is a noteworthy point in that it brings this literature even closer (at least in exter-

---

[103] In this verse of Ps. 7, both דין and שפט are used and the use of κρινεῖ and κρῖνον respectively, suggest that there is some connection between דין and שפט, at least thematically. This would seem to be the case precisely because there does not appear to be any distinction in meaning between דין and שפט in this context.

[104] Fensham, "Widow, Orphan...." p. 130.

nal similarities) to the relationship between justice, king and Yahweh in Israelite religion. The vertical-horizontal association alludes to the fact that the executing of justice on behalf of the oppressed is not a concept which is established by the State, but rather by divine interest.[105]

In essence, it can be seen that in both Near Eastern and Israelite contexts, there is a relationship between king and deity with respect to the administration of justice. The roles of the deities are distinctive, for whereas, in Israel, Yahweh participates to the point of establishing the laws, in the Ancient Near East the deity is more of an honorary figure. Shalom Paul notes that Yahweh "is not merely the guarantor of the covenant, as the deities are in the epilogues to Mesopotamian legal collections and treaties; he is the author of the covenant who directly addresses his people."[106] Moreover, as opposed to justice being the responsibility of one god in the pantheon, "Yahweh is regarded as the only protector. He is even placed in opposition to the gods of foreign nations and hailed as the only true supreme Judge of the world."[107] It is Yahweh who saves and delivers Israel out of Egypt and it is

---

[105] For a different view, see Paul D. Hanson, "The Theological Significance of Contradiction Within the Book of the Covenant" in *Canon and Authority*. eds. George W. Coats and Burke O. Long (Philadelphia: Fortress Press), 1977. Hanson suggests that, "Civil law, as expressed for example in the actual body of laws in the Codex Hammurabi, was a strictly secular institution, having nothing to do with the cultic officials or deity." p. 120. Hanson's view appears to be somewhat inadequate. Even though the "king-god" relationship in Mesopotamia is not identical to that obtaining in Israel, nevertheless the "king-god" connection in Mesopotamia is a relationship. In some fashion, the gods in Mesopotamia are involved in the affairs of the people. Hanson's position appears to falter particularly in the light of the Šamaš-Hammurabi relationship. Against Hanson's position, see E. Hammershaimb, "On the Ethics...." p. 79. However, an important distinction needs to be made here. See Hans Jochen Boecker, *Law and the Administration of Justice in the Old Testament and Ancient East.* trans. Jeremy Moiser (Minneapolis: Augsburg Publishing House), 1980. Boecher makes a useful observation when he says, "although Hammurabi for example acted by divine commission, it is as king of Babylon that he wrote his code and expressly described himself as lawgiver." p. 41. This must be seen in the context of Yahweh being the sole legislator in Israel.
[106] Shalom S. Paul, *Studies in the Book of the Covenant in Light of Cuneiform and Biblical Law.* SVT XVIII (Leiden: E.J. Brill), 1970, p. 37.
[107] Fensham, "Widow, Orphan...." p. 138.

Yahweh who enters into covenant with the people; this is the God of Israel who seeks justice. Justice, however, is not his sole portfolio, he is the God of all creation, and it is this God who shows concern for the poor and oppressed.

The presence of common elements in the literature of the Ancient Near East and the Old Testament, specifically as it relates to justice, can be an invitation to conclude that the Old Testament received its orientation in this regard from its neighbors. There is at least one scholar who has concluded that in fact the Old Testament's message regarding justice and care for the oppressed by the king is procured in its entirety from Canaanite religion.[108] Somewhat more judiciously one may suggest that Israel, because of circumstances, inherited many of the customs of its neighbors. Fensham notes:

> It was a common policy, and the Israelites in later history inherited the concept from their forbears, some of whom had come from Mesopotamia, some had been captive in Egypt, and others had grown up in the Canaanite world. In the Israelite community, this policy was extended through the ethical religion of Yahweh to become a definite part of their religion, later to be inherited by Christians and Muslims.[109]

This view is not to suggest that Israel is using its neighbors as a means for handling its internal situation, but rather to point to the fact that it is inevitable that there would be traits inherent in

---

[108] Hammershaimb, "On the Ethics...." p. 93. There is no doubt that there are many inferences, explicit commands and statements in Canaanite texts regarding this idea, nevertheless it would be too sweeping a conclusion to suggest that the Old Testament usage is a wholesale transportation of the Canaanite texts. At one level, it would appear that Hammershaimb's conclusion has merit, and if this study were focused solely on external similarities and evidence, then it would be true. However to agree with Hammershaimb's statement, there would need to have been an in depth study of factors such as the *Sitz im Leben*, the contexts and circumstances. While the external evidence expresses similarities, the variables make it difficult to concur with Hammershaimb's conclusion.
[109] Fensham, "Widow, Orphan...." p. 139.

Israel's attitude towards matters such as justice, precisely because of its ancestral ties and contiguity to other nations.

There is certainly incontrovertible evidence demonstrating the similarity between Israel and its neighbors regarding justice. With all of the distinctiveness which each religion displays, still there is enough similarity on important elements which are helpful. It is certain that there are contextual similarities between דין and שפט and this only serves to underline the consensus regarding justice in the Ancient Near East and Israel.

III. Use of שפט in the Old Testament

The use of שפט is an essential aspect of this chapter, particularly because of its dominant use in the Old Testament (208 occurrences), but also because משפט is derived from it. The following discussion will enable us to see the meanings of שפט and whatever development there is. One area in which there are still many questions to be answered concerns the role of the שפטים in Judges. The discussion of שפט in Judges will point to a crucial use in the Old Testament and will inevitably lead to a picture which outlines an early use of שפט and indicate also the later developments.

A. The שפטים in Israel

One of the perplexing questions which arises when an attempt is made to discuss the use of שפט in the Old Testament, is the way שפטים is employed. The most logical starting point is with the book of Judges, where the title שפטים is neither representative of the contents of the book nor the functions of the characters. Who then are the שפטים? The function of the שפטים in Israel is dependent on what שפט is supposed to have meant in Ancient Israel. First though, a word must be said regarding the "major" and "minor" judges.

Chapter II

1. "Major" and "Minor" שפטים

The fact that the שפטים are divided into two categories (based on the information provided about them in the Bible) only succeeds in creating greater difficulties. Opinions regarding the relationship between the "major" and "minor" שפטים vary. Ishida, for example, finds no essential difference between the "major" and "minor" שפטים and supports his thesis by pointing to "the fact that both Tola and Jair, who belonged to the so-called 'minor judges' 'arose (ויקם)' (Judg. 10:1, 3) shows that they were both deliverers like other 'major judges.' (cf. 2:11, 16, 18; 3:9, 15) Indeed, as for Tola, it is written: 'He arose to save (להושיע) Israel.'"[110] Thus Ishida would conclude that functionally, there is no difference between the "major" and "minor" שפטים. According to Malamat however, the essential difference between the "major" and "minor" שפטים is based on the literary sources out of which they are drawn. For example, the "major" שפטים are from folk narrative, while the "minor" שפטים are from family chronicles.[111] The most commonly held theory proposes that the "major" שפטים are not שפטים at all, but are incorporated into the list of שפטים by the author of the deuteronomistic chronicle because Jephthah is listed in both groups.[112] In the description of Jephthah in Judg. 11:1-11, he is not called שפט [113] but is given the generic title ראש and then the rarer one קצין.[114] The

---

[110] Ishida, "The Leaders of the Tribal Leagues." p. 517.
[111] Malamat, *World History*, p. 131.
[112] See Martin Noth, *The History of Israel*. trans. Stanley Godman (London: Adam and Charles Black), 1958, p. 101. See also Rudolf Smend, *Yahweh War and Tribal Confederation* trans. Max Gray Rogers, (Nashville: Abingdon Press), 1970. Smend says that the title שפט which is used to describe the "minor judges" was of course transferred by the Deuteronomic author of the book of Judges to a number of war heroes, whereby next to the true, but "minor," there appeared the figurative, but "major" judges. p. 47. See also A.D.H. Mayes, *Israel in the Period of the Judges*. SBT 29 (London: SCM Press), 1974, p. 61.
[113] Even though the שפטים are said to have "judged" Israel, there is no instance in the book of Judges where the term שפט is used to refer to one of these individuals, except in the introduction (2:16-18) where the writer speaks of Yahweh raising up שפטים, and in reference to Deborah in 4:4.
[114] It is obvious that the initial interest in Jephthah is for military matters. Upon examination of the biographical sketch of Jephthah, at least two impor-

fact that Jephthah appears both as a "major" and a "minor" שפט is not indicative of the custom of being either a "major" or a "minor" שפט, but rather that Jephthah's situation is exceptional. Noth's view, therefore, which is predicated on the inductive argument that because Jephthah appears as a "minor judge," all military heroes also have judicial functions, is untenable.[115] There is no indication that any שפט is a military leader and a civil leader simultaneously. As such, there is no mixing of responsibilities, and, as Smend notes, "the non-political-military office of the Judge of Israel is not the direct continuation of the charismatic leadership, and it is not surprising that Jephthah is the only case where with certainty a major judge has become a minor one."[116]

It is certain that the "major" שפטים are military heroes and whether or not they performed any judicial functions during their tenure is unknown. What is well known and accepted is that they arose during times of military crises and came to the rescue of Israel. Moreover, it must be noted that during the period when the שפטים functioned, there were other leaders in existence, the most notable being the elders. It is perhaps the presence of the elders which helps to discount the notion of judicial activity on the part of the שפטים. It is true that during the period of the Judges, the office of the elder was not one of national significance, but one generally associated with the city. (e.g. Judg. 8:14,16) In fact, if there were a need for judicial functions, then the elder would act, and this was the case in all local communities. Weinfeld observes that, "in purely local matters such as family affairs, levirate marriage,

---

tant factors emerge. After being driven from his house, Jephthah's profession would have been classified as "outlaw" and as an illegitimate son, he is also an outcast of society. Historically, in the life of Israel, these two factors would certainly be against him. Yet, implicit in this episode regarding Jephthah's appointment is the extraordinary circumstances in which Israel finds itself, for even Jephthah is surprised that he would be sought out for military leadership. It is clear that while the initial interest in Jephthah is for military maneuvers, he would be a leader of a different sort in Israel; hence after being a ראש and קצין, he is said to have "judged" Israel.

[115] Martin Noth, *The Deuteronomistic History*. JSOTS 15 (Sheffield: JSOT Press), 1981, pp. 42-43.

[116] Smend, *God War*, p. 52. Smend is suggesting that 1) the minor judges have nothing to do with military matters and 2) the minor judges are simply those who are leaders in civil matters.

blood redemption and defamation of the virgin, the elders themselves acted without resorting to officials....Similarly, when central authorities were involved, the 'judges' and the 'elders' acted together."[117] Thus, it would appear that the שפטים were not involved in going from one place to the next in order to adjudicate in cases. As de Geus notes, "the Judge was first of all a municipal official, a ruler whose authority rested upon the power of the council of elders."[118]

However, by the time of Samuel, the role of the elders took national prominence. When Israel decided that the time had arrived for a different form of government, and the choice was for a king, it is the elders who take the request to Samuel. (I Sam. 8:4) Further, the importance of the elders is also seen in the context where Abner speaks with the elders regarding the enthronement of David as king. (II Sam. 3:17) In addition to this, the national significance of the elders is seen when they travel to Hebron, for the covenant-making with the new king. (II Sam. 5:3) What these examples of the role of the elders at both the local and national levels indicate is the fact that they are principally the ones who administer the affairs of Israel.[119]

While much has been said so far regarding the major שפטים in the book of Judges, there is very little which is said about the "minor" שפטים.[120] For many years, Martin Noth's theory of the amphic-

---

[117] Moshe Weinfeld, "Judge and Officer in Ancient Israel and in the Ancient Near East," *IOS* 7 (1977), p. 81.
[118] C.H.J. de Geus, *The Tribes of Israel* (Amsterdam: Van Goraim, Assen), 1976, p. 206.
[119] For other examples of the role of elders, see, Exod. 24:1; Isa. 3:2-4; Hos. 7:7; Mic. 7:3; Zeph. 3:3; Job 9:24, 12:17.
[120] Malamat, says that in the book of Judges, "the term *shofet* and the verb *shafat* both refer to a leader of the people, whether a major judge or a minor judge and such activity indeed included the office of arbitrator and judge in the legal sense of the word." *World History*, p. 131. In this statement, Malamat attempts to unify the functions of both the "minor" and "major" שפטים. However, one element which he overlooks is the fact that the activity of the "major" שפטים was determined by the prevailing military circumstances. It must be assumed that in times of peace that there was some system of judicial authority which was in existence. It would be inaccurate to presuppose that with the ascension of a new שפט, primarily because of the need for mili-

tyony was axiomatic. Noth suggests that the amphictyony in Ancient Israel had its foundation in law and it is the judges who were the instruments in charge of executing this law. Moreover, Noth claims that "they appear as the bearers of an office which was administered by one man; and the list mentions six such judges, who filled the office of judge in an uninterrupted sequence."[121] One of Noth's main supports for his theory of the amphictyony is the presence of a central sanctuary in Israel and it is supposedly in this setting that the minor שפטים functioned. In recent times many scholars have been critical of Noth's view and have generally rejected it.[122] This rejection of Noth's theory raises once again the question of the role of the "minor" שפטים. If, as the many critics of Noth's theory have observed, there is no evidence to support central sanctuary, or amphictyonic law, then Noth's conclusion regarding the function of the שפטים is seriously flawed.

Noth believes that the amphictyony concept was so well known in Ancient Israel that the writers did not need to mention it directly.[123] This is the basis on which he constructs his theory of the function of "minor" שפטים. Two points must be registered here regarding Noth's framework. First, the argument from silence is

---

tary leadership, that the existing judicial system would become inoperative and the newly selected leader would assume also, the role of legal arbitrator.
[121] Noth, *History of Israel*, p. 101. See also M.S. Rosenberg, "The Šōfᵉṭim in the Bible," *EI* (1975), pp. 77-86.
[122] See for example, Harry M. Orlinsky, "The Tribal System of Israel and Related Groups in the Period of the Judges" in *Studies and Essays in Honor of Abraham A. Neuman* (Leiden: E.J. Brill), 1962, pp. 375-387; also, Wolfgang Richter, "Zu Den Richtern Israels," *ZAW* 77 (1965), pp. 40-71. Richter suggests that there was no central sanctuary and functionary over a tribe, but rather a civil leader of a small town. See also, George W. Anderson, "Israel: Amphictyony: 'AM; KAHAL; EDAH" in *Translating and Understanding the Old Testament* (Nashville: Abingdon Press), 1970, pp. 135-151. Also Mayes, *Israel in the Period of the Judges*; James D. Martin, *The Book of Judges* (Cambridge: Cambridge University Press), 1975, and Sean Werner, "The period of the Judges Within the Structure of Early Israel," *HUCA* 47, (1976), pp. 57-79. Warner notes that there was no shrine with national significance, and the three shrines at Mizpah, Gilgal and Bethel were all equal in importance and status. p. 65. He does note, however, that while this was true of the period of the שפטים, it was not the case in the time of Samuel, when there was a cultic center at Shiloh, which had national significance. See Sam. 1:1-28.
[123] Noth, *History of Israel*, p. 97.

not an idea entirely unknown and in fact it has been used to substantiate points which would otherwise remain dubious. For example, the term ברית is found nine times in the Eighth Century prophets, (Isa. 24:5; 28:15; 33:8; Hos. 2:20; 6:7; 8:1; 10:4; 12:2; Amos 1:9) with Hos.8:1 being the only explicit reference to a covenant with Yahweh. However, to make a collective judgment that the prophets of this era knew nothing of the covenant with Yahweh would be unjustified. Rather, argument from silence in this instance would be ill advised, the reason being that the concept of covenant was well known in Ancient Israel. Second, Noth's theory is seriously impeded, precisely because it is grounded on a flawed premise. Heuser correctly submits that, "arguments from silence must be used with extreme caution and only in conjunction with corollary circumstance that render it probable."[124] It is apparent that both the "minor" and the "major" שפטים existed during this period in Israel's history and there is reason to believe that they did so simultaneously precisely because they functioned differently, and it was the latter element which distinguished them, not their titles. Rather than being involved in a central sanctuary, they were in fact leaders in a localized government. Thus both the "major" and "minor" שפטים were leaders, but with different responsibilities.[125] This theme will become clearer when the idea of "שפטים as rulers" is examined later in this chapter.

2. שפטים as Saviors

The idea that the שפטים are actually saviors or deliverers is rooted in the several instances in which the term הושיע is used in association with שפטים. Moreover, there are references, such as I Sam. 24:16 and II Sam. 18:19, where שפט has the contextual meaning of "deliver;" these occurrences lend credence to this theory. Even though the subject of these references is Yahweh, neverthe-

---

[124] Alan J. Heuser, "The 'Minor Judges' - A re-evaluation," *JBL* 94 (1975), p. 191. See also George Anderson, "'AM; KAHAL; EDAH," for a critique of the "argument from silence." p. 148.

[125] See, H.C. Thompson, "Shopheṭ and Mishpaṭ in the book of Judges," *TGUOS* 19 (1961-62), pp. 74-85.

less, it is quite probable that if שפט is used to mean "deliver" and the "judges" are called שפטים, then the implication is that "delivering" is an element in their overall function.126 This thesis, which is in particular reference to the "major" שפטים is not easily justified, even though there are scattered instances in the Old Testament which support it. This notwithstanding, Oskar Grether has proposed a solution to this question. According to Grether, one must distinguish in the book of Judges between the function of the "greater" שפטים and the "lesser" שפטים. The "lesser" שפטים can be compared to the *Gesetzsprecher* of Iceland, being "appeal judges," whose decisions carry the force of law.127 The "greater" שפטים are "charismatic leaders" and Grether thinks that their primitive title may have been מושיע, "savior." It was later that the two functions were confused, resulting in the charismatic leaders and the *Gesetzsprecher* both being called שפטים.128 Even though Grether concludes that מושיע is only in reference to the charismatic leaders, there is also an instance in which הושיע is used in reference to a minor שפט. Regarding Tola, it is said that he arose (ויקם) to save (להושיע) Israel.129

From Grether's view and the example of Tola it is clear that there is an element of "saving" or "delivering" in the functions of the שפטים. Yet, this does not explain convincingly the role of שפטים as "saviors." Two other opinions must be noted regarding this question. Van der Ploeg posits an explanation which makes a distinction between the use of שפט (when used in a context meaning "save") in reference to Yahweh and the שפטים. According to van der Ploeg, Yahweh "judges" but because one cannot appear before his tribunal, שפט means above all for him to "do justice," meaning that he either punishes or recompenses. Each time that Yahweh exer-

---

126 It must be noted here that the instances in which שפט is used to mean "deliver" are not in the book of Judges.
127 See Oskar Grether, "Die Bezeichnung 'Richter' für die Charismatischen Helden der vorstaatlichen Zeit," *ZAW* 57 (1939), pp. 110-121. Grether's theory regarding the role of the "minor" שפטים is purely speculative, for there is no basis for this position.
128 Ibid., p. 110.
129 See Judg. 10:1, where Tola is mentioned and in 10:3 where Jair is described as "arising" also.

cises his justice, one can say that he is "judging." When the oppressed people appeal to him and ask him to "judge" them, it can be equated with an appeal to "save" them. As such, van der Ploeg argues that when Yahweh "judges" an individual or nation, שפט generally means "save."¹³⁰

Van der Ploeg notes that "to save" and "to judge" are entirely different and while it is sometimes said that Yahweh "judges," that is, "saves," it is only because Yahweh is situated above the parties involved. Hence, when an individual is absolved by him, he or she is simultaneously "saved" from the adversary. The "judges" on the other hand represent only one party and for them "to judge" the people was not "to save" them.¹³¹ Second, Orlinsky concludes that the role of the "major" שפטים "was to deliver (*hōshīă*) from the enemy the Israelites who were affected; then they 'judged' (*shāpᵉṭū*), i.e. ruled as Chieftains, those whom they had militarily delivered."¹³²

Several observations are necessary at this point. First, Orlinsky's position provides a neat chronological order for the functions of the שפטים which however simply does not exist. His suggestion that they were both "judge" and "deliverer" at designated times is untenable.¹³³ Second, both Grether and van der Ploeg overlook crucial elements in their discussions and, consequently, in their conclusions. The distinction which is created by Grether is biblically untenable, for there is clearly no indication that the "major" שפטים were deliverers, while the "minor" שפטים were judicial functionaries. In fact, the references to Tola discounts Grether's claims that הושיע is a term which is reserved for the "major" שפטים. Van der Ploeg's concept of Yahweh is one which suggests that

---

¹³⁰ See J. van der Ploeg, "ŠĀPAṬ et MIŠPĀṬ," *OTS* 11 (1943), p. 147.
¹³¹ Ibid., pp. 147-148.
¹³² Orlinsky, *Studies and Essays*, p. 378.
¹³³ It must be noted that there is no indication which verifies the theory that the שפט first functioned as a "deliverer" then as a "judge." In Judg. 2:16, 18, for example, the noun שפטים is used with the verb ויושיעום, while in Judg. 3:9, it says that Yahweh raised up a deliverer (מושיע) who delivered Israel (ויושיעם). In other words, the question centers around the reason for having two different subjects attached to הושיע, if in fact, all שפטים were initially "deliverers;" certainly then there would be no reason for the specialist מושיע as is the case in 3:9.

Yahweh is set apart from his people almost in an Olympian manner and from there administers judgment and salvation. This perception however is quite erroneous, for Yahweh, from every biblical indication, is the God who is constantly among his people, and the fact that Israel is his people, *ipso facto* necessitates that he act on their behalf. However, "acting on Israel's behalf" does not exclude judgment. In other words, judgment and salvation are not exclusive of each other, and this understanding applies both to Yahweh and to the שפטים. That is to say, that the שפטים "judged" Israel clearly includes the element of "saving" and "delivering."[134] It is therefore to be noted that the use of הושיע is not a new element in the responsibilities of the שפט but rather an integral part of their very role.[135]

---

[134] It is helpful to keep in mind here that being a שפט does not exclude the primary functions of an individual. This hypothesis is borne out by Eli's role as both priest and שפט. The description of Eli has always been that of priest, yet in I Sam. 4:18, after Eli dies, it is said of him:

שפט את ישראל ארבעים שנה

which says, "He had judged Israel forty years." The term שפט had never been used in relation to Eli prior to this and some scholars, for example, Henry Preserved Smith, *A Critical and Exegetical Commentary on the Books of Samuel*. ICC (Edinburgh: T and T Clark), 1899, have concluded that the deuteronomistic redactor attempted to include Eli as one of the שפטים. However, the idea of Eli as priest is preserved consistently, and so it raises the question as to whether the redactor was in fact interested in Eli as a שפט as Smith speculates. It would appear that if the redactor were interested in this, then why were the references regarding Eli as priest not deleted? It is with this in mind that one is inclined to agree with Rosenberg, who suggests that the logical probability of Eli being a שפט should not be ignored. "The *Šōfᵉṭim* in the Bible." p. 78. See also, H.W. Hertzberg, *I and II Samuel*. OTL (London: SCM Press), 1964, who says that "there is no evident reason why he, the priest of the most eminent sanctuary, should not also have held the office of judge." p. 49.

[135] Of the eighteen occurrences of מושיע in the Old Testament, four are found in the book of Judges (3:9, 15; 6:36; 12:3) and while it is true that in each instance a particular שפט is named, it does not set these individuals apart as primarily "deliverers." Rather, as שפטים, the idea of "saving" and "delivering" their people would be of paramount importance. It is also significant that the שפטים who are mentioned as מושיע are also noted as having "judged" (שפט) Israel. Moreover, to suggest as van der Ploeg does, that the "major" שפטים were the מושיעים exclusively, is clearly an overstatement. In fact, the term מושיע is not reserved for the שפטים, for in several instances it is used in reference to Yahweh. See, for example Isa. 45:15 and Ps. 17:7.

B. שפט as Judicial Term

The use of שפט to mean "judge" has for long been the center of a centrifugal debate and even though recent scholarship has managed to focus this debate somewhat, nevertheless there are many questions which still remain. A century ago, Henry Ferguson argued that the idea of judging and deciding questions is in fact the primitive meaning of שפט and all other meanings were subsequently added. As such, the original meaning of שפט is used in the context of deciding questions judicially and in administering justice, and the person who does these things is referred to as a שפט.[136] After Ferguson, there have been many others who have attempted to establish the meaning of שפט in the Old Testament as being forensic in its orientation.

Perhaps the most important proponent of this view was Grether.[137] In his study he attempts to defend the theory that "judge" is not only the primitive but the only meaning of שפט. Accordingly, he argues that שפט appears as "judging," "delivering judgment," (that is, giving what is right) "sentence," "punishment" and the general duty of the judge. In essence, Grether's interpretation is entirely forensic in overtone.[138] He notes two important factors in his discussion, both of which he employs as favorable elements for his theory. First, he observes that the root שפט occurs two hundred times[139] in the Old Testament, but of these, he sees only three occurrences as having the meaning "rule"[140] while most of the others have a judicial connotation.[141] From this he concludes that at least statistically, it is impossible that שפט could mean "rule." While this kind of inductive reasoning has some merit, it is clear that Grether's method is based on an interpreta-

---

[136] See Henry Ferguson, "The Verb שפט," *JBL* (1888), p. 131.
[137] Oskar Grether, "Die Bezeichnung...." pp. 110-121.
[138] Ibid., p. 111.
[139] The number does not include the occurrences of משפט in the Old Testament.
[140] The idea that שפט in its earliest use meant "rule" will be discussed later in this chapter. Since it is the other main meaning which is ascribed to שפט Grether focuses his discussion in response to this.
[141] Grether, "Die Bezeichnung...." p. 113.

tion which looks superficially at the texts, without engaging in the task of critical examination. For example, he sees the two occurrences of שפט in Ps. 96:13 as meaning "judge."

לפני יהוה כי בא כי בא לשפט הארץ
ישפט-תבל בצדק ועמים באמונתו

"Before the LORD, for he is coming, for he is coming to judge the earth. He will judge the world with righteousness, and the peoples with his truth."[142] שפט in this context is assumed by Grether to mean "judge" and thus the function of Yahweh with regard to הארץ and תבל is judicial in nature. Because each use of שפט has in this context a personal object, namely "earth" and "continent," the connection to the concept of "land" is quite noticeable.[143] Moreover the use of "peoples" can hardly be viewed as being Israelite in its reference. Hence, Grether's implication that שפט in this context means "judge" is not persuasive.[144] It appears that Grether's conclusions are established on purely external evidence. Moreover, Grether does not find the Ras Shamra texts helpful in determining the background of שפט, but nevertheless concludes that in fact these texts which were published at the time of his writing indicate that the meanings associated with שפט are "judge," "help to right someone," "judicial functionary" and also "jurisdiction" and "משפט."[145] Thus, the conclusions which are drawn have been de-

---

[142] This is a simple text and it is grammatically straightforward. However, contextually, a literal translation does not reflect the intended meaning. It is interesting that the NRSV provides a literal meaning.
[143] The Hebrew words which are used for "earth" and "continent" are הארץ and תבל respectively. The NRSV renders תבל as "world" and thus imposes something of a cosmic connotation, perhaps to create a sense of uniformity with הארץ, which can certainly be understood to have cosmic proportions. It is also interesting to note that the LXX renders תבל as οἰκουμένη rather than κόσμος, the former indicating that תבל signifies much more of a particularity rather than universality.
[144] See Schmidt, *Das Königtum*, p. 30.
[145] Grether, "Die Bezeichnung...." p. 112.

rived from the use of שפט in both the Old Testament and Near Eastern texts.146

Many other scholars after Grether have agreed with his thesis and have pursued his line of thought. Van der Ploeg, for example, notes that in the instances in which שפט is used with Yahweh as the object, the meaning is neither "rule" nor "judge" but rather "to do justice."147 Yet, he argues that the meaning of שפט in the Old Testament is "judge." In other words, since the meaning "judge" does not fit every category, then excuses are given, such as the one which explains the apparent problem of having Yahweh associated with שפט. Moreover, van der Ploeg concludes that since שפט has a judicial meaning, then משפט must mean "judgment." He says:

> Puisque שפט signifie toujours "juger," il s'ensuit que le sens primaire de משפט est "jugement". Et comme "juger" ne signifie pas seulement "prononcer une sentence," mais s'étend a tout ce qui accompagnait ou suivait immédiatement la procédure primitive, il s'ensuit que משפט ne designe pas seulement la sentence du juge, mais tout le procès et ses conséquences immédiates.148

More recently Donald McKenzie has pursued the theory which Grether espoused. McKenzie notes two points of significance. He suggests that there is no indication outside the book of Judges that the verb שפט ever means "to help to justice by defeating an enemy in battle."149 McKenzie's implication in this state-

---

146 Grether's conclusions regarding the meaning of שפט in the Near Eastern texts are untenable. The earlier discussion of שפט in the Near Eastern texts shows conclusively that in fact the primary meaning of שפט is not "judge," but "rule."
147 Van der Ploeg, "ŠĀPAṬ et MIŠPĀṬ." p. 147.
148 Ibid., pp. 151-152.
149 D.A. McKenzie, "The Judge of Israel," *VT* 17 (1967), p. 118. See also McKenzie's article, "Judicial Procedure at the Town Gate," *VT* 14 (1964), pp. 100-104. In this latter article, McKenzie notes that the noun משפט based on the meaning of שפט refers to (1) decision of the judge, (2) guilt of a condemned person, (3) judicial proceedings, and (4) simple justice. See also, Ludwig Köhler, *Hebrew Man*. trans. Peter Ackroyd (London: SCM Press), 1956. Köhler says, *"shaphaṭ* originally means 'to decide between,' *mishpaṭ* means in most

ment is twofold. First, it intimates that the שפטים of Israel are judicial functionaries and not "rulers" as some have suggested, and second, he notes that throughout the Old Testament, the meaning of שפט is a direct derivation of its earliest meaning, "judge." Second, McKenzie develops the thesis that Samuel was a judicial functionary, the final one. His example is taken from I Sam. 8:5-6, where the people seek a change in their form of government, and asks Samuel to be their advocate to God. According to McKenzie, it is the rigor of traveling from Bethel, Gilgal, Mizpah and Ramah to deliver judgments, that become too demanding on the physical strength of Samuel, and since Samuel's two sons do not help, the people seek a new leader.[150] This of course is connected with McKenzie's earlier point regarding the role of שפטים in Israel. In both instances, McKenzie is convinced that it is the judicial function which is described when שפט is used.

Several observations are necessary regarding the views of Grether, van der Ploeg and McKenzie. Grether's discussion on the use of שפט is somewhat incomplete and oversimplified. He notes at the beginning of his study that he will examine each theory (on the meaning of שפט) individually, but in essence he simply makes superficial reference to them without any critical examination. For example, in his examination of שפט as "rule" or "reign," he observes that in Aramaic, שפט cannot be found (though there is an occurrence in Ez.7:25, and many examples in non-biblical Aramaic), but that it is found in Canaanite literature. However, he does not refer to, or discuss any examples. He simply points to Lidzbarsky who says that "to reign" and not "to judge" is the meaning of שפט. Grether, moreover, notes in passing that the Ras Shamra texts use שפט to mean "judge," but once again he does not illustrate his point with any specific examples. This is the extent of Grether's discussion of the theory of the double meaning ("judge," "rule") of שפט. After such a discussion he concludes that the comparison with the languages of Near Eastern neighbors does not lead to a double

---

cases, 'a decision which is valid for a person.' From this can be derived quite naturally the two most common meanings, 'a legal decision, judgement,' and 'a legal claim which someone has.'" p. 157.
[150] McKenzie, "The Judge of Israel." pp. 118ff.

meaning of שפט in Hebrew, but he also observes that there is no evidence against it.[151]

Second, the views of van der Ploeg are heavily influenced by Grether, and not surprisingly, he endorses many of the points of Grether. However, he does make certain independent observations, the most important of which were discussed earlier. Van der Ploeg notes that שפט, when used in reference to Yahweh cannot mean "judgment" but rather means "to do justice." It is certainly true that the idea of "doing justice" can be attributed to Yahweh, but it is clearly not the only meaning which can be derived. Van der Ploeg presupposes that in order for there to be judgment by Yahweh, a person or nation must be involved in a physical tribunal. This view is rather myopic and oversimplifies the use of שפט in reference to Yahweh. There are in fact many instances in which Yahweh is involved in a lawsuit, and the evidence clearly indicates that it is not necessary for there to be a physical trial. One of the most notable examples of an open conflict between one party and Yahweh is found in the story of Job. If one were to take Job's questions seriously, then one is led to conclude that in these instances, the complaints are against a God who delivers "judgments," judgments which clearly do not fall within the category of "doing justice." Van der Ploeg's theory therefore is not particularly persuasive. Moreover, in his conclusion, van der Ploeg, like Grether, notes that, "La racine שפט se recontre un grand nombre de fois dans la texte massoretique de l'A.T....Or dans tous ces textes, la verbe שפט a toujours le sens de 'juger,' ou un autre sens qui en est directement dérivé. Il s'ensuit que 'juger' est bien la signification primitive en même temps que primaire de שפט."[152] It is in fact a conclusion which is drawn from little discussion.

Third, in McKenzie's discussion regarding the meaning of שפט, he notes that שפט, when used to describe the role of the שפטים refers to a judicial function. In this context he suggests that Samuel is the last of the judicial functionaries and attempts to explain the request of the people in I Sam. 8:5 as one which in-

---

[151] Grether, "Die Bezeichnung...." pp. 111-112.
[152] Van der Ploeg, "ŠĀPAṬ et MIŠPĀṬ." p. 146.

volves the appointment of a person to execute judgments. If the reason for wanting to replace Samuel and his sons is primarily because of their inability to execute judgment, then surely what is needed is a שפט[153] and not a מלך. In I Sam. 8:5ff, Samuel is asked by the people for a new king to govern (שפט) them. It is true that they seek a מלך, but the use of שפט together with מלך indicates that שפט is clearly not meant to be understood simply as a judicial term. The people are certainly not seeking a new member of the judiciary, for if this individual were meant to execute judgment between parties, then Samuel would be a prime candidate despite his age,[154] precisely because wisdom would be one of the primary criteria for such a position. The fact that Samuel is "too old" has nothing to do with his ability to execute judgment (if that were his role), but it is evident that a מלך "to judge" implies much more. That Samuel is "too old" is indeed indicative of the probable function of the individual sought and in the process confirms the theory that a שפט in Israel functioned as a leader, and not only as a judicial functionary. שפט, from the contextual evidence, simply cannot be construed to mean "judge." True, it is the king who is the one ultimately responsible for executing justice, but there is no evidence to support a theory that it is his main function, and there is certainly no evidence to suggest that being a king entails functioning as a "judge." It is perhaps the words of I Sam. 8:20 which finally solves this question. In this instance, the people are adamant about the person they seek and the functions of the prospective candidate. They are seeking someone to govern them (שפט) and fight their battles. This is the clearest evidence of Samuel's role (in part), and thus McKenzie, is incorrect in supposing and concluding that Samuel is a judicial official.

What Grether, van der Ploeg and McKenzie have attempted to do is to prove that "judge" is the only possible meaning which

---

[153] In fact, even if a שפט is sought and he is understood to be a judicial functionary, then one would have to explain the element of Samuel's sons being eligible to replace him, precisely because the position of the שפט in Israel is not a hereditary one.

[154] One could also argue that in fact if Samuel were suffering from mental senescence, then surely the elders would not have approached him regarding his replacement; some other measure would have had to be taken.

Chapter II 135

can be derived from שפט. Consequently, they have overlooked crucial instances in which the presence of שפט simply does not fit the mould which they have created. The critique of their positions therefore is not so much a rejection of any possible truth there might be in their thesis, but rather a criticism of their methodology and their overlooking of fundamental factors.

C. שפט as "Authority"

It is perhaps in the area of שפט as "rule" that שפט as "authority" receives its most significant arguments. This position finds its greatest and most formidable support from the association between שפט and terms such as שר (chief, prince), יועץ (advisor), מחקק (leader), מלך (king), and רזן (official, governor). In this section several specific examples will be discussed in order to illustrate and give credence to שפט as "authority." Before the association between שפט and the terms above is discussed, three general examples will be examined. Earlier in this chapter it was shown that the role of Samuel was not a narrow prescribed judicial one, but a more general one as ruler. In that discussion, it was pointed out that the reason the people wanted a king to rule (שפט) them was precisely because of the nature of the שפט's rule; it was not judicial but oriented more in the area of leadership and military affairs. This view is further enhanced by Samuel's words in I Sam. 12:1-5. In the rhetorical questions which Samuel poses to the people of Israel, it becomes clear that Samuel is a good leader and this is seen through the words of the people, "You have not defrauded us or oppressed us or taken anything from the hand of anyone." (I Sam. 12:5) Oppression, fraud and corruption are generally associated with those in leadership positions. The fact that Samuel's questions and Israel's answers are given from the point of view of Samuel as a capable and well respected ruler is seen in two instances in I Sam. 12:2. In this verse, Samuel says that מתהלך לפניכם המלך and אני התהלכתי לפניכם; Samuel's description of his role is identical to that of the king. In the first instance, it is the king who leads and in the second instance it is Samuel who leads.¹⁵⁵ This context clearly suggests that Samuel was a leader though the title "judge" is used in reference to him.

Several specific examples will further demonstrate the use of שפט in the context of "rule." One such example is seen in the conspiracy involving Absalom. (II Sam. 15:1-4)¹⁵⁶ In this instance, Absalom comes to the realization that executing משפט as he conceives of it is the responsibility of someone with authority and in this particular case he acknowledges that person to be the king. As a result, when Absalom says, "If only I were judge (שפט) in the land," he is in fact hoping to be king. This becomes clear when it is so understood in the context of II Sam. 15:2, where someone needing משפט comes to the king! This example is not to suggest that there is no need for the judiciary, but rather to note the association between "rule" and שפט.

As was noted above, there are several words indicating leadership which are associated with שפט; an example of each will be discussed in turn. In II Ki. 15:1-5, there is the description of Azariah's demise for allowing idolatry during his reign. After Yahweh punishes him by making him leprous, his son Jotham is made king. The text in II Ki. 15:5b reads:

ויותם בן-המלך על-הבית שפט את-עם הארץ

"And Jotham, the king's son was in charge of the palace, governing (שפט) the people of the land." There is no doubt as to the association between שפט and מלך here. The function of the king is to rule, and in this instance, שפט is the verb used.

A second example of this association is in II Sam. 7.¹⁵⁷ In this context, Yahweh sends a message to king David telling him

---

¹⁵⁵ The NRSV translates both מתהלך and התהלכתי as "walk." It is true that הלך could mean "walk" but in this context "lead" is a better rendering. If "walking before" is meant to convey the definite idea of leadership, only then would the NRSV's translation be acceptable.

¹⁵⁶ Whether or not Absalom is wrong in believing that everyone who comes to him will have משפט is not the concern here.

¹⁵⁷II Sam. 7 has been held to be a late addition and thus cannot be taken as true historical material of the period to which II Samuel is attributed. How-

not to build a temple for the ark; Yahweh points out to his prophet Nathan that in all the years in which he has been with the people of Israel, the ark had always been in a tent and he never asked the judges[158] who were "shepherding" his people to build a house for the ark. It is this point which makes Yahweh's words regarding the judges particularly crucial to this discussion. In the earlier days, it was the שפטים who were the leaders and this is evident from the fact that they were the ones who were shepherding[159] Yahweh's people. This of course ties in with the context to produce strong evidence for the association between "rule" and שפט.[160]

In addition to this, the noun is used in parallel to שפט. In Hos. 7, there is a description of the chastisement of Samaria because of its wickedness. In this description, several authorities are mentioned together. In vv. 3,5 "princes" and "kings" are mentioned and in v.7 "rulers" (שפטים) and "kings" are mentioned together. This context suggests that those in positions of leadership are responsible for the wickedness in Samaria's society; there is no reason to believe that שפטים in this instance is used in particular reference to members of the judiciary. Rather, in addition to the מלך, the שפט is meant to be representative of those who lead the people. This association between מלך and שפט is seen also in Ps. 2. In this Psalm, the kings and rulers are warned that they should be faithful to Yahweh, the one who has given them power. Here, מלך is used twice, once in parallel to רזן (leader, ruler v.2) and the other time with שפט. (v.10) The context once again clearly suggests that it is the rulers who are being pointed to. Perhaps a phrase in Ps. 2:10 will help to demonstrate this point. The phrase...שפטי ארץ...refers to more than simply judicial functionaries, for the context involves national rebellion and terms such as "nations," "peoples," "earth,"

---

ever the literary features which are found here are nevertheless useful for the purposes of this discussion.
[158] The word שפטים does not appear in the Hebrew, but this text clearly has a reference to II Sam. 7:11, where שפטים is used.
[159] The concept of "shepherding a people" has traditionally been used to mean "leading a people" in the Ancient Near East, and this is precisely what is meant here. For other similar references in the Old Testament, see, e.g. II Sam. 5:2 (I Chron. 11:2), Isa. 44:28; Jer. 3:15; 23:4; Mic. 5:4; Ps.78:72.
[160] The text is repeated in I Chron. 17:6.

are used and...שפני ארץ...reflect this. ארץ alludes to a national rather than a local problem.¹⁶¹

In addition to these instances, שפט is also used in parallel to שר. In Exod. 2, the incident in which Moses reprimands the two Hebrews for fighting is outlined. After Moses scolds one of the Hebrews for striking the other, the one replies with these words:

מי שמך לאיש שר ושפט עלינו (Exod. 2:14)

These words immediately give the impression in a sarcastic manner that Moses was displaying attitudes which implied leadership or overseeing. Superficially, one might notice the use of שפט and assume that the view of the individual who speaks is in reference to Moses' decision that one Hebrew had struck the other, and is thus guilty.¹⁶² However, שפט must be understood in the light of Moses' place in the household of Pharaoh and the position of power which he held there. The Hebrew's sarcastic question is meant to refer to Moses as a person of power and authority and not judicial functionary.¹⁶³

These examples show conclusively that the root שפט is used primarily in the sense of "rule" and "authority." This is of course particularly applicable to the period of the Judges where the phrase וישפט את ישראל occurs several times in reference to the שפטים. This phrase must be understood as an expression of the rise of the שפטים as rulers.¹⁶⁴ In these instances then, שפט simply means

---

161 For similar examples of occurrences of מלך and שפט together, see Isa. 33:22; Ps. 148:11.
162 The NRSV translates שפט in this context as "judge" but clearly the term "ruler" would be a more appropriate rendering.
163 For similar examples of שר used in parallel with שפט, see Amos 2:3, Mic. 7:3; Zeph. 3:3; Prov. 8:16; II Chron. 1:2. Note also that there are instances in which שפט is used in parallel with both שר and מלך. See, e.g. Hos. 13:10; Ps. 148:11.
164 Ishida concludes that, "šāphaṭ in wayyišpoṭ 'eth-yiśrā'ēl in the book of Judges and I Samuel also signifies not 'to judge' in a narrow sense of the term but 'to rule,' in which the function 'to judge' is included." "The Leaders of the Tribal Leagues...." p. 520. See also, Rosenberg, who notes that וישפט involves more than simply giving judgment; it has to be understood to mean that he exercised authority. "He became the Chieftain over Israel." "The Šōfeṭim...." p. 77.

"ruler" and the degree of importance which is afforded a שפט is dependent on the subject with whom he is associated. For example, when שפט is in reference to שר or מלך or Yahweh, then the rule is supreme and carries great authority. However, when the reference is to *suffete* or the like, then the function is commensurate with the limited power inherent in that office.

It is true that שפט is connected in some manner with jurisdiction, but certainly not in a narrow sense. It has to be understood in the light of its association with some figure of authority. Generally, "to be judged" or "to be vindicated" is not necessarily understood negatively within Israel. For example, in Ps. 7:9 [8] the individual seeks the judgment of Yahweh, clearly not for punitive measures, but for Yahweh's mercy and continued relationship. As such, even if שפט in this context has a judicial overtone, still its basis would be in the person of Yahweh, the ultimate authority. In other words שפט means not so much that a guilty individual is given well deserved punishment but that it refers to someone's restoration. This is precisely where the idea of authority is essential, for only one in authority can restore.

In the widest sense of the word שפט points to the action which reaffirms and sustains an individual's משפט. This is primarily the reason why the leaders of pre-state Israel are called שפטים. Their function is to deliver and restore Israel, for in deliverance and restoration a relationship is healed, maintained, sustained. This would be the primary *raison d'être* for the שפטים. It is this meaning of שפט which is later associated with the kings who are responsible for the welfare of the people, working to ensure that the right relationship between individuals is maintained, as well as the relationship between Yahweh and Israel. The king seeks the guidance of Yahweh in this matter, and this once again underlines the idea of authority and the importance of this authority for the sustaining of the covenant relationship. In I Ki. 3:9, there is a description of Solomon seeking wisdom from Yahweh in order to govern (שפט) his people, to discern between good and evil. The use of שפט in this context makes it clear that the meaning has to do with rule and not with the judicial function, though of course this latter element can be contained in the former.

The discussion of שפט in this chapter has pointed to "rule" as the primary and oldest meaning of שפט. It is true that not all the elements of Ancient Near Eastern usages of שפט are identical to the Old Testament ones, but this is to be expected, precisely because of the different cultural and religious orientations. Orlinsky is one scholar who believes that it is idle to use this kind of study, and points specifically to the futility of the comparison between the שפט of Israel and the *suffete* of Carthage. He argues that with a period of over a thousand years separating them and the difference in historical circumstances and social structures, surely a comparison cannot be viable.[165] This comparison would indeed be an idle task, if the primary interest is in comparing external similarities to arrive at a usage which is identical. However, this is neither the interest nor the aim of this study, and in comparing the שפט with the *suffete*, the interest is to see whatever movement in meaning there is, taking into account elements such as contexts and connotations. Since the Old Testament says very little about the function of the שפטים, then it is essential to resort to the analogical method of determination and in using this method, the use of שפט in the Ancient Near East proves crucial. As the following chapter focuses on the use of משפט, the impact of the discussion of שפט on the use and meaning of משפט will become apparent.

---

[165] Orlinsky, *Studies and Essays*, p. 379.

Chapter III

I. Occurrences of משפט in the Old Testament

A survey of the occurrences of משפט[1] in the Old Testament will give some indication of the different meanings, contexts and connotations which are associated with this term. It will also bring into focus the various subjects which are used with משפט; whether it is Yahweh, Israel, or the individual. In addition to these factors, perhaps the most important element which will be derived from this examination and analysis is the functional use, namely the motivational force behind משפט, whether subscription to a norm or the sustaining of a relationship.

GENESIS

There are three occurrences of משפט in Genesis, and each has a distinctive meaning. In 18:19, Abraham and his children are charged with "doing משפט," a command given with the sole purpose of sustaining the relationship with Yahweh. This is explicit in this verse, as it points to the fact that "doing משפט" is directly tied to the expectation of "keeping Yahweh's way." In 18:25, Yahweh is described as the "judge of the earth" who does משפט. This indicates clearly the important aspect of Yahweh's relationship with the world, and involvement in the affairs of the world.[2] It must be noted that the doing of משפט may include a punitive element, something which becomes evident in the demise of Sodom. In this instance, their relationship with Yahweh depends on the cleansing of Sodom. As we witness in the discourse between Abraham and Yahweh, it Yahweh's intent always to choose life in the face of death. This however is not done outside of human commitment

---

[1] In the following examination of the occurrences of משפט, the term משפט will be used to refer to both the singular and plural forms, unless there is the need to make a technical distinction. Later on in this chapter, there will be a discussion specifically on משפטים.

[2] In this context, Yahweh is described as ruler of the earth and thus perhaps משפט here has to do with *"cosmic justice"* or *"cosmic harmony."*

and responsibility. In 40:13, מִשְׁפָּט is used in a non-technical sense of "customary." This also must be understood as that which is expected in order to sustain the ceremony associated with the placing of the cup in Pharaoh's hand. Thus, while the context requires a rendering of "customary," it does connote some degree sustaining a relationship.

EXODUS

Of the eleven occurrences, four (28:15, 29, 30 [2x]) are in chapter 28 and three of these are in reference to the 'breastplate of judgment.' In 28:15, מִשְׁפָּט is used in a context which simply describes the physical nature of the breastplate. In 28:29, and the first instance in v. 30, Aaron is described as wearing the breastplate, but it is not for his personal relations, but rather that of Israel. The second instance of מִשְׁפָּט found in v. 30 makes this clear. Aaron, as he appears before Yahweh in his capacity as priest, represents Israel and brings its מִשְׁפָּט with him. מִשְׁפָּט in this instance can be rendered by one of many terms, such as "cause," "case" or any element which is necessary to bring to Yahweh, perhaps even in the form of a confession in order to maintain rightly the relationship with Yahweh.

In three instances (15:25; 21:1; 24:3), מִשְׁפָּט is used to mean "ordinance," but on each occasion, the context is different. In 15:25, Moses prays to Yahweh for water and Yahweh gives a מִשְׁפָּט which if followed would keep the people in good standing with him; the alternative being punishment similar to that which Egypt receives. In 21:1, מִשְׁפָּט is used in the context of determining that which is necessary in order to have the proper relationship between master and slave. מִשְׁפָּט in 24:3 is used to mean "ordinances," and these are given by Yahweh as expectations of those who would be in a covenant with him. The idea of entering into a covenant relationship becomes clear in 24:8. Twice (21:9, 31), מִשְׁפָּט is used to mean "dealing" or "judging." Both of these occurrences exemplify the importance of sustaining a proper relationship between different parties and the way these parties are dealt with; they reflect the issue of relationship, and not the subscription to a norm. In Exod. 21:9, it would be simple to render משפט as "norm,"[3] but if this were to be the case, it would certainly detract from the context. That is to say, משפט is used here in the context of relationship between a master and a former slave. The sustaining of this particular relationship is dependent on משפט which then is clearly being used in the sense of "custom." If it were merely a "norm" which was being alluded to here, then it would make the actions of the master rather detached and meaningless.

In 23:6, there is the command to do משפט to the oppressed and not pervert it. This is perhaps the one occurrence of משפט in Exodus which is most definitively used in the context of relationship. Perversion and corruption of משפט introduce the element of oppression in society, and this goes against the very nature of the covenant relationship. Finally, in 26:30, משפט appears to be used in its most technical sense, meaning "plan." Even in this reference, the concept authority is evident, precisely because it is Yahweh who is the original designer of the tabernacle and it is this which is shown to Moses. Moreover, this experience further reflects the relational aspect between Yahweh and those who are participants in this cultic affair.

LEVITICUS

There are fourteen occurrences of משפט and of this number, eleven (5:10; 9:16; 18:4, 5, 26; 19:37; 20:22; 25:18; 26:15, 43, 46) can be translated as "statutes" or "ordinances." Of these 18:4, 5, 26; 19:37; 20:22; 25:18 call for the "doing of Yahweh's ordinances." In all of these instances, the doing of משפט is directly connected with Israel's faithfulness and responsibility to Yahweh. They are clearly not being asked to subscribe to cosmic norms, but rather the doing of Yahweh's משפט sets Israel apart as his people. In 5:10 and 9:16, משפט is used in the context of presenting offerings to Yahweh. Offerings are done according to Yahweh's משפט; משפט in

---

[3] Rosenberg says, regarding the משפטים in Exod. 21-23, that they are to be viewed "more properly as a collection of case decisions than as a code. The degree to which these *mišpāṭīm* become binding was probably determined by how normative they became for the society." *Diss.*, p. 135.

this case points to that which is necessary for the offerings to fulfill the desired function. Also, in 26:46 the use of משפט while being rendered "ordinances," clearly has a covenantal overtone, for it is in reference to the bond between Yahweh and Israel.

The remaining three instances (19:15; 35; 24:22) occur in contexts which plead for non-discrimination against the poor. In 19:15, משפט is stressed as being essential in the area of "judging;" partiality and deference are abhorred. In 19:35, it is used in the context of "weights and balances," an area in everyday life which is crucial for the welfare and sustaining of the people. If there is corruption in this area, relationships are not only broken, but invariably a chasm between the rich and the poor develops. In 24:22, Moses makes it clear to the people that Yahweh expects the same משפט to be used for the stranger and the native, clearly an admonition which is intent on preserving equity and thus a right relationship. Hospitality is thus construed as an essential component of any relationship.

NUMBERS

There are nineteen occurrences of משפט here and of this number, fifteen (9:3, 14; 15:24; 27:11; 29:6, 18, 21, 24, 27, 30, 33, 37; 35:24, 29; 36:13) are in reference to the various ordinances. All of the ordinances pointed to in chapter 29, are used in the context of the different offerings. These occurrences of משפט indicate once again the element of relationship, for Yahweh has expectations and demands of his people and the keeping of these guarantees a right relationship. Not abiding by the משפט of Yahweh in the offering implies opposite consequences. In 15:16, the use of משפט is similar to Lev. 24:22, where it is noted that there must only be one משפט for the native and the stranger alike. In this way there is no chance of discrimination or the prospect of creating inequities. That is, matters such as ethnicity must not shape hospitality. In 27:5, it is used in the context in which Moses brings the משפט of the people to Yahweh, and in this instance משפט can be rendered as

Chapter III 145

"case," though this does not necessarily imply a forensic use.⁴ In 27:21, משפט is used in the context of Joshua's preparation for leadership, and in this capacity Israel is to obey him.⁵ Finally, in 35:12, משפט is used to mean the "judgment" which is meted out to a killer. In this context, the slayer must submit himself to a process of משפט. The section (vv. 16-23) which follows this verse might unwisely be taken to be the "norms" which have to be met, but in fact, they are necessary elements for the sustaining of relationships within society.⁶

DEUTERONOMY

There are thirty-five occurrences here and of this number, seventeen (4:1, 5, 8, 14, 45; 5:1; 6:1, 20; 7:11; 8:11; 11:1, 32; 12:1; 26:16, 17; 30:16; 33:10) are used to mean ordinances. Most of these occurrences have implicit references to the importance of keeping these ordinances in order to sustain a healthy relationship with Yahweh. There are also explicit references such as in 5:1 where Moses admonishes the people to learn and do the משפטים of Yahweh. The reason for this becomes evident in 5:2 where he reminds Israel of the significance of keeping the משפטים.

יהוה אלהינו כרת עמנו ברית בחרב

---

⁴ This is a helpful occurrence of משפט, and a cursory glance at the context does not suggest any uniqueness. However, a closer study of this text indicates that the use of משפט here is instrumental in explaining the way in which "the laws of Yahweh" are initiated. The fact that Moses is the one who hears the case, implies that the local judges have already administered a verdict which is subsequently being appealed. Moses, not being able to arrive at a decision on his own, appeals to Yahweh and it is Yahweh's words which become a משפט.

⁵ Rosenberg observes that, "*mišpāṭ* when associated with *hōšǎn* 'breast-plate' or the '*Urim*' or '*Tummim*' is an oracular decision. This decision is not limited to priestly or cultic matters buy may extend to all areas of life." *Diss.*, p. 99.

⁶ The idea of משפט being used in a punitive sense for restoring a relationship is not unusual. See, e.g. Jer. 10:24 and 46:28.

"The LORD our God made a covenant with us at Horeb." The implications of this are clear, and there is no doubt that the משפט of Yahweh has an intrinsic connection with this covenant.

Five other occurrences (1:17 [2x]; 16:19; 24:17; 27:19) are used in reference to the perversion of משפט. In 1:17, the focus is on "partiality of judgment," and the context suggests a use which is judicial, but once again, the argument against partiality is precisely because of the destruction of the existing relationship among the people and a subsequent division into "classes."[7] The occurrence in 16:19 is similar to this and contains the same concern for those who are in a position to administer משפט, and also a concern for those who are on the receiving end of "perverted" משפט. In 24:17, the theme is also similar to these, but the objects on this occasion are "the widow," "the orphan," and "the resident alien." In 27:19 this last theme is repeated and it is perhaps in this context that the importance of משפט to the oppressed is underlined. Those who pervert משפט are not merely scolded or even abhorred, they are cursed (ארור), a term which is reserved for extreme situations.

On three occasions (17:8, 9, 11) משפט is used to mean "decision," and refers to that which is handed down by a judge and the Levitical Priests. Even in these instances, the "decision" which is executed is done specifically to protect the individual who has been hurt and needs to be restored.[8] The occurrence in 16:18 is used in similar fashion, and, as a follow up, the people are reminded that this protection involves the covenantal promise of the land. In 32:4, משפט describes the actions of Yahweh, while in 33:21,

---

[7] Rosenberg suggests that, "the priests and magistrates are not to be afraid to render any verdict, for in reality 'the decision' is not theirs but God's. They are merely divine instruments acting on his behalf." *Diss.*, p. 99. What Rosenberg's view once again underlines is the fact that even when a supposed judicial term such as "decision" is used, it has to do with authority, rather that "judging." In this instance it is the highest authority which is spoken of, namely Yahweh's.

[8] Rosenberg observes that "the use of *tora* 'instruction' and *mišpāṭ* 'decision/bearing' in v.11 should not be taken to infer that the court was divided into two clearly demarcated judicial bodies, where the former pertained only to priests and religious matters, and the latter to lay magistrates and non-ritual and civil questions. The context indicates that the priests were involved in civil disputes as well." *Diss.*, p. 101.

it is used in reference to the decrees of Yahweh. Of the remaining five occurrences, משפט is used in identical manner in 19:6 and 21:22. In these two contexts it is used to refer to the consequences of a particular crime. Because each crime which is committed affects a relationship, then משפט is necessary in each instance to restore the injured party or provide compensation to the family of the dead person. In 19:6 and 21:22, the prescribed משפט is death. In 21:17 the use of משפט focuses on the משפט of the first-born; this instance illustrates clearly that the importance of establishing the right (משפט) of the first born is precisely in order to establish and ensure the correct relationships within the family. In 25:1, משפט is used to mean the place where justice is to be executed and in 32:41 it means "judgment" without any technical overtone.

JOSHUA

There are three occurrences and each is used in a different context with a distinctive meaning. In 6:15, משפט can be translated "manner" and a brief overview gives no indication of a larger context outside of the immediate reference to the manner in which Joshua marched around the wall. However, when this occurrence of משפט is seen within the greater context of the surrounding chapters, it becomes evident that the משפט of marching came from Yahweh, thus bringing משפט once again into association with authority. In 20:6, משפט is used in the context of a congregation executing משפט to an individual and in this instance it has to do with protection rather than condemnation.⁹ Finally, the occurrence in 24:25, is in the context of covenant-making, where Joshua after making a covenant with the people gives his משפט as expectations and expressions of the covenant. Once again, חק ומשפט are set down by Joshua in order to keep the covenant relationship intact. חק together with משפט is not unique to this situation however.¹⁰

---

⁹ It is interesting to compare the use of משפט in Josh. 20:6 with the use in Num. 35:12. Both occurrences are in reference to "judgment" given by the congregation but in the Numbers occurrence it involves a punitive element while in Joshua, it has to do with a degree of innocence.
¹⁰ See, e.g. Exod. 15:25; Num. 27:11; 35:29; Ez. 7:10.

JUDGES

There are three occurrences here and two of these (13:12; 18:7) can be rendered as "manner," but each is in a distinctive context. In 13:12, it is used in the context of Manoah asking the angel about the משפט of life the child Samson is to live. From the surrounding context, it becomes clear that Samson's manner (משפט) of life has a direct connection with Yahweh and thus his משפט will be of a nature that will keep him in this special relationship as a Nazarite. In 18:7, the משפט of the people of Laish reflects a sense of peace and satisfaction. In this instance, it might be argued that משפט is used in a secular sense, however the context suggests that there is harmony, and a healthy relationship among the people. The third occurrence is in 4:5 where Deborah gives משפט to someone who comes to her with a case. It is not certain whether or not Deborah was a שפט but at least in this instance she seems to be fulfilling a judicial function.

I SAMUEL

Of the seven occurrences, three times (8:9, 11; 10:25) משפט is used in a context describing the reign of a king. In all of these contexts, the people are told about the משפט of the king, in this instance the king being Saul. The importance of expressing the משפט of the king to the people is twofold. First, this is their first king, hence the orientation. Second, and perhaps more importantly it indicates the responsibility of the king to the people, a responsibility which finds its most significant element in the sustaining of his relationship with his people, and his nation's relationship with Yahweh.[11] The occurrences in 2:13 and 27:11 can both be rendered

---

[11] Even though these occurrences of משפט are in contexts which speak of the "ways" of the king, nevertheless the connotations are not identical. In 8:9, 11 משפט can be rendered as "ways" or "customs," and these terms do not indicate whether the "ways" or "customs" are good or evil. However, the context clearly suggests that because of the circumstances surrounding the appointment of the king, his "ways" (משפט) are seen in a negative light. In 10:25, even though משפט appears to be used in a similar fashion, the context clearly suggests that the משפט of the king is positive.

as "custom" but the context are different. In 2:13 משפט is used in the context of describing the משפט of the priests in relation to the people while in 27:11, it is in a context which describes David's משפט when he raids countries. In 8:3, the context speaks of the perversion of משפטם; in this instance it is the sons of Samuel who are the guilty ones. The importance of not corrupting and perverting משפט is reflected in the elders' request for a king. Finally, in 30:25, it is used to mean "ordinance" and occurs in a context in which David urges a sense of equity regarding the spoils which are received on an expedition. The ordinance (משפט) which David makes is meant specifically to establish equality between those who remain in battle and those who remain behind.

II SAMUEL

Of the five occurrences, three (15:2, 4, 6) are found within the section engaged with Absalom's conspiracy. In these instances, משפט is once again associated with authority. Absalom desires to be an adjudicator, but is unable to do so, because he perceives himself, despite his role of prince, as an average citizen.[12] In 8:15, משפט is used in a context describing David as administering justice to all. There are several noteworthy elements in this occurrence. משפט is here associated with the king, the highest authority, and in this capacity he administers משפט. The king is the primary figure who is responsible for the execution of משפט not only in the capacity of filling the highest human leadership institution, but also as the one who acts on behalf of God. Also, in this particular instance, the specific reason behind David's execution of משפט is to create equity and sustain a proper relationship among the people. Finally in 22:23, David says that he has kept the משפט of Yahweh, and the implication here is that this is instrumental in his continued relationship with Yahweh.

---

[12] Absalom's deep desire to be an arbiter probably blinds him to the need for impartiality in his judgement. He hopes to declare innocent anyone who comes to him with a ריב or משפט.

I KINGS

There are seventeen occurrences and four of these (2:3; 6:12; 9:4; 11:33) can be rendered simply an "ordinances" and all refer to Yahweh. All of these references though are in contexts which focus on Yahweh's relationship with the king of Israel. The use of משפט in 2:3 epitomizes the use in the other three instances and sets the pattern for the uses in 6:12; 9:4; 11:33. When it was time for David to die, he gave advice to Solomon and this included the keeping of Yahweh's משפט. The reason for this is clearly spelled out by David when he points out to Solomon that keeping the משפט of Yahweh is essential for the continuation of the relationship.

Five other occurrences are found in chapter 8 (45, 49, 58, 59 [2x]) and all are in the context of Solomon's prayer that Yahweh might maintain the cause (משפט) of his people. In these instances, Yahweh is not simply upholding Israel's משפט in an objective manner, but the covenantal relationship presupposes on Yahweh's part that he will maintain Israel's משפט, particularly if the משפט of Yahweh has been kept. So, when Solomon prays to Yahweh, he is calling on him to maintain a relationship with Israel even when Israel has sinned.

There are three other occurrences (3:11, 28 [2x]) which are once again associated with Solomon, but in these instances, they are in reference to his responsibility to execute משפט. There are two important points which must be noted here. First, in 3:11, it is clear that Solomon understands the fundamental nature of his kingship and this is reflected in his request from Yahweh. He seeks the element of "wisdom" which is not only necessary for his rule to be successful, but also points to the fact that Solomon does not set out on a pilgrimage of self-fulfillment.[13] Second, in 3:28, the demonstration of משפט is perceived by the people as a gift from Yahweh. This, once again indicates the connection between the

---

[13] In this context, Solomon seeks משפט from Yahweh in order to help him discern between good and evil. He is certainly not seeking the ability primarily to decide correctly in judicial cases (though this aspect is not excluded), but rather he is seeking that which is essential for him to be a good ruler. Thus the renderings of the LXX (κρίμα), Vulgate (*judicium*) and the KJV (judgement) are inadequate.

מִשְׁפָּט which is to be administered to the people and the ultimate source, Yahweh.

In 5:8 [4:28], מִשְׁפָּט can be rendered as "charge" or "responsibility" and is found in a context which points to the servants fulfilling their מִשְׁפָּט (that which is expected of them). In 6:38 it is used to mean "specifications." A cursory look at this occurrence does not suggest anything unusual, but in fact מִשְׁפָּט here centers on the importance of "right relations." It is true that מִשְׁפָּט in this instance is used in a secular sense, but it nevertheless underlines the important aspect of all the parts of the structure being in the correct relationship to each other. The occurrence in 7:7 is used in the phrase "Hall of Justice." In 10:9, the queen of Sheba remarks that Yahweh has made Solomon king, so that the latter might execute מִשְׁפָּט. This context once again underlines the basic responsibility of the king and the primary expectation which Yahweh has of him. In 18:28, מִשְׁפָּט can be rendered as "custom," with a negative overtone. The מִשְׁפָּט of those who worship Baal is to cut themselves with swords and lances, but this apparent indignity must not overshadow the fact that these worshippers are doing that which they believe keep them in relationship with Baal. Finally in 20:40, מִשְׁפָּט is used to mean "judgment" in a punitive sense.

II KINGS

Of the eleven occurrences, eight (17:26 [2x], 27, 33, 34 [2x], 37, 40) are in chapter 17. The occurrences in vv. 33, 34 and 40 can be rendered as "custom" or "manner." These contexts make it clear that both Yahweh and other gods have מִשְׁפָּט, but it is not a matter of choice for Israel, for Yahweh's מִשְׁפָּט is the point of reference for Israel's relationship with Yahweh. In these instances, the custom (מִשְׁפָּט) of the other gods has a negative overtone, and following this custom, as Samaria does, brings dissociation from Yahweh. In vv. 34 and 37, מִשְׁפָּט is used to mean "ordinances" and these are in the same context as the previous three. On these occasions, Samaria is described as not having kept the מִשְׁפָּט of Yahweh, a condition necessary for a right relationship. In 17:26 and 17:27 מִשְׁפָּט is described as that which is essential for the foreign nations to know, in order not to experience death. This context once again distinguishes between what might have been the משפט of other nations, and Yahweh's משפט. Moreover, in this context it is obvious that the משפט of Yahweh brings life.

Another occurrence is in 1:7 and the context requires a translation such as "manner."[14] Even this term however does not fully capture the meaning of משפט in this context. It is true that 1:8 describes the manner in which the man is dressed, but the meaning of משפט must be understood in the context of what Elijah says, for it is not the clothing which makes Elijah distinctive, but his משפט, which points to his association with Yahweh. In 11:14, משפט is rendered as "custom," and in 25:6, it is used to mean "sentence" in a punitive judicial sense.

ISAIAH 1-39

There are twenty-three occurrences of משפט in this book and eleven of these (1:27; 4:4; 5:16; 9:6 [7]; 16:5; 26:9; 28:17, 26; 30:18; 33:5; 34:5) are in reference to the "justice of God." Of these occurrences, only 5:16 is employed in an inactive sense; that is, it is seen more as an attribute. All the other references to the "justice of God" are in contexts which either point specifically to the משפט of Yahweh on behalf of Israel or allude to it.[15] Five other occurrences (3:14, 10:2, 28:6 [2x]; 32:7) are used in contexts which emphasize the need for justice (משפט) for the poor and oppressed. These occurrences give an indication of the many areas in which משפט is needed. The occurrence in 10:2 is tied to the "woe" in 10:1; this is the consequence of not giving justice to those who are most in

---

[14] The NRSV renders משפט in this instance as "sort," which is used to inquire about the nature of the person. This word, however, does not capture the connotation of משפט in this context, for it does not seek to find out about the physical nature or even the individual's presentation, but rather the individual's entire orientation.

[15] See L.W. Batten, "The Use of מִשְׁפָּט" JBL XI (1892), pp. 206-210. Batten sees משפט in the Old Testament as having to do with a moral quality. He notes that the occurrence of משפט in Isa. 30:18, where Yahweh is referred to as a "God of משפט," refers to Yahweh's moral attribute. p. 207. By suggesting that this is the primary use, Batten overlooks the central significance of משפט in the sense of moral attribute.

Chapter III

need. Two important points may be noted from the occurrences in 28:6. In v.6, it is clearly spelled out that the one who executes משפט needs to have the spirit of משפט that comes from Yahweh. This instance once again gives a perfect indication of the relationship between the משפט of Yahweh and that which is desired for the people. Both of the uses of משפט in v.6 tie into v.7 and form a biting condemnation of those in authority; those who are in a position to execute משפט to the people, and do not. The prophet and priest, people whose integrity are expected to be above reproach are singled out here as among those who are the principal players in the perversion of משפט. This is also tied in closely to the occurrence and use of משפט in 3:14. In this instance, it is the elders and princes who are singled out for Yahweh's משפט. There is no doubt that in this context משפט has a punitive connotation. It is not a judicial use, for it is the lack of משפט for the poor that brings punishment to the offender.

Two other occurrences are found within the context of Isaiah's observation of the degradation of Israel. In the first instance, in 1:21, it is used as a part of a pair of parallels. Israel's degradation has moved from a position of "faithfulness" to one of "harlotry;" the nation has moved from being full of משפט to being the abode of murderers. The extremes in this context are striking. The second occurrence in 5:7 is a part of Isaiah's "Song of the Vineyard" where the prophet tricks Israel into self-condemnation. משפט in this context forms part of a poignant picture in which Yahweh's extraordinary love for Israel is demonstrated. The special relationship is established in 5:1, where it says: אשירה נה לידידי....[16] With this special relationship, Yahweh expects משפט but finds משפח instead.

In 1:17, משפט is employed in a context which exhorts the people of Israel to "seek משפט" and this involves the care of the poor and oppressed.[17] This occurrence gives a clear indication of the ac-

---

[16] This phrase could be translated as "Let me sing for my friend," but the NRSV's use of "beloved" rather than "friend" misses the general orientation of the parable.

[17] The statement in Isa. 1:17 which says, שפטו יתום is rendered by the NRSV as "defend the orphan." This translation unfortunately neither captures nor re-

tive and concrete nature of משפט and the need for this to be an essential component in every aspect of life. In 26:8, it is used in the context of those who remain in the משפט of Yahweh. The occurrence in 32:1 points to the future rule of the princes and kings of Israel. In one respect this can be seen as a contrast to the reference in 3:14 where the princes are shown to be corrupt. The context suggests that this new age of justice is meant to be understood as one which will be in the life of Israel in the foreseeable future. It is not explicitly a messianic oracle. Finally, in 32:16, with the coming of an age where the leaders will execute משפט, not only will the people benefit, but so will all creation.

ISAIAH 40-66

Of the twenty occurrences, six (42:1, 3, 4; 49:4; 53:8; 54:17) refer to the "suffering servant" of Yahweh. Three of these 42:1, 3, 4, are a part of the first servant song.[18] Twice in these verses it notes clearly that the servant will bring משפט to the "nations" and establish משפט in the "earth." There is every reason to believe that Israel was the primary concern of Yahweh, but in these references, the "earth" and "nations" establish Yahweh's universal concern.[19]

---

flects the essence of משפט. The earlier part of the chapter has made it clear that the Old Testament use of שפט is more in the area of "rule." As was pointed out, "rule" is a concept which by its nature is meant to include the overall responsibility for the ruler's constituency. When many of those who are being "ruled" consists of the poor and powerless, then "care" is also clearly an essential component of "rule." In this instance, the people are not asked merely "to defend" (though this is important) but rather to take care of. When משפט is understood in this sense, it fits the context well, for surely "the orphan" have none to care for them and thus the need for people "to rule" (take care of) over them is natural.

[18] In this first "servant song," it is not entirely clear to whom the servant's beneficent acts are directed. It could of course be the people of Israel now that they are in exile. Even though there is the development of the theory of individualism (e.g. in the sense of righteousness and accountability to Yahweh) nevertheless the common element in their present existence is bondage and thus it would be à propos to postulate that in fact the object of the servant's beneficence would be the people of Israel, as a community. Perhaps, it would be better to say that in the first instance Israel is the beneficiary.

[19] See Volkmar Herntrich, "κρίνω: The O.T. term מִשְׁפָּט," *TDNT* ed. Gerhard Kittel, Volume III (Grand Rapids, Michigan: Eerdmans Publishing Company),

Chapter III 155

In this servant song, the עבד will bring משפט, coming silently and not overriding the weak but rather respecting them. In some ways, the care of the weak is the point of departure for determining the truth of the משפט. Moreover משפט in these references is seen as something which will be established on earth by Yahweh. It is not the establishment of some objective religion as van der Ploeg suggests,[20] but rather, when משפט is used in this context, it refers to that which is an ultimate aspect of Yahweh's relationship with his people, namely, the deep care and concern for them. The other three references to the "suffering servant" (49:4; 53:8; 54:17) all develop the suffering aspect of the servant's role. Both 49:4 and 53:8 point to the suffering of the servant, but at two different levels. In 49:4, there is a sense of self doubt about the effectiveness of the servant's role, while 53:8 describes the theme which was begun in 53:7, namely the suffering of the servant at the hands of the people. Finally in 54:17, the confidence of Yahweh in the servant is underlined by the fact that the servant will be vindicated against all oppressors.

Five other occurrences are found in chapter 59 (8, 9, 11, 14, 15). All of these focus on the absence of משפט in society. The first four of these occurrences contain specific images which are associated with the lack of משפט. In v. 8, the lack of משפט affects שלום;[21a] in v. 9, lack of משפט brings darkness;[21b] in v. 14 the absence of משפט has caused the level of truth to decrease and in v. 11 the lack of משפט is directly related to the people becoming like animals. In 59:15, these are all brought to the fore and the consequences be-

---

1965, pp. 922-933. Herntrich observes that, "the comprehensive significance of מִשְׁפָּט is shown especially in the fact that the prophet uses it in the absolute. מִשְׁפָּט is a comprehensive term for the revelation of God in which is grounded not merely the relationship of Yahweh to his chosen people, but also his relationship to the nations." p. 933.

[20] Van der Ploeg, "ŠĀPAṬ et MIŠPĀṬ." p. 155.

[21a] See, von Rad, who notes that שלום, "is not adequately rendered by 'peace,' for the word designates a state where things are balanced out, where the claims of a society are satisfied, a state, that is, which can only be made effective when protected by a society governed by justice...." *Theol.* I, p. 372.

[21b] Rosenberg notes that the משפט of Yahweh is often used in the context of light. *Diss.*, p. 105. The idea of light infers certain particular images when used in the same context as משפט. See e.g. Isa. 51:4, Zeph. 3:5; Ps. 37:6.

come clear: Yahweh is displeased. The image of Yahweh in an angry mood expresses the great importance of having משפט.

Three other occurrences (40:14; 51:4; 61:8) are used in reference to Yahweh. In 40:14, משפט is a part of a rhetorical question which makes it clear that משפט originates with Yahweh. In 51:4, Yahweh's משפט will be a light unto the nations. This image of light conveys a sense of freedom and of course the ability to see clearly which in turn brings truth to the fore.[22] In 61:8 it is made clear that Yahweh loves משפט and will bring משפט to all who need it. משפט also occurs twice in 58:2, and in very strong words Israel is condemned for its sins. The irony in this context is that Israel appears to be blind to its transgressions and carries on with its association with Yahweh as if nothing were amiss. These references establish that Yahweh is not interested in the outward show of obedience and worship but rather Yahweh desires משפט, and when this is missing, all else is in vain.

The remaining four occurrences are all used in different contexts with different meanings. In 40:27, Israel is reminded that its complaints about the hiddenness of Yahweh and thus the discarding of its right (משפט) are unfounded, for Yahweh is the omniscient Creator. In 41:1 משפט is used to mean "judgment" and in this instance the executor of "judgment" is Yahweh, and it is used in a forensic manner. Yahweh is the ultimate judge, and it is Yahweh who decides the case between Israel and its oppressors. In some ways, it seems to be more of a demonstration to convince Israel of Yahweh's concern; the coastlands have been defeated and the gods and rulers (Israel's oppressors) have been dismissed. This occurrence in 41:1 is connected with 41:21-29 where there is a court hearing.[23] In 50:8 משפט is used together with בעל to mean "adversary." משפט in this context may be taken to mean "case" and בעל thus is the person who attempts to stifle the servant's "case"

---

[22] Rosenberg's idea that משפט here refers to the doctrine of Yahweh is unclear and perhaps misses the point of the light imagery. *Diss.*, p. 105.

[23] See W.A.M. Beuken, "*Mišpāṭ*. The First Servant Song and its Context," *VT* 22 (1972), pp. 1-30. Beuken notes that the "they" and "us" motif makes it clear that this is a judicial matter, and, most important, it states unambiguously whose side Yahweh is on. p. 15.

(משפט). In this context, the servant is sure of Yahweh's vindication. Finally, in 56:1, Israel is told "to do justice," (משפט) and this is tied directly to Yahweh's salvation and deliverance.

JEREMIAH

There are thirty-two occurrences and of these six (1:16; 4:12; 39:5; 48:21; 51:9; 52:9) can be translated as "judgment." Four of these occurrences refer to Yahweh. In 1:16 and 4:12 the משפט of Yahweh is the element which punishes Israel for apostasy; in these instances it is clear that Yahweh's משפט includes a punitive element. However, punishment must not be understood as an end in itself, for the משפט of Yahweh works for the restoration of Israel and punishment is but one step to that end. In 48:21, judgment (משפט) has come upon Moab and in 51:9, Yahweh has also brought his משפט against Babylon. In these instances, the primary reason for judgment against these nations, is for the deliverance of Israel from the grasp of Moab and Babylon. Thus once again, the punishment against these nations is not an end in itself. The occurrences in 39:5 and 52:9 are identical and one simply repeats the other. In this context, Nebuchadrezzar delivers "judgment" against Zedekiah, and here משפט is used in a judicial sense.

Three other occurrences (5:4, 5; 8:7) are used in the context of those who do not know משפט. In the first two instances, Jeremiah seeks on behalf of Yahweh anyone who knows the law (משפט) of Yahweh. The prophet is unable to find anyone, rich or poor, who knows Yahweh's משפט. In 8:7 Israel's apostasy is described in a striking manner. The people do not know the משפט of Yahweh and this is seen in parallel to the animals who are aware of that which is critical for their existence. The implication here is clear; the people have neglected that which is essential to them.[24] The ex-

---

[24] The NRSV translates משפט in this instance as "ordinance" but this does not capture the fullness of the concept. Rosenberg suggests that the people simply did not adhere to the norm of Yahweh, Diss., p. 164. This however is also missing the main point, for there is some indication that the people did not know the way (משפט) of Yahweh; that is to say, they were overlooking Yahweh's covenantal involvement in their lives. See also, Eliezer Berkovits, "The Biblical Meaning of Justice," *JUDAISM* 18 (1969), pp. 188-209. Berkovits

tent of the neglect is seen in stunning clarity, being set alongside the animals' ability to discern what is important to them.

In three other occurrences (7:5; 22:3, 15) there is a stress on the importance of "doing justice" (משפט). There are two elements which are particularly important in these occurrences and which must be noted. First, the idea of "doing justice" is not made in a vacuum but rather it is said with the context of particular neglected groups: the alien, the orphan, and the widow. These people are not to be oppressed, but משפט must be shown to them. Second, there are ultimata and promises which are given to Israel depending on whether משפט is done or not. In 7:5, the promise is to allow Israel to dwell in the land of its ancestors. The implication for not obeying is self-evident, for the land which is the very the quintessential expression of the identity of Israel will be taken away. In 22:3, 15; the importance of doing משפט is stressed. In 22:3, the doing of משפט is concerned with the maintenance of the Davidic dynasty and clearly involves the relationship between God and king. In 22:15, משפט is used in the context of a rhetorical question and points to the importance of doing משפט as the means of well-being. In two other instances (4:2; 9:23 [24]) it is used in reference to Yahweh, as one who loves משפט. In 4:2, משפט forms a part of a confession which says that Yahweh loves משפט.

In 17:11 and 22:13 (concerning king Jehoiakim), the individual who becomes rich does so without doing משפט, and at the expense of those around him. These two references make it clear that it is futile to amass wealth and not do משפט. On two occasions (23:5, 33:15) משפט is used in the context of the "righteous branch." These references epitomize what is expected and demanded of the king. The "righteous branch" reflects this and משפט is perceived as the main element which is associated with the king. The two occurrences, 26:11, 16 are both used in a judicial sense, within the

---

suggests that in this context, "the *mishpaṭ* of the Lord is a cosmic principle of measured, balanced relatedness which applies to the whole of life, to the realm of the Spirit, no less than to the realm of nature....These seasonal birds know their appointed time; they sense the orderliness and interrelatedness in nature; thus they know when to come and when to go, but Israel does not acknowledge the same *mishpaṭ* as it prevails in the spiritual life of the world." p. 204.

context of a judicial hearing concerning the fate of Jeremiah. In both instances the issue at stake is whether Jeremiah's preaching and pronouncements have created a rift in the relationship between the people and Yahweh. If it is determined that Jeremiah is in fact guilty, then the crime is punishable by death; on the other hand, if he is deemed innocent as is the case in v.16, then he is allowed to proceed. There are also two occurrences in chapter 32 (vv. 7,8) in which משפט is used to mean "right" in the sense of duty. In this case משפט is in the context of Yahweh's sign to Jeremiah through the purchase of a field. In this instance it concerns the relationship between the family and land.

The occurrences in 30:11 and 46:28 are used in identical contexts and are in reference to Yahweh. In these instances, Israel's sin notwithstanding, Yahweh will bring salvation. However, before this happens Israel will first be chastened, according to that which is deserving. This is what משפט means in these contexts. This is an important occurrence in that משפט is used in a punitive sense, but it is also a step towards restoration.

The remaining seven occurrences are all found in separate contexts. In 5:1, משפט appears as that quality which is essential yet which is missing from among the people. In 5:28, the anger of Yahweh is seen when it becomes apparent that there is no משפט in society, and all have become corrupt. In 10:24, it is used as a part of Jeremiah's prayer to Yahweh, for sparing Israel; rather than correct with anger, Yahweh is asked to correct with משפט. The implicit indication here is that it is משפט which is essential for this restoration. In 21:12, the king is exhorted to do משפט to the people and to take care of those who are being oppressed. In 30:18, it is used in the context of Yahweh's promise to Israel to restore the nation; the fact that the citadel will stand in its rightful site, demonstrates in a peculiar way the idea of restoration in a manner which seeks to hold in proper unity the necessary components of life. When something is restored, e.g. a friendship, a relationship, it means that it returns to the way it is intended to be. The restoration of the city and citadel exemplify this. Moreover, restoration also involves the essential element of harmony - thus the citadel and the city will once again exist in an original situational relationship.[25] Finally, in 49:12, משפט is used within the context of Yahweh's oracle against Edom. In this sense it may be rendered as "fate" or what is deserving in particular circumstances.

EZEKIEL

Of the forty occurrences of משפט, nineteen (5:6 [2x], 7 [2x]; 11:12 [2x], 20; 18:9, 17; 20:11, 13, 16, 18, 19, 21, 24, 25; 36:27; 37:24) are used to refer to the ordinances of Yahweh. In these instances what is certain is that Israel has not kept the משפט of Yahweh and this has resulted in a brokenness in their relationship. Israel is specifically set up in the center of all the nations, perhaps even as an indication of Yahweh's rule as being the axis of the existence of all nations. The presence of Israel in this position is meant to underline Yahweh's power, but instead Israel does not follow Yahweh's משפט. But not only does Israel neglect the expectations, but follows the ways of the neighboring nations. (11:12) Thus it is not a situation where Israel unconsciously forgets the משפט of Yahweh but consciously rejects it in favor of its neighbors'. The rejection of Yahweh's משפט is in essence a rejection of Yahweh and a breach of the covenant relationship.

On four occasions (5:8; 7:27; 16:38; 39:21) משפט is used in the context of the "judgment of Yahweh." The occurrence in 5:8 is directly connected with the occurrences in 5:7 which point to Israel's apostasy. The breaking of the relationship and the rejection of Yahweh bring destruction to Israel. The metaphor of harlotry in 16:38 forms a powerful indictment against Israel, and, as part of the judgment (משפט) of Yahweh, Israel will be sunk to its lowest level and made to suffer indignation before the other nations.

In four other occurrences (23:24 [2x], 45 [2x]) it is used in the context of Yahweh allowing others to judge Israel for its wickedness. They occur in the allegorical story of Oholah and Oholibah, the two fictional characters representing Samaria and Jerusalem. Since Jerusalem has apostasized and committed idolatry, it is handed over to the nations to be judged. In these instances, it is

---

[25] See Fahlgren, Ṣedāḳā, p. 126.

once again clear that not only does Yahweh have משפט but other nations have their משפט as well. In this case too, it includes a punitive element.

In four other occurrences (18:5, 8, 27; 33:16) משפט is associated with life. In 18:5, 8, whether an individual lives or not is conditional on several factors, including doing what is lawful or just (משפט). Being "just" involves care for the underprivileged and even executing justice between individuals. What is notable in this context is that doing משפט involves the sustaining of others. The instances in 18:27 and 33:16 note that even though an individual was once wicked, משפט could change the person and bring life. In one other occurrence (44:24) it is used in the context where priests are told that they can execute משפט. The fact that they will give judgment in a controversy suggests by implication that the priest is to "right the wronged person." In this context the use of משפט has a forensic overtone.

The remaining seven occurrences are used in a variety of contexts. In 7:23, it is used to describe the extreme desolation and corruption of Israel. It is used in a technical sense here referring to the nature of the crimes, in this case, "bloody crimes."[26] In 18:19, it is used in a context which establishes that doing משפט is the essential element in the question as to whether one lives or not. In this reference it is made clear that the doing of משפט removes the possibility of the child suffering for the parent's iniquity. In 21:32 [27] it is used in a sense which means "right of ownership" and even though it is used in the context of Yahweh's judgment, it is not a forensic use, but refers to the ruler whose right of ownership (משפט) it is. This use thus points to a figure whose orientation is shaped by Yahweh's משפט. In the occurrence in 22:29, it is used in the context of those who oppress unjustly (משפט) the poor. In 34:16, משפט is used as a part of the metaphor of the shepherd and sheep, and "feed them with משפט." The image of "feeding with משפט" paints a picture of sustaining that which is

---

[26] Rosenberg observes that משפט דמים refers to the act of the criminal. The city is full of blood crimes (משפטי דמים) and thus the punishment must be משפט מות, that is, the death penalty. See, *Diss.*, p. 126. For similar instances see, e.g. II Sam. 16:8; Jer. 26:11; Nah. 3:1.

necessary to keep Israel well.[27] The occurrence in 42:11 is used in the description of the temple. In this occurrence משפט is used in a context which not only outlines the various aspects of the structure of the chamber, but also the relationship between these parts. In 45:9, Yahweh calls for משפט for the people rather than violence and oppression, and in this instance, the "princes" are singled out for criticism; this however could be a reference to all those in leadership positions. The use of משפט here points to two elements of "relationship." There is a sense of the relationship between the rulers of Israel and Yahweh and thus the expectations which Yahweh demands of them. Also, the relationship between Yahweh and Israel is underlined by the use of עמי.

HOSEA

Of the six occurrences, three (5:1, 11; 6:5) refer to the judgment of Yahweh. The judgment of Yahweh is against Israel for its transgressions and apostasy. Those from whom משפט is expected in society are singled out for rebuke. The priests, the kings and the prophets are the leaders, and from them is expected the sustaining of Yahweh's covenant, thus setting an example for the rest of the people. There is no doubt that the judgment (משפט) of Yahweh here is punitive in nature, but it is also evident that the reason has to do with the breaking of the covenant. (6:7) The nature of this covenant relationship will not allow final destruction, but these periods of chastisement are more to cleanse and bring Israel back to the right path. In 2:21 [19], משפט is used in a context in which Yahweh speaks of the restoration of the faithless spouse, Israel. Israel will be restored in a covenant which will involve all of creation and it will be one which is based on righteousness (צדק), justice (משפט), steadfast love (חסד) and mercy (רחם). The occurrence in 10:4 refers to Yahweh's destructive judgment. The imagery of "poisonous weeds" in the furrows of the field describes the effect of

---

[27] This reference to "feeding them with משפט" does not indicate disciplinary action, as Rosenberg suggests. See *Diss.*, p. 127.

the judgment on Israel. Finally, in 12:7 [6], משפט is used in the words of Yahweh to Jacob: "hold fast to love and justice" (משפט).

JOEL

No occurrences.

AMOS

There are four occurrences, two of which (5:7; 6:12) refer to the perversion of משפט. In 5:7 and 6:12 משפט, which is supposed to sustain life and relationship, is turned into poison, and this in turn has led to the downfall of the society. Israel has succeeded in corrupting משפט, a central element in the relationship with Yahweh. In 5:15, it is used specifically in the context of executing משפט "in the gate." In some ways this is particularly crucial precisely because the oppressed go to the "gate" for their only chance of redress, and when משפט is corrupted at this level, then there is no hope for the oppressed. Finally, in 5:24 it is a part of the imagery of the constant ever-flowing stream. Rather than have משפט be dried up, Yahweh urges Israel to have it become dynamic and vibrant.

OBADIAH

No occurrences.

JONAH

No occurrences.

MICAH

Of the five occurrences, two (3:1, 9) are used in reference to the rulers of Israel. In 3:1, משפט is used in a rhetorical question and points to the fact that it would have been better for these rulers to know מִשְׁפָּט.28 The occurrence in 3:8 is used in a context which is in contrast to 3:1 and 3:9. In 3:8, the prophet Micah compares himself with the seers and diviners but unlike them, he has the Spirit of Yahweh and this includes Yahweh's מִשְׁפָּט. In 6:8, the prophet points to that which is required by Yahweh in maintaining a proper relationship. Included in the expectations is the doing of מִשְׁפָּט and this is seen in contrast to the quantity and quality of offerings and sacrifices.29 Finally in 7:9, מִשְׁפָּט is used in the sense of "cause," and the language portrays Yahweh as involved in a tribunal. Micah's intention is to suggest to those around him that Yahweh will in fact act on his behalf.

NAHUM

No occurrences.

HABAKKUK

All four of the occurrences are found in chapter 1. It is used twice in 1:4 in reference to the perversion of מִשְׁפָּט. In this context, the prophet protests to Yahweh that the latter does not appear to be involved in the affairs of the people. Habakkuk notes that there is destruction, violence, strife, contention and perversion of מִשְׁפָּט. In 1:7, מִשְׁפָּט is in a context which describes the self-oriented nature of the Chaldeans' (neo-Babylonians) justice. The prophet observes that the מִשְׁפָּט of the Chaldeans proceeds from themselves and thus implies not only a difference from Israel but more notably, that Israel's מִשְׁפָּט comes from Yahweh. Finally in 1:12, it is used in the context of Yahweh using the Chaldeans as the instruments of his judgment (מִשְׁפָּט) against Israel.

---

28 Even though thematically 3:1 and 3:9 may appear identical, it may be that these rulers are quite different from each other.
29 Batten, notes that passages such as Mic. 6:8, where the prophet speaks of "doing justice," have a moral sense. "The use of מִשְׁפָּט" p. 208. This is too narrow a view, for the doing of מִשְׁפָּט encompasses everything that affects life.

Chapter III

ZEPHANIAH

There are four occurrences, each of which is used in a different context. In 2:3, there is a warning to seek Yahweh and do משפט and thus be spared from the wrath of Yahweh. In 3:5, the constancy of Yahweh's משפט is seen in sharp contrast to the corruption of Israel's leaders. While the prophets, priests, and judges are oppressing the people, Yahweh remains just and righteous. In 3:8, the meaning of משפט is unclear but the context suggests a time of judgment, perhaps final judgment. If this is the correct sense then משפט means "sentence" or "decision" and carries punitive overtones, tying in with Yahweh's indignation. Finally in 3:15, משפט is also used in a punitive sense, but it is reserved, thus suggesting the idea of restoration.

HAGGAI

No occurrences.

ZECHARIAH

Both of the occurrences are in reference to judgment. In 7:9, Yahweh says to the people through Zechariah that they should render true judgment (משפט). One is led to believe that here it is used in a judicial sense. The view is engendered by the use of the terminology "render judgment." However the context suggests that what is necessary is the care and well-being of the disenfranchised. In 8:16, Yahweh tells the people what is expected of them; included in this catalogue of demands is "render judgment." However unlike 7:9, it says here that "judgment in the gate" is necessary and as such this reference has a judicial overtone.

MALACHI

There are three occurrences and each is used in a different context. In 2:17 Yahweh is wearied by the constant complaints of Israel, always asking where is the God of justice. This occurrence is a part of a larger context which develops the relationship between Israel and Yahweh, using the metaphor of marriage. Yahweh does not believe in divorce (the breaking of the covenant), yet this is what Israel has done. In 3:5 משפט is used to refer to the final judgment where Yahweh will judge all those who have lived contrary to his way. Finally in 3:22 [4:4], it is used in the sense of "ordinance."

PSALMS

There are sixty-two occurrences here and of this, twenty refer to the ordinances of Yahweh (18:23 [22]; 19:10 [9]; 81:5 [4]; 89:31 [30]; 119:7, 13, 20, 30, 39, 43, 52, 62, 102, 106, 108, 160, 164, 175, 147:19, 20). These ordinances of Yahweh are not mere norms and are not static, but rather they are concerned with the relationship between Yahweh and Israel. In 18:23 [22], for example, keeping the ordinances of Yahweh has resulted in a reward and is also associated with the deliverance from the enemy (18:18 [17]ff). In other words, the ordinances of Yahweh are intimately connected with the elements of daily life. The reference in 89:31 demonstrates the converse effect. This is a particularly important occurrence precisely because it contains several significant elements. If the ordinances are not kept, then the perpetrators will be punished. Thus, not only are those who keep the ordinances affected (positively) but also those who fail to do so (negatively). However, the punishment inflicted on the transgressors will not lead Yahweh to violate the covenant relationship; for he will always be faithful to his promises and thus the punishment is more an instrument of restoration that an instrument of vengeance.

Fourteen other occurrences (1:5; 7:7 [6]; 9:8 [7]; 9:17 [16]; 10:5 48:12 [11]; 76:10 [9]; 97:8; 119:75, 84,137; 122:5; 143:2; 149:9) are used in contexts which refer to Yahweh's judgment. However, this judgment varies, for it can have both positive and negative overtones. For example, the occurrence in 1:5 points to the fate of the wicked person and it says that this individual will not be allowed to participate in the judgment (משפט) of Yahweh, but "the righteous" will. Certainly in this sense, משפט has a positive connotation and probably refers to a time when those who have been faithful to Yahweh will gather together. Most of these fourteen occurrences have a similar overtone, but the occurrence in 143:2 gives an indication of Yahweh's judgment (משפט) having a punitive or negative element. In this instance the Psalmist prays for deliverance and pleads with Yahweh not to enter into judgment (משפט) with him.

On seventeen other occasions (9:5 [4]; 25:9; 33:5; 36:7 [6]; 37:28; 89:15 [14]; 94:15; 97:2; 99:4; 101:1; 103:6;111:7; 119:32,91,149,156; 140:13 [12] it is used to point to the various expressions regarding the justice (משפט) of Yahweh. In 33:5 there is the point regarding Yahweh's love of משפט, while in 36:7 the משפט of Yahweh is seen as being unfathomable. The foundation of Yahweh's throne is built on משפט and צדק; this reference (89:15) makes it clear that משפט is not a by-product of Yahweh's actions but it is the basis of them. In 99:4, where Yahweh is described as one who loves משפט, it also points to the fact that Yahweh has established equity. This משפט and the concern for all individuals to be equal and enjoy the same standards are tied together. Similar to this is the instance in 103:6 in which Yahweh is described as working משפט for those who are oppressed.

On two other occasions (37:30; 112:5) it is used in the context of those who do justice (משפט). Both of these occurrences focus on ordinary individuals who are righteous. In both instances the righteous individual is the one who does משפט and consequently is the one who is rewarded. In two other occurrences (17:2; 37:6) משפט is used in the sense of "vindication" but the contexts are different. In 17:2 it is used in a prayer to Yahweh for vindication while in 37:6, the psalmist pleads with the people to trust Yahweh, and acknowledges that if they do, Yahweh will surely vindicate them.

The two occurrences in 72:1-2 are part of a Royal psalm and in this instance the king is praying to Yahweh, seeking the ability to judge the poor with משפט and צדק. משפט and צדק are clearly seen to be the essential elements for a successful reign.[30] The occur-

---

[30] See I.H. Eybers, "The stem ŠPṬ in the Psalms," *OTWSA*, 1963, pp. 58-63. Eybers believes that משפט in this context should mean "judicial power" or "capacity to judge." p. 60. Eybers' view is too narrow to reflect fully the king's

rence in 105:5, points to the actions of Yahweh for the people while in 105:7 it refers to Yahweh's משפט in all the earth.[31] In this context, the משפט of Yahweh is closely connected with the covenant relationship between Yahweh and the people. (cf. 105:8) The occurrences in 106:3 and 146:7 point to the need for there to be justice (משפט) to the poor and oppressed. In both instances the person who does משפט is referred to as אשרי. Finally in 119:13, משפט is used as a part of an individual's confession to Yahweh.

JOB

There are twenty-three occurrences, all found in the poetic dialogue. Seven of these occurrences (8:3; 9:19; 19:7; 34:12, 17; 36:17; 37:23) can be rendered simply as "justice" and refer to Yahweh, but with a variety of contextual considerations. In 8:3 and 34:12, משפט points to the fact that Yahweh does not pervert justice (משפט) but implies that in every relationship Yahweh is just. Similar to these are the occurrences in 9:19; 34:17 and 37:23 in which Yahweh is seen as a God of משפט. In 19:7, Job cries out that there is no משפט and makes it clear that he has declared Yahweh as an enemy who holds the power of משפט but has chosen to destroy him.

There are also five occurrences (27:2, 34:4, 5,6; 36:6) which are used to signify one's "right." In 27:2, Job continues to plead his innocence (משפט) in the face of all that is happening. In the four other references, Elihu attempts to demonstrate to Job that it is impossible for him to be innocent in the eyes of Yahweh, precisely because Yahweh does not pervert justice; by implication therefore, Job must have done something wrong. Like the other counselors,

---

request. In fact, in Ps. 72:2, דין is used to mean "judicial ability" and is clearly meant to be distinct from משפט, in this context. Here משפט is a function of דין. The idea of משפט in this occurrence is not so much a request for ability to determine legal matters, as it is the ability to preserve covenantal relations by ensuring that those who are apt to be oppressed, receive משפט from the king.

[31] The difficulty in translating משפט is reflected in the NRSV's rendering of משפט in Pss. 105:5 and 105:7. In both instances, it is translated as "judgments," but clearly these contexts are different and "judgment" does not capture the essence. See Eybers, who says that in 105:7, משפט ought to be rendered as "just rule" or "righteous dominion." "The stem ŠPṬ in the Psalms," p. 60.

Elihu thus falls back on the theory of retribution. In three other occurrences (9:32; 13:18; 23:4), it is used in a judicial sense. Job, in order to defend his integrity hopes for a trial (משפט) between himself and Yahweh (9:32) and he is confident because his case (משפט) is prepared and he knows that he will be vindicated. (13:18; 23:4) Even though these instances are used in a judicial sense, the underlying idea is to restore the broken relationship between Job and Yahweh. In three other occurrences (14:3; 22:4; 34:23) it is used in reference to the "judgment" by Yahweh. Note two elements here. First, it is Yahweh who ultimately determines the affairs of humanity and as such it is he who makes the decisions regarding the appropriate times for events to transpire. Second, "judgment" in these references has a punitive overtone and even has an element of finality to it.

In two occurrences (29:14; 35:2) משפט is used in reference to Job. In 29:14, Job continues to plead his case and observes that he did all that was expected of an individual, for his entire life is made up of משפט and yet he is suffering. In 35:2, Elihu attacks Job's belief that his punishment is unjust. The occurrence in 31:13 is in the context of Job's search for a possible reason for his suffering and he wonders if it could be because he had not pursued the cause (משפט) of his servants.[32] The occurrence in 32:9 is used to mean "what is right" as opposed to "what is wrong." It is not a question as to whether one party is "right" over against the other, but rather it involves the factors which are essential for a sound relationship. Finally in 40:8, משפט is used in a rhetorical question by Yahweh to Job. In this context Yahweh accuses Job of denying that he (Yahweh) has משפט. (i.e. is in the right)

PROVERBS

Of the nineteen occurrences, six (2:8, 9; 16:11, 33; 21:3; 29:26) refer to Yahweh, but each is used in a distinctive context. In 2:8, Yahweh is described as guarding the path of משפט for those

---

[32] Job's servants are in a similar social strata to the widow, orphan and poor in that there is generally no one to plead on their behalf.

who follow him. There is a parallelism here between ארחות משפט and דרך חסידיו which suggests that the חסיד is someone who has משפט. In 16:11, the context illustrates the involvement of Yahweh in the mundane things of everyday life; in this instance it is in reference to "scales, balances and weights."[33] This occurrence reiterates the interest of Yahweh in preserving the lives of those who are poor, for it is this group of people who are most apt to suffer from false weights and balances. The use of משפט in 16:33 indicates clearly that regardless of what happens in the lives of the people, it is Yahweh who dictates the final picture.[34] In 21:3, the "doing of משפט" has more meaning and relevance to Yahweh than does sacrifice, and in 29:26, it points to the fact that in Yahweh an individual receives משפט, and this is seen in contrast to the favors which are received from rulers.

Three other occurrences (17:23; 19:28; 24:23) speak of the perversion of משפט, and each instance focuses on a particular area of perversion and corruption. In 17:23, it points to the individual who secretly accepts a bribe with the specific intention of corrupting משפט. In 19:28, it refers to the witness who does not take seriously the task of telling the truth and maintaining justice; rather such a person makes משפט a mockery. In 24:23, it refers to "partiality in judging" which presupposes that one party is not being granted משפט when it should be. All three of these occurrences are used with a judicial overtone.

Twice (12:5; 21:15) it is used as an attribute of the "righteous." In 12:5, the thoughts of the "righteous," are described as משפט. 21:15 describes the joy of the "righteous" when justice (משפט) is done. In two other occurrences (16:10; 29:4) it is used to underline the fact that the king administers judgments and executes justice. The king, by being the epitome of משפט is able to have

---

[33] Rosenberg notes that, "in association with 'balances' and 'scales' *mišpāṭ* bears the meaning of 'correct, honest, accurate' or some such term as would yield the opposite of 'corrupt' or 'dishonest.' It is here employed as a specialized extension of 'just'." *Diss.*, p. 152.

[34] The NRSV's rendering of משפט in this context as "decision" is probably not the best translation, for it does not capture the essence of the context, and, moreover, it gives a forensic connotation to its use.

peace and stability (29:4) in his land; his judgments (משפט) are done with honesty and integrity. (16:10)

The remaining six occurrences are all used in different contexts with particular references. In 1:3, which is a part of the editorial introduction, there is outlined the nature of the instruction. משפט is clearly one of the important elements in the instruction, for it is only one of four concepts which is specifically noted. In 8:20, wisdom says that she walks in the paths of משפט. The occurrence in 13:23 refers to the injustice which is the cause for the shortage of food for the poor. Even though there is enough food, the corruption of משפט has resulted in the subsequent shortage. In 16:8, it points to the futility of amassing wealth through injustice. The occurrence in 21:7, pits the violence of the wicked in antithesis to doing what is just (משפט). Finally in 28:5, משפט is clearly associated with those who seek Yahweh and is set in sharp contrast to those who are evil. In this context, understanding משפט is closely tied to being in relationship with Yahweh. Those who do not seek Yahweh, consequently do not understand משפט.

RUTH

No occurrences.

SONG OF SONGS

No occurrences.

ECCLESIASTES

There are six occurrences, used with different connotations. In 8:5, 6, משפט is used to suggest that there is always an appropriate way (משפט) for every situation. In these occurrences, משפט therefore refers to "proper course of action."[35] The occurrences in 11:9 and 12:14 focus on the judgment of Yahweh. In 11:9, a warning is

---

[35] Rosenberg suggests that, "the force of *'et* 'time' in the hendiadys is to supplement *mišpāṭ* so that one knows not only 'how to proceed, but also when.'" *Diss.*, p. 152.

attached to the admonition to enjoy youth. This cautionary word suggests that the enjoyment of youth has to be balanced and kept in perspective, for surely it will have to face the reality of Yahweh's judgment; the punitive implication is evident. In 12:14, the judgment of God seems to be neutral in that everything will be judged, regardless of good or evil.

The thoughtful observation of Qoheleth is evident in 3:16, as he says that instead of justice (משפט) there is wickedness. In 5:7 [8] this cynicism is again witnessed as the Qoheleth points to the high officials as being the ones who are responsible for the corruption of משפט. In this instance, Qoheleth observes that it is the highest official who is ultimately responsible.

LAMENTATIONS

Both of the occurrences (3:35, 59) of משפט are used within a forensic context. In 3:35, משפט is used to mean "right" in the sense of an individual's position within a case, while in 3:59, it refers to an individual's "cause."

ESTHER

No occurrences.

DANIEL

The one occurrence (9:5) involves Daniel's confession to Yahweh and this includes two significant elements. First, Yahweh is described as one who keeps the covenant and steadfast love (9:4) and second, this is done in specific relation to those who keep his ordinances (משפט). This is ideally the situation which Yahweh would wish, but Daniel's words in 9:5 indicate that the people have gone astray, and thus, in the process, have broken the covenant relationship.

EZRA

Both of the occurrences (3:4; 7:10) are used to mean "ordinances." In 3:4, it is used in the context of the "feast of booths" where burnt offerings are offered up according to the ordinance (מִשְׁפָּט). The use of מִשְׁפָּט in this instance points to the fact that there is a proper manner in which an offering must be presented and only when this is done is it acceptable to Yahweh. In 7:10 Ezra pledges to teach the ordinances (מִשְׁפָּט) of Yahweh to Israel. This must be understood in the context of Ezra's knowledge of Yahweh's מִשְׁפָּט and its importance for the relationship between Israel and Yahweh.

NEHEMIAH

There are five occurrences (1:7; 8:18; 9:13, 29; 10:30 [29]), all of which refer to the "ordinances of Yahweh." In 1:7, it is a part of Nehemiah's confession of Israel's corrupt nature; this corruption is shaped by the Israel's disobedience and not having kept the commandments, statutes and ordinances (מִשְׁפָּט). In 8:18, מִשְׁפָּט is used in the context of the "feast of booths" according to the ordinance (מִשְׁפָּט), that is, according to the manner which is proper. (cf. Ezra 3:4) In 9:13, it refers to the ordinances (מִשְׁפָּט) which were given to Israel by Yahweh at Sinai. This occurrence is connected to the one in 9:29 where it points to the fact that Israel has sinned against these ordinances. This, however, is not a reference to keeping a particular norm, for the consequences are not merely hurt feelings by Yahweh but damaged relationship. Yahweh who is the constant party in this relationship is always ready to forgive and restore Israel. Finally in 10:30 [29], the use of מִשְׁפָּט is in reference to the doing of Yahweh's מִשְׁפָּט. This is in direct relation to the covenant making in 10:1 [9:38].

I CHRONICLES

Of the eight occurrences, two (16:12, 14) are in reference to the judgment of Yahweh. The text of I Chron. 16:8-22 is identical to that of Ps. 105:1-15. For a discussion of I Chron. 16:12,14, see above discussion of Ps.105:5, 7. Both of these occurrences are understood in the context of 16:15 where it is noted that Yahweh is concerned about, and remembers his covenant. The occurrence in 6:17 [32] is used in the context of describing the various duties which are assigned to the Levites. In this particular instance, the individuals chosen have the responsibility to perform the service of song according to the expected order (משפט). This is not so much a prescription of the order of the worship, as it is the necessary משפט which is essential for keeping it in harmony with all other elements in the temple. In 15:13, it is used in reference to the care of the ark of God and in this instance it is pointed out that there is a particular way (משפט) in which to care for it. This "way" is very important precisely because the "wrong way" involves a broken relationship with Yahweh, as 15:13 points out.

The occurrence in 18:14 refers to David's reign; as king he executed משפט and thereby maintained equity among the people. In 23:31, it refers to the required number of burnt offerings for them to be proper and acceptable to Yahweh. In 24:19, it is used in the context of the division of priests, with each having a duty to perform according to the "procedure" (משפט) which is given for the respective duties. In 28:7, משפט is used to mean "ordinances" and is in the context of Yahweh's promise to David that his throne will be established forever if the משפט of Yahweh is kept.

II CHRONICLES

Of the thirteen occurrences, five (7:17; 8:14; 19:10 33:8; 35:13) are used to mean "ordinances," though the contexts vary. In 7:17 it is a part of Yahweh's promise to Solomon that if he keeps the ordinances (משפט) of Yahweh as David did, then he too will enjoy the fruits of the covenant which was made with David. In 8:14, it refers to the ordinance for the division of priests and in 19:10 to the role of priests in situations that involve the execution of judgment. In 33:8, the promise of Yahweh to Israel hinges on the doing of Yahweh's ordinances (משפט). In 35:13, it refers to the proper way (the ordinance) of roasting a lamb for sacrifice.

In two other occurrences (4:7, 20), משפט is used to mean "according to a particular manner," and are in the context of Solomon making the lampstands according to the משפט. In 6:35, 39, Solomon in his prayer asks Yahweh to maintain the cause (משפט) of the people. (See, I Ki. 8:45, 49) Two other occurrences (19:6, 8) refer to the action of judges. In these instances, משפט is used in a judicial sense; the judicial functionaries are warned against partiality and perversion of justice. In 9:8, the reference is to Solomon's responsibility for the execution of justice (משפט) to the people. (cf. I Ki. 10:9) Finally, in 30:16, it is used to refer to that which is "customary."

There are several observations to be made regarding the occurrences of משפט in the Old Testament. First, this study enables us to see the variety of uses, and the subjects and objects associated with משפט. It sets the stage for the following discussion regarding the use and meaning of משפטים. It also places in perspective both the subject and the object who are mostly associated with משפט and indicates the originator of משפט.

Second, משפט as is noticed from this discussion, occurs in many different contexts, and thus this study enables us to see both the immediate and the larger contexts. Occasionally משפט occurs in a context which, when studied by itself, may only indicate a specific and particular connection to an immediate object, as in the use of משפט in reference to offerings, or to the building of the temple. However these occurrences set the stage for the next section when the particularity of these references will be examined in a wider perspective.

Third, this examination of the occurrences gives a clear indication of the preponderance of uses in the respective books and at the same time the differences and similarities in meanings become evident. For example the predominant rendering of משפט in Leviticus and Deuteronomy is "ordinance" while in First Isaiah it is "justice." The task in the next section is to take the variety of uses, meanings and contexts and examine them in the light to Yahweh's relationship with Israel.

II. Excursus on משפטים

It is primarily the use and meaning of the singular noun משפט which is of particular importance in this study. However, in the distribution and examination of the occurrences of משפט the plural form is also included, and as such a brief discussion of the use of משפטים will prove useful. It is to be noted that משפטים is found for the most part in the Pentateuch and particularly in Deuteronomy. In Deuteronomy, and in other occurrences as well, it carries the exhortation for Israel to keep the משפטים of Yahweh. There is an implicit element suggesting that the keeping of the משפטים of Yahweh is what is of importance, not the following of the prevailing human customs and norms. It is thus essential that the use of משפטים is kept in proper perspective. These משפטים must be seen as a reflection of Yahweh's love for Israel, for in these משפטים Yahweh provides for Israel a basis for doing משפט.

The משפטים are an expression of Yahweh's will, and when they are seen in this sense, they point in the direction of Yahweh's expectations. Consequently, when משפט is lacking, frequently it is because the משפטים of Yahweh are disregarded, and this results in a breakdown in relationship. The idea of "relationship" is often overlooked, particularly when seen in the context of משפטים, probably because the term is generally rendered in English as "ordinances." This translation of משפטים gives it a somewhat static and legalistic connotation, rather than something which is inherently associated with covenant relationship. It is perhaps this perspective which prompts Rosenberg to note regarding the משפטים, "as an efficient leader, Moses provided the people with a collection of norms (mišpāṭim) which is to serve as an instrument for the establishment of a just order."[36] Or, as he concludes, "in reality these mišpāṭim were decisions handed down in individual cases which

---

[36] Rosenberg, *Diss.*, p. 140.

were intended to serve as precedents for similar situations in the future."37

These views of Rosenberg overlook the larger and more important contextual considerations. McAvoy notes, "Yahweh's ordinances are never arbitrary because the basis of them is a covenant which unites Yahweh to Israel."38 That is to say, the מִשְׁפָּטִים of Yahweh are not meant to be a display of codes which may or may not be used. They are not a detached set of norms, which, as Rosenberg suggests, is there simply as a guideline. They must be seen within the context of the covenant relationship, as claims and expectations of that relationship. It is clear that the מִשְׁפָּטִים are a direct result of the relationship between Yahweh and Israel; they are given primarily to uphold this relationship. The fact that the claims of the covenant are expressed as מִשְׁפָּטִים suggest by implication that they are not laws which are applied in a detached and generic manner, but rather as the term indicates, they have to do with מִשְׁפָּטִים. Herntrich observes, "because this relationship is always the basis when the O.T. refers to מִשְׁפָּט and מִשְׁפָּטִים, the reference is never to a binding norm of a general morality."39

Moreover, when the מִשְׁפָּטִים of Yahweh are spoken of, it is not so much a set of written legal codes, or a collection of case decisions[40] that is being alluded to; rather they are referring to the infraction of expectations and demands of the relationship between Yahweh and Israel, and between covenantal kins. They are elements which have become customary and are essential for the health of the individuals involved in a relationship. As such, when there is no מִשְׁפָּט or when it is corrupted, then invariably there are legal implications, in that its absence implies that certain legal requirements are being eroded. This legal overtone, moreover alerts us to the brokenness in the relationship. As such, one may argue that מִשְׁפָּטִים *does* have a legal connection, but only insofar as it is one factor in the overall picture of Yahweh's covenantal expecta-

---

37 Ibid., p. 143.
38 H.W. McAvoy, *Diss.*, p. 45.
39 Herntrich, "κρίνω: The O.T. term מִשְׁפָּט." p. 927.
40 See Rosenberg, *Diss.*, pp. 137-138.

tions. Herntrich observes this when he says, "On the revelation of God's will, i.e. on His משפט there rests the obligation of the whole people and of each individual and also the legal claim of each individual (e.g. the poor) and of the whole people."[41]

It can be said therefore, that while משפטים is generally rendered as "ordinances," it does not have a static or legalistic sense; rather it expresses and reflects Yahweh's covenantal expectations. Because the covenant incorporates all of life, then by its nature it involves a legal reference, but it is certainly not oriented primarily on a legal basis.[42]

III. משפט and the Functional Locus

The discussion in this section of the chapter intends to demonstrate the principal function of משפט. The meanings and contexts of משפט will be examined aiming to show the role of "relationship" in these uses. However, the meaning of משפט is rather complex, and the fact that contemporary studies have ascribed certain meanings to משפט does not facilitate matters. It is therefore necessary to delve beneath these many renderings and trace the main functional locus. With this in mind meanings which are generally associated with משפט will be discussed, and this will subsequently lead into the final discussion of the theme of "משפט as relationship."

A. משפט as Custom

Many of the occurrences of משפט in the Old Testament are used in the sense of "custom" and even in the covenant code, the

---

[41] Herntrich, "κρίνω: The O.T. term מִשְׁפָּט." p. 927.
[42] This brief excursus has focused exclusively on משפטים as they relate to Yahweh and the way they ultimately reflect his claims on the members of the covenant relationship. Also, it must be noted that משפטים is not only in reference to Yahweh but it is also associated with neighboring nations. For example, in Ezek. 11:12, Israel rejects the משפטים of Yahweh in favor of the משפטים of the surrounding nations.

מִשְׁפָּטִים of Yahweh is often referred to as "customs."[43] This use of מִשְׁפָּט is not reserved for earlier texts; indeed something of a transition is seen in Isa. 28:26, where מִשְׁפָּט expresses the "appropriate way" for the cultivation of a field. It is important to discuss briefly, instances in which מִשְׁפָּט is used to mean "custom" or "manner." One such occurrence of מִשְׁפָּט that is well known is in Judg. 13:12. In this instance, מִשְׁפָּט can be rendered as "manner" or even "custom," but the context clearly suggests that it is not merely an objective "manner" which is being spoken of by Manoah, but rather a particular one which would keep Samson in a special relationship with Yahweh. It is not so much the "rules" or "norms" which must be obeyed, but rather that special מִשְׁפָּט which is necessary to launch Samson as one who is intimately associated with Yahweh.

In addition to this, מִשְׁפָּט is used in Gen. 40:13, where Joseph interprets the dream of the chief butler, and tells the latter of the particular customary (מִשְׁפָּט) way of placing the cup in Pharaoh's hand. Once again, the use of מִשְׁפָּט here may appear to be in reference to a special code, but in fact it refers to that element which is necessary to maintain everything correctly, that is, the right manner. Also, in II Ki. 11:14, the custom (מִשְׁפָּט) of the king has to be understood in the context of those around him. There is a particular and customary place reserved for the king, but this is not to be understood as an objective norm which must be obeyed regardless of circumstances. Rather, it is the customary position, precisely to show the relationship between different ranks; in this case the king's position shows his superiority as ruler. In order to maintain a true perspective of the relations, there is the custom (מִשְׁפָּט) which is followed.[44]

A common element in these last two instances is the emphasis on the importance of striving to sustain and upkeep these

---

[43] See, e.g. Exod. 21:1; Lev. 18:5-6; 25:18; Deut. 4:5; 8:11. See also, Osborne Booth, "The Semantic Development." pp. 105-110.
[44] Van der Ploeg, suggests that the use of מִשְׁפָּט in these contexts indicates that it means something from which "one is not able to escape." "ŠĀPAṬ et MIŠPĀṬ." p. 154. One is not able to escape, precisely because of the demands and expectations of a relationship.

customs. At least this would appear as the most noticeable external element. However, there is an obligatory character which threads together these references. They are far from being detached customary rites or laws which must be fulfilled; rather it is the following of a משפט which is designed by Yahweh.[45]

Even though משפט is occasionally rendered as "custom" or "manner," it still has to do with relationship and in this sense it refers to every person who is a part of a relationship and who participates in its maintenance. As such each individual has his or her משפט, and often when it is used in this sense it is rendered "custom." The king has his משפט (e.g. I Sam. 8:9); the priests have their משפט (e.g. Deut.18:3; I Sam. 2:13); used in this latter context, משפט refers to the custom which allows the priests to have a certain share of the sacrificial meal. This custom sustains the relationship between priest and people. The first-born also has his or her משפט.(e.g. Deut. 21:17) The משפט of the Phoenicians is to live in peace and security. (Judg.18:7) In addition to categories such as these, there are instances where the individual has a particular משפט. Elijah has a משפט (II Ki. 1:7); Samson has a משפט (Judg. 13:12) and there is the משפט of David. (I Sam. 27:11)[46]

As evidenced by the preceding discussion "custom" or "manner" is used quite often, but the contexts clearly point to the concept of harmony within a particular relationship. It is only when this element is overlooked that משפט becomes static, legalistic and detached from Yahweh.[47]

---

[45] Fahlgren, concludes that the "manner" of an individual can become the "custom" of a people. He notes that in Judg. 18:7, the five Danite spies notice that the people of La'ish live after the משפט of the Sidonians." "S^{e}dāka," p. 125. There is no verification of this thesis and while a specific example may fit this view, it appears to have little general biblical support.

[46] For a fuller discussion of this view of משפט and its association with parties and individuals, see Pedersen, *Israel I-II*, p. 350.

[47] Jacob, notes that, "the conception of *mishpat*, evolving in the direction of custom, rule, law, into the character of what is obligatory and constraining, became incapable of expressing all that was meant by the righteousness of Yahweh." *Theol.*, pp. 97ff. Jacob's view may appear acceptable and valid in the light of this discussion but in fact it is only a superficial reference to "custom." He does not consider the larger context but rather draws a conclusion based on an immediate context. See also Snaith, who likewise overlooks the covenantal aspect when he says that תורה and משפט, "are synonymous to

Chapter III 181

B. משפט as Judicial Concept

A cursory examination of the occurrences of משפט in the Old Testament, and particularly the way in which משפט is rendered (by terms such as "justice," "judgment," "decision,") might indicate a dominant judicial overtone. One scholar who believes that משפט has such a judicial connotation is Eliezer Berkovits. He argues that the primary meaning which is associated with and derived from משפט is forensic in overtone. In order to understand the position which Berkovits has taken, it is important to examine several of the biblical examples to which he refers.

In I Ki. 3:11, Solomon seeks משפט from Yahweh in order to govern the nation and this request is granted to him. Berkovits dismisses the theory that משפט in this context could mean "justice" or "judgment," and then proceeds to say that what Solomon asked Yahweh for is the ability "to hear wisely with proper insight, the suits brought into his court."[48] What Berkovits is saying, in effect, is that Solomon, as king, is also a judicial functionary. This, in fact misses the point of Solomon's request. Solomon is clearly not primarily seeking the ability to execute judgment or to listen to a lawsuit; rather, he is aware of his main function, namely, king of Israel, and it is with this in mind that he seeks משפט. In this sense משפט is not only judicial but covers every element associated with ruling.

In addition to this, in Deut. 1:16-18, where Yahweh admonishes the judges to be impartial and just, in their execution of משפט, Berkovits believes that משפט in this context is not in reference to "judgment" but to the "entire suit." He translates Deut. 1:17a thus: "Ye shall not respect persons in *mishpat*."[49] But it is clear that the context points to commands which are given explicitly to judges. Deut. 1:17 certainly refers to the probability of the judges

---

the extent that both are the declared word of God. They are different in that *torah*, at this early stage, meant an original pronouncement, whilst *mishpat* meant a decision according to precedent....Because of this idea of precedent the word *mishpat* can mean 'manner, custom.'" *The Distinctive Ideas of the Old Testament*, p. 75.

[48] Berkovits, "The Biblical Meaning of Justice." p. 188.

[49] Ibid., p. 188.

being influenced by the more powerful of the two parties in question. The fact that the first use of משפט in 1:17 refers to "judgment" is underlined by the second occurrence of משפט which undeniably refers to the "judgment" of Yahweh. It would certainly be an error to suggest that משפט in reference to Yahweh, means "entire suit."

In these two examples, as in the others which Berkovits cites, there is one common element. Even though Berkovits sees משפט as having a judicial connotation, he believes it to be much more encompassing than merely the pronouncement of judgment. He believes that משפט refers to the entire judicial procedure. Berkovits sums up his position in this way: "In all the cases which we have quoted, and in numerous others, *mishpaṭ* stands for the strictness of the law and the implementation. And God is the judge who executes such justice and law."[50] The idea of legal arbitration and pronouncement of judgment must be understood only as elements which are essential for the proper sustaining of a relationship. As such, when a judge executes משפט it is not so much a punitive action against one party (though this is often a secondary factor), but rather a means of repairing a broken relationship, and sustaining justice. This exists in situations which involve Yahweh and Israel, individual versus individual, and individual versus state. Abraham Heschel notes:

> Justice is not important for its own sake; the validity of justice and the motivation for its exercise lie in the blessings it brings to man. For justice...is not an abstraction, a value. Justice exists in relation to a person, and is something done by a person. An act of injustice is condemned, not because the law is broken, but because a person has been hurt.[51]

Thus, fundamentally, when משפט is used in a context which may suggest a legal sense, it must not be taken as the precise ad-

---

[50] Ibid., p. 190.
[51] Heschel, *The Prophets*, p. 216.

ministration of law by a judge.⁵² It is helpful at this point to discuss briefly examples of משפט having a forensic overtone. In Lev. 19:15, the command to execute justice when pronouncing judgment is seen to be associated with those members of the society who are most likely to be oppressed. In effect, this is a warning not to create power classes and establish divisions which inevitably lead to the oppression of certain sections of the society. In Isa. 3:14, Yahweh enters into judgment (משפט) with the elders and princes, and it is true that the picture is a judicial one, but the judgment which is meted out to them is entirely because of their involvement in the systemic oppression of the poor. Thus the immediate reason for the use of משפט is forensic, but the primary motivation is for the restoration of those who have been hurt. One other example will suffice here. In Prov. 16:33, the use of משפט refers to the action by Yahweh against those who have perverted justice. Here, it appears that משפט is used in a judicial sense and insofar as Yahweh is the supreme judge and he delivers judgment, it is correct. However, that Yahweh comes to a "decision" in this matter is due entirely to the fact that some individuals have perverted justice and in the process have hurt others. As Cazelles notes, "we are not dealing with the judicial and forensic, but with supernatural ontology."⁵³ And at its roots, this ontology involves and includes the sustaining of the covenant people.

Finally, a word needs to be said regarding the judicial element in the book of Job which focuses on Yahweh and the individual. There are many instances in which the use of משפט and the language used depict a judicial connotation. For example, there is language such as, "...we should come to trial (משפט) together" (9:32); "I have indeed prepared my case (משפט)" (13:18); "...and bring me into judgment (משפט)" (14:3); "I would lay my case (משפט) before him." (23:4) These examples, together with others, indicate

---

⁵² See G. Pidoux, "Judgement: O.T.," *Vocabulary of the Bible*, ed. J.J. von Allmen (London: Lutterworth Press), 1958. Pidoux notes that even on the occasions where there is a judicial overtone, it is inseparable from the concept of covenant. p. 209.
⁵³ H. Cazelles, "A propos de quelques textes difficiles relatifs à la justice de Dieu dans l'Ancien Testament," *RB* 58 (1951), p. 171.

Job's deep frustration with the silence and apparent absence of Yahweh, and in his speeches, he envisages himself as being involved in a lawsuit. While this is the picture which emerges from the book, it is not Job's fundamental concern, nor is it the concern of the book itself.[54] The main concern in the book focuses on the broken relationship between Yahweh and Job and on Job's subsequent questions. The judicial language and overtone are, then, expressions of Job's quest for a confrontation with Yahweh, rather than true reflections of the aim of the book.

It is evident, that even though there are many instances in which משפט is used in an apparently judicial context, the fundamental question reverts to the concept of relationship, and inevitably it involves the healing of a broken relationship and the restoration of a hurt party.

C. משפט and Authority

As has been pointed out earlier, the background of שפט is associated with "rule" and "authority," both in the Ancient Near East and the Old Testament. It is therefore not surprising that משפט also has a close affinity with "authority." The "judgment," and "justice" of Yahweh, both reflect the משפט of Yahweh and so do "vindication" and "deliverance" by Yahweh. Yahweh is the ultimate authority, and it is from him that the nations receive unblemished משפט. The fact that Yahweh dispenses justice and judgment clearly indicates his authority.

There are many different contexts in which the משפט of Yahweh is used. In Job 8:3, Bildad, one of Job's friends, in a pair of rhetorical questions emphasizes the fact that Yahweh is a God of משפט. Also, in Job 37:23, Elihu, speaking about Yahweh reminds Job that Yahweh is a God of משפט. The importance of these references to the משפט of Yahweh is seen in the knowledge that Yahweh is the ultimate authority and is involved in Job's destiny. The implication is that Yahweh would not execute any משפט which is cor-

---

[54] See H.W. Hertzberg, ZAW 41 (1923), pp. 42-50.

rupt, nor would he participate in a situation which by its very nature makes משפט perverse.

These however are not only instances in which משפט is associated with Yahweh; certainly one of the overwhelming uses of משפט with reference to Yahweh concerns his משפטים. These are the expectations and demands which become part of Yahweh's people, both for this sustaining of their relationship with Yahweh and for a proper relationship with each other. Once again, it is noted that the משפטים are from the highest authority. One other example will suffice at this point. In II Ki. 17:26, the nations which are placed in Samaria by the King of Assyria find that they are being "thrown to the lions," precisely because they do not know the משפט of Yahweh, who is clearly the highest authority.

In addition to Yahweh being the principal figure of authority, there is also the king, whose function and responsibility it is to epitomize משפט and ensure that, at all times, the people, and in particular the oppressed, have משפט. In his position, the king becomes the chief administrator of משפט, and in this capacity he is also Yahweh's deputy. This position of authority and his role as Yahweh's anointed is developed in the narrative of I Sam. 9. This narrative, which focuses on the appointment of Saul as king, illustrates the essential elements of the king. Yahweh says, "He shall save my people," (I Sam. 9:16) a statement which indicates one of the requirements of the king. Immediately after this, Yahweh tells Samuel, "Here is the man of whom I spoke to you," (I Sam. 9:17) a statement which points to the second prerequisite of kingship, namely, the king as Yahweh's anointed.

While these examples establish the role of the king in a general way, that is, "ruling" and "saving," it is perhaps the reference in Jer. 22:3 which epitomizes the crucial functions of the king. In his message to the king of Judah, Yahweh says "Do justice (משפט) and righteousness and deliver from the hand of the oppressor him who has been robbed. And do no wrong or violence to the alien, the orphan, and the widow, or shed innocent blood in this place."(Jer. 22:3) The idea of doing משפט is thus clearly spelled out as a primary function of the king, the highest figure of authority, after

Yahweh.⁵⁵ This reference also notes those parties for whom the execution of משפט is most important. They are the ones who need משפט most of all and it is to them that the king has his greatest obligation. The fact that the ruler is accountable to Yahweh and is responsible for the execution of משפט is further attested in Eccles. 5:8.

However, while משפט is seen to be associated with authority, and hence the natural link with the use of שפט, this is not the primary concern. Even more important than this, is the motivation behind the משפט of Yahweh and the king. Fundamentally משפט has to do with covenant relationship and to this we now turn.

D. משפט as Relationship

The previous chapter examining the use of שפט in the Ancient Near East and the Old Testament serves to establish the primary meaning of שפט as "rule" or "authority." However, while the authoritative figure associated with שפט has changed through the ages, the term itself still refers to authority. Moreover, the discussion of משפט as "rule" in the Old Testament, has conclusively shown that Yahweh is the ultimate authority who is associated with שפט. In addition to שפט, the noun משפט is also associated with Yahweh, and once again Yahweh is seen to be the highest authority from whom משפט comes. משפט is certainly an essential and important aspect of Yahweh's character; later in this chapter examples of the use of משפט in this regard will be examined. As was noted earlier, שפט is often associated with Yahweh, where it is used as a title or to describe an action. (e.g. Yahweh judging) Given this, it is essential to establish the fundamental function of Yahweh's judgment; that is, what is the ultimate motivation behind the description of Yahweh as a judicial functionary. In this section, examples of context in which שפט occurs in reference to Yahweh will be examined, in order to demonstrate that the underlying principle behind this use is one of relationship.

---

⁵⁵ For similar references, see, e.g. Isa. 16:5; Prov. 31:9.

1. Examples of שפט as Relationship

The narrative of Gen. 16, describes the actions of Sarai and Abram, in their attempt to aid Yahweh in his promise to provide an heir for Abram. In their quest to be of assistance and take the initiative in bringing about the fulfillment of the promise themselves, Sarai make a unilateral decision to use Hagar, her slave woman and orders Abram to have a child with her. However, when Hagar conceives the child, the new found esteem which she discovers creates a rift in the relationship between the two women and between Sarai and Abram, "May Yahweh judge (שפט) between you and me." (16:5)

From the immediate context, it might be perceived that this statement has judicial overtones and thereby has to do with the question as to whether Abram or Sarai is to be blamed for the incident with Hagar. This would certainly be a logical perception, precisely because both Sarai and Abram are involved in the use of Hagar. The consequence of Hagar's new self esteem is reflected in the fact that there is a breakdown in the relationship between Sarai and Abram. The child whom Hagar bears is intended by Sarai and Abram to be the fulfillment of the promise of Yahweh. However, they come to the realization that while the son of Hagar is fathered by Abram, he cannot be a child of the promise. Hence, Sarai's comment, "May Yahweh judge between you and me" is more of a hope on her part that her relationship with Abram might be restored, rather than a suggestion for judicial action. Abram's reaction confirms this, when he shows Sarai that their relationship will continue as before, by his acknowledgment of Sarai's charge over Hagar. Sarai's fear focuses on the possibility that Abram might hold Hagar in a special esteem, because she conceives his child and the affection which Abram has for her as his wife would have to be shared. This is dispelled by Abram who assures Sarai that she still has power over Hagar; Sarai thus reasserts herself and repairs the broken relationship with Abram by her harsh treatment of Hagar.

The relationship between Sarai and Abram however, is not the only one which is referred to and affected in this context. In

Gen. 15:18 Yahweh reiterates the promise and makes a covenant with Abram and promises that his descendants will inherit the land. It is this promise (cf. Gen. 12:1-4) which includes the component of descendants, that brings to the fore for Sarai and Abram the realization that Sarai is unable to have a child and that in their calculations, and finite time-line, Yahweh's promise is likely to remain unfulfilled. Rather than have this happen, Hagar is allowed to conceive for the purpose of producing an heir. In their actions, Sarai and Abram overlook the maker of the promise and the originator of the covenant; they do not include in their plans the fact that Yahweh's promise to Abram is an integral aspect of the covenant. Moreover, they do not consider the fact that the time-line with which they were limited, albeit understandable given their advanced years, is not the one by which Yahweh was bound. When Sarai says, "May Yahweh judge between you and me," this is also indicative of the realization that they have acted contrary to the intention of Yahweh. Sarai's words must be understood also as an expression of the division between Yahweh on the one hand and Sarai and Abram on the other. Seeking the judgment of Yahweh here must indicate the desire to restore the relationship. Sarai's words must therefore be understood to have a two-fold implication; the restoration of Abram and Sarai's relationship and their relationship with Yahweh.

A second example of the use of שפט with reference to Yahweh is in Exod. 6:6. A cursory look at this text might suggest that it is primarily concerned with punitive measures against Egypt. However, a closer examination indicates otherwise. In this respect, it is helpful to look at Exod. 6:5 where Yahweh says, "I have also heard the groaning of the Israelites whom the Egyptians are holding as slaves and I have remembered my covenant." These words express clearly the unnatural combination of "covenant" and "bondage;" it is evident from Yahweh's words that being in bondage goes against the grain of the covenant. Yahweh says that Israel's redemption and deliverance will come from great acts of judgment. It is the "judgment of Yahweh" which is clearly the element employed in procuring the release of Israel. However, when the "judgment of Yahweh" is employed here, it is not merely an instrument of punishment for Egypt and the subsequent deliverance of Israel, nor is it a reflection of the righteousness of Israel and the evil of Egypt.

To be sure, Israel suffers and Egypt is oppressive, but these are only secondary elements in a much larger picture. When Yahweh decides to act, he is not being an objective, detached judicial functionary, executing judgment to nations, but rather Yahweh's actions in this instance are a direct result of his relationship with Israel. The elements which are pointed to are "bondage" and "covenant." The existing situation which creates a fractured relationship is the bondage of Israel, and the motivation for deliverance by Yahweh is the ideals of the covenant relationship. Of paramount importance, is the sustaining of the covenant relationship, not the punishment of Egypt, though this becomes an instrument. It can be seen then that even though the language and in some ways the context suggest a judicial overtone, it is clearly the concept of relationship which is the locus.

A third example of the use of שפט in reference to Yahweh is in Isa. 2:4. Like the instance in Gen. 16:5, the occurrence in Isa. 2:4 is also used together with ריב and once again this would be an external indicator of a forensic use. However, the use of ריב here is not a true indicator of the focus of the context. Isa. 2:1-4[56] can perhaps be called an "oracle of peace," one which describes the state of the nations during this particular period. Rather than swords and spears, there will be pruning hooks and ploughshares, and war will cease. The question which arises here has to do with the instrument which will be used to procure this peace. Isa. 2:4 says: ...ושפט בין הגוים... [Yahweh] will judge between the nations. This certainly does not refer to a tribunal where Yahweh will decide which of the nations is "righteous" and which is "wicked," but it refers to that element which Yahweh will use to ensure peace.

It is not the punishment of one or the vindication of another; in other words, שפט in this instance is not used in a sense which establishes the "right" of one nation over against the other. Yahweh judges the nations with the sole purpose of establishing peace and

---

[56] See also, Mic. 4:1-3.

this is not done through punishment nor through the judiciary. When Yahweh "judges," as in this instance, the fundamental issue at stake is "proper relationship," and the idea of peace underlines this, for the relationship between nations cannot be right if there is war and tension and strife. The changing of weapons into instruments of peace (and particularly agricultural instruments) is indicative of the very deep change which is imperative for there to be a right relationship. It is certainly "peace" which is spoken here, but important though this is, it is only an expression of a right relationship. When there is war, there is hurt, and parties become involved in destruction and hatred and these are factors which are expressions of a splintered relationship. In Isa. 2:1-4, peace is the expression which points to the restoration of a broken relationship.

2. Examples of משפט as Relationship

The following discussion focuses on select texts which include the use of משפט and which provide different contextual considerations. Each text will be examined in detail with the primary focus on demonstrating that the functional locus of משפט is "relationship."

There are three occurrences of משפט in the Old Testament which are used in contexts that are associated with architecture. These occurrences underline the use of משפט in the sense of relationship, outside of covenant. In I Ki. 6:38, the temple is described as having been completed. The sense of harmony and relationship is seen here, in that the finished temple has all the different parts in correct relationship to each other. In Jer. 30:18, the restoration of Israel involves the restoring of the city and the citadel will be in its former state. Finally, in Ezek. 42:11, משפט is used within a context which refers to the relationship of the parts of the structure to each other. The extensive description of the temple (chapters 40-46) and the detailed outline of the parts and their relation to each other emphasize the importance of a sense of "wholeness" and harmony.

When משפט is used in Leviticus, it is evident that predominantly it refers to "ordinance(s)"[57] of Yahweh. These are generally regarded as "norms" or "laws" which must be subscribed to. Two examples of משפט in Leviticus will be examined, to confirm the hypothesis that the functional locus of משפט in these occurrences is relationship rather than the static norm or law.

In Lev. 9:16, Aaron is described as having presented, and offered the burnt offering according to the משפט. A cursory examination of this text in its context suggests that משפט may be rendered as "ordinance," but this term does not explain the primary factor. The sacrifice of animals, the sprinkling of blood (Lev. 8:19, 30) and the eating of the flesh (Lev. 8:31) are all elements traditionally associated with covenant-making, and this episode involving Aaron as priest fits this framework. In other words, the presentation of this offering according to the משפט is done precisely in order to confirm the relationship between Yahweh, priest and people. As such, "ordinance" as a rendering of משפט in this context must not be taken to refer to a generic norm, but rather to a necessary element which is involved in the establishing and sustaining of relationships. Thus, when an offering is presented in a proper manner, according to the משפט, then the relationship between Yahweh and his people is maintained or restored as the situation may warrant.

A second example of the use of משפט in Leviticus which will be helpful here is in 18:26. Yahweh says to his people that they should keep his משפט.(cf. 18:4) Israel is given an indication of the expectations and demands of Yahweh. These demands are given with the sole intention of sustaining the relationship between Israel and Yahweh. Yahweh must not be perceived as one of two options (the other being the Canaanite god). It is certainly not a question of Yahweh wishing to impose a set of norms on Israel and not allowing a freedom of choice. The position of Israel with regard to its sustenance, makes choosing one from two sources a non-viable option. By following the ways of Canaan, it is not so much

---

[57] See above, in the section on "Occurrences of משפט" where משפט in Leviticus is discussed. The occurrences clearly verify this assertion.

making a positive decision as it is rejecting the covenant with Yahweh.

Another example is in II Ki. 17:26. On a purely external level it would appear that משפט means "custom" in this context, but on a deeper level, it becomes evident that the "משפט of Yahweh" is not merely a norm or custom which must be adhered to. The consequences of not "knowing" the משפט of Yahweh indicate clearly the nature of this משפט.

First, those who have come into Samaria are obviously strangers and are not expected to know the "ways" of Samaria or the משפט of Yahweh. The fact that they do not know the משפט of Yahweh, underlines the difference between these people and the people of Yahweh.

Second, "knowing" משפט cannot be understood to mean "an awareness of a particular standard." The use of ידע implies a close relationship with a party and not simply an "objective knowledge." ידע is also used to express a sexual relationship, as in Gen. 4:1 and thus the use here, while not sexual in connotation still clearly refers to relationship. This would certainly explain the lack of knowledge (ידע) on the part of the incoming nations, for inherent in this idea of "knowledge" is the fact that there is some relationship with Yahweh.[58] In other words, "knowing" encompasses the elements of involvement and commitment, both of which are obviously lacking on the part of the incoming nations. Perhaps the consequences of the lack of knowledge of *Yahweh's* משפט underline most powerfully the essence of the term. The fact that these foreign people are killed suggests clearly the extreme significance of this משפט.

Third, the use of the משפט of Yahweh rather than the משפטים of Yahweh is an important factor. In this context, the use of משפט suggests that it is pointing to a singularly most important element. It is not the "ordinances" of Yahweh which are being spoken

---

[58] It is perhaps noteworthy that while it is the משפט of Yahweh which is being referred to, it is אלהים and not יהוה which is used. The fact that it is the generic term which is used points further to the lack of knowledge on the part of these nations. Yahweh is clearly a term which is reserved for those who are in relationship with him.

of here, and it is certainly not the "ordinance," or "custom" or "law."⁵⁹ There are certainly "customs" which might give an indication of what is expected of the people of Yahweh, customs such as "offerings" and "worship," but these are only significant insofar as they represent the much greater משפט of Yahweh. In this case, the משפט is indicative of that which is essential and crucial for there to be any knowledge of Yahweh, namely, to be in covenant relationship. It is only with this as the foundational element, that knowledge and all of the expectations and demands can be attained.

The occurrence of משפט in Jer. 22:3 is in a context which includes all of the elements which have been discussed so far. First, there is the presence of the two main sources of authority, namely Yahweh and the king, and in Jer. 22:1, it is clear that it is Yahweh who give the orders and administers the commands and in so doing, indicates who is the ultimate authority. Also, the role of the king is crucial in executing משפט to the people and in this respect, the king clearly appears as Yahweh's deputy.

Second, the admonition which is given to the king outlines specifically what is necessary for the relationship between Yahweh and Israel to continue in good stead. At the same time the consequences of not heeding the words of Yahweh are pointed out. One of the foremost requirements is for the king to do משפט to all those who are powerless and without authority; only if this is done will the relationship be sustained. Once again, implicit in this demand is the fact that for the covenantal relationship to be maintained in the manner in which it is meant to be, then all parties must be true to their responsibilities. This means that the people must therefore be responsible for the welfare of each other and follow the expectations of remaining in good relationship with

---

⁵⁹ The difficulty in interpreting and translating משפט in this context is further exemplified through the different renderings in various versions. The JB translates משפט as "worship;" the NRSV translates it as "law;" the KJV translates it as "manner" and the NEB translates it as "established usage." See also, Leon Morris, "Judgement and Custom," *ABR* 7 (December 1959), pp. 72-74, who renders משפט as "custom." So too, John Gray, *I and II Kings*. OTL (London: SCM Press), 1964. While not giving a specific translation, Gray suggests that "*mišpāṭ* here signifies the duly regulated order maintained by authority, here of Yahweh in his own land." p. 594.

Yahweh. The consequences of not fulfilling the expectations and following the word of Yahweh is devastation.

Breaking the relationship is not punishment in itself, for in addition to this, Yahweh will make the nation desolate. (v.5) Only in adhering to the values of the covenant relationship is the nation of any essence. When the covenant is not adhered to and the authorities become corrupt and irresponsible then destruction is inevitable. Jer. 22:8-9 place the use of משפט in its proper relational perspective. The contiguous nations will ask why Yahweh dealt so harshly with Israel and the answer will be, "because they forsook the covenant of Yahweh." And of course the covenant is forsaken when משפט is absent.

The occurrence of משפט in Ezek. 44:24 is another example of the use of משפט in a context which apparently has little to do with relationship. The Levitical priests are given all the guidelines regarding the manner of life they are to live. Included in these guidelines, is also a word regarding the role of the judge, and in this respect, it notes that whatever is decided must be based on the משפט of Yahweh. There are three important observations to be noted here.

First, the priests do have the authority to pronounce judgment, but the ultimate authority is clearly Yahweh. Even though it is the priests who are the instruments in executing משפט, the משפט itself must be from Yahweh. Second, the first point is significant, precisely because the משפט of Yahweh is what is essential in order to sustain the right relationship between the people and Yahweh. Also, the משפט of Yahweh is crucial in the context of judging, in order to nullify the chance of any partiality in the case of the judges. Third, in order that the relationship between individuals is sustained or healed as the case may be, it is imperative that they be "judged" with the משפט of Yahweh, which at its core, is about relationship. To judge according to the משפט of Yahweh means that there is impartiality, so that whatever controversy there is between individuals, is resolved, and a proper relationship is restored. If the relationship between individuals is fractured, then it will certainly affect the relationship with Yahweh. In order to keep both in harmony, the משפט of Yahweh is essential in executing any form of justice.

In Zeph. 3, there are three occurrences of משפט and all are associated with Yahweh. The references in 3:5 and 3:8 will be examined briefly. The prophet Zephaniah, in a woe oracle against Israel, points to the corruption of all those in authority. As a contrast to this, Zephaniah emphasizes the משפט of Yahweh, who is portrayed as faithful and ever-present. (v. 5) What is clear in this description of Yahweh and Israel is the chasm which divides them and thus causes the brokenness in the relationship. It is, of course, notable that the actions of the leaders of Israel are directed primarily against the citizens and go against the fiber of the covenant. Thus, not only are they corrupt in the eyes of the people, but moreso in the eyes of Yahweh, the originator of the covenant. The fact that Yahweh is constant in his משפט indicates what is expected of those entrusted with the responsibility. As is usually the case when the relationship between Yahweh and his people is broken, it is Yahweh who is the one to restore it, despite the fact that it is Israel who is the offender.

In Zeph. 3:8, the משפט of Yahweh is to gather the nations and kingdoms and purge them. Once again, in this context, it is evident that the משפט[60] of Yahweh is the important element necessary to cleanse the nations and consequently to have a righteous remnant in Israel. The primary reason for Yahweh's משפט is not so much the punishment as it is cleansing of elements in society which are a hindrance to a right relationship. In other words, in this context the משפט of Yahweh is essential for maintaining Yahweh's relationship with Israel. Certainly משפט in this context has nothing to do with judicial activity, even though Yahweh speaks of himself as a witness (עד), a term which might have prompted the NRSV to render משפט as "decision." It is true that it is the witness who separates the truth from the untruth and thereby establishes the righteous. In the case of Yahweh, it is his משפט which is the instrument that will do this, for the sole purpose of once again estab-

---

[60] The NRSV translates משפט in this context as "decision," and this gives it something of a forensic connotation. The context does not require a judicial act by Yahweh, and thus this particular translation is overly narrow.

lishing a nation true to the demands and commitments of the covenant.

The final example of משפט for discussion is from Dan. 9:5, an occurrence which is part of a prayer of confession to Yahweh. This is one instance in which the concepts of ברית and משפט are clearly shown to be connected with each other. In Dan. 9:4, Yahweh is described as the one who keeps the covenant and in 9:5, Israel is described as a people who has rebelled and turned aside from Yahweh's משפט. Thus, while Yahweh maintains the covenant, Israel rebels and injures the covenant relationship by not keeping the משפט of Yahweh. The brokenness in the relationship is evidenced in terms such as "treachery" [מעלם] (9:7); "shame" [בשת] (9:8); "sinned against you" [חטאנו לך] (9:8); "rebelled" [מרד] (9:5, 9); "transgressed" [עבר] (9:11), all of which are indicative of Israel's rebellion against Yahweh. These terms clearly express more than not simply subscribing to a norm.

Daniel's prayer is a confession of the majesty and greatness of Yahweh on the one hand, and the sinfulness of Israel on the other. The turning away from Yahweh's משפט has resulted in the desolation of Israel. Once again, this context indicates that even though Israel has sinned and not kept the expectations of the relationship (including משפט), nevertheless through the mercy of Yahweh, Israel is restored as an active party to the covenant. While it is true that it is only through the mercy of Yahweh that Israel is restored, Daniel's words of 9:5 presuppose that since it is the absence of the keeping of Yahweh's משפט which is responsible for the brokenness, then it would have to be the presence of this משפט which will renew the relationship after Israel restored.

Several observations might be drawn from the discussion thus far. The preliminary discussion of the use of *špṭ* in Ancient Near Eastern literature serves two important functions. First, it is evident that the use of *špṭ* is primarily in texts and situations which are associated with some form of authority, whether it is king, governor, or *suffete*. Second, in demonstrating the meaning of "rule" as its focus, we can see that the judicial meaning of *špṭ* is secondary. This examination of the background of *špṭ* sets the stage for the subsequent discussion of שפט in the Old Testament.

Chapter III 197

It is clear that the religious and social framework of the Ancient Near Eastern societies are different from that of Israel, the most specific and significant distinction being in Israel's relationship with Yahweh. This distinction notwithstanding, it is crucial to have this background discussion, precisely because many of the elements of Israelite society are similar to, if not identical with those of its neighbors. In the case of language and its references, the situation is no different.

The discussion of שפט in the Old Testament is important for two reasons. First, the similarities to its use in the Ancient Near East are striking and the meaning of "rule" is confirmed. This discussion established that fundamentally שפט has to do with authority, and this is clearly seen in the period of the שפטים. Second, the importance of knowing the primary reference of שפט is seen not only for its own sake, but particularly for the foundation which it sets for the discussion of משפט. At the outset, as one would imagine, משפט has to do with the basic meaning of שפט which has been demonstrated as having to do with the idea of authority. Since the primary intent of this chapter is the examination of משפט, it is important that the brief discussion of שפט be done in order to place the meaning of משפט in correct historical and linguistic perspective. Even though the background of שפט indicates that it has to do with authority, this should not, of course, be taken to be indicative of the overall reference of משפט. What it does, is to point to the background and set the stage for discussion.

In addition to this, the section on the occurrences of משפט is particularly essential to the overall direction of this thesis. It enables us to see in a contextual setting the many and varied uses of משפט. The systematic distribution of משפט places its use in perspective and allows us to recognize the versatility of the concept. That is to say, this categorization clearly distinguishes the many ways in which משפט is rendered (e.g. judgment, justice, ordinance, decision, case) and the subjects with which it is associated. (e.g. Yahweh, king, judge) This discussion not only outlines the quantitative distribution of משפט, but in so doing dispels the commonly held view that משפט means "justice" in a narrow forensic sense. The different meanings which are testified to here, also demonstrate the movement and development in meaning. Moreover, such a distribution is necessary if in fact the attempt to determine the functional locus is to be successful. It is important to show that it is not only the occurrences which overtly refer to the covenant that allude to relationship, but rather all occurrences.

It is true, as Beuken says, that משפט may be classified in two categories and that one may envisage "*mišpaṭ* as a situation, an event to be realized, a process and its execution resulting in relations of righteousness, the background obviously being this: that the present situation is devoid of justice."[61] And then of course there are numerous occurrences where משפט is thought to be an ordinance or a law to be obeyed or proclaimed. However, to make such a classification and attempt to find the functional locus would be futile and ill-advised. Thus, a categorization such as Beuken's, provides only a partial overview.

Finally, it can be seen that משפט is not an objective norm which must be subscribed to, whether in legal, cultic or religious affairs. Rather, everyone is involved in some form of relationship. The individual and the community are both expected to do משפט, but this expectation is effected through Yahweh's משפט which is inherent in his covenant. This involves commitment to the covenant and knowledge of Yahweh. For the individual, משפט embodies the expectations both of Yahweh and others of the covenant relationship. As Eichrodt notes, "*mišpāṭ* is no abstract thing, but denotes the rights and duties of each party arising out of the particular relation of fellowship in which they find themselves. In this way, everyone has his own special *mišpāṭ*." [62]

---

[61] Beuken, "*Mišpāṭ*." p. 7.
[62] Eichrodt, *Theol.* I, p. 241.

Chapter IV

I. Salient Features of צדק, שפט, משפט

The study of *ṣdq* and *špṭ* in the Ancient Near East together with that of משפט and צדק in the Old Testament, provides a comprehensive account of the uses, connotations and meanings associated with these concepts. In this examination, several elements have emerged as being integral to these concepts, elements which are germane to the ensuing discussion of the use of צדק and משפט in the Eighth Century prophets, and particularly their use with regard to the social critique of the prophets.

A. צדק

The examination of *ṣdq* in the Ancient Near East indicates that this concept, while being used in religious, ethical and forensic contexts, refers in some form to "relationship." In no. 287 of the Tel el-Amarna tablets, Abdu-Hiba makes a plea to the king regarding his relationship with the Kasi people. In this instance *ṣdq* refers to Abdu-Hiba being "in the right." Also, in the Aramaic text of Nerab, the relationship between king and deity is reflected in the latter granting the king a good name and a prolonged life. Moreover, the idea of "straightness" as regards *ṣdq* in pre-Quranic Arabic, also, as Achtemeier argues, refers to a responsibility within a relationship.[1]

This idea of צדק is centered in "relationship" within a variety of contexts. In the Old Testament צדק is used in reference to Israel and the individual, but the ultimate source of צדק is clearly Yahweh. Whatever righteousness Israel may have is derived entirely from being in a covenant relationship with Yahweh. That is, Israel is צדק only insofar as Yahweh is צדק. The righteousness of the individual is similar to this, in that the individual also derives his or her צדק from Yahweh.

---

[1] See above, chapter 1.

B. שפט

The use of *špṭ* in the Ancient Near East indicates that its background is centered in some form on the idea of "authority." The discussion of the use of *špṭ* in Mari suggests clearly that the root *špṭ* with its many derivatives has to do with authority and acts of authority. Ideas such as "governing," "ruling," and "giving orders" are all associated with *špṭ*. The use of *ṭpṭ* in Ugaritic gives the closest parallel to שפט in the Old Testament. *Ṭpṭ* in the Aqhat tale refers to king Dan'el, and in the text discussed in Chapter 2, of this study, Dan'el is pictured as administering justice to the widow and the orphan. While this particular use has a forensic overtone, *ṭpṭ* is used in reference to the king and not to a judicial functionary. Thus, the king in executing justice for the widow and the orphan may be perceived to be one on whom the responsibility for the care and protection of the powerless lies. Moreover, the discussion of the Phoenician inscription of Ahiram concludes that the use of *špṭ* in that context refers to "rule" rather than "judge." It is the "royal" not the "judicial" authority which is being spoken of here. Even in the relatively late Carthaginian use of *špṭ*, there is a sense of "rule" rather than a specific judicial orientation.

The discussion of the use of שפט in the Old Testament points to the fact that it is used in several contexts. Traditionally, the use which is generally associated with שפט is judicial in connotation. However, this examination points to two other significant conclusions. First, שפט as "authority" is found in many instances in the Old Testament and second, שפט is found in several contexts in the Old Testament, within the framework of "relationship." The examples discussed earlier indicate that שפט as "relationship" involves both Yahweh and Israel on the one hand and the relationship between individuals on the other.

C. משפט

While משפט is not used in entirely the same manner as שפט, nevertheless, it finds its most significant occurrences in connection with "authority" and "relationship." Both of these uses are

Chapter IV

particularly important for the discussion on the Eighth Century prophets, precisely because both of these areas are developed as integral parts of the prophets' message. The authorities generally associated with משפט are Yahweh and the King, and this serves as a foundation on which the Eighth Century prophets expand on their idea of "authority." Most often, it is the relationship of Yahweh and King with the people which involves the use of משפט.

What is clear from the study of these three terms is the fact that they all involve the matter of authority and the concept of relationship. In these terms, the question of relationship connotes a positive element. Whether it is the relationship between Yahweh and Israel or between individuals, there are either positive acts which are noted or positive expectations which are looked for. The salvific acts of Yahweh point not only to the covenantal responsibility of Yahweh, but also includes that important element of care for his people. "Care" and "concern" are also implicit elements in the use of שפט and משפט as "relationship." Whether it is the restoration of the relationship between Abram and Sarai or Yahweh's admonition to the king of Israel to "do justice," the implication in these examples is not to create an artificial relationship or restore artificiality to a relationship but to demonstrate care and concern.

II. Occurrences of צדק and משפט together in Old Testament Contexts -Exclusive of the Eighth Century Prophets

LEVITICUS

The one occurrence of צדק and משפט together is in 19:15. This is a part of the "Holiness Code" and here Yahweh admonishes those with the responsibility of executing justice, to do so impartially.

לא תעשו עול במשפט לא-תשא פני-דל ולא תהדר
פני גדול בצדק תשפט עמיתך

משפט is used here in a judicial manner, in an active sense. צדק is the source from which the משפט should be executed. Being in צדק implies that impartiality in justice will take place. The use of צדק and משפט in this context intimates that they affect the people in a concrete way. The text clearly implies that משפט has its source in צדק (בצדק תשפט).

DEUTERONOMY

There are six instances in which צדק and משפט occur together. In 4:8; 32:4 and 33:21, צדק and משפט refer to Yahweh. Both 4:8 and 33:21 underline the nature of Yahweh's ordinances and decrees. 32:4 describes the character of Yahweh (צדיק) and his ways (משפט). In none of these instances is there any indication of a possible relationship between צדק and משפט. In 16:18 and 16:19, צדק and משפט are both used in a forensic sense. In 16:18, the judges are admonished to give "righteous judgments." While צדק is used in this instance to describe the nature of the משפט, there is no obvious relationship between the two. However, the presence of צדק and משפט in 16:19 does shed some light here in that "partiality" is seen in opposition to צדיק. In this sense, the subject matter is similar to Lev. 19:15. Once again, there is no particular relationship between צדק and משפט which is established here. Finally, in 25:1, צדק and משפט are used in a forensic sense and while the terms are clearly connected contextually, there is no ground for determining a relationship between the two.

II SAMUEL

The two occurrences are in 8:15 and 15:4. In 8:15 צדק and משפט are used as two elements which characterize David's reign over Israel. The significance of this is seen in that it implies that David is a great king (8:13, 14) and צדק and משפט are the elements which exemplify his kingship. There is no indication of a relationship between צדק and משפט, but together they are used to express the nature of the relationship which David has with his people. In this occurrence, both צדק and משפט come from David, and are used with an active overtone. The second occurrence in 15:4 involves Absalom's interest in giving צדק to those who have a cause (משפט).

I KINGS

The single occurrence is in 10:9. In a way, this occurrence is similar to the one in II Sam. 8:15. While there is the implication that David is a great king, because of צדק and משפט, Solomon is perceived by the Queen of Sheba as having been made king precisely in order to execute צדק and משפט. On this occasion, both צדק and משפט are expected to be executed, since both terms are governed by the word לעשות. There is no indication that צדק and משפט are used synonymously here nor is there any indication of a possible relationship between the two.

ISAIAH 40-66

There are seven instances in which צדק and משפט occur together. In 50:8 צדק is used to mean "vindicate" and refers to Yahweh, while משפט is used with a negative overtone to mean "adversary." While both צדק and משפט appear in this context, there is no apparent relationship between them. In 54:17, both צדק and משפט are used in a similar fashion to 50:8.

In 56:1, the prophet urges the people to listen to the words of Yahweh, to...שמרו משפט ועשו צדקה. This is in connection with the promise of salvation and deliverance by Yahweh. In this verse, again there is no indication regarding a possible relationship between צדק and משפט, but both terms are used in a context which suggest action and has practical implications. In 58:2, both צדק and משפט are used twice, but the connotation of each pair is distinct. In the first instance, Yahweh rebukes the people for acting as if they live in צדק, yet they forsake his משפט. In this context, משפט is the expectation of Yahweh and the nation cannot disregard משפט and still presume to live in צדק. In this sense, משפט comes from צדק and the neglect of the former, adversely affects the latter. The second instance in 58:2 refers to the nature of Yahweh's judgments

(משפט). צדק is in a construct relationship with משפט, that is, Yahweh gives righteous judgments (משפטי צדק).

The final two instances are in 59:9 and 59:14, and appear to be connected. Both 59:9 and 59:14 use an imagery of "space" or "distance" and in both instances צדק and משפט are said to be in the distance. A second similarity is the parallelism which is used in both contexts. In 59:9, the absence of משפט and צדק is associated with darkness (חשך) and gloom (אפלות) while it is implied that the presence of משפט and צדק brings light (אור) and brightness (נגהות). In 59:14, there is the implication that the absence of צדק and משפט has led to the ruin and disappearance of truth (אמת) and uprightness (נכחה). There is no indication in either of these occurrences that there is a possible relationship between צדק and משפט.

JEREMIAH

There are eight occurrences in which צדק and משפט are used together. These eight occurrences may be divided into four groups; in one group, צדק and משפט refer to Yahweh; second, they refer to a king; third, they refer to those who pursue wealth through injustice, fourth, they are used in the form of an oath. In 9:23[24], צדק and משפט are described as active characteristics of Yahweh. Here, there are two important elements which are noteworthy. First, in 9:22[23], the prophet speaks about the glory which is unacceptable, that is, "wisdom," "might," and "riches" of the individual. Rather, the glory which is advocated is one which knows Yahweh and which will bring people to the realization that Yahweh is a God who practises צדק and משפט. This use in 9:23[24] is somewhat reflected in 12:1, where Yahweh is described as צדיק and as one who listens to those who have a cause (משפט). Clearly, it is entirely because Yahweh is a God of צדק that he listens to these causes. While these uses give some indication of צדק and משפט as active concepts, perhaps even related in some manner, there is no indication of the nature of the relationship.

In three other occurrences (22:3; 23:5; 33:15) צדק and משפט are in reference to the monarchy. In 22:3, Yahweh makes it clear that he expects צדק and משפט from the king of Judah. The king is ex-

Chapter IV   205

pected to employ and demonstrate צדק and משפט as elements necessary for delivering the oppressed. The idea of צדק and משפט as Yahweh's expectation from a king is further testified in 23:5 and 33:15; Yahweh himself will send a king and once again the qualities which are singled out are צדק and משפט. צדק and משפט are not static qualities; salvation and security, for Judah and Israel respectively (23:6), will be as a direct result of the king's צדק and משפט.

In 4:2 צדק and משפט are used in the form of an oath, while in 22:13, Jeremiah uses הוי as a way of executing judgment on those who have pursued their own financial interests through unrighteousness and injustice. This lack of צדק and משפט is reflected in the oppression of others. The condemnation in 22:13 serves as a direct contrast to 22:15-16, where צדק and משפט, when practised, lead to the well-being of both king and subjects, according to the MT. Moreover, צדק and משפט in the life of a king, are expressed in the care and concern for the poor.

None of these four categories indicate a possible relationship between the two terms צדק and משפט. However, in all the categories, there are instances which suggest clearly that both צדק and משפט are practical factors in life.

EZEKIEL

There are seven instances in which צדק and משפט occur together. Five of these occurrences (18:5,9,19,27; 33:16) refer specifically to individual responsibility. If the individual does what is "lawful and right," and if the individual keeps the ordinances of Yahweh, then the individual will live. These occurrences do not indicate that there is any particular relationship between צדק and משפט. In 23:45, צדק and משפט are in reference to the judgments given by the righteous against those who commit adultery. Here again, there is no suggestion of a relationship between צדק and משפט. Finally, in 45:9, Yahweh admonishes the leaders to replace violence and oppression by צדק and משפט respectively. The leaders are expected to pursue actively this course. Just as violence and oppression reflect active means of suppressing the existence of the people, so צדק and משפט will actively alleviate these injustices and restore the people to an acceptable manner of living.

While none of these instances suggest a possible relationship between צדק and משפט, there is no indication of synonymity either.

HABAKKUK

The one instance in which צדק and משפט occur together is in 1:4. משפט occurs twice in this verse and on both occasions, it refers to something essential which is either absent or perverted. The cognate of צדק which is used is צדיק and here it is contrasted with the wicked. צדק and משפט, while occurring in the same verse, have no obvious relationship, and, in fact, their uses may be construed to be even detached from each other.

PSALMS

There are twenty-one instances in which צדק and משפט occur together. Nine of these (9:5 [4]; 19:10 [9];119:7, 62,75,106,137,160, 164) refer to the righteousness of Yahweh and allude specifically to his judgments and ordinances. That is to say, the ordinances and judgments of Yahweh are righteous; they are related to his nature. צדק describes both the nature of Yahweh and his acts, precisely because they are inseparable. Six other occurrences (33:5, 37:6; 89:15[14]; 97:2; 99:4;103:6) have both צדק and משפט in relation to Yahweh. There are three elements to note here. Yahweh not only loves צדק and משפט (33:5), but his throne is established in them. (89:15 [14]; 97:2) He executes צדק and משפט to the oppressed (99:4; 103:6), and for those who trust in him, he will vindicate them and bring them their right. (37:6) These examples indicate clearly, that both צדק and משפט are concepts associated with Yahweh, in a descriptive manner and in an active manner. There is no suggestion from these examples of a possible relationship between צדק and משפט.

Chapter IV

There are three occurrences (1:5; 37:30; 94:15)[2] in which צדק and משפט are used in regard to the benefit of being a צדיק. In all three instances, the צדיק will enjoy in some form, משפט, or live by it. It is clear from 1:5 that insofar as the wicked and sinners do not participate in משפט with the צדיק, משפט is thus clearly something which is set apart for the צדיק. Both 37:30 and 94:15 indicate that משפט is an element which is reflected in the צדיק, precisely, because that person is a צדיק. In these examples, there is no indication of a relationship between צדק and משפט. Whether it is a question of judgment as in 1:5 or justice in daily life as in 37:30 and 94:15, it appears that משפט is only present and available if the subject is a צדיק.

There are two occurrences in 72:1,2. It is not entirely clear whether Ps.72 is of Solomonic origin or whether it is in fact a description of Solomon's rule. What is certain, is that in 72:1 Yahweh is asked to give צדק and משפט to the king. V. 2 expresses a wish that the king might practise צדק and משפט in his rule. One of the recipients of צדק and משפט is the עני. Two points are to be noted here. First, עניי is used in this context to refer to Yahweh's poor. The inference here is that Yahweh is on the side of the poor, and the call for משפט to be given to the עני implies that this does not always happen. Second, it must be noted that both צדק and משפט, according to 72:1, have their source in Yahweh. There is no way of deciphering a relationship between צדק and משפט here, for they are both given by Yahweh and they are both expected to be used by the ruler.

צדק and משפט are also used together in 106:3. In the light of what Yahweh expects of his people, it is imperative that they practise צדק and משפט; he will not accept anything less. In this occurrence, אשרי is used in conjunction with the doing of צדק and משפט. אשרי has often been used as a parallel to הוי.[3] When הוי is used in Amos and Isaiah, it is often in the context of those who oppress

---

[2] See BHS *ad loc.* where צדיק is suggested as a better reading, with MS and versional support.

[3] See, Erhard Gerstenberger, "The Woe-Oracles of the Prophets," *JBL* 81 (1962), pp. 249-263, and Wolff, *Amos the Prophet.* trans. Foster R. McCurley (Philadelphia: Fortress Press), 1973, pp. 17ff.

the poor and needy.⁴ In this occurrence, צדק and משפט are both active qualities and the individual or community who upholds these qualities will be "blessed." Once again, there is no indication of a possible relationship between these concepts. Finally, in 119:121, צדק and משפט are spoken of as the nature of certain acts. Both צדק and משפט determine the actions of the individual, but once again there is no evidence of a relationship between the two.

JOB

The six occurrences of צדק and משפט together may be placed in two categories. In 13:18; 29:14; 34:5 and 35:2, צדק and משפט are used in contexts which speak of Job's innocence. In 13:18, Job believes that a verdict of innocence will come to him from Yahweh because of the strength of his case (משפט); this is a forensic use. In 29:14; 34:5 and 35:2, both צדק and משפט are seen to be characteristics of Job and 29:14 in particular illustrates the fact that צדק and משפט are integral to Job's life. In none of these instances is there any indication of a possible relationship between צדק and משפט.

The two other occurrences are in 8:3 and 37:23. In 8:3, as a part of his reprimand of Job for the latter's claim to innocence and being in the right, Bildad remarks that Yahweh does not pervert צדק or משפט. In neither of these two contexts is צדק and משפט used synonymously or is there evidence of a relationship between them.

PROVERBS

There are four occurrences of צדק and משפט together, and in each instance the intent is different. In 1:3, this editorial use reflects the importance of צדק and משפט in the book of Proverbs. Both צדק and משפט are areas in which the youth are instructed. In 12:5, צדק and משפט are used to describe the just (משפט) thoughts of the righteous (צדיקים). In 16:8 צדק is used in contrast to בלא משפט. Even though a little is gained in צדק, it is better than much בלא משפט. It is implied here that משפט is being used synonymously with צדק. The

---

⁴ See, e.g., Isa. 5:8, 22; 10:1-2; Amos 6:1, 4. cf. 5:18.

Chapter IV   209

final occurrence is in 21:15, where משפט is described as a joy to the
צדיק.

ECCLESIASTES

There are two occurrences, in 3:16 and 5:7[8]. In 3:16, צדק
and משפט are seen by Qoheleth, to have been replaced by wickedness. In this instance, there appears to be a somewhat tenuous
connection between צדק and משפט. Both are used in parallel to רשע
and are opposed to it, hence there is some indication that are used
synonymously in this context. In 5:7[8], צדק and משפט are singled
out as elements which might be taken away from the poor, thus
oppressing them. It is clear that both משפט and צדק are essential
for a proper means of living for the poor, but there is no indication
of a possible relationship between them.

I CHRONICLES

There is one occurrence in 18:14 and it is an exact repetition
of II Sam. 8:15. See above for discussion.

II CHRONICLES

The one occurrence in 9:8 is a repetition of I Ki. 10:9. See
above for discussion.

This examination of the occurrences of צדק and משפט together
serves to underline two important points. First, צדק and משפט have
been used both in early and later Old Testament literature; however, there is no consistency in their usage, and often then, there
appears to be no connection between "righteous ordinances" and
the "doing of justice and righteousness." There is, moreover, no
uniformity of contexts for which צדק and משפט are used together. In
differing contexts, צדק and משפט refer to characteristics or attributes of Yahweh; at other times, they express acts of Yahweh,
and on other occasions they describe the nature of the laws of

Yahweh. In addition to these, צדק and משפט express the expected behavior of the people to each other.

Second, there is no straightforward indication of a particular relationship between צדק and משפט. As is noted in the occurrences, צדק is often used as a way of describing משפט, as in righteous ordinances (משפט צדק). In this sense, perhaps, there is a relationship, but the use of construct relationships only serves to give the occasional functional pattern. What is not evident is any indication suggesting which of the two is the prior term or if the effect of one is derived from the other. There are however, three isolated examples, which might be helpful in this respect. In Lev. 19:15, there is an indirect reference to משפט having its source in צדק; in Prov.16:8 and Eccl. 3:16, there is an implication of synonymity.

This examination of the occurrences of צדק and משפט together, in the Old Testament (except the Eighth Century prophets) sets the stage for a discussion of their use in the Eighth Century prophets.

III. The Relationship between צדק and משפט in the Eighth Century Prophets

The examination thus far of צדק and משפט has demonstrated the general use of these terms in the Old Testament. Both concepts function in concrete situations and both are used to articulate in a clear manner, the notion of relationship. What is evident from this study is that צדק and משפט exist primarily as elements of relationship, both divine-human and human-human. However, to this point this study has not endeavored to show the possible connection between צדק and משפט. In order to discuss the function of these terms within the framework of the Eighth Century prophets, it is important to discern their relationship to each other, as they are used by these prophets.

There are sixteen instances in which צדק and משפט are together in the same context in the Eighth Century prophets. This is particularly notable, on realizing that צדק occurs a total of thirty-nine times and משפט thirty-eight times in these prophets. That is to say, in approximately two-fifths of all the occurrences, צדק and

משפט occur together. Only the Psalms, with twenty-one occurrences of צדק and משפט together has a higher total than the Eighth Century prophets, but, the actual percentage of this work-pair in the Psalms is less than that of the Eighth Century prophets.[5] The use of צדק and משפט in the Eighth Century prophets is integrated in an inseparable manner into the message of the prophets. Every instance in which צדק and משפט occur together in the these prophets, refers either to their absence in Israelite society and the consequences therein or to Yahweh and what is expected as behavior from his covenant people.[6]

In most of the instances in which צדק and משפט are together, the contexts and usage do not allow for a development of an understanding of the relationship between the two terms. It is obvious from the preaching of the prophets that they are not particularly interested in creating new definitions of צדק and משפט, nor are they intent on outlining the relationship between the two terms. However, this is not to suggest that a relationship does not exist. Some scholars have concluded that there is no difference in meaning between צדק and משפט and that, when they are used together, they are meant to be synonymous.[7] On the other hand, there are scholars who perceive a difference in these concepts, but whose explanation and interpretation do not extend in detail. For example, Heschel observes that, "it is exceedingly difficult to establish the exact difference in meaning of the biblical terms *mishpat,* jus-

---

[5] The Psalms have one hundred and thirty-four occurrences of צדק and sixty-four occurrences of משפט. That is, one-sixth of all occurrences of צדק are with משפט, while the percentage of occurrences of משפט with צדק is one-third.

[6] It is true that צדק for example, in these prophets, is not seen explicitly in an active sense, in reference to Yahweh (as in Deutero-Isaiah, where צדק in reference to Yahweh generally conveys the idea of "deliverance" or "salvation") nevertheless, its relation to Yahweh makes his expectation clear.

[7] See e.g. Pedersen, who does not argue extensively for the synonymity of צדק and משפט, but who nevertheless notes that, "*mishpāṭ* right, justice, virtually means the same as *ṣedhek*. Both expressions inform us of the state of the soul and the resulting relation to other souls." *Israel I-II.* p. 352. See also Sidney Rooy, "Righteousness and Justice," *ERT* 6 (1982). Commenting on the use of צדק and משפט in Amos, Rooy says, "Amos in a typically hebraic, poetic way uses justice (*mishpat*) and righteousness (*tsedaqah*) as synonyms." p. 263. Rooy goes on to conclude "justice is righteousness and righteousness is justice." p. 265.

tice and *tsedakah*, righteousness (which in parallelism are often used as variants). However, it seems that justice is a mode of action, righteousness a quality of the person. Significantly, the noun derived from *shafat* (to judge) is *shofet* which came to mean a judge or arbitrator; while the noun from *tsadak* (to be just) is *tsaddik*, a righteous man."[8] While Heschel's observation regarding justice as a "mode of action" and righteousness as a "quality of the person" is perceptive, his explanation of the general meaning and connotation of צדק and משפט does not capture fully the essence of the terms. It is clearly an oversimplification to reduce צדק and משפט, even with his distinction, to the realm of judicial activity.[9]

Moreover, there are scholars who have recognized the essential elements which unite צדק and משפט. Koch points to a fundamental aspect of the relationship between צדק and משפט, when he notes that, "both *mišpāṭ* and *ṣᵉdāqā* appear as spheres of power which already exist in advance of human actions."[10] Even though Koch does not pursue this point at any length, it is nevertheless a valid one and the correct point of departure for initiating a discussion on the functional relationship between צדק and משפט as they are used in the Eighth Century prophets. Mays stretches this point of Koch's even further when he says that צדק and משפט express the quintessence of Yahweh's will.[11] Moreover, Mays observes, regarding Amos's use of צדק and משפט, that "Amos coordinates *mišpāṭ* so closely with *ṣᵉdāqa* because the latter is the source of the former; *mišpāṭ* is the fruit of *ṣᵉdāqā*."[12] Mays' assertion regarding this relationship is surely one which has merit, but he does not substantiate his observation by proceeding with examples, nor does he give a relevant discussion. Furthermore, Mays appears to weaken his assertion by suggesting that, "*mišpāṭ* means the judicial process of establishing in a case before the court what

---

[8] Heschel, *The Prophets*, pp. 200-201.
[9] See conclusion regarding use of שפט as discussed in Chapter 2 of this study.
[10] Klaus Koch, *The Prophets* I, p. 58.
[11] See, James Luther Mays, *Amos*. OTL (Philadelphia: Westminster Press), 1969, p. 92. Also, Jean-Luc Vesco, "Amos de Teqoa, défenseur de l'homme," *RB* 87 (1980), pp. 481-513. Vesco notes, "Les deux termes expriment la quintessence de la volonté divine." p. 497.
[12] Mays, *Amos*, p. 92.

Chapter IV 213

the right is (and therefore who is in the right), and rendering that opinion as the judgement of the court."[13]

Immediately noticeable from the scholarly views expressed here, is the diversity of opinion, the lack of consensus, not to mention the lack of unanimity and the realization that much more needs to be said by way of understanding and relating these concepts.[14] The following discussion is an attempt to discern the relationship between these concepts as they appear in the Eighth Century prophets. Four examples of contexts in which צדק and משפט appear together, will be examined. The examples are particularly helpful in showing the relationship between צדק and משפט.

A. Amos 5:7

> Ah, you that turn justice (משפט) to wormwood and
> bring righteousness (צדק) to the ground!

In discussing the use of צדק and משפט together here, it is essential that the imagery be understood correctly. The clue lies in the prophet's reference to those who have wantonly discarded צדק. From the context, it is evident that at one time Israel had צדק or, as Koch more aptly puts it, "the Israelite did not *possess* righteousness; he was *in ṣedāqā*."[15] What is clear is that Israel was in a specific and special relationship which was bonded in צדק. Thus, when צדק is thrown to the ground, there is the image of Israel disrobing itself of that which has kept and sustained it in a special relationship with Yahweh. The casting away of צדק becomes the point at which Israel has rejected the binding element with Yahweh. The relationship is not annulled, but it is broken.

With the discarding of צדק, it is inevitable that משפט will be affected adversely. Even though Mays points out that משפט is the prior word in these word-pairs in Amos,[16] nevertheless, in this in-

---

[13] Ibid, p. 132. The discussion of שפט and משפט in chapters 2 and 3 of this study, suggests that Mays' conclusion is not entirely convincing.
[14] See, Koch, *The Prophets* I, p. 58.
[15] Ibid., p. 58.
[16] Mays, *Amos*, p. 92.

stance it is imperative that the use of צדק be understood first. Mays asserts that the word-order of these concepts is important, and he establishes his assertion on the word order of צדק and משפט as they appear in the MT of Amos, and he maintains this order as the basis of a cause and effect relationship between צדק and משפט. Mays further presupposes that in Amos 5:7, "the cry seeks the attention of all those who turn justice (*mišpāṭ*) into wormwood and thereby discard righteousness (*ṣᵉdāqā*) as something worthless."[17] This view suggests that it is the corruption of משפט which consequently leads to the rejection of צדק. Initially this may give the appearance of a logical movement, however it is difficult if not impossible to argue that Israel was always in צדק until the time of the perversion of משפט. If Israel were constantly in צדק, then משפט would not be corrupted. In order for the corruption of משפט to transpire, Israel must already have abandoned צדק. In effect, צדק is the prior word and it is out of צדק that משפט has its force.

While Amos 5:7 is rendered in the NRSV as, "Ah, you that turn justice to wormwood and bring righteousness to the ground," a more suitable interpretation might be: "In bringing righteousness to the ground, you have turned justice into wormwood." (See below, discussion of Amos 6:12) Clearly this does not correspond to the grammatical Hebrew structure of the MT, but it enables us to diagnose the relationship between the two words. It allows us to realize that the act of rejecting צדק is precisely that factor which is directly responsible for the transformation of that which is necessary for sustaining a relationship (משפט) into that which leads to calamity and death (לענה).

B. Amos 5:24

> But let justice (משפט) roll down like waters and
> righteousness (צדקה) like an everflowing stream.

It is the imagery in this verse which is the element that facilitates the understanding of the relationship between צדק and משפט.

---

[17] Ibid., p. 91.

Chapter IV

There is a tendency to conclude and a danger in so doing that since both צדק and משפט are expressed in terms of water imagery in the same context, they are synonymous. Naturally, this would be superficial for while "water" appears to a make them synonymous, it is "water" which distinguishes them and provides the basis for the relationship. The consciousness of movement, constancy, dynamism, liveliness is powerfully expressed here. The imagery of water is particularly suitable as there is the underlying realization that there could be stagnancy or for that matter a drought. While there is an inherent danger in dissecting an imagery, nevertheless, there is something to be said about pursuing the water imagery here in order to discern the relationship between משפט and צדק.

The idea of משפט "tumbling over" or "cascading"[18] paints a picture of משפט as a waterfall and thus presupposes that there is a source out of which it comes. Anyone who has seen a powerful waterfall realizes that its majestic fall, its power, its ability to be perennial are all determined by the source of the water. It is with this in mind that the description of צדק takes on particular importance. In this occurrence, צדק is portrayed as an "ever-flowing stream," which is precisely what is necessary in order to keep משפט "tumbling down." In other words, the constancy and power of משפט are derived from צדק. This imagery of water makes it clear that משפט and צדק necessarily exist together. There cannot be משפט without a source, and likewise, if there is perennial צדק, it will, by its nature continue to flow. The absence of one presupposes the absence of the other, or at least affects its presence. It is no surprise therefore, that there is no instance in the Eighth Century prophets where the absence of צדק is denounced, but where משפט is present. Conversely, there is no occurrence which points out that משפט is present but not צדק. While the use of משפט and צדק in Amos 5:24 indicates (from this discussion) a cause and effect relationship, it must be noted that this does not epitomize all occurrences

---

[18] See, Hans Walter Wolff, *Joel and Amos.* trans. Waldemar Janzen et al. (Philadelphia: Fortress Press), 1979, p. 259.

of this word-pair. However, what it does epitomize is the necessity for the co-existence of צדק and משפט.¹⁹

C. Amos 6:12b

> But you have turned justice (משפט) into poison
> and the fruit of righteousness (צדקה) into wormwood.

This is perhaps the one instance in the Eighth Century prophets which gives the clearest indication of the relationship between משפט and צדק. Even though both משפט and צדק are used in this context, the prophet is primarily preoccupied with משפט, the perversion of it. Amos 6:12a: "Do horses run on rocks? Does one plow the sea with oxen?" points to the dramatic transformation of Israelite society, for now even the impossible is possible. This theme is closely connected with Amos's criticism of the perversion of משפט; the perversion and destruction of משפט was once assumed to be impossible, but Israelite society has managed to do the impossible. As he did in 5:7, Amos's primary concern is to indicate the extremity of the perversion and this is demonstrated poignantly through the use of "poison" and "wormwood." The first line of 6:12b voices the prophet's words regarding the radical transformation of משפט. In essence, the second line of 6:12b is a repetition of the previous line. In this regard, it is necessary once again to reflect on the words of Amos 5:7. There, it is noted without being shrouded in imagery, that משפט has been turned into wormwood. The parallel between the two verses is revealing.

ההפכים ללענה משפט (Amos 5:7)
כי הפכתם...ופרי צדקה ללענה (Amos 6:12b)

---

[19] See, Paul Ramsey, "Elements of a Biblical Political Theory," *JR* 29 (1949). On Amos 5:24, Ramsey concludes: "here plainly justice must be understood as the same thing as righteousness, expressed differently in poetic parallel lines." p. 275. Ramsey's view is untenable, as it overlooks the relationship between the two concepts and simply relegates their use together as poetic.

In 6:12b, וּפְרִי צְדָקָה is used as a synonym for מִשְׁפָּט, and thus Amos declares on both occasions that something has been turned into wormwood. It is clear from 6:12b that it is not צְדָקָה itself, but the fruit of צְדָקָה which is being corrupted.

Amos's use of צְדָקָה in 6:12b is entirely as a point of departure for recognizing the corruption of מִשְׁפָּט. In so doing however, the prophet invites us to witness the integral relationship between מִשְׁפָּט and צֶדֶק. Being described as "the fruit of צְדָקָה," it is manifestly apparent that מִשְׁפָּט is not the prior element. Amos conceives of צֶדֶק as that which bears or gives rise to the possibility of מִשְׁפָּט in the community, as prior.

D. Isaiah 28:17a

> And I will make justice (מִשְׁפָּט) the line,
> and righteousness (צְדָקָה) the plummet.

The use of מִשְׁפָּט and צְדָקָה in this context may conceivably be the clearest example in Isaiah of the relationship between these concepts. The architectural imagery[20] which is employed here is particularly useful in aiding the determination of the relationship between מִשְׁפָּט and צֶדֶק. מִשְׁפָּט is described as "the line" and צְדָקָה as "the plummet" and both "line and plummet" are engaged in the establishing of equilibrium of balance. In order to do so, each has to function in its own right, yet together they constitute an intrinsic unity. The unity between the two is not predicated on both being uniform in their function and being. The function of the "line" and the "plummet" illustrate not only the basic purpose of מִשְׁפָּט and צֶדֶק, but also the relationship between the two. This reference in Isa. 28:17a makes it clear that in order for there to be equity in a society, both צְדָקָה and מִשְׁפָּט must be in tandem and work together. The metaphors of "line" and "plummet" suggest that the presence of one without the other renders it incapable of proper functioning. They are both indispensable for the functioning of the other.

---

[20] See, R.E. Clements, *Isaiah 1-39*. NCBC (London: Marshall, Morgan and Scott), 1980, p. 231.

צדק as the משקלת, by its nature and function will determine the accuracy and correctness of what is to be allotted. When the משקלת has completed its function, then the קן is able to allocate correctly. If the קן is used first or by itself, then the accuracy of the measurement will in all likelihood be faulty. As the element which is responsible for correctness and accuracy, צדק becomes the prior article. It is true that the imagery of משקלת and קן creates a picture of rigidity, but this is not to suggest stagnancy and legalism but propriety and correctness.

The relationship between משפט and צדק in this context also contains one additional element which compounds both the nature and importance of the relationship. Here משפט and צדק are woven into the elements associated with the covenant of Yahweh. In Isa. 28:14ff, the prophet notes that the rulers have made a covenant with Sheol, which immediately presupposes the rejection of Yahweh's covenant. When Yahweh re-establishes משפט and צדק among his people, the covenant with Sheol will be annulled. In order to restore Israel from its state of apostasy, the establishment of צדק and משפט is essential. What is clear is that the restoration of Yahweh's covenant is inexorably connected to צדק and משפט.

The discussion of these four instances, in which צדק and משפט occur together provides evidence which indicates several factors about the relationship of these concepts. First, it is clear that there is a distinction between the use of the concepts, and they are not intended to be synonymous. Moreover, there is indeed a relationship between these concepts as they are used in the Eighth Century prophets. Second, the incontrovertible evidence suggests that neither צדק nor משפט can exist without the other. Inevitably when צדק disappears from the community, משפט follows, and restoration comes with the appearance of צדק first, followed by משפט. Third, it has become evident that משפט is not a self-authenticating concept, but צדק authenticates it. That is to say, צדק is the element which bonds the individual, the community, the nation with Yahweh in a covenant relationship. The presence of צדק presupposes that משפט will also be present and function in a manner which reflects its relationship to צדק. In a sense, משפט functions in a manner similar to that of a parent. Once an individual has become a parent, thus establishing a special relationship, there are expectations both from the parent and from the child. One may suggest that parent and child, now that they by nature and necessity live with each other, do not constantly ask whether a good deed, or thought should be bestowed on the other. The nature of the relationship precludes questions such as these. It is irrelevant to ask whether they *should* love each other. Likewise, once צדק establishes the relationship, the question of משפט is naturally assumed; it is never relevant to determine whether משפט is engaged in the relationship. Regardless of the situation, it is צדק that is the prior term and does the establishing of any relationship, and משפט follows, and sustains this relationship.

One final example will suffice here. In Isa. 1:21, the prophet laments the fact that at one time צדק lodged in Israel,[21] but now murderers have taken the place of צדק. When צדק was in Israel, there was משפט, it was "full of משפט." However with the rejection of צדק, משפט also disappeared. Now instead of צדק, there is מרצחים (murderers), and it is not surprising that the absence of משפט directly corresponds to מרצחים with the presence of משפח (bloodshed) ((Isa. 5:7). The corresponding term here is particularly helpful, precisely because there is something of a cause and effect relationship which is outlined. When there is צדק, משפט follows and likewise when there are מרצחים, משפח follows, which is of course a natural consequence.

Before we go to the discussion of צדק and משפט with regards to social critique, a brief look at the role and function of the Eighth Century prophets will set the stage for understanding the prophets' message.

---

[21] See, N.W. Porteous, "The Basis of the Ethical Teaching of the Prophets" in *Studies in Old Testament Prophecy*. ed. H.H. Rowley (Edinburgh: T and T Clark), 1950, pp. 143-156. Regarding the use of צדק in this context, Porteous notes that, "it is not inconceivable that the Hebrew conception of צדק, so prominent in the prophetic oracles, bears some relation to the pre-Israelite cult of El-Elyon in Jerusalem, a deity who...was probably regarded as a personification of צדק. If this were so, there would be a special significance in the fact that Isaiah speaks of Jerusalem as the city in which righteousness once lodged and which may again becomes the city of righteousness." p. 155.

Chapter V

The Role and Function of the Eighth Century Prophets

This is hardly a new question, yet it is one which continues to have widespread interest as these prophets maintain a contemporary relevance within church, the larger society and scholarly circles. Given this, it is important to reflect on some of the roles which have been assigned to them.

In an attempt to determine the role and function of the Eighth Century prophets it is essential they be not placed into any strait jacket of contemporary systematization. Neither the prophets nor their message can be reduced to fulfilling prescriptive norms or standards which have been designed retrospectively. A perusal of the prophets' message testifies to the fact that their message was not delivered and shaped to fit certain norms. The prophets are not systematic theologians and therefore their message cannot be taken and studied as systematic theology.[1] Indeed, the category of "Eighth Century" overlooks many distinctive features of these prophets.

The fact that these are prophets who preached in the same century hardly qualifies them to be contemporaries, but that is the category which has been ascribed to them. It would be as if in the next century, all the US presidents of the 20th century will be placed into a large pot and melted together. Needless to say, if this were done a warped sense of history will be espoused.

To be sure, there are many similarities in the message of the prophets, nevertheless their different foci point to the spontaneous and contextual nature of their message. While we have inherited their message as part of scripture, it was first delivered within a particular time in history to a particular people. And while the prophets employ well known conventions, they can no more be classified as adherents of a set standard and their message be un-

---

[1] See, Gene M. Tucker, "The Role of the Prophets and the Role of the Church," *QR* (Winter 1981), pp. 5-22. Tucker notes that "the prophets were not theologians, but their message contain and are founded upon powerful theological content which is difficult to ignore." p.13.

derstood from this angle, than someone who employs the rhyming couplet be heralded a protégé of Alexander Pope.

Further, a basic presupposition among scholars today is that not all the words which we find in the text can be ascribed to the prophets. This naturally only serves to compound the problem, because the system of redaction and refinement not only creates textual and redactional speculation, but adds an element of incoherency to the already complicated interpretive issue.

It is therefore evident that the question of placing the prophets in well rounded categories is impossible. Depending on the emphasis which is placed, the prophets have been called "ethicists," "revolutionaries," "reformers," "traditionalists," "Yahwists," "poets," among others. This wide range of possibilities in itself underlines the difficulty which exists. Clearly to posit the prophets as exclusively, or even primarily one of these, is to run the risk of overlooking significant textual evidence which might indicate differing notions.

It is the hope that this brief overview will serve two main functions. First, it seeks to demonstrate the multifaceted nature of the prophets, and second it might question rigorously those arguments which seek to reduce the prophets as one dimensional and again bring this issue in the main arena of biblical scholarship. If only for the sake of Old Testament scholarship, these points are important, but moreso they are consequential for the implications of the prophets' message for the church and its relation to society. I shall look briefly at five different categories and indicate the salient features of the arguments which have been proposed.

A. The Prophets as Social Reformers

The reform of Israel's society has been perceived by many scholars to be the central focus of the prophets' message. This direction is shaped in large part by the sharp invectives which are hurled by the prophets against those who would treat unjustly members of the covenant community. Involuntarily, the proponent of this view is encumbered with the presuppositions of contemporary or at least recent reformers. Several scholars, with varying conditions support this theory.

To some degree, this position is in response to Julius Wellhausen, who some one hundred years ago, proposed that the prophets were creators and innovators of the faith of Israel.[2] Donald Williams suggests that in fact these prophets," are to be regarded more correctly as 'reformers,' attempting to bring Israel back to its theological heritage, which was grounded in the Mosaic covenant. Amos is one of the first of the 'reformers;' however Amos is not a systematic theologian....Moreover Amos speaks with the radical dictum of a reformer, not working out the logical conclusions of his theology."[3]

This argument is predicated on the premise that Amos and other Eighth Century prophets already had a theological and experiential foundation on which their preaching was established. In effect they did not institute anything new but rather, they served simply as prodding instruments of reform. What therefore was important for the prophets was the concern to keep alive the traditions of ancient Israel. "While Amos does not quote the Decalogue, the interpreter of Amos immediately is cognizant of the fact that his strident denunciations find their source in Mosaic law."[4]

In addition to this view, others interpreters have suggested that the use of certain terms and words point to a borrowing from already existing traditions. Arvid Kapelrud observes that, "the very important expressions 'good' (ṭob) and 'evil' (rå') are not explained at all, nor is 'justice' [mišpaṭ]. Amos presupposes that these terms and what they imply are known to his audience. He could not have done so if he had intended to bring something new....What the prophet wanted was to see the people live together in the way

---

[2] See Julius Wellhausen, *Prolegomena to the History of Ancient Israel* (New York: The Meridian Library) 1957, pp. 473-474. See also Ernest Nicholson, "Israelite Religion in the Pre-exilic Period: A Debate Reviewed" in *A Word in Season*. eds. James D. Martin and Philip Davies (Sheffield: JSOT Press) 1986, pp. 3-34. Nicholson re-examines Wellhausen's thesis in the light of recent inquiry and suggests that greater merit is to be given to it than that which has been given in the last 50 years.

[3] See, Donald L. Williams, "The Theology of Amos," *RE* 63 (1966), p. 393.

[4] Ibid., p. 394

they had done...according to ancient principles....[5] Like Williams, Kapelrud clearly presupposes that there is something to which Israel must return, and this then is the focus of the prophets' message.

Still others suggest that it is the social legislation of the Pentateuch that is foremost in the mind of the prophet. Many of the laws which govern and shape the various aspects of life are seen to be virtually salvatory in nature. The destruction of the laws therefore is assumed to be responsible for the demise of the society and the fundamental reason for the prophetic critique.

John Lucal intimates, that on one hand, the legislation of the Pentateuch, with its prohibition of alienation of land, the charge of interest on loans, its prescription for the indigent to have the remains of the harvest, a year for rest and remission of debts, and the freeing of slaves after six years is incorporated into Israel's society as measures which would sustain the balance among the different categories of individuals.[6] According to Lucal, "this program aimed at reducing inequalities of wealth and reducing social distress, as well as preserving a bit of democratic egalitarianism which Israel had known in the nomadic period."[7]

On the other hand with the establishment of the monarchy, many of the legislations which shaped the identity of the people were neglected or forgotten. The monetary flow created a taste for luxury and this coupled with the increasing chasm between the powerful and the powerless, led inexorably to the widening of the gap between the rich and the poor; the inequalities were sure to follow and indeed they did.

Proponents of this position contend that the movement away from the pentateuchal legislation and the rise of the monarchy together with the inevitable class distinctions occupied the attention

---

[5] Arvid S. Kapelrud, *Central Ideas in Amos* (Oslo: Universitetsforlaget) 1961, p. 66

[6] See John A. Lucal, "God of Justice: The Prophets as Social Reformers," *TBT* 32 (1967), pp. 2221-2228. See also Joseph G. Bailey, "Amos: Preacher of Social Reform," *TBT* 19 (1981), pp. 306-313. Although Bailey does not discuss or even mention the principles of social reform, he nevertheless views Amos as a social reformer.

[7] Lucal, p. 2222.

of the prophets most of all. Lucal takes his position one step further. "That the prophets were social reformers is further attested to by the influence which their writings have had on Jewish thought ever since. It is a commonplace in American political history and sociology that the prophetic tradition has held the vast majority of American Jews to espouse programs of social legislation such as the New Deal."[8]

Moreover, he suggests that if "social reformers are univocally equated with secularist and humanitarian liberals who have specific plans for social progress, then the prophets cannot be put in this category....At the other extreme, if social reformers are only those who subordinate the social and political to the moral order and insist on the necessity for a supernatural regeneration of society before true justice can be achieved, the prophets can be classified as social reformers, provided that no specific plan of progress be required."[9]

Some observations are necessary at this point. The concept of reform by its very nature presupposes at least two basic premises. First, reform entails the removal of abuses or the misuse of power, and it could be that the object of reform has some antecedent from which there has been some departure. Thus, reform has to do with the return to a particular basis. Second, reform involves not only the return to an ideal, but a program which invariably departs from the historical ideal. Thus, a social reformer might be regarded as one who has a specific program which seeks to return to an existing institution in a corrected form.

The twentieth century christian church attests this. Not only did the 16th century reformers such as Luther and Calvin strike out against many of the practices and traditions of the church in their day, but while they sought to recover the elements which characterized it, they also implemented new ideals which set them apart from the establishment. Reformation by its nature involves elements both of the old and the new. Given these general expectations and orientation of reformers, it is apparent that the

---

[8] Ibid., p. 2222.
[9] Ibid., p. 2227.

Eighth Century prophets were not inclined in this specific direction. Others have suggested that the absence of new programs or laws or even solutions that detail particular programs invalidate the notion of the prophets as reformers.[10]

Still, others point out that the issues in the society were so deeply embedded in the psyche of the people that reform was not even a viable option. To be sure this is something of an educated guess, for while the society faced the critical matter of its identity, one cannot be sure that the death of the society was what was necessary.[11] While the extremity of this view can certainly be challenged, the point is well taken, for the people seemed to be beyond reform, and in any event, there is no indication that the prophets were called to reform. In this regard, there are two texts in Amos which are relevant for consideration.

> And I raised up some of your children to be prophets,
> and some of your youths to be nazarites.
> Is it not indeed so, O people of Israel? says the Lord.
> But you made the nazarites drink wine,
> and commanded the prophets saying,
> "You shall not prophesy." (2:11-12)

Moreover, the prophets make it clear that God had tried many different ways in which to reform the people and their ways, and in each of these, the people turned their backs. Amos 6: 6-11 spells this out very clearly; the refrain of "you did not return to me" expresses powerfully the obstinacy of the people to any kind of reform of their lives and indeed of the society.

---

[10] James Luther Mays, "Justice: Perspectives from the Prophetic Tradition," *Interp* 37 (1983), pp. 16-17. See also H. Eberhard von Waldow, "Social Responsibility and Social Structure in Early Israel," *CBQ* 32 (1970), pp. 182-204. Von Waldow notes, "The prophets do not proclaim a kind of new social reform program. Rather, they recognize the deteriorated social and economic situation of their present and match it against the will of God...." p. 203. A similar view is espoused by John Bright, *Jeremiah*. AB (New York: Doubleday) 1965, p. xvi.

[11] Klaus Koch, "Origin and Effect of Social Critique of the Pre-exilic Prophets," *BTF* 11 (1979), p. 94.

B. The Prophets as Revolutionaries

While the idea of reform would tend to link the tradition with a new program, the idea of revolution, by it nature rejects existing institutions and replaces them with new ones. Or at least revolutionaries call for the replacement of the status quo. Martin Cohen has argued that the prophets have to be understood from a "sociopolitical typology" which presupposes that the prophets are not loners in their execution of their task. In sustaining this thesis, he postulates that the prophets are supported, if not maintained, by structures, implying some sort of following. Accordingly, he asserts that, "without the megaphone of structure, even the most cogent voices are muffled. When such loners can be heard, they are regarded by the establishment as mere nuisances and shunted off unheeded into expedient oblivion. Rarely do loners have an opportunity to deliver themselves of their ideas at official gatherings such as those in which in Amos, Isaiah, Jeremiah and also, almost most certainly Hosea and Micah participated."[12]

Intrinsic to the position by Cohen, is the fact that the prophets are successful only insofar as they are supported by systemic structures of some sort. Consequently, Cohen would say that this is the reason why prophets such as Amos and Micah among others were not martyred; their structural and corporate power prevented such an event. Moreover, that they were involved both in government and Temple also indicate their status as revolutionaries. "Among the Biblical Hebrews, Temple and government were merely different dimensions of a single organism of state, with the Temple serving as the major ceremonial center of the polity. Within the Temple, the cult was the quintessential sociopolitical symbol, the flag, so to speak, of the ideals and the hopes of the united society."[13] In effect then the critique of one was essentially a critique of the other. The words of Amos in 7:10-13 which might

---

[12] Martin A. Cohen, "The Prophets as Revolutionaries," *BAR* 5 (iii 1979), p.16.
[13] Ibid., p. 16.

ordinarily be considered as treason is perceived as words of a revolutionary. Cohen encapsulates his argument thus:

> ...they were in fact revolutionaries. As such they were interested not in the correction but in the overthrow of what they regarded to be a corrupt government. If they were revolutionaries, the indictment of the cult was not objective but symbolic; that is, what they said of the cult, they meant for the national government. Since their plan for the national government was its dissolution, their symbolic articulation of this goal could have called for nothing less than the dissolution of the cult.[14]

Some observations are necessary at this point. Cohen's arguments which typify proponents of the revolutionary theory are based entirely on the premise that the prophets were intent on abolishing some of the institutions of ancient Israel. With this as a fundamental presupposition, it is easy to follow the argument of Cohen and others with a similar view. Because revolutionaries have traditionally replaced existing institutions with new ones and in so doing they themselves become part of the new establishment, Cohen argues that, that is also the case with the prophets.

To reduce the prophets to being revolutionaries and members of the establishment surely is an oversimplification; indeed one may suggest that the prophetic office is narrowed considerably with this kind of perspective. Even the basic premise in this position is imprecise. It is not at all a consensus that the prophets were seeking the abolition of the cult. Moreover, even if this were true, other elements in the argument are speculative. Cohen's sociopolitical analysis of the prophets' need for a structure misjudges the prophetic role and indeed the notion of the call by Yahweh.

Even if one were to argue that there was a structure on whom the Eighth Century prophets depended, and these consisted primarily of those for whom the prophets advocated, still this proposition would not be enhanced. While the marginalized of the

---

[14] Ibid., p. 16.

society would be most logical structural force, still their voice and potency would not in themselves be much support. This position would also intimate that the prophets themselves lacked power, and had it not been for the structure which Amos had at his side, Amaziah would have had him executed. (Amos 7:10)

This view is clearly untenable, and the overall orientation is much too influenced and shaped by a methodology which is distinctively contemporary. As Mays suggests, "the [prophets] were not...political activists or revolutionaries....Their concentration on the demand for change in the lives of the people and their trust in the work of God in overturning the old impossibilities to make way for the new was too unrelieved."[15]

One must however acknowledge that the message of the prophets was revolutionary in the light of the situation that was prevalent at the time. Perhaps also, because of the baggage which this word now carries, it can hardly accurately capture the essence of the prophetic role. The Eighth Century prophets were not guerrillas or even for matter anti status quo *per se*.

C. The Prophets as Traditionalists

Many scholars support the theory that the prophets were fundamentally preservers of the traditions of ancient Israel. Primarily the concern in this view is to show that the prophets are so inextricably tied to the traditions of Israel that their message can only have credibility when viewed as a call to renew and restore the neglected traditions. Hence, Albrektson suggests that, "the deepest motive underlying the political statements of the prophets were not political but religious, rooted in the holy traditions which

---

[15] Mays, "Justice...." p. 17. See also B. Alger, "The Theology and Social Ethic of Amos," *Scripture* 17(1965), pp. 109-116. Alger observes that, "The prophets were not...revolutionaries trying to overthrow the established order...." p.111. Also, Edmund Jacob, "The Biblical prophets: Revolutionaries or Conservatives," *Interp* 19 (1965), pp. 45-47. Jacob notes that, "there are considerable differences between the revolutionary orators and the biblical prophets. The prophets do not call the crowds...to rise up against a tyrant or against an unjust social order." p. 49.

formed the religious foundation of the Israelite state."16 The Exodus tradition is referred to often as manifesting the dependence of the prophets on the central act of the life of ancient Israel. For example, in the case of Amos, he is perceived to be dependent on the Exodus tradition because he refers to the saving power and providence of Yahweh (2:9-11); his reminder to Israel regarding Yahweh's elective grace (3:1b-2), and his view of Yahweh as a creator God. (9:7) References such as these are also found in Hosea, where the grace of God is noted (9:10; 11:1; 13:5), and a reference to the beginning of the relationship between Yahweh and Israel. (12:10[9]; 13:4) While Isaiah does not appear to rely much on the Exodus tradition, nevertheless he is perceived to have "maintained a firmer contact with the traditional modes of thought and feeling than did either of his eighth century predecessors."17

From this position it would seem that the prophets are held within certain traditional limitations or boundaries. Moreover the reference to, and the use of tradition, suggest a dependence on tradition. The message of the prophets is therefore shaped in varying degrees by the traditions which they inherited. One of the main trends in this school of thought is the tracing of the prophetic message to the rootage in the tradition. So, as Henton Davies notes, "the presence in the J and E documents of ideas later to be found in the prophets, confirms the probability of their dependence upon the tradition."18

However the dependence which is advocated does not end with the realization that there are traces of traditional elements but proceeds to assert that the message of the Eighth Century prophets is in fact shaped Israel's tradition. Von Rad champions this position and adverts, "that the eighth century prophets must already have fallen heir to a certain tradition, a heritage which

---

16 Bertil Albrektson, "Prophecy and Politics in the Old Testament" in *The Myth of the State*, ed. Haralds Biezais (Stockholm: Almquist and Wiksell), 1972, p. 55.
17 G. Henton Davies, "The Yahwistic Tradition in the Eighth Century Prophets" in *Studies in Old Testament Prophecy*, ed. H. Rowley (Edinburgh: T&T Clark), 1950, p. 41.
18 Ibid., p. 44.

furnished them with the subjects on which the prophets spoke."[19] Von Rad assumes that the common elements in Amos and Isaiah indicate that to a great extent, the prophetic way of Isaiah was already paved for him by Amos. Likewise, the way for Amos is already paved for him by his predecessors, though, of course of these there is no written record. In any event the Exodus tradition which is seen to have influenced Amos suffices to express the dependence on tradition.

This position leaves considerable space for critique. There seems to be a subjection of the prophets' message to a prescribed norm. There are numerous examples in history (e.g., in literature and music) where certain original forms have become axiomatic. It would be an oversimplification to suggest that anyone who is exposed to and uses an established literary or musical form will be classified as being in debt to the initiator of that particular form. There is no doubt that the Eighth Century prophets preached on subjects which were not new to the people; however to say that they were "furnished with subjects" subordinates both their call and message to a prescribed convention. A study of the Eighth Century prophets in the light of other Old Testament literature clearly disputes this.

It is noteworthy that both Amos and Isaiah are particularly knowledgeable of the cult and monarchy respectively. Some scholars even believe that Amos was part of the cult.[20] While not impossible, it is highly improbable that Amos would be a part of the cult and yet become so extremely critical of Israel's cultic affairs. The assertion of these scholars must be viewed within the context of the prophet's call. The point is that the "call" must be taken seriously and not be understood as a mere sanctioning of the status quo. The differences in the prophets' call experience attest the distinctiveness of their call; it is entirely possible that "cleansing" may

---

[19] Gerhard von Rad, *Old Testament Theology* II. Trans. D. M. G. Stalker. (Edinburgh: Oliver and Boyd), 1965, p. 149.
[20] A. S. Kapelrud, *Central Ideas*, p. 70. See also Ivan Engnell, *Studies in Divine Kingship in the Ancient Near East* (Oxford: Basil Blackwell), 1967, p. 87 and John Gray, *I and II Kings*, p. 434. Cf. G. H. Jones *I and II Kings*. NCBC (London: Marshall, Morgan and Scott), 1984, p. 393.

not be the decisive point in determining the prophets' involvement in, or abstention from the traditions. James Williams rightly contends that, "a position within or without any of the voluntary or involuntary associations of society is no certain clue to one's self-understanding or ideology, or vice-versa."[21]

One expects that a prophet of Israel would echo traditional elements in his preaching, but that hardly suggests dependence. This is apparent, for example in Amos's critique of the society; there is no clarion call for the preservation of Israelite laws, though clearly the laws of Exod. 22-23 are presupposed in his preaching. Amos, like his contemporaries never launches into a discussion of the efficacy of the laws; that is never his intention. Knowledge of the traditions, versus dependence must be distinguished. Amos's words in fact mirror his concern that the people were using the laws as façades behind which to hide; these fortifications were standing in the way of doing what was right. This is particularly evident in the critique of the cult by all of the Eighth Century prophets. The people were worshipping in a way which subscribed to all the traditions, but worship remained meaningless and empty.

There is in fact much that is new in the prophets' message. It is to expected that an element of Israel's history would be reflected in the prophets' message, but it would be inaccurate to say that the prophets were preaching for a return to the practice of divine law. But it is not only the legal tradition that is in dispute here. Some scholars have argued that the wisdom tradition is the background and basis from much of the preaching of the Eighth Century prophets.[22] Koch who opposes this view, contends that, "the attitude of the sages of Israel towards the poor is ambiguous. The poor demand charity but otherwise he is the cause of his own poverty and therefore deserves his destiny."[23] Koch's point spells out one of the difficulties in insisting on the wisdom tradition as a back-

---

[21] James G. Williams, "The Social Location of Israelite Prophecy," *JAAR* 37 (1969), p. 156.
[22] See, in particular Hans Walter Wolff, *Amos the Prophet* (Philadelphia: Fortress Press), 1973, and Johannes Fichtner, "Jesaja unter den Weisen," *Th. Lz* 74 (1949), pp. 75-80.
[23] Koch, "Origin and Effect...." p. 97.

ground for the prophetic message against social injustice. For example, Prov. 22:22 states, "Do not rob the poor (*dal*) because they are poor (*dal*) or crush the afflicted('*ani*) at the gate." On the other hand, Prov. 10:4 says, "A slack hand causes poverty, but the hand of the diligent makes rich." The ambiguity is self-evident.

One cannot overlook the use of the tradition, for in a real sense it serves to bring the prophet in touch with the audience. This is essential not only for the recognition of the common heritage, but more importantly to jolt the people into the realization and acknowledgment of their ways. Hence, many of the images and metaphors which are used are well known, but the message is not a repetition of traditional axioms.[24] Norman Porteous subscribes to the view that the prophets were not traditionalists and gives a probable reason for his assertion. He notes emphatically that the prophets "were much more than traditionalists. In fact to use the word of them at all is to run the risk of grave misunderstanding. It has become necessary to emphasize the element of tradition in their teaching just because of the tendency to ignore or minimize it. The balance must now be restored by an equally emphatic insistence that they were men who had a tremendous personal experi-

---

[24] See, Bernhard Lang, *Monotheism and the Prophetic Minority*. SWBAS (Sheffield: The Almond Press), 1983. Lang points specifically to one element in the prophets' preaching to underline this point. He notes, "In imagining the Day of Yahweh the prophets create a counter balance to the old retrospective tradition, such as the elections of the patriarchs and the Exodus from Egypt." p. 78. Also, the recalling of Israel's experience in Egypt is of course important for the remembering of the covenant relationship with Yahweh and Yahweh's deliverance. However, recalling this event is also a point of irony; for those who were once slaves in Egypt have become enslavers and oppressors. The difference here is that the enslaved and oppressed are their own people. See, also von Rad, who observes correctly that, "the prophets most decidedly took as their starting point the old traditions of Jahwism....Thus as far as the old Jahwistic traditions were concerned, the prophets and their hearers were on common ground: but they differed in their interpretations of these traditions, which the prophets believed were far from ensuring the Israel's salvation." *Theol.*II, p.179.
Moreover, von Rad notes, "The old traditions said that Jahweh led Israel into her land, founded Zion, established the throne of David, and this was sufficient. No prophet could any longer believe this; for between him and those founding acts hung a fiery curtain of dire judgements upon Israel, judgements which in the prophets' opinion, had already begun; and this judgement had no basis in the old Jahwistic tradition." p. 185.

ence with God."[25] While "tremendous personal experience" is not necessary as a means of countering the "tradition" argument, nevertheless Porteous's point is à *propos*. This category has elements that are necessary for a total understanding of the prophets' message and orientation, but it is no more acceptable by itself than the other categories previously discussed.

D. The Prophets as Yahwists

The primary motivation for this hypothesis is the belief that Israel was accommodating apostasy and syncretism in its worship practices. One of the prophets for whom this understanding is apt is Hosea. In Hosea, it is clear that both syncretistic religion and the rejection of Yahweh are prominent. But Hosea is not seen in isolation in this regard. Several scholars see the Eighth Century prophets as a group focusing their message on the revival of Yahwistic religion. Johannes Lindblom notes:

> In the light of the fundamental idea of the special relationship between Yahweh and his people, the new discovery of the pre-exilic prophets...was that Israel had fallen away from Yahweh, her God, had been rejected as a nation and would be punished. This is the presupposition for a right understanding of the prophets. To begin with anything else (monotheistic doctrine, moral admonitions, or even 'messianic' promise) is to miss the way to a real understanding of pre-exilic prophecy.[26]

Lindblom's underlying premise is the abuse and misuse of the promise of Yahweh to the people of Israel, regarding their chosenness. The covenant relationship has been broken and the aim of the prophets was to restore the elements necessary for a renewal

---

[25] N. W. Porteous, "The Basis of the Ethical teaching of the Prophets" in *Studies in Old Testament Prophecy*, ed. H.H. Rowley (Edinburgh: T&T Clark) 1950. p. 151.
[26] Johannes Lindblom, *Prophecy in Ancient Israel* (Oxford: Basil Blackwell) 1963, p. 312.

of the relationship. Thus the prophets' critique of the cult, oracles against the foreign nations, criticism of social injustices must be seen as various expressions of the elements constitutive in the demise of Yahwism.

Norman Porteous also advocates this position. He suggests that the prophets were proponents of Yahwism in the light of the influence of Canaanite religion in Israel. He argues that the way of life in Israel was being conformed to the ways of the neighboring nations and these have in turn led to compromises in the sphere of religious practices. He notes that, "in the eighth century BCE the situation had become more critical, and in the life and death struggle with Baalism in which the prophets were Israel's chief protagonists, these men came to an ever deeper and more creative understanding of what the God-ordained Israelite way of life involved."[27]

In essence the prophets were involved in a situation which concerned the very survival of Israel, a survival which had its antagonist in the form of foreign religion. Syncretism, the removal of which occupied the preaching and attention of the prophets. Everything which was said and done by the prophets must either be regarded as secondary or deriving its importance from the prophets' Yahwistic insistence.[28] This position can also be seen in an early view of Mays; he has two arguments. First, in dismissing the fact that Amos was involved in the initiation of a new religion, he maintains that the prophet was engaged "in the radical revival

---

[27] Porteous, "The Basis...." pp. 152ff.
[28] For similar developments of the primacy of the prophets' message on Yahwism, see Snaith, who says, "God first, ethics second, was the order of their preaching." *The Distinctive Ideas of the Old Testament*, p. 60. See also E. Clinton Gardner, *Biblical Faith and Social Ethics* (New York: Harper and Brothers), 1960. Gardner notes, "Their ethical teaching, as important as it is, was almost incidental, for they were first of all religious prophets." p. 33.
Cf. James Luther Mays, "Words about the Words of Amos," *Interp* 13 (1959), pp. 259-272. Even though Mays' article is specifically oriented around Amos, nevertheless his remarks would be paradigmatic for the Eighth Century prophets--for those who argue with Yahwism. Mays notes, "the ethic of Amos is through and through religious; orthodox-Yahwism is the basis of his critique." p. 269.

in the ancient election covenant theology and the application of it to the contemporary situation which Israel's social development and political history have created."[29] Mays is certainly cognizant of the importance of the prophet's political and social environment but, in any event, sees Yahwism as the core of the prophet's message, which is to repair the brokenness in the society. Second, Mays notes, "careful examination of the relevant texts seems to show that Amos denounced Israel's worship because it was syncretistic and abetted the social wrongs which he found so odious."[30]

Again, some observations are necessary at this point. Lindblom's view regarding the apostasy of Israel is a valid one, but his theory that the message of the pre-exilic prophets is one of judgment and doom because of the apostasy is inadequate. To be sure, there are several expressions of rejection (Hos. 9:1; Amos 8:2; Mic. 3:12), but these must be understood in the larger framework of the prophets' overall message. To reduce the entire message of the pre-exilic prophets to one of judgment and doom is to overlook major components.

Moreover, to suggest that apostasy and subsequent punishment be the starting point for understanding these prophets immediately compels the question as to whether the breakdown in the demands for social justice is as a result of apostasy or alternatively whether the absence of social justice leads inevitably to a fracture in the relationship with Yahweh. The latter alternative must be a viable option. Also, the reduction of the problem to a confrontation between Yahwism and Baalism is itself too myopic. While it is clear that apostasy is a factor which features prominently in the problems of Israel, it can hardly be ascertained that it is Baalism that leads to this apostasy, let alone prove that the entire structure of Israel's relationship is ridden with Baalism. As a factor, Baalism has to be seen alongside the severe internal problems which Israel was experiencing at the time, problems which adversely affected the relationship among the citizens and consequently the relationship with Yahweh.

---

[29] Mays, "Words...." p. 268.
[30] Ibid., p. 270.

Finally, regarding this view, the prophets' accusations and the announcements of Yahweh's judgments are to be seen as punishment which are commensurate with the crimes committed. The themes of prophetic accusation do not parallel those that we find in Jonah, where repentance is sought. The revival of election theology is not the primary purpose of the prophets, and at best it is a secondary inclination. The brokenness of the covenant is surely one of the consequences, if not the primary one, of the prevalent social injustices. It is not the prior brokenness of the covenant relationship which leads to the social injustices but the reverse.

Further, there is really no indication that syncretism is the point of contention in the polemics against the cult in Amos.[31] Whether it is an entire rejection of the cult that Amos seeks or whether he criticizes its shallowness, the point remains that Amos is denouncing the unfounded belief that sacrifices, offerings and all that the cult entails in and of themselves are sufficient for a proper relationship with Yahweh.

E. The Prophets as Ethicists

For many, this is the most obvious starting point for an understanding of the Eighth Century prophets, the reason being that their message is usually conceived of as being in relation to the absence of social justice and its many expressions. From the discussion in the preceding pages, it is evident that many scholars regard the prophets as something other than ethicists. In major part this is due to the fundamental belief that the prophets as individuals are called by Yahweh. The true prophetic role thus presupposes an alignment with, if not a source in Yahweh. On the other hand, to call the prophets ethicists does not necessarily signify either their secular or religious association. In fact, it is often assumed that

---

[31] See, von Rad who notes that "Amos was apparently quite unmoved by Hosea's main topic, the threat of Jahwism from the Canaanite worship of Baal." *Theol.* II, p. 176. See also Werner H. Schmidt, *Introduction to the Old Testament*, trans. Matthew J. O'Connell (London: SCM Press) 1984. Schmidt observes that "unlike Hosea...Amos does not base his criticism of the cult on the defection to the cult of Baal." p. 199.

ethicists need not have a direct association with the Divine, precisely because the theory of ethics does not have its roots in the religious realm.

Thus the title of "ethicists" for the prophets is regarded as incomplete and does not allude to the essential elements of the role of the prophets. For example, Snaith can say, "religion first, ethics second"[32] as a way of ordering the function of the prophets. The element of ethics in the prophets' message is perceived to be a reflection of the nature of Yahweh's covenantal expectations and not simply the preaching of sound humanitarian values. Despite the many articles focusing on the ethical component,[33] it is not a category which has found much favor.

The discussion of these categories has indicated the strength and the many limitations which each has in turn. It is clear that the Eighth Century prophets did not conform blindly to any of the prescriptive norms where were available at the time. If then the prophets are not reformers, revolutionaries, traditionalists, Yahwists or ethicists, then the question must be asked, "who are they?"[34]

---

[32] See above, note 28.

[33] For example there are articles and studies with titles such as: John Barton, "Ethics in Isaiah of Jerusalem," *JTS* (1981), pp. 1-18; E.W. Davies, *Prophecy and Ethics: Isaiah and the Ethical Traditions of Israel.* JSOTS 16 (Sheffield: JSOT), 1981; N.W. Porteous, "The Basis of the Ethical Teaching of the Prophets;" E. Hammershaimb, "On the Ethics of the Old Testament Prophets," *VTSup* 7 (1959), pp. 75-101; and F.J. Huey, "The Ethical Teaching of Amos, Its Contents and Relevance," *SWJT* 9 (1966), pp. 57-67.

[34] In the last couple of decades other categories have been suggested. David Robertson, *The Old Testament and the Literary Critic* (Philadelphia: Fortress Press) 1977, suggests that the prophet is in fact a poet. This is seen to be the case in part because of the poet's ability to be critical of society or country or ruler, and through his or her "poetic license" not be held accountable to any authority. It is true that the prophet as poet captures the essence of what it means to someone who demonstrates a literary prowess and espouses an awareness of the injustices in society. And, indeed, many of the prophetic books have striking literary qualities, but these elements, while important, are hardly the central core of the prophets' message.
In the quest for determining the prophets' function, scholars have sought out functional similarities between Israelite prophets and their Ancient Near Eastern counterparts. In this regard, see, Klaus Baltzer, "Considerations regarding the Office and Calling of the Prophet," *HTR* 61 (1968), pp. 567-581. Baltzer concludes in this article that the Israelite

Many of the personalities in the OT are placed within convenient categories, and while there may be some debate, there are certain basic elements on which there is general agreement. For example, the question of the $šofᵉṭim$ (judges, rulers) and their role remains unresolved, but there are some basic criteria on which their functioning might be ascertained. Similarly, the categories of elders, kings and priests all appear to have some consensus regarding their respective roles. However, the same cannot be said about the prophets. There is no doubt that there are sharp differences in approaches, messages, contexts and historical circumstances between the pre-exilic, exilic and post-exilic prophets. What this indicates is that a broad categorization of these prophets serve no great positive purpose, but rather it tends to overlook their distinctiveness.

It is commonly assumed that the Eighth Century prophets have an intrinsic connection through their time and message. Even though there are essential elements which link them (such as the corruption of צדק [righteousness] and משפט [justice], both of which are spelled out by the prophets to be indispensable for a proper relationship) nevertheless, these prophets are clearly individuals. Isaiah for example, is from the city. He is interested in world politics; he spends much effort in the oracles against foreign nations; he views world politics as being an integral part of Yahweh's larger scheme of things. There are distinct traits which indicate his interest in the monarchy and in fact he looks for a new king who would epitomize צדק and משפט. Still in the Northern King-

---

prophet is akin to the Egyptian vizier. The question as to the function of the prophets has clearly gone through much consideration. As early as the second century BCE this question was contemplated upon. In the Mishnaic treatise *PIRKE AVOT* it is said, "Moses received Torah at Sinai and handed it on to Joshua, Joshua to elders, and elders to prophets. And the prophets handed it on to the men of the assembly." This translation is taken from Jacob Neusner, *Torah from our Sages, PIRKE AVOT* (New York: Rossel Books) 1984, p. 24. Modern scholarship has deemed this mishnaic view as not very helpful. See, e.g., Joseph Blenkingsopp, *A History of Prophecy in Israel* (Philadelphia: The Westminster Press) 1983, who says, "On this showing, the primary function of the prophet was to bridge the gap between the primordial revelation at Sinai and the rabbinic leadership. Like the sages who succeeded them...the prophets were therefore custodians and traditioners of the law." p. 24.

dom, Hosea comes from a farming background, and in fact, it would appear that he is opposed to anything which is monarchical. His particular interest is in the purifying of the sacral tradition of Israel; he is intent on cleansing the cult of its irregularities and restoring it to its ancestral orientation. Unlike Isaiah, he has no great desire to concern himself with world affairs and international politics.

In the Northern Kingdom, Amos, the sheep herder from Tekoa, shows clearly that he is more than a country rustic. He inveighs strongly against the social injustices in the society; he is critical of the cultic institution, though syncretism is not a pressing concern, and does not devote any time to the alliances which Judah strikes up with the foreign nations, a concern which is quite evident in Isaiah. Micah like Amos, does most of his preaching in the Northern Kingdom (though he too like Amos is from the South) and shares many of the latter's concerns. His invectives against the rulers, the affluent and wealthy landowners show a striking similarity to the critique of Amos. Micah however, unlike Isaiah, appears to be certain of the annihilation of Jerusalem and its subsequent disappearance from the pages of history.[35]

One of the elements that becomes clear with a comparison such as this is the reality that the prophets cannot be placed and subjected to categories which impose particular limitations on the content of their message. Certainly all the categories which have been discussed have important factors which must be reckoned with, and while the prophets do not fit exclusively in any them, they do encompass all of them. What is therefore most helpful is to consider the prophetic office.

Because of the nature of Israelite prophecy it is to be expected that the prophets were immersed in the Yahwistic traditions and even a part of the institutions. Tradition must therefore be seen as a presupposition and a not a rigid framework. In other words, one does not have to seek to justify the prophets' Yahwistic inclination; this is a basic premise of the prophetic call. What is consequential is the direction of the message, the elements focused on, and the in-

---

[35] See von Rad, *Theol.* II, p. 176.

trinsic tie these elements have to the relationship Yahweh has with the people. Hence an attempt to explain why Isaiah hopes for a new Jerusalem and why Micah predicts its destruction points to a difference in context and elements unique to the prophetic office. So while the prophet might encompass a number of features from the different categories, he does not fit exclusively in any of them.[36] The prophet remains fundamentally a messenger[37] who proclaims and interprets Yahweh's word in the light of the situation in which he finds himself.

---

[36] See Walther Zimmerli, "Das Gottesrecht bei den Propheten Amos, Hosea und Jesaja" in *Werden und Wirken des Altes Testaments*, eds. Rainer Albertz, Hans-Peter Müller, Hans Walter Wolff and Walther Zimmerli (Göttingen: Vandenhoeck and Ruprecht), 1980, pp. 216-235. Speaking specifically about Amos, Zimmerli suggests that this prophet does not look exclusively to one institution or one code, rather he utilizes all the traditions which are at his disposal and adapts them to suit his message. pp. 218-220. See also Arvid Kapelrud, "New Ideas in Amos," *VTSup* 15 (1966), 193-206, who says that Amos, "was neither a founder of a new ethical religion, nor just a bearer of ancient traditions. He was something in between. He was an intelligent man, devoted to the service of God and well versed in the ancient traditions of his people and in its way of living....He combined old and new points of view and drew up lines, which came to be determining for the religion of Israel in *saecula* to come." p.206.

[37] For a discussion of the prophet as messenger, see James F. Ross, "The Prophet as Yahweh's Messenger" in *Israel's Prophetic Heritage*, eds. Bernhard W. Anderson and Walter Harrelson (New York: Harper and Brothers) 1962, pp. 98-108. In this article Ross points to some of the reasons why the Eighth Century prophets have not been referred to as "messengers." See also Claus Westermann, *Basic Forms of Prophetic Speech* (Philadelphia: Westminster Press), 1967.

Chapter VI

I. צדק, משפט and the Social Critique of the Eighth Century Prophets

The high incidence of צדק and משפט in the Eighth Century prophets is in itself indicative of the importance of these terms to the prophets. As was pointed out earlier, the prophets, though prophesying within the framework of Israel, are nevertheless individuals and in many ways quite distinctive. Even though their starting points might be different, they do have one factor in common (with the apparent exception of Hosea),[1] and that is their piercing critique of social injustice. In their message the unacceptability of social injustice is seen alongside Yahweh's expectation of משפט and צדק. The starting point of the prophets' social proclamation is acutely tied to the need for משפט and צדק.[2] Isaiah, in being strongly critical of the injustices in Israel, notes on several occasions that either משפט and צדק are missing or that they are necessary. In 1:21, he deplores the state of Jerusalem by noting the way in which משפט and צדק are corrupted and erased from society. In 1:27, where he indicates what is necessary for the restoration of Jerusalem, two elements feature prominently, משפט and צדק. The absence of משפט and צדק in society is directly related to the injustices which are prevalent. This is an obvious cause and effect relationship, effectively expressed in 1:21-23. It is because of the lack of משפט and צדק that everything has become adulterated in society, and those with the primary responsibility for the caring of the poor and disenfranchised are the ones who appear to be the most corrupted. This connection between צדק and משפט and social justice is further underlined poignantly in Isaiah's "Parable of the Vine-

---

[1] Because there is no difference between cultic and social critique, Hosea's critique of the cult may be understood as a social critique.

[2] See, Svend Holm-Nielsen, "Die Sozialkritik der Propheten" in *Denken der Glaube*. ed. Otto Kaiser (Berlin: Walter de Gruyter), 1976, pp. 7-23. Holm-Nielsen notes, "Ausgangspunkt für die soziale Predigt der Propheten sind die Worte צדק and משפט. Recht und Gerechtigkeit sind der Hintergrund für die Strafpredigt der Propheten, nicht nur in sozialen Zusammenhängen, sondern auch in kultischen Zusammenhängen...." p. 13.

yard." The absence of משפט and צדק in Israel (5:7) is directly related to the decay of societal values and uninhibited greed. (5:8)

This association is also developed in Amos. The connection between 5:7, where the corruption of צדק and משפט is strikingly described, and 5:10-12, where the various expressions of social injustices are inveighed against, is unmistakable. Those who have corrupted משפט and צדק are the ones who are actively involved in establishing social injustices. Moreover, in Amos, צדק and משפט are found in contexts in which the cult is criticized. In Amos 5:21-24, the façade of cultic activity as it is found in Amos's society is seen to be in sharp contrast to משפט and צדק.[3] It is highly probable that these words of Amos against the cult are tied to his critique of social injustices. As is evident throughout Amos, those involved in cultic matters are also the ones using this sanctity as a means of self-indulgence.[4]

Even though צדק and משפט occur only once together in Hosea, it is a pivotal occurrence. In 2:21[19] Yahweh says that the relationship with Israel will be re-established in צדק and משפט. The importance of this use is reflected in the immediate juxtaposition with the reference to Baalism. However, צדק and משפט must also be regarded as affecting all other elements of Israel's life. Like Hosea, צדק and משפט occur together only once in Micah and in this particular instance (7:9) it does not refer to social critique. However, the

---

[3] This unit will be discussed in greater detail in the section "Religiosity and the Cult" later in this chapter.

[4] Against this view, see, Philip Hyatt, "The translation and meaning of Amos 5: 23-24," ZAW 67-68 (1955-56), pp. 17-24. Hyatt suggests that in Amos 5:23-24, the use of צדק and משפט does not have any reference to ethics or social justice. He attempts to justify this assertion by alluding to the many different uses of צדק and משפט in Deutero-Isaiah, that refer to "salvation," "deliverance," originating in Yahweh. pp. 19-20. Hyatt's methodological principle is, at this point, suspect. It is certainly inadvisable to determine the meaning of a concept in one context by pointing to the way it was used in another, overlooking the political, social, and religious circumstances at the time. Regarding the use of צדק and משפט in this context, and in fact generally in Amos, Koch remarks, "it is already noticeable that the phrase is used in the context of *the cult* and not in connection with social criticism." *The Prophets* I, p. 58. Koch's statement overlooks the connection between 5:4-6 and 5:10-15, where צדק and משפט are clearly related to the social critique of the prophets. To say that צדק and משפט are only used in the critique of the cult, is neglecting a fundamental insight of Amos.

Chapter VI

different forms of injustices which are denounced by Micah are almost identical to those of his counterpart Amos. Oppression by the affluent (2:1ff), the irresponsibility and corruption of the leaders (3:1ff) and the cult (6:6-8) all appear in Amos in similar forms and associated with צדק and משפט. משפט in fact occurs in every context in which Micah calls for justice in society. Mic. 3:1 indicates the need for the leaders to know משפט; 3:9 continues this theme, while 3:11 points to the corruption of משפט in the avenues of power. The occurrence of משפט in 6:8 may be regarded as a part of the prototype of Yahweh's expectations. What is clear from these examples is the fact that משפט is that element which is expected from the people as a response to Yahweh's relationship and of course that which is necessary to keep others in a right relationship.

These occurrences indicate clearly that the emphasis on צדק and משפט is there precisely because of its association with the subject of social justice. The prophets are obviously aware of the number of times that these terms are being used and clearly intend them to be viewed in the light of their message. Even though not every use appears to correspond specifically to every context, and in Micah's case צדק does not appear with משפט in contexts denouncing social injustices, nevertheless, there is little doubt about the connection.[5]

II. The Intertwining of Socio-Economic and Cultic Expectations

The relationship between the social and religious polemics of the Eighth Century prophets has often been seen as two distinct areas. Werner Schmidt most recently adopted this stance.[6] He makes something of an absolute distinction between cultic and social criticism. Commenting on these themes in Amos, he notes:

---

[5] See, above Chapter I, where it is pointed out that even though ברית is only found twice in the Eighth Century prophets with reference to Yahweh's covenant, still it would be an error to conclude that these prophets are uninterested in the concept of ברית. The parallel here with the presence of צדק and משפט in every context, is self-evident.

[6] Werner H. Schimdt. *Introduction to the Old Testament*, p. 199.

> When we describe Amos as a prophet of social justice, we put our finger on the principal but not the only theme of his arraignment. There is also...a criticism of the cult....Like the later prophets, he makes the special idiom of the priests his own for polemical purposes and attacks the sacrifices and feasts (4:4f; 5:21ff; 8:10; cf. 2:8). Like his criticism of society, his criticism of the cult cannot be left in isolation; it is integrated into his message regarding the future (5:5, 27; 8:10) and thus into his prophetic understanding of God. For this reason, we may ask whether the motto Justice and Ethics instead of Cult is not in the final analysis, inadequate, even though it does capture part of his message.[7]

The motto "Justice and Ethics" would be inadequate only in so far as the criticism of the cult is seen as being entirely divorced from the realm of social justice and ethics. Schmidt's distinction[8] at this point surely misses the close integration of different elements of the prophets' message. On a superficial level, it would appear that the cult has little to do with social justice, but the words of Amos certainly link them together, not necessarily in a "cause and effect" relationship but nevertheless in a manner in which one affects, and is affected by the other.

The separation of social justice from the cult is also alluded to by Hyatt, where he refers specifically to Amos 5:23-24. Even though he does not create as sharp a distinction as Schmidt does, nevertheless implicit in his view, is the notion that Amos 5:23-24 is entirely in reference to the cult and Yahweh's relationship. He contends that, "the prophet is saying to the Israelites that they must cease their preoccupation with feasts, festal gatherings, offering, etc., in order that Yahweh may cause to flow down upon

---

[7] Ibid., p. 199

[8] Also Koch, points to one important distinction: "Criticism of religious practices and criticism of social conditions are not on the same level. Whereas Amos uses the genre of prophecy for the latter, religious criticism is expressed more seldom and then through texts that are priestly in character." *The Prophets* I, p. 51. This, however, is a distinction which has to do with genre and form and not with thematic association.

them His deliverance and salvation. Their elaborate ceremonialism is a barrier to God's salvation. When his *mishpāṭ* and *ṣᵉdāqā* come upon them, there will be 'social justice.'"9 Hyatt's argument posits a theory of cult and social justice which is indicative of a general misunderstanding of the theology of Amos, and specifically of 5:23-24. There is no indication that Amos's critique of the cult is tied to Yahweh's deliverance and salvation. In fact, it is abundantly clear that the ideas of "deliverance and salvation" are not preoccupations of Amos. There is no doubt that "deliverance and salvation" coming from Yahweh to Israel is preached in other contexts, such as Deutero-Isaiah, but it is certainly not in Amos. The ceremonialism is not a barrier to their reception of Yahweh's deliverance, but it is a barrier to the presence of צדק and the flow of משפט to members of the community.

Rather than the position of Schmidt and Hyatt, it must be reckoned that the denunciation of the cult cannot be separated from the overall denunciation of the attitude of the whole people. The cult and its orientation become for the prophets a microcosmic expression of the larger problem of brokenness and anthropocentric idealism. There is no material difference in the decay of the society, both the social and cultic aspects.10 "The cult must be viewed within the wider cadre of everyday life of the people exactly because the cult was moulded by 'popular theology.'"11 In essence, the prophets seek to emphasize that the cult has become so much of a human oriented institution and is being used to satisfy misguided and selfish feelings, that its theocentric nature ceases to function. What is absent from the cult is precisely that which is absent from society as a whole, namely צדק and משפט. Everything which transpires in Israel is intricately connected with

---

9 Hyatt, "...Amos 5:23-24." p. 24

10 See, Holm-Nielsen, "Die Sozialkritik der Propheten." p. 13.

11 C.J. Labuschagne, "Amos' conception of God and the popular theology of his time" in *Studies on the Books of Hosea and Amos, 7th and 8th meetings of OTWSA*, 1964-65, p. 130. Labuschagne's definition of popular theology is that it "considered Yahweh to be there for the sake of the people, serving them unconditionally. Naturally this conception of God was an opiate to the people, causing them to relax, to feel secure; no one could touch them - not even God." p. 128. See also, Kapelurd, *Central Ideas*, p. 76.

the people and thus even the cult, that which is meant to bring the individual into communion with Yahweh, becomes no more than a personal achievement. It is no surprise therefore that Amos, in many of his invectives, points to the anthropocentric nature of the cultic practices. Hence his language is self-explanatory: *your* tithes, *your* sacrifices (4:4), *your* feasts, *your* solemn assemblies, *your* burnt offerings, *your* fatted breasts, *your* songs, *your* harps. (5:21-23; cf.8:10) This turning of cultic events into moments of self-gratification[12] indicates clearly the implicit need which these worshippers see as important. The cult becomes a means of sanctioning their activities in social life.

This connection between the social and aspects of Israel's life may be illustrated with two specific examples. The gift of the land to the people by Yahweh, was implemented through "salvation history;"[13] it is this gift of the land which is associated with cultic places. Bethel and Gilgal, places where cultic festivals occur, have become sites for the expression of injustices. The land, which has become locations of cultic events, is the same land that is essential for the sustenance of the poor; it is their only means of surviving. Koch notes, "the inherited land is central to the remarks about the situation of the *dallîm*; it is the condition that makes a free life possible."[14] Moreover, Koch raises the questions as to whether the land issue is connected with fixed ideas about the significance of cultic places. He observes that, "the fruitful earth had its 'centre' in the temple at Bethel....What took place there spread out like ripples over the whole area. It is therefore hardly by chance that the social criticism often culminates in the accusation that holy places and seasons are being violated in the course of these outrages."[15] The imagery of the "fruitful earth" having its center in the Temple is apposite in the light of the steady disappearance of

---

[12] See, Hans Walter Wolff, *The Old Testament: A Guide to its Writings.* trans. Keith Crim (Philadelphia: Fortress Press), 1973, p. 88.

[13] Koch, *The Prophets* I, p. 55.

[14] Ibid., p. 56. See also, R.E. Clements, "Temple and Land: A Significant Aspect of Israel's Worship," *TGUOS* 19 (1961-62), pp. 16-28, especially p. 26.

[15] Koch, *The Prophets* I, p. 50. Even though Koch concludes that צדק and משׁפט only refer to the cult, nevertheless he sees the combination between the cult and social justice.

land from those who need it most of all, the poor. Now, the "fruitful earth" is no longer providing for the poor, the "people of the land," but is taken over by the powerful. The Temple, as the center of the "fruitful earth," has become the haven for those who continue to view it in its traditional relationship to the land, precisely because the worshippers are the ones who own the land. The land, as a gift from Yahweh and as an element which is the right of every Israelite, now becomes the exclusive property of the rich. The cultic activities are directly shaped by this new ownership and come to be understood in the light of this development.

Another example, which in some ways focuses sharply on the relationship between cult and social justice, is in Amos 2:8. This is a particularly important reference in that it combines three elements, all essential for a complete understanding of the prophet's social critique. First, there is the question of pledges and their use by creditors; in this regard, it is clear that Amos looks to the law codes as his guide. In Exod. 22:25[26]ff, it is clearly stated that a garment which is taken in pledge must be returned "before the sun goes down" for the individual needs it for warm covering during sleep.[16] There are certain items which are prohibited from being taken in pledges, for these are regarded as essential for collaterals. This idea must have been on the mind of Amos as he reproaches those who impugn this element of covenant responsibility. Even though Amos does not point specifically to the disregard for the pledged garments it must be concluded with Mays that "the use of the pledged garments for couches at the shrine, seems to presuppose its violation."[17]

Second, there is sharp irony in the fact that it is the אביונים, the דלים, and the ענוים, collectively the disenfranchised of the land, who are the ones that need the beds on which to lie and the garments to wear. While they are being deprived of these, the rich and powerful people use the items as superfluous trimmings for their feasting and lavish lifestyle. Third, there is the combination

---

[16] See also, Deut. 24:6.
[17] Mays, *Amos*, p. 47. For a different view, see M. Dahood, "To pawn one's garment," *Biblica* 42 (1961), pp. 359-366. Dahood suggests that, "Amos is here condemning the practice of sacral prostitution." p. 365.

of social and economic injustice on the one hand and cultic indulgence on the other. The irony in the prophet's words is biting: "they lay themselves down beside every altar on garments taken in pledge; and in the house of their God they drink the wine bought with fines they imposed." Amos not only denounces this blatant expression of injustice, but also the false notion of communion with Yahweh. This striking portrayal of the excesses of social and economic injustices "shows that these worshippers felt no incongruity between what they did in the legal economic realm and the God worshipped with feasting and sacrifice."[18] This is surely an expression of ignorance, for outside of their inappropriate behavior in a Temple, they also believe that their cultic association will keep them in good stead with Yahweh. Amos's interest in underlining the connection between socio-economic affairs and cultic practices is clearly spelled out here. What Amos evokes here is not unique to him but rather epitomizes message of the Eighth Century prophets. The everyday routine of life cannot be separated from the cultic events.[19]

The discussion on the relationship between צדק and משפט in the Eighth Century prophets and the use of these concepts within the framework of the prophets' social critique now set the stage for a discussion of the various contexts in which צדק and משפט are seen to be absent, neglected or corrupted. Moreover, the brief examination of the role of the Eighth Century prophets endeavors to show the unique approach of these prophets to the task of prophesying. The elements which together make up their message clearly set them apart from any prior existing institutions or traditions. The verification of this is seen amply in their attitudes to the societal values and expectations.

---

[18] Mays, *Amos*, p. 47.
[19] See also, Isa. 1:13-17; Amos 3:13-15; 5:21-24; Mic. 6:6-8.

III. Elements of Social Critique

The critique by the Eighth Century prophets covers several aspects of the social, economic and cultic life of Israel, all of which are intricately tied together. One of the critical elements which must be noted right at the outset is the fact that the basis of the brokenness within society can be traced to a brokenness in the people's relationship with Yahweh.

A. The Rejection of Yahweh - Isa. 5:1-7

Isaiah's "Song of the Vineyard" has long been recognized as one of his most poignant and well-known denunciations of Israel. For the discussion to follow, it will be helpful to examine Isa. 5:1-7 and use it is a paradigm of the Israelites' movement away from Yahweh and consequently from each other. It is important that this text be seen as a parable and not as an allegory, that is, that the many items pointed to in the story be not viewed as corresponding to historical events in Israel.[20] Essentially, this parable contains three central parties: a friend, and two other characters all of whom feature prominently.[21] The importance of rendering ידיד as "friend" is seen in the fact that the song is sung by a third party on a friend's behalf, hence it is a song about love, rather than a love-song in the traditional sense.

This "Song of Love" consists of three important and inseparable elements. First, there is a graphic description of the care which

---

[20] Against, Otto Kaiser, *Isaiah 1-12*. OTL (London: SCM Press), 1983. Kaiser sees the "Song of the Vineyard" as being said in retrospect, thus denoting what has been done to Israel rather than what is to be done. He sees it as a "theology of salvation history." p. 93. The inadequacy of Kaiser's view is that it moves subtly into the framework of an allegory. See also, Gale E. Yee, "The Form-Critical Study of Is. 5:1-7 as a Song and Juridical Parable," *CBQ* 43 (1981), pp. 30-40. Yee sees this "Song of the Vineyard" as both "a song and a juridical parable." p. 40.

[21] The word ידיד is translated "beloved" in the NRSV and "loved one" by G.B.Gray in *The Book of Isaiah 1-39*. ICC (Edinburgh: T and T Clark), 1912, p. 82; a preferred translation is "friend." This fits the context better, since it is a "friend" and not a "beloved" on whose behalf the speaker tells the story. See, Clements, *Isaiah 1-39*, p. 58 and Kaiser, *Isaiah 1-12*, p. 93. Also Heschel, *The Prophets*, p. 84.

is given to the vineyard. In v. 2a, "digging," "clearing," "planting," "building a tower" all indicate the systematic care with which the vinedresser has tended the vineyard. In fact, only choice vines are planted, once more suggesting that only the best is reserved for the vineyard. Yahweh, the vinedresser, has given all that is necessary for a proper response from the vineyard Israel, and now it is the latter's turn to respond in a manner which is commensurate with the care applied. Second, the expected response by Yahweh and the actual response by Israel is encapsulated in one sentence. "He looked for it to yield grapes, but it yielded sour grapes."[22] In planting the vineyard with choice vines, it is the vinedresser's expectations that the best grapes would be yielded. What is in the question here is not the wrong species of grapes, as "wild grapes" would suggest, but a very poor quality of grapes. Israel as the vineyard has not responded in a manner which reflects the care and special providence with which it is tended. Rather, in a way, the yielding of sour grapes suggests that Israel has done that which is contrary to its inherent qualities. This rejection by Israel is clearly spelled out in v. 5:7b where the nature of Yahweh's expectations is specified. In the care which Yahweh gives to Israel he expects צדק and משפט in return. These two elements set the pattern for the prophet's entire social critique, for it is the absence of צדק and משפט which has affected all of Israel's society. In substituting

---

[22] The NRSV uses the term "wild grapes." So also, Kaiser, *Isaiah 1-12*, p. 89. Gray, also incorrectly, renders it as "wildings." *The Book of Isaiah*, p. 82. On the other hand, Clements, says that "bad grapes" is a more suitable rendering. Heschel opts for "sour grapes." *Isaiah 1-39*, p. 58. *The Prophets*. p. 84. It is perhaps Driver who makes the most pointed distinction. See. G.R. Driver, "Difficult Words in the Hebrew Prophets" in *Studies in Old Testament Prophecy* ed. H.H. Rowley (Edinburgh: T and T Clark), 1950, pp. 52-72. According to Driver it is "not 'wild grapes' since a cultivated plant cannot produce wild fruit,...but bad, diseased grapes,' i.e. spoiled by anthracnosa which makes the cluster disgusting to the eye and inedible...." p. 53.

משפח 23 and צעקה,24 Israel has overturned everything which is invested in it. The righteous God has been replaced by those who are murderers (cf. 1:21) with the likely outcome. Rather than צדק which binds Israel in relationship with Yahweh, now there is צעקה, outrage; the reflection of צדק is missing, the fruit of צדק has been turned into a cry from the oppressed. Once again it is the element which binds Israel and Yahweh in relationship which is missing and which subsequently leads to "cry" by the oppressed.25

Third, there are the consequences which follow naturally from such a rejection of Yahweh and the nurtured relationship which he provides. Even so, Yahweh does not immediately abandon Israel; he calls on the people to decide for themselves who is at fault. The rhetorical question in v. 4a underlines the completeness of Yahweh's case and at the same time presupposes that the answer from the people is in Yahweh's favor. Vv. 5-6 describe graphically the extent of the punishment inflicted on Israel and have an implicit reference to the military siege which will come upon Israel. The elements of protection (hedge, wall) will disappear, and the care which is spelled out in v. 2a will be reversed. (v. 6a) The one element which is fundamental for the vineyard's survival, namely rain (v. 6b), will be stopped. Even though there is no indication that Israel will be decimated entirely, still the punishment described has a tone of finality.

While the three points discussed here are all integral for a full understanding of the "Song of the Vineyard," for the purpose of this study, it is not so much the punishment by Yahweh which is of interest, as it is the caring act by Yahweh and the contrary reaction by Israel. In this regard, it is v. 7b which is of paramount importance, for here, there is outlined clearly what Yahweh expects (צדק, משפט) and that with which Israel responds (צעקה, משפח).

---

[23] In his translation of משפח, Kaiser renders it "injustice." *Isaiah 1-12*. p. 90. While this encompasses the entire gamut of brokenness, it misses the verbal similarity with 1:21. There is no reason to assume that משפח is not meant to be "bloodshed," something specific in the mind of the prophet.

[24] See, Carl Graesser, "Righteousness, Human and Divine," *CTM* 10 (1983), pp. 134-141. Graesser suggests that צעקה, "is virtually a technical legal term for the oppressed person's cry to the court for redress." p. 137.

[25] See Heschel, *The Prophets*, p. 85

This expectation and response is the basis for the prophetic critique of Israel's society.[26]

B. Religiosity and the Cult

The cult has traditionally been the core of Israel's existence and as such plays a central role in the understanding of Israel's religious and social life. In the Eighth Century prophets the cult can be perceived to be the center of the prophets' criticism of injustices, precisely because it is the hub of what ever transpires in daily existence. Unlike the traditional view of the cult, where cultic practices and rituals are clearly outlined and shown to be important, in the Eighth Century prophets it is precisely these practices which are inveighed against. The primary reason for the prophets' criticism of the cult may perhaps be expressed in Rooy's observation that, "grave social crimes cannot be remedied by grand cultic ceremonies."[27] It is this separation of cultic ceremonies from social responsibilities that incite the prophets to hurl invectives against the cult and its practices. It is as Hyatt correctly concludes, "much of the prophetic criticism of the worship of their time can be summed up in the statement that they objected to its failure to proclaim the moral demands of a sovereign God who wished to be worshipped by the whole of Israel's life and not simply by that which took place within the formal cult."[28]

It is important to note that even though each of the Eighth Century prophets is critical in some way of Israel's cultic practices,

---

[26] See, William Creighton Graham, "Notes on the Interpretation of Isaiah 5:1-14," *AJSL* 45 (1928/9), pp. 167-178. Commenting on 5:7 where Isaiah laments the absence of משפט and צדק, Graham notes that "it is doubtless the allusion to the מִשְׁפָּה [sic] and צְעָקָה which characterize the social order of the day, which leads the prophet in verse 8,9 into the economic aspect of his theme." p. 171. Even though Graham is implying a distinction between the social and economic aspects of the prophet's critique, he nevertheless observes the clear connection between 5:7 and what follows. Kaiser, notes also that 5:7 is closely tied to the seven prophetic woes, *Isaiah 1-12*, p. 58.

[27] Rooy, "Righteousness and Justice." p. 272.

[28] J. Philip Hyatt, "The Prophetic Criticism of Israelite Worship" in *Interpreting the Prophetic Tradition*. ed. Harry M. Orlinsky (Cincinnati: The Hebrew Union College Press), 1969, p. 217.

it is not to be assumed that they merely repeat each other or that their perspectives and pronouncements are identical. As was noted earlier, there is no doubt that there are common elements which are fundamental to their critique, but this is not a reason or basis for the dismissal of their distinctiveness. It is with this understanding that each of the Eighth Century prophets will be discussed in turn, focusing on the critique of the cult.

1. Isa. 1:10-17

This unit in Isaiah serves as a paradigm of his critique of cultic practices during his time. The prophet singles out the rulers (קצין) for ridicule, though people in general are spoken to. However the "people" who concern the prophet at this stage are specifically the rulers, and they are those of Sodom and Gomorrah, here referring to Jerusalem.[29] To align Jerusalem with Sodom and Gomorrah is to give a clear indication of the sinful nature of Jerusalem. The rulers and ruling classes in Jerusalem are perceived to be in a similar situation to their counterparts in Sodom and Gomorrah, namely that there are few that are righteous. In this instance, the lack of righteousness is reflected in their cultic practices. It is the elaborate and sophisticated worship practices, the extensive ritualizing by these leaders which are being criticized. The prophet's words in vv. 11-15 outline clearly the many aspects of the cultic practices which are being adhered to rigorously by these leaders, and these are precisely the elements which come under criticism. It is a somewhat misguided belief which suggests that "formal observance of ritual and cultic duty would suffice to maintain the people in a state of blessedness."[30] The prophet makes it clear that sacrifices, offerings, incense, assemblies are all useless to Yahweh and will make no impact on him. The formality of "right times" in terms of the moon are of no significance, and even the special feasts and prayers are perceived to be despicable. The irony here is that these leaders are doing exactly what is pre-

---

[29] See e.g., Clements *Isaiah 1-39*, p. 32; Hans Wildberger, *Isaiah 1-12* (Minneapolis: Augsburg Fortress Press), 1991, p. 39.
[30] Clements, *Isaiah 1-39*, p. 32

scribed for proper cultic practices, yet they are overlooking the fundamental issue crucial for a proper relationship with Yahweh. Isaiah makes it clear that *this kind* of ritualizing is not only inefficacious, but downright distasteful to Yahweh. Every element which is a part of the cultic practice has been rejected by Yahweh. It is the juxtaposition of hands which pray and make offerings and which are at the same time "full of blood" that stuns the prophet in its very incongruity.[31] The underlying message here is that Yahweh will not accept any element of worship is done by "hands full of blood."

In vv. 16-17 the prophet provides the solution both for "hands full of blood" and for expectations of Yahweh. These rulers are to wash themselves clean, and this is to be understood precisely in relation to "hands full of blood." The imagery of "washing" has most naturally to do with the act of cleansing, and this in itself involves a sense of newness, removing that which is unnatural. (e.g. dirt) In this instance, in order to be in a proper and natural relationship with Yahweh and with each other, it is a time of cleansing that is necessary, and this means a dramatic turning around. In other words, on the one hand, cease what is being done, and on the other, do justice, correct oppression, care for the orphan, plead for the widow. (v. 17) The critical element here is the "blood," for in this is expressed the sin committed by the rulers and inherent in the idea of "washing" is the return and re-establishment of משפט. The worthlessness of the cultic practices appears to be tied to the fact that the participants have blood on their hands.[32]

---

[31] The reference to "hands full of blood" may have two possible explanations. Both of these involve worship and those who participate there. First, it may refer to the rulers as the ones held responsible for the suffering and oppression of many. The latter may be the group against whom crimes and injustices have been committed. It is interesting to note that the blood imagery is also alluded to in Isa. 1:21 and referred to in 5:7. Second, and in some respects the most obvious reference is to the blood of animals which have been killed for sacrificial purposes; it is in this possibility that the irony lies. These fatted animals are being fed, only to be slaughtered, all to no avail, meanwhile the poor are being starved.

[32] See, Hans M. Barstad, *The Religious Polemics of Amos*. SVT 34 (1984), p. 115. Also, Edmond Jacob, who notes that "To lift in worship hands that are

Chapter VI 257

The words of Isa. 16b-17 on what is expected, pose the question as to the relationship between these words and the cult. James Williams suggests that, "however we may interpret this oracle, we must agree that Isaiah does not even hint in his closing exhortation to combine moral uprightness *and* cultic faithfulness. Here as elsewhere, he simply presents in hortatory form, the wisdom known not only in Israelite culture, but among all peoples: 'wash! clean up!'"33 Williams' view does not include the co-existing of cult and משפט, but sees the idea of washing as being done in משפט. This presupposes a distinction between משפט and the cult and suggests that together they are conflicting forces. Whether Williams' view is entirely tenable will be discussed later, but what is clear is the idea that "washing" occurs in the seeking of משפט.34 There is no doubt about Isaiah's disputation regarding the legitimacy and efficacy of Israel's cultic practices. However, in 1:17 as sharp as the prophet's critique of the cult is, there is no indication that it is being done in opposition to the cultic practices *per se*. That is to say, for example, 1:17 does not begin with an adversative *waw*.35 Essentially, there is no clear polarization between cultic practices and the need to do משפט. Clearly the underlying theme is the importance of doing משפט, but the question as to whether it must be done *instead of* cultic practices is not made entirely clear by Isaiah. What is made clear in Isa. 1:10-17 is that the prevailing cultic practices and conventions are useless, implying no salvific validity. From this criticism the prophet indicates what is needed, namely משפט.

2. Hos. 6:6

The expression of Yahweh's demand in Hos. 6:6 serves as a paradigm for the ingredients of a proper relationship with Yahweh. It is clear that Hosea's critique of the cult involves the matter

---
covered with blood is both a sin and meaningless." "The Biblical Prophets...." p. 53.
33 James Williams, "The Social Location...." p. 162.
34 Ibid., p. 162.
35 Contrast, Amos 5:24.

of syncretism primarily, but the words in 6:6 reflect the demand of Yahweh, regardless of whether the cult is being corrupted through Baalism or social injustice within Israel. Hos. 6:6 includes two elements also found in the criticism by the other Eighth Century prophets, namely, "offerings" and "sacrifices." Whether or not they are being offered according to the prescribed way of the Israelite tradition or according to Canaanite religious practice does not make a material difference here. While משפט and צדק do not occur in Hosea, within the context of his critique of the cultic practices, nevertheless 6:6 includes the ingredients which parallel the critique of the other Eighth Century prophets. Both "sacrifices" and "offerings" are set in opposition to חסד and דעת אלהים. חסד and דעת as used here, are clearly meant to be in contradistinction to the sacrifices and offerings which are presented to Yahweh as elements to sustain the covenant relationship.[36] At least in this way Hosea's words can be understood to parallel those of his contemporaries. What is certain is that the cult in Hosea's estimation, is being used in a manner which departs from its traditional efficacious use. It is as Ward notes, "Hosea's climactic line [6:6], which contrasts the efficacy of ḥesed with that of burnt offerings, implies that the cult has been distorted into a mechanism for exploiting God's power. As such, it fails not only to achieve its objective, but actually jeopardizes the faith and moral integrity of the participants."[37] Thus, what is evident is that חסד and דעת involve the element of morality while sustaining the integrity of the presenter, and this is precisely what is missing.

3. Amos 4:4-5; 5:4-5, 21-24

The sharp critique by Amos against the cultic practices in Israel has traditionally been seen as paradigmatic of the critique of the Eighth Century prophet in general. However, there are ele-

---

[36] See, Nelson Glueck, *Ḥesed in the Bible*. trans. Alfred Gottschalk (Cincinnati: Hebrew Union College Press), 1967. According to Glueck, חסד is in the same category as צדק and משפט as far as relationship to Yahweh is concerned. p. 57.

[37] James M. Ward, *Hosea* (New York: Harper and Row), 1966, p. 121.

ments in Amos which are unique to Amos and hence must be examined separately. The sarcasm in 4:4-5 demonstrates the disgust which Amos has for cultic practices. Amos takes a traditional call to worship and reverses its use and intent in order to provide for Israel a clear indication of the extent of its sinning. While coming to a center of worship originally meant an occasion for adhering to Yahweh's expectations, here, "tithing," "sacrifices," "offerings" have all become elements of self-satisfaction. This prophetic intrusion by Amos is certainly meant to overturn all expectations, and the declatory formula in v. 5, "...for so you love to do, O people of Israel" is also a sharp contrast to the usual declaration. In effect, what Amos is saying is that, "the sacrificial cult has nothing to do with Yahweh. It is not the Lord, but the self of Israel which is the ground of their worship."[38] The increased frequency of the rituals only serves to increase Israel's transgressions on the one hand and satisfy its personal quest on the other.

Amos 5:4-5 must be understood within the context of this fulfillment of the religious needs of the self in separation from Yahweh. The worship centers of Bethel and Gilgal are denounced, and Amos indicates that in order to "live," Israel must seek Yahweh, a command which implies clearly that the many cultic activities of 4:4-5 have failed to match up to Yahweh's expectations. It would appear that it is impossible to "live" through the cult, but it is unclear as to whether the cult is irrelevant for "life." Yahweh's admonition of "seek me and live" in 5:4 suggests the need for a change, once again placing this in opposition to the cultic centers. The alternatives are clear, namely, "Seek (דרש) Yahweh" or "Seek (דרש) Bethel," the former will give life while the latter will "come to naught." It may be as Mays notes, that "to seek Yahweh" involves "holding on to Yahweh" as a way of life.[39] The juxtaposition of 4:4-5 and 5:4-5 establishes clearly that Israel is merely proceeding

---

[38] Mays, *Amos*, p. 75. See also, Norman K. Gottwald, *A Light to the Nations* (New York: Harper and Row), 1959. Gottwald suggests that what Amos attacks is "the irreligion of the religious, that coarse religious utilitarianism in which the greedy and frothy-minded simply see their own powers magnified and validated by the gods they worship." p. 289.

[39] Mays, *Amos*, p. 87.

through the motions in a manner which is divorced from the expectations of Yahweh's covenant. Brueggemann correctly observes that Israel is involved in "renewal without genuine encounter with the Lord of covenant....Israel is indicted for careful adherence to the motions of covenant-making without substance in them."[40]

While the words of 4:4-5 and 5:4-5 are indicative of Amos's sharp opposition to the cultic practices, it is perhaps in 5:21-24, where there is the most powerful condemnation of these practices. In this context, he makes clear the connection between the cultic ceremonies and the need for משפט and צדק. This is the only instance in the Eighth Century prophets where combined polemical language such as "I hate, I despise..." is used as a form of denunciation. These words leave no doubt about Amos's rejection of the cultic practices. In this critique, Yahweh's pronouncements attack all the elements of Israel's worship, for it is not only the feasts or assemblies or offerings or songs that smack of hypocrisy, but everything within the cult.[41]

This denunciation of the cultic practices here is unequivocal, however its connection with משפט and צדק is quite different from that of Isa. 1:10-17. In Amos 5:21-24, the transition between the critique of the cult and v. 24 is through the use of an adversative *waw*. To translate the *waw* as "and" would be to miss the impact and intent of Amos's words; the LXX uses καὶ in this instance. Amos shows a sharp contrast between that which is *thought to be*

---

[40] W. Brueggemann, "Amos IV: 4-13 and Israel's Covenant Worship," VT 15 (1965), p. 9. See also, Alger, who notes that, "The requirements of God's justice were that within the covenantal framework there should be right behavior and this involved more than externalism in religion. It demanded a right way of living together with one's neighbours." "The Theology and Social Ethic of Amos." p. 113.

[41] In Amos 5:22, even the so-called "peace offerings" are rejected. This is particularly important precisely because the term used for "peace offerings" here is שלם (which is also the term used in Lev. 3 [שלמים]). The significance of this lies in its root meaning, the sense of wholeness. See, Helmer Ringgren, *Israelite Religion*. trans. David Green (London: SPCK), 1966. Ringgren points out that the nature of the שלם offering is that it establishes communion with God, or rather, this is the intended purpose, pp. 170-171. The significance of this is that it rejects that sacrifice which is ultimately meant to bring the individual in communion with God, precisely because this sacrifice is divorced from social justice.

efficacious and that which *is* important and essential. Whether this adversative *waw* connotes "instead of" or "in addition to" will be discussed later. Wolff notes that this critique cannot be separated from the references in 5:7 and 6:12 where משפט is turned into wormwood and poison. This משפט "was meant to effect blessing and prosperity among the people, just as the streams and rivers of a land bring the gift of fertility and life."[42] The presence of משפט and צדק in 5:24 serve as a clear reminder of the elements which are necessary for life, seen alongside the emptiness of the cultic rituals. "One could not worship God truly without an active commitment to the welfare of others."[43] It is precisely this failure which is being criticized in 5:21-24.

4. Mic. 6:1-8

Mic. 6:1-8[44] is a perfectly self-contained example of the mistakenness of Israel's priorities. The unit 6:1-5, might be regarded as a court scene, with two witnesses (the mountains and the hills), together with Yahweh and Israel. Micah summons the people to hear what Yahweh has to say and then breaks the news to them that Yahweh is involved in a lawsuit and Israel is the defendant. The speech by Yahweh is not a polemical and abrasive one but a lamenting, reflective one which outlines the positive elements that have brought Yahweh and Israel closer together in the past. Moreover, these are all occasions in which Yahweh was the deliverer and Savior, and Israel, the delivered, the recipient of saving

---

[42] Wolff, *Joel and Amos*, p. 264.

[43] James M. Ward, *Amos and Isaiah* (Nashville: Abingdon Press), 1969, p. 71. For a different understanding of Amos 5:24, see Mariottini, who suggests that, "The word משפט involves the juridical right of the individual in the court of law, while צדקה involves the norm of right living." *Diss.*, p. 96. Mariottini's view creates a severe limitation on the scope of צדק and משפט in this context and in so doing misses the overall direction of Amos's message.

[44] The question regarding the unity of Mic. 6:1-8 is still in debate. However, most scholars agree that 6:1-8 is a unit. See, e.g. Leslie C. Allen, *The Books of Joel, Obadiah, Jonah and Micah*. NICOT (Grand Rapids, Michigan: Eerdmans), 1976, p. 362; Ralph L. Smith, *Micah-Malachi*. WBC (Waco, Texas: Word Books), p. 50; H.W. Wolff, *Micah* (Minneapolis: Augsburg Fortress Press), 1990, p. 164. Against this view, see Mays, *Micah*, p. 128.

action. With this reflective tone, this unit is not unlike Isa. 1:2ff, which even though it too is a court scene, nevertheless is not harsh but has a tone of lamentation. Yahweh in vv. 3-5, clearly sets the scene for the response of the people in vv. 6-7. Even though the recapitulation by Yahweh of his acts of deliverance does not focus particularly on cultic events, it is precisely the cultic events and activities that are perceived by the people to be the main element in question.[45]

In the people's response in vv. 6-7, it is evident that they have misunderstood the words of Yahweh. From Yahweh's opening statement, it is clear that something has gone awry in the relationship with Israel and that it is the fault of the latter. Israel realizes this, and both this realization and the desire to restore the relationship lead the people to offer a catalogue of cultic possibilities, attesting to their belief that this is the necessary constituent for the relationship. The question which begins v. 6 illustrates clearly the disposition of the questioner.[46] This individual assumes, in a tone which suggests some degree of dissatisfaction, that Yahweh is displeased because of the quantity and quality of the cultic offerings. The question loses its genuine quest for an-

---

[45] See, J.T. Willis, "Review of Th. Lescow, Micha 6, 6-8," *VT* 18 (1968), pp. 273-278. Regarding the link between vv. 1-5 and vv. 6-7, Willis believes, "that a good case can be made in favor of the idea that vv. 6-7 represents a spontaneous response of Micah's hearers to his *Gerechtrede* in vv. 1-5 in the form of a "Torliturgie" with which they had become so familiar in the Jerusalem cult. This would explain the ' breathless' emotional character of these questions." p. 277.

[46] See Hans Walter Wolff, *Micah the Prophet*. trans. Ralph D. Gehrke (Philadelphia: Fortress Press), 1981. Regarding the use of the singular "I" in vv. 6,7 and אדם in v. 8, Wolff says, "every individual must gain clarity about what is good for humanity." p. 105. This is an important observation, for the individual here represents more than a single person; the individual is an expression of all people. The fact that it is an individual who is being addressed makes the words of Yahweh pointed and seeks to show the essence of the message as it applies to all people. Perhaps, to have spoken to "his people" or "my people" might have blunted some of the sharpness of the words. See also James L. Mays, *Micah*. OTL (London: SCM Press), 1976. On the use of אדם in 6:8, Mays notes that this "reflects the generalizing and paradigmatic intention of the saying as a whole; its teaching is meant for any *man* in Israel." p. 141. This is also reflected in Barstad's notion that, "these words of Micah do not seem to stand in any particular context or to be regarded as a general theological statement of the prophet." *The Religious Polemics*, p. 114.

swers from Yahweh by having the questioner propose a list of possible answers, moving from the commonly used, to the most outrageous, that of the offering of a first born. What is immediately apparent in the answer of the questioner is that all the possibilities are associated with some form of cultic offering. There is a clear sense that sacrifices and offerings function in an *ex opere operato* manner.

This response is intricately associated with Yahweh's ריב against Israel. It might be said that in vv. 3-5, it is Yahweh who is presenting his side of the ריב while the people respond in vv. 6-7. The people are obviously attuned to a tradition which presupposes that brokenness in the relationship with Yahweh is repaired through the offering of sacrifices. Hence, the people ponder whether it is the quantity (thousands of rams; ten thousands of rivers of oil) or the quality (a first-born child) of the offering which is in question.[47] There are two implications here. First, as was noted earlier, the words of Yahweh in vv. 3-5 are perceived to refer to the inadequacy of the cultic practices. Second, there is, inherent in the people's response the belief that the sacrificial system is a panacea for all the brokenness in their relationship with Yahweh. It appears only to be a question of quality and quantity. Israel however, is not allowed to continue in this misguided belief that it is through the sacrificial cult that a proper relationship with Yahweh can be maintained.[48] The requirement of Yahweh is pronounced in v. 8. This requirement is not only concretely outlined, but it appears to reject every iota of the worshipper's suggestions. The second half of v. 8 has the underlying implication that outside of משפט and צדק, nothing else is required. There is no indication however, whether v. 8b is meant to be "instead of" or "a part of" the cultic practices of vv. 6-7.

---

[47] It may be true as Mays notes, that the worshipper wishes to humble himself or herself before Yahweh, but it still remains that "self-humiliation" and submission to Yahweh are seen only in terms of cultic offerings, *Micah*, p. 139.

[48] See, E. Hammershaimb, "Some leading ideas in the Book of Micah" in *Some Aspects of Old Testament Prophecy from Isaiah to Malachi* (København: Rosenkilde og Bagger), 1966, pp. 36ff.

The discussion to this point has focused on the critique of the cult and the alternative expectation pronounced by the prophets. While the invectives and denunciations are sharp, there is no word of punishment. In this regard, Amos 8:3a is helpful. It may be translated as "The Songs of the temple shall become wailings in that day...."[49] Mays notes that, "the hymns of the temple were songs of exuberant joy and hope in Yahweh, but under the lash of Yahweh's wrath the sound of wailing, the howling chants of lamentation, would replace them."[50] This is the critical point here, for that which was once held to be an element of joy and communion with Yahweh will become no more than a funerary lament. The judgment entails a total reversal of expectations. This is the matter which is the focus of the next section.

---

[49] This is from the NRSV. See also, Mays, who translates it, "they wail the hymns of the temple in that day...." *Amos*, p. 140. However, Wolff, translates it, "then the songstresses of the palace will wail." *Joel and Amos*, p. 317. There are two important points to note here. Wolff emends the text at this point, so instead of שירות, the text now reads שרות. This of course, is translated as "songstresses," and given this emendation, "palace" is a natural translation of היכל. Wolff assumes that שירות is a scribal error and that the original word was שרות. One reason given for this conclusion is that שירות (songs) is unlikely to be the subject of "wail." p. 317.
However, there is no other reference in Amos where שרות is used and there is certainly no other occurrence of שירות in Amos which may be used to support Wolff's argument. As such, there is no reason to depart from the use of שירות in the MT. Moreover, היכל can be translated either as "temple" or "palace." There are six occurrences of היכל in the Eighth Century prophets and on three occasions (Isa. 6:1; Amos 8:3; Mic. 1:2) the contexts demand the translation of "temple" and the other three occurrences (Isa. 13:22; 39:7; Hos. 8:14) call for "palace" as the likely translation. Using only this external evidence, there is no reason why היכל should particularly be translated as "palace" in 8:3. What is essential in determining the most likely meaning, is the context.
When 8:3 is understood in the light of Amos's overall condemnation of cultic practices, then it is clear that שירות must be upheld and rendered as "songs" as an expression of worship and היכל as "temple" in order to correspond to the meaning of the text. "The songs of the temple shall become wailings in that day."

[50] Mays, *Amos*, p. 141. See, also Shalom Paul, *Amos*. (Minneapolis: Fortress Press), 1991, who notes with graphic detail that, "The whining is occasioned by the dreadful sight of heaps of corpses shrewn all about. The prophet does not indicate the cause of their death, whether by pestilence or by the hand of some enemy....Masses of bodies are cast about unburied or disinterred. Because the greatest ignominy and disgrace is not to be brought to a proper burial, all the prophet can utter is (הַס) hush...." p. 255.

5. The Cult: Cleansing or Abolition?

It has become increasingly clear from this discussion that the prophets' social critique involves an extensive attack on the cult. All of the Eighth Century prophets have shown that, "the participants in the sacrificial rites follow the rules laid down for cultic celebrations, but they do not follow the rules laid down by Yahweh for moral and social behavior. Able to bring offerings, they are at the same time unable to do justice towards the weaker ones among their fellow citizens."[51] The people see the cultic rituals as sufficient for a continued relationship with Yahweh and for the securing of his goodwill. The people who are being criticized for their cultic practices without משפט and צדק are the affluent and powerful, and it is their affluence and power which suggest to these people that they are enjoying Yahweh's favor. Their prosperity has allowed them to secure great offerings (Mic. 6:6-7), but, as Waterman observes, "in their zeal to secure the means for costly offerings the people were not concerned about any principle of economic justice involved in getting them; as a result ruthlessness was condoned in everyday life while its direct antagonism to true religion was not even suspected."[52] It is this discontinuity between the cultic practices and the social life of the people which is the primary concern of the prophets' critique. However, in this critique of the cult because of the absence of משפט and צדק it is not entirely clear whether the prophets are calling for an abolition of the cult or a re-ordering of its priorities.

Scholars who argue that the prophets are preaching an abolition of the cult generally look to Amos and Isaiah as their *point d'appui*. James Williams suggests that Amos's anticultic polemic is more that a denunciation of the cult in its present form, that is, only ritual faithfulness and no social justice. Rather, he contends that Amos 5:21-24 is directly dependent on 5:25. Amos's rhetorical question regarding the bringing of sacrifices in the wilderness implies the answer "no." Williams uses this argument to arrive at

---

[51] Barstad, *The Religious Polemics*, p. 115.
[52] Leroy Waterman, "The ethical clarity of the Prophets," *JBL* 64 (1945), p. 299.

the conclusion that Amos is saying, "sacrifices are completely invalid now, whether they are offered by morally blameless hand or not."[53] The use of Amos 5:25 as support for the thesis that sacrifices and offerings were not originally a part of Israel's response to Yahweh's covenant is also supported by Lindblom. He sees Amos 5:25 as indicating that, "the entire cult, as it was celebrated at the sanctuaries, was alien to the genuine Yahweh religion and detested by Yahweh."[54] In effect, the cult not only fails to affect Yahweh, which is what it is meant to do, but it stands in the way of a relationship with Yahweh. The rhetorical question in v. 25 suggests implicitly that Yahweh's care and provision for the Israelites while they were in the wilderness were not effected by the cultic practices of Israel. Hence, it is unnecessary now, particularly since it prevents the essential elements of the relationship. What is argued here is that Yahweh does not need sacrifices and offerings, and that these have no covenantal validity.[55] With this presupposition, Amos 5:24 is seen not in conjunction with, but in contradistinction to 5:21-23. In this regard the *waw* which begins 5:24 is seen as meaning "instead," rather than "in addition." Moreover, Shalom Paul perceptively observes that, "...This total disavowal of the cult is expressed anthromorphically by the Lord's shutting off so to speak, several of his own senses: smell (v 21 אָרִיחַ לֹא), sight (v 22 לֹא אַבִּיט), and hearing (v 23 לֹא אֶשְׁמָע)."[56]

Similarly, Isaiah's criticism of the cult is understood to be a complete rejection of it. Ward argues that the critique in Isa. 1:10-17 "cannot be mitigated by appealing to Isa. 6....Chapter 6 does indeed prove the importance of the temple and formal acts of atonement in Isaiah's own experience and faith, but it does not constitute an endorsement of animal sacrifices."[57] Ward thus sees

---

[53] James Williams, "Social Location...." p. 160.
[54] Lindblom, *Prophecy in Ancient Israel*, p. 353.
[55] See, Irving M. Zeitlin, *Ancient Judaism* (Cambridge: Polity Press), 1984, p. 221. See also, John Skinner, *Prophecy and Religion* (Cambridge: Cambridge University Press), 1922. Skinner argues that, "Not only is sacrifice of no avail as a substitute for righteous conduct, but a perfect religious relationship is possible without sacrifice at all." p. 181.
[56] Shalom Paul, *Amos*, p. 192.
[57] Ward, *Hosea*, p. 122.

the presence of the temple in Isa. 6 as being distinct from the critique of the cult. This is further supported by the fact that within the critique of the cult, there appears to be no questions of the purification of the cult. Ward holds that, "ritual modes of access to God are wholly rejected...and the active pursuit of justice is upheld as the sole legitimate means of appropriating God's blessing."[58] The question here is not whether sacrifices, pilgrimages, festivals and prayers are rejected in principle; to pursue this is to miss the point. It is not the principle which is in question, but that they are modes of access to God.[59] In other words, the intrinsic validity of these rituals is in question. Scholars who pursue this view, see the cult on the one hand, and משפט and צדק on the other, as antithetical.[60]

The lack of consensus on the question of the critique of the cult is reflected in the sharply divided positions held by scholars. The idea that the prophets preach for a retention of the cult, once cleansed, is also held by many scholars. The basic point in this position suggests that the prophets are calling not so much for the abolition of the cult, as for משפט and צדק to be reflected in cultic practices. One of the early proponents of this position was William Harper.[61] In his introductory section on Amos, Harper notes, "to have opposed sacrifice in itself would have meant opposition to the only method yet known to humanity of entering into communion with deity, in a word the abolition of all tangible worship....It was therefore, not sacrifices in general that Amos opposed."[62] The argument is that Amos is not interested in abolishing worship or sacrifices, for if he had been interested in doing so, he would have indicated this plainly. As Kapelrud suggests, what is clear is that the prophet is critical of the form of the cult of Yahweh. He notes

---

[58] Ward, *Amos and Isaiah*, p. 233.

[59] Ibid., p. 235. See also, Zeitlin, *Ancient Judaism*, p. 226.

[60] For a brief word on the abolition of the cult in Micah and Hosea, see Glueck, *Ḥesed in the Bible*, p. 61.

[61] William Rainer Harper, *A Critical and Exegetical Commentary on Amos and Hosea*. ICC (Edinburgh: T and T Clark), 1905. See also, H.H. Rowley, "The Nature of Prophecy in the Light of Recent Study," *HTR* 38 (1945), pp. 1-38.

[62] Harper, *Amos and Hosea*, p. cxix.

that, "It has become a rich temple cult, dominated by sacrifices and feasts which overshadow other important features, first and foremost the ethical demands."[63] It is this element of "ethical demands" which is seen to be the point of interest, rather than the cult itself. What is necessary is a renewal of the relationship with Yahweh which will bring a corresponding response to other individuals within the framework of social justice and which in turn, will bring meaning to the sacrifices and worship. The hollowness of the cult and its separation from social justices is precisely what makes it ineffective and unacceptable. However, as Rowley suggests, "there is no reason to suppose that they [the pre-exilic prophets] held that no other sacrifices could be offered by men whose hearts were right with God."[64] Inherent in being "right with God" is "being right" with one another.

This school of thought does not believe that the cult is in tension with social justice, but that they are intended to be interrelated. Thus when the cult becomes an act unrelated to the society and its needs, then a critique of the cult is a moral responsibility. The fact that the cult, which is the central location for communion between God and the individual, can become "a carnival of human activity"[65] attests the absence of Yahweh and the futility of the rituals. The automatic and self-contained nature of the cult

---

[63] Kapelrud, *Central Ideas*, pp. 75-76. See also, R.E. Clements, *Prophecy and Covenant*. SBT (London: SCM Press), 1965, who notes, "We must understand the prophetic criticism of the cult, therefore not as signifying that the prophets themselves desired a new kind of non-cultic religion on Israel's part. If we may conjecture what kind of reforms they would have sought to introduce, they would not have introduced the abolition of all cult, but its transformation to become a vehicle of a more ethical and responsible attitude toward Yahweh....The condemnation of the cult lay not in the fact of its existence but in the fact that it had abandoned the covenant tradition of Israel's past." p. 100. See also, Ivan Engnell, "Prophets and Prophetism in the Old Testament" in *Critical Essays on the Old Testament*. trans. John T. Willis (London: SPCK), 1970, pp. 123-179. Engnell suggests that, "these so-called anti-cultic sayings refer to special cases: they are directed either against certain definite forms of the cult...or against a cult whose advocates are incriminated in one way or another, especially in their inferior ethical and social practices." p. 139.

[64] H.H. Rowley, *The Unity of the Bible* (London: Carey Kingsgate Press), 1953, p. 43.

[65] Wolff, *A Guide*, p. 85.

is precisely the action which results in a breakdown in the vertical and horizontal relationship. It is under these circumstances that the cult is seen to be under criticism, for the value of the cult can be gauged only from its effect on the participant to pursue social justice. Thus it is claimed that a cleansing of the cult is what is necessary.[66]

Certain observations are necessary at this point. It is clear that the matter of social justice and the cult are closely intertwined; both schools of thought at least agree on this fundamental point. Those who argue that the prophets are seeking an abolition of the cult are in fact implying that these prophets are revolutionaries. An individual who seeks to bring to an end an institution which is basic to the religious needs of the people and which traditionally has served positively within the lives of the people, can only be seen as a revolutionary. Yet, there is no need to believe that the abolition of the cult would be the answer. To pursue this line of thought may in fact lead one to overlook the main interest of the prophets. The prophets are concerned about the relationship between the cult and social justice, and they see this relationship in a proper form, as an integral part of Israel's life. To have abolished the cult would, in a different manner, also ruin the relationship. "Cult in itself was not sufficient, it had to be combined with ethics."[67] The reverse is equally unacceptable, for ethics divorced

---

[66] Reflecting on Hosea's critique of the cult in 6:4-6, Barstad, notes that, "Hosea simply states that there are certain qualities which Yahweh wants from the Israelites other than the cultic ones....It is more appropriate to say that this prophet makes the value of the cult relative than to claim that he rejects it." *The Religious Polemics*, p. 113. Also, Engnell, who notes that "the demand for righteousness is a demand involving cultic responsibilities. In fact it includes a demand for cult, for a *right* cult, of Yahweh, a genuine Yahwistic cult, unmixed with foreign elements and combined with ethical and social blamelessness." "Prophets and Prophetism." p. 138.

[67] Kapelrud, *Central Ideas*, p. 76. See also, Jacob, who suggests that, "whenever formalism...succeeded in installing itself in the cult, when it became a system at the disposal of man which he felt to be sufficient to put right with God, then it became dangerous. For once settled in the interior of a system, man closes his eyes to reality and no longer sees that the divine presence goes infinitely beyond the cultic framework." "The Biblical Prophets..." p. 53. Also Engnell, who says, "The prophets do not demand righteousness *instead of* the cult, but righteousness *and* cult, right cult." "Prophets and Prophetism." p. 138.

from the cult leaves the actions of the people detached from the relationship with Yahweh. Both are necessary for Israel.

The argument for the retention of the cult together with משפט and צדק is a valid one. What needs to be understood in this position is that, "the value of true worship is beyond estimate, as the source of power and direction for all of life."[68] The fundamental nature of "true worship" is that it is rooted in Yahweh, a connection which has implications for the well-being of the society. In holding to this position, two comparisons may be made.

One aspect of Israel's life which comes under attack by Isaiah in particular, is the monarchy. It is clear from Isaiah's words that the monarchy is involved both in internal and external matters which do not reflect Israel's relationship with Yahweh. The critique of the monarchy is relevant to the discussion here, in that, with all its faults, the prophets do not seek the abolition of the monarchy. Rather they seek a just and loyal king. This can be understood at two levels. First, there is the messianic oracle of Isa. 11:1-4 which refers to the coming of the messiah rather than to an earthly king of Israel. Second, there are the references in 9:6-7;[69] 16:5; 32:1, 16-17 which point clearly to future kings[70] in Israel. Moreover, one's attention is called to the fact that each of these four occurrences notes that the king will rule in משפט and צדק. The significance of the prophesy is that these kings will not merely rule, but rule with משפט and צדק. This makes for a particularly useful comparison with the critique of the cult. Like the monarchy, the cult also comes under attack, but while scholars do not argue for the abolition of the monarchy, the cult does not enjoy a similar position. However, in many respects the critiques are similar; like

---

[68] Wolff, *A Guide*, p. 85.

[69] The Christian Church has taken 9:6-7 as a prophetic oracle, referring to the coming of the Messiah. However, historically it was meant to refer to an earthly king. See e.g., Clements, *Isaiah 1-39*, p. 104 and Kaiser, *Isaiah 1-12*, pp. 204ff.

[70] In 16:5, מלך is not used, but clearly the implication is there through the use of כסא. In 32:1, מלך is used together with ימלך, and these words are the source for the description in 32:16-17. There will be צדק and משפט once there is a מלך who reigns with צדק and משפט.

the monarchy, the cult needs the essential elements which enable it to function properly.

The second observation regards the parallel with the prophets' critique of the "judicial system." This aspect of judicial functioning is an essential part of Israelite life; qualification to participate as a judge here is closely related to one's status in society. This inbuilt structure is a channel for the many expressions of social injustice and, like the cult, comes under severe attack from the prophets. (Isa. 5:23; Amos 5:12) While the prophets are disgusted by the corruption in this aspect of the judicial system, it would be an oversimplification to suggest that they are seeking an abolition of the judicial system. Despite the inherent problems, this system is necessary, and, as in the case of the cult, the prophets' attack focus on the element of cleansing, not abolition.

The cult being the center of Israel's life is by its nature theocentric, and this is exactly the point which is made by Amos in 5:21-24. The צדק is missing from the cult, and this immediately indicates that the element which brings Israel into relationship with Yahweh and sustains this relationship is absent. This has a twofold effect. First, with the absence of צדק, the cult becomes strictly anthropocentric, and the values which emanate from it are expressions of humanism rather than of the covenant with Yahweh. Second, it is impossible for משפט to be reflected in the lives of these people, precisely because משפט has its source in צדק. Hence, the critique of the cult is one which calls for the cleansing of the cult, and this can be accomplished only through the restoration of the relationship with Yahweh.

C. Affluence at the Poor's Expense
   Isa. 3:18-24; Amos 3:14-15; 4:1; 5:11; 6:4.

The prophets' critique of the excessive luxury of some in Israel is closely tied to the punishment of these individuals by Yahweh. The crass over-indulgence and the extravagance are seen as wholly unacceptable in the light of the stage of the poor and oppressed, those from whom the affluent can afford their luxurious living. As Bernhard Lang notes, Amos, "does not only attack wealth, but also *la dolce vita*;"⁷¹ it is this whole lifestyle which comes under attack. In examining the prophets' critique of the corrupting influence of affluence and luxury, it must be understood that the prophets are not members of a particular economic class at odds against another. It is certainly not the case that the prophets are placing the poor on a pedestal and proclaiming the advantages of being poor. Moreover, they are not ideologically against wealth, but they *are* opposed to certain ways of procuring riches and maintaining affluence. As Mays explains, "if [wealth] fostered conspicuous consumption at a level of luxury that was enjoyed in heedless unconcern for the needs of others, it was wrong. If it was gained by the violation of the rules of righteousness which set the value of personal relations above profit, it was iniquitous. If wealth became the dominant motivation of those responsible for social well-being, because they held power, that was sin."⁷² It is the acquisition of wealth at the expense of the poor and the maligning of צדק and משפט which come under attack.

The scene for this discussion is set within the detailed outline of the fine jewelry and luxurious ornaments which are a part of the superfluous needs of the rich.⁷³ (vv. 18-23) In this context, it is the women who are being criticized, but the critique clearly extends from v.13. The theme of vv. 14-15 cannot be separated from the critique of vv. 18-23. The punishment outlined in v. 24 clearly corresponds to the critique of Isaiah, for those who have perpetuated for themselves great luxury at the expense of the poor, will now be made to live in the manner of the poor.⁷⁴

---

⁷¹ Bernhard Lang, "The Social Organization of Peasant Poverty in Biblical Israel," *JSOT* 24 (1982), p. 54.

⁷² Mays, "Justice...." p. 14.

⁷³ Most scholars agree that vv. 18-23 is an interpolation. See, e.g., Clements *Isaiah 1-39*, p. 50; Kaiser, *Isaiah 1-12*, p. 79; Wildberger, *Isaiah 1-12*, p. 151. However, even though these verses may not be Isaianic in origin, they are nevertheless in the spirit of vv. 16-17, 24.

⁷⁴ Kaiser, says that, "it is not clear that the prophetic critic has anything but feminine variety and delight in jewelry in mind; this, along with an exaggerated self-consciousness, causes him offense." *Isaiah 1-12*, p. 79. Kaiser, in this view overlooks the larger connection between this luxury and the corresponding poor.

This denunciation by Isaiah is one which has a distinct similarity to Amos 4:1 ff,[75] but in the latter's case there is the sharp juxtaposition between the "cows of Bashan" on the one hand and "the poor" on the other. Because of this explicit contrast, an examination of this context would be appropriate for this discussion. Bashan in Transjordan is a region traditionally noted for its fine cattle and rich fertile land.[76] Bashan stands out as a place of quality, and the products of Bashan are generally considered superior. It is therefore no surprise that these women whose primary interest is in luxury and drink are described as "cows of Bashan," for they are out to secure the best for themselves. It is clear that these "cows of Bashan" are upper-class "women of the elite social stratum of the capital city."[77] This notwithstanding, Amos is clearly not interested in dwelling on the quality of the women, lest it be surmised that he is viewing them in a complimentary way. The use of "cows"[78] must be conceived of in reference to the animals of Bashan and it is this image which is superimposed on the women. So traditionally, while it is the cattle of Bashan that are the most well-fed, and of good size, now it is the women of Samaria who fit this description. Bashan probably still has good land and fine cattle, but the excessiveness of the women's desires has overshadowed this traditional point of reference. These women have become like the fat well-bred cows and "like replete cattle, they willfully trample down their pastures, the lower classes of the people, on which their existence in fact depends."[79]

If the over-eating and over-drinking is particularly repugnant in these women, still worse is the fact that this kind of rev-

---

[75] Kaiser, notes that the critique of Isaiah does not have the same social slant as Amos does. *Isaiah 1-12*, p. 79. However it must be stated that there is a reference to trampling of the poor in Isaiah's critique of the affluent. See later discussion of Isa. 3:12-15.

[76] See, e.g. Deut. 32:14; Ps. 22:12; Ezek. 39:18; Mic. 7:14.

[77] Wolff, *Joel and Amos*, p. 205.

[78] Mays suggests that "cow" is not a derogatory name for women in the Ancient Near East, for here the women are referred to as "cows" in a complimentary manner. "Justice...." p. 72. See also, Jean-Luc Vesco, who suggests, "'vaches de Basan' souligne leur prospérité...." "Amos de Teqoa...." p. 496.

[79] Koch, *The Prophets* I, p. 46.

elry is made at the expense of the poor and defenseless who are exploited mercilessly.[80] The women of Samaria are able to continue in the luxury and excess in which they live, only through this exploitation of the poor. The attitude of the women to their husbands is also quite revealing, for the women's demands are so constant that the husbands have no choice but to procure enough wealth to sustain their drinking.

As in Isa. 3:24, the punishment in Amos 4:2f. is quite appropriate. Even though the terms צנות and סירות are not clear in their meaning, the generally accepted renderings of "hooks" and "fishhooks" respectively fit the context well. What is of essence here is the extremity of the punishment, which corresponds with the actions of the recipients.

Outside of the particularity of the "cows of Bashan" and the luxury of the women, there is also a general and larger expression of the affluence within society. In Amos 3:14-15, the juxtaposition of the cult and the affluence of some, is once again a clear commentary on the connection between these two aspects of life. Punishment is meted out both to the cult and to the affluent. The outlining of the different kinds of houses in v. 15 is indicative of the great wealth which is being enjoyed at the expense of the poor. This relationship between the oppression of the poor and the corresponding increase in affluence of the powerful is clearly spelled out in Amos 5:11. It is only because the דלים are trampled that the economic extravagances of the powerful can be afforded. The building of "houses of hewn stone" (cf. 3:15) and the planting of pleasant vineyards are directly related to an economic trampling of the דלים. However the judgment of Yahweh will ensure that the luxuries of these affluent people will never be enjoyed; they will be deprived of the pleasures which are expected from their wealth. Even those who have begun to bask in their luxurious living will not enjoy it forever. The stark contrast between the "ruin of Joseph" and the affluent is particularly poignant in Amos 6:4-6, where there is the reference to "beds of ivory" and the eating of

---

[80] See, P.J. Balduino Kipper, "A evolução econômico - social em Israel e a pregação das profetas," *RCB* 20 (1977), p. 315.

lambs and calves, the choicest and most tender meat, excessive drinking and the lavishness of finest oils. The extent of this kind of luxury and living is seen only in the light of the plight of the poor. While the wealthy are living in excesses, the poor have their garments taken away in pledges. (2:8) The poor lose the source of their livelihood (5:11) while the rich eat and drink in excessive amounts.

It is therefore no surprise that on every occasion where there is a description of the affluence of Israel, there is a corresponding indictment and judgment. The procuring of wealth, with a disregard for the condition of the poor, is seen as a direct affront to the relationship with Yahweh and to the inherent expectations.

D. Monetary Economy, Merchants and Rich Landowners
   Isa. 3:12-15, 5:8; Amos 2:6-7; 5:11; 8:4-6; Mic. 2:1-2

The ever-widening gap between the rich and poor, is for the Eighth Century prophets a major concern. In some respects, it is the most crucial aspect of their message, for it involves at its very core the question of economics. This in turn is connected with the cult and also with the legal assembly. The main economic factor which affects the poor is the lack of land. The importance of land and property cannot be overemphasized, for it is the landowning citizens who constitute the legal assembly of the towns. In order to be counted as a member of a particular community, a person has to be a propertied citizen of that community.[81] The difficulty of the poor person is self-evident, for in having no property or land, membership in the community is nullified as is the opportunity to be a member of the assembly. Thus, the non-propertied persons are caught in a web which sets them on the periphery of society. This, however, is but one difficulty, for there are others which are fundamentally associated with the covenant with Yahweh.

---

[81] See, e.g., Gen. 23 and the situation of Abraham. Also, Lang, *Monotheism*, p. 126.

1. Early Exploitation

The international, external indicators of success during the Eighth Century suggest that Israel was a successful nation and much of this was based on the exploitative orientation of Israelite society. What in effect was transpiring, judged by apparent success, was a growing division within the society, separating those who were the small family landowners from the wealthy entrepreneurs. Moreover, as Kaiser points out, "as a results of Uzziah's foreign policy, the tributes of neighboring countries and the latifundia economy practised by the king brought ready money into the country."[82] With this economy built on a readily available flow of money, the wealthy landowners are the ones capable of procuring greater assets, primarily land from the poor at the latter's expense. The small landowners find that they cannot support themselves from the resources of their land and thus become increasingly dependent on their wealthier counterparts who take advantage of their situation. It is a system which thrives on the flow of capital and in then long term creates a damaging rift in the society. The pursuit of power and affluence blind these entrepreneurs to the ills which are becoming widespread, directly as a consequence of their actions. The poor landowners become ready preys for quick investment, and the responsibility for the poor and powerless is neglected as are the expectations of the covenant relationship with Yahweh.

However, not only do these actions against the poor contradict the expectations of the covenant, but the securing of land from the poor for financial gain is fundamentally contrary to Israel's existence. The prophets' opposition to this attitude of land-grabbing by the wealthy landowners clearly presupposes, "the ancient tribal concept of political and economic life, in which distribution of property was more equitable."[83] During the period of the tribal

---

[82] Kaiser, *Isaiah 1-12*, p. 65.
[83] James G. Williams, "The Alas-Oracles of the Eighth Century Prophets," *HUCA* 38 (1967), p. 85. See, also, Delbert R. Hillers, *Micah* HERMENEIA (Philadelphia: Fortress Press), 1984. Hillers notes that, "the economic and social ideal of ancient Israel was of a nation of free landowners - not debt-

system in Israel's history, property, including land and means of sustenance, was considered to be inalienable for everyone. The customs by which the people lived involved caring for each other.[84] These are the elements which are now absent from Israelite society. The right to ownership of land appear as myth, and the obligations which are a part of tribal customs are forgotten.

Some scholars view the rise of the monarchy as the primary catalyst for this sharp division in Israelite society. De Vaux, for example, argues that the advent of the monarchy and its firm establishment in the life of Israel has within it the elements which spark off a monetary economy involving the rich and poor. According to him, with the centralization of the monarchy, "the play of economic life, business deals and the sale of land, destroyed the equality between families, some of whom became very rich, while others sank in poverty."[85] Archaeological evidence has verified this division. Whereas, excavation of Tenth Century Israelite

---

slaves, share-croppers, or hired workers - secure in possession, as a grant from Yahweh, of enough land to keep their families." p. 33.

[84] See, Edward Neufeld, "The Emergence of Royal-Urban Society in Ancient Israel," *HUCA* 31 (1960), p. 33.

[85] Roland de Vaux, *Ancient Israel: Its Life and Institutions*. trans. John McHugh (London: Darton, Longman and Todd), 1961, p. 68, and Siegfried Herrmann, *A History of Israel in Old Testament Times*. trans. John Bowden (London: SCM Press), 1981, p. 236. Also, Robert B. Coote, *Amos Among the Prophets* (Philadelphia: Fortress Press), 1981. Coote argues that the plight of the poor in the Eighth Century was due to two main factors. First, there was "the shift from the predominance of patrimonial domain to prebendal domain and [second], the role of the ruling elite in encouraging and profiting from this shift." p. 26.

Essentially, Coote notes, the movement away from the inalienable rights to land, towards its commercialization. He points out that, "the way the ruling elite of Israel exercised prebendal domain has been called rent capitalism. The peasant occupiers of the prebendal estates had not only to pay tribute for the use of the land, but also rent for the various means, or factors, of production like water, seed, work animals, tools, human labor for assistance...." p. 29. See also, Leslie C. Allen, "Amos, Prophet of Solidarity," *Vox Ev* 6 (1969), who notes that, "The bonds of the old tribal amphictyony had been loosened with the result that the traditional norm of social justice had collapsed. An economic boom caused by territorial expansion and new fields of commerce was enjoyed by certain sectors of the people. There developed a two-tier society, comprising an elite class of unscrupulous and irresponsible opportunists and the lower classes, exploited by the barons of commerce and agriculture." p. 46.

towns has shown that all the houses are of the same size and arranged in a similar manner, "the contrast is striking when we pass to the eighth century houses on the same site: the rich houses are bigger and better built and in a different quarter from that where the poor houses are huddled together."[86] Such is the situation which prompt the prophets to hurl invectives against the rich landowners.

In this discussion regarding the rich and the poor and the widening division between the two, it must be noted that it is not only the economic, but the religious question which is of great importance. The gift of the land harks back to Israel's deliverance from Egypt. In a fundamental sense, the amassing of land is not only a blatant injustice against the other person, but it is an act which seeks to usurp the position of Yahweh as the ultimate landowner. It is Yahweh who promises Israel the land, and it is Yahweh who guides them to it. Hence, the land belongs to all of Israel as a gift from Yahweh and to use this gift as an instrument of oppression against others not only defeats the original intent, but defies Yahweh's own action. The land cannot be presumed to be under the ownership of any individual or be under the governing auspices of a particular group. "The land shall not be sold in perpetuity, for the land is mine; with me you are but aliens and tenants." (Lev. 25:23) To secure land from the poor is therefore not only an unethical breach of the responsibilities of the rich, but is a blatant usurpation of that which is Yahweh's. Because the land belongs to Yahweh, it can neither be bought nor sold. "The prohibition of the sale of land was meant to keep in being the sound economic and social structure of the people."[87] In addition, how-

---

[86] De Vaux, *Ancient Israel*, pp. 72-73. See also, Neufeld, who notes that, "houses of wealthy townsmen had carved wooden ornaments representing human figures, there were winter houses and large summer houses made of ashlar or cedar or panelled with cedar wood, decorated with artistic panels made of ivory and painted with vermilion. This growing love of luxury, pretentiousness and ostentatiousness was in striking contrast to the simple unsophisticated and natural life traditional to the old pre-monarchical Israel and still fully maintained in the villages." "The Emergence...." p. 44.

[87] Kaiser, *Isaiah 1-12*, p. 66. See also, Herrmann, who notes, "that in Israel the land really belongs to Yahweh: every free Israelite who had land of his own administered it as the gift of Yahweh to himself and his family." *A His-*

ever, the land is a symbol of Yahweh's promise to and presence with Israel; it is an element involved in the covenant relationship. The land, as it is intended to be, serves as a unifying factor between Yahweh and Israel and then one section of the people and another. Thus the force of an exploitative ideology which has enveloped Israelite society, in addition to creating an unnatural rift within society, is simultaneously rejecting the covenantal demands of Yahweh and the ideals of Israel's existence. It is clear that the exploitation, practised by the rich landowners is alien to Israel's economic and social life.

2. Loans, Debtors and Usury

The use of loans by rich landowners is the single most effective way of procuring land while simultaneously oppressing the poor. Because of various circumstances the poor landowner is often compelled to borrow money in order to continue the work on the land, and the source of the loan is invariably the rich landowners. This is the point at which the small landowner's problems begin. To be a small landowner is to be in a state of oppression, precisely because of the difficulty of providing for one's family with such limited means. However, once the small landowner becomes a debtor and is in the firm grasp of his wealthy counterpart, that is the point at which oppression of a different nature begins.

This is the first step towards the possible acquisition of the poor person's land, and in this first step are involved two major factors. First, there is the unscrupulous nature of the transactions of the wealthy landowners. The primary motivational force behind their transactions with the poor landowners is concern not for the latter's welfare, but for their own self-interest. The wealthy landowners are determined to create an oligopoly of land, and the people who are the prime targets for insolvency are the small landowners. Second, there is nothing illegal about this kind of

---

tory of Israel, p. 236 and A. Alt, "Der Anteil des Königtums an der sozialen Entwicklung in den Reichen Israel und Juda" in *Grundfragen der Geschichte des Volkes Israel* (München), 1979, pp. 367ff.

transaction, and in fact there are laws which cover contingencies of this nature. Lev. 25:39-40 makes it clear that self-enslavement or debt slavery carries with it protection by the creditor; the debtor has to be treated at least as a hired servant or a sojourner. This law may be understood as giving legitimacy to the procuring of land from the poor. Thus, what the prophet is critical of is not the breaking of the law, but something much more fundamental, namely the lack of care and concern for the poor person. The wealthy landowner is driven by his own greed to have more for himself, regardless of the consequences to the poor. These entrepreneurs can only be content when "there is room for no one but you." (Isa. 5:8) Regarding the protection of the small farmer who takes out a loan, it is conceivable that most of the laws are kept, but there are clearly occasions in which the keeping of the law on the one hand and its avoidance on the other, lead to the demise of the Israelite small landowner.

The laws regarding the giving of loans allow for the seizure of goods and property from the debtor. This is perhaps the single most important factor which is responsible for the landless state of the poor. When the debtor is unable to repay a loan, then his property and other possessions become targets for seizure. Legally there is nothing untoward here, but once again, it is not the legality which is being questioned. In fact, the extent to which the possessions of the debtor are at the disposal of the creditor is spelled out in the words of Deut. 24:10-17. The implication here is that virtually everything owned by the debtor is within conforming limits as far as repayment is concerned. That the creditor is forbidden to take a widow's garment in pledge is indicative of the extremes. The widow is a classic example of poverty within the Ancient Near Eastern context, and a garment represents the last of the basic essentials. Even if the garment is not taken, still the plight of the poor is not particularly enhanced. Certainly when the law is viewed in this light, it is evident that its protective powers are minimal. It still depends heavily on the humaneness of the creditor. Invariably, there is a lack of humaneness in the transactions between rich and poor, and there is no escape once the small landowner is in the snare of his wealthy counterpart. This, however, is not a sad commentary on the misguidance and ill-judgment of the poor, for they have no choice. Not to borrow from the wealthy landowner, particularly in the wake of a poor crop or a crop failure, would be a sure expression of hopelessness and destruction.

However, it is not the taking out of the loan which is entirely responsible for the oppression of the small landowners. It is noteworthy that there is only one instance in the Eighth Century prophets against usury, and this is a disputed one. (Isa. 3:12) This, perhaps, may be taken to mean that at least there is some respect for the laws against usury.[88] After all, Israel departs from the traditions of the neighboring nations by condemning and disapproving of interest on loans. On the other hand however, it may be that the crimes against the poor are so overwhelming that details such as exorbitant interest rates are not singled out for criticism.[89] It is certainly difficult to envisage a wealthy landowner loaning money without interest, particularly since the pressure is on the small landowner to borrow, not the wealthy landowner to lend. The difference in socio-political climate between the time when the laws were created and the Eighth Century is clearly noted by Hillel Gamoran:

> Part of the explanation...as to why Israel had a law against interest...is that Israel's laws were formed during a period of less developed political and economic life....When Israel created its laws against interest, the only loans that were given were loans to the poor and hungry. There was no demand among the Israelites for commercial loans....A more advanced economy required

---

[88] See, e.g. Exod. 22:24 [25]; Lev. 25:35-38; Deut. 23:20-21 [19-20]. It is interesting to note that in the prohibition against interest, money is the one common element in all three references.

[89] For an alternative suggestion, see, Davies, who says that "it is possible...that the creditors of Isaiah's day had designed other methods of deriving benefits from their loans - methods which would have provided them with an incentive to lend money without resorting to the prohibited practice of usury." *Prophecy and Ethics*, p. 68.

loans for business purposes and not merely to alleviate poverty.[90]

Without doing so directly, Gamoran's idea points to the change in Israel's society, for no longer are the people involved as a pastoral community, but rather, the new economy distinguishes between the rich farmers and landowners on the one hand, and the peasant farmers on the other.[91] With this distinction there also emerges business pursuits, which mean that loans are not being given as aid to the poor but as a business transaction.

Even so, it must be noted that there is nothing inherently immoral or unethical about interest charged on loans. Rather, it is the interest which is charged against those persons with whom the lender supposedly shares a special relationship, grounded in Yahweh, that is in question. This is implicit in the Exodus and Leviticus references, and it is made explicit in Deut. 23:20-21 [19-20]. Interest may be charged against persons from other nations, but not against other Israelites.[92] The prohibition as stated in Deuteronomy in not specifying a particular economic class, allows for a better understanding of the importance of the relationship which is to exist among the Israelites. It is apparent in Lev. 25:35-38 and in Exod. 22:24[25] that the primary concern is for the poor,

---

[90] Hillel Gamoran, "The Biblical Law against Loans on Interest," *JNES* 30 (1971), p. 128. See also, S. Stein, "The Laws on Interest in the Old Testament," *JTS* 4 Part II (October 1953) pp. 161-170, especially p. 164.

[91] See, Neufeld, who notes that the fertile lowlands were inhabited and owned by the rich while the rocky highlands were inhabited by the poor, thus adding to the economic divisions. "The Emergence...." p. 44.

[92] Gamoran, notes that there is an important distinction to be made between נכרי and גר. The נכרי is "the foreigner who came to the land for a limited period of time and the *ger* the alien who permanently settled among the Israelites." "The Biblical law against loans on Interest." p. 130. The term which is used in Deuteronomy is נכרי. See, also, Edward Neufeld, "The prohibitions against Loans at Interest in Ancient Hebrew Laws," *HUCA* 26 (1955), pp. 355-412. Neufeld notes that, "the *nokri* stood in no relation to the tribe and could claim no legal rights; he was not included in the human laws in Deuteronomy for the protection of the poor and needy; he had neither home nor right in Israel." p. 389. Thus the נכרי could be charged interest on loans precisely because the נכרי is not presumed to be under Israelite law and even more important, because the נכרי is clearly not a member of the covenant relationship with Yahweh.

but in Deut. 23:20[19], the concern is for all Israel; the intrinsic element of care which accompanies the covenant relationship is evident.[93]

What appears certain from this discussion is the realization that the rich landowners are sinning legally. The small landowners are enmeshed in a situation which results in their loss, either way. If they borrow money from their wealthier counterparts, their agony is only prolonged, and if they refuse to take a loan, the end is swift. This is the nature of the law when approached in a detached and objective manner.[94] This is the point at which the prophets become sharply critical, for while the "letter of the law" might be adhered to, there is no צדק and משפט. In other words, the elements which are essential for the sustaining of the relationship between Israelites on the one hand, and between Yahweh and Israel on the other, are absent.

3. Isa. 3:12-15; 5:8

It still remains largely unresolved among scholars as to whether Isa. 3:12-15 is a unit. Some scholars[95] have suggested that 3:12 is a lament and forms a transition between the preceding verses and 3:13-15. Others view vv. 12-15 as a unit.[96] For the purposes of this discussion 3:12-15 will be taken as a unit, the significance of which will become apparent. In some ways, v. 12a holds the key to this unit. Scholarship regarding the meaning of this section of v. 12 is still in a state of flux. Most English transla-

---

[93] In other biblical references, it is clear that "interest" is frowned upon. See, e.g., Ezek. 22:12 and Ps. 15:5, both of which suggest that the taking of interest on a loan is tantamount to the acceptance of a שחד.

[94] See, Davies, who notes that in the Naboth incident (I Ki. 21:1-16) all of the necessary legal elements are present. Naboth is placed on trial by the monarch; two witnesses are found; Naboth's answer may be construed as blasphemy and the penalty of blasphemy is death by stoning. In addition to this, execution outside the wall is legal. *Prophecy and Ethics*, p. 78. Yet despite all of this, Naboth is innocent!

[95] See e.g., Clements, *Isaiah 1-39*, p. 49 and Wildberger, *Isaiah 1-12*, p. 138.

[96] See e.g., Kaiser, *Isaiah 1-12*, p. 74.

tions⁹⁷ follow the MT; however, the three textual variants⁹⁸ which are mentioned in the BHS on this verse are followed instead by the NEB.

> Money-lenders strip my people bare,
> and usurers lord it over them. (NEB)⁹⁹

This rendering of v. 12a not only provides a perfect unity with v. 12b, but shows clearly the connection with vv. 13-15. In vv. 12-15, several categories of those in power and authority are specified: money-lenders, usurers, leaders, elders and princes. What in fact is clear from these verses is the prophet's criticism of those who have responsibility to the poor and powerless, inherent in their office (leaders, elders and princes) and those who use the other citizens to further their own ambitions (money-lenders and usurers). In any event, it is evident that the poor are exploited and oppressed in order that the wealthy and powerful might continue to expand their monetary horizons. The unit makes it clear that the "poor" are Yahweh's people. This is seen in the presence of עמי three times and עמו twice,¹⁰⁰ and used twice in parallel to these, is עני. The idea of "crushing," "grinding," "misleading" points to the extremity of the poor's plight.

---

⁹⁷ See e.g., the NRSV and KJV.

⁹⁸ One of the key word in this verse is נגש - to exhort. (BDB) The MT reads נגשיו which misses the essence of the verse and certainly does not fit in the overall context. On the other hand, the variant נגשים in the BHS is a much more sensible choice. In this regard, see, G.R. Driver, "Linguistic and Textual Problem: Isaiah I-XXXIX," *JTS* 38 (1937), pp. 36-50. He suggests that the sense of the verse is only discovered with the use of נגשים. p. 38. See also, the LXX which uses πράκτορες, "tax-collectors." With the use of נגשים, then it follows that מעולל should be seen to come from עול and not עלל as is commonly done. The use of עול makes it clear that the context has to do with "exacting more than is just" and "imposing a burden." p. 38. Finally, the use of וְנֹשִׁים as opposed to MT's וְנָשִׁים brings out the complete sense of the sentence. Both the Targum and LXX prefer וְנֹשִׁים (usurers) to וְנָשִׁים (women).

⁹⁹ See also, Kaiser, "My people - everyone of their governors is a plunderer, and usurers rule them," *Isaiah 1-12*, p. 74, and Wildberger, "O, my people! Its tyrants are 'people fleecers,' and 'extortioners' rule over it." *Isaiah 1-12*, p. 137.

¹⁰⁰ עמו is the textual variant in v. 13; this fits the context better. (cf. LXX τὸν λαὸν αὐτοῦ) The MT reads עמים.

Chapter VI

> Ah, you who join house,
> who add field to field,
> until there is room (מקום) for no one but you,[101]
> and you are left to live alone[102]
> in the midst of the land.

Isa. 5:8 points clearly to the exploitation in Israel, where the wealthy continue to expand and the poor are left isolated with little in terms of property. Miller notes that the result of the "rapid expansion of one's wealth by acquiring more and more houses and land...was a breakdown in the order of Israelite society, increasing discrepancy between rich and poor and a fundamental violation of Yahweh's intention for the relationship between people and land."[103] What Israel is guilty of is both direct and indirect impugnment of Yahweh's role in Israel' s life. By appropriating what is not inherently theirs, the rich are turning the poor into slaves and thus creating an indirect affront to Yahweh. By seeking to secure the land for themselves, the wealthy landowners are directly rejecting Yahweh's ownership of the land.

It may be that the connection between 5:8 and 10:1 is evident here. The connection between these two texts is widely recognized by scholars.[104] Thus, the reference in 5:8 to the joining of "house to house" and the adding of "field to field" may be closely

---

[101] See, W. Johnstone, "Old Testament Expressions in Property Holding," *Ugaritica 6* (1969), pp. 308-317, who notes that מקום has a technical meaning referring to "estate" or "property" in addition to its general meaning of locality, place or spot. p. 314. Johnstone supports this thesis by alluding to the following biblical examples: Gen. 23:20; Judg. 9:55; 19:28; I Sam. 2:20; 27:5; 29:4; II Sam. 19:40 [39].

[102] See, Norman K. Gottwald, *The Tribes of Yahweh* (Maryknoll, New York: Orbis Books), 1979. In this volume, Gottwald has an extensive study on the use of ישב and its derivatives in the MT. (pp. 511-535) He suggests that ישב means "to rule" and is generally used in a negative sense, e.g. "ruling abusively" or "ruling oppressively." p. 531. It would appear therefore that הושבתם in Isa. 5:8 connotes more than "you are made to live;" rather, it points to a more oppressive act of forcing the small landowner to function without land.

[103] Patrick D. Miller, *Sin and Judgement in the Prophets*. SBL. Monograph Series 27 (California: Scholars Press), 1982, p. 43.

[104] See, e.g., Clements, *Isaiah 1-39*. p. 60; Kaiser, *Isaiah 1-12*, p. 96 and Wildberger, *Isaiah 1-12*, pp. 195-196.

tied to the iniquitous decrees of 10:1-4, which are denounced by Isaiah. By having decrees which are inherently unjust and unethical and which are targeted against the poor, the rich and powerful are able to obtain more properties, while simultaneously making the poor into non-entities. Even if a reasonable price were to be paid for the property (and this is improbable) still the basic covenantal principle is in question, for in taking the property of the poor, the rich inevitably succeed in taking the only source of income and livelihood of the small landowner. With the monopolizing of land and property the poor and powerless become marginalized members of society.[105]

4. Amos 2:6-8; 5:11; 8:4-6

In these three passages, the prophet Amos graphically describes the manner in which the affluent members of society oppress the poor, for their own gain. In each instance, the poor[106] are described as being trampled upon for the economic interests of the rich. Particularly in 2:6-8 and 8:4-6, there is evidence of the

---

[105] See, H. Donner, "Die soziale Botschaft der Propheten im Lichte der Gesellschaftsordnung in Israel," *OA* 2 (1963), pp. 229-245. Donner called this accumulation of land (5:8), an early form of capitalism (*Art Frühkapitalismus*). Cf. also, B. Duhm, *Das Buch Jesaja* (Göttingen: Vandenhoeck and Ruprecht), 1892, p. 36.

[106] In Amos 2:7 and 5:11, the term used for "the poor" is דל while in 8:4 "the needy" trampled upon are the אביונים. The economic references in these texts indicate clearly that the דלים are the poor in an economic sense. That the דלים are peasant farmers is attested in II Ki. 24:14. The אביונים are those in need of help. This term connotes a lack of "physical and material necessities," essential for one's livelihood. See, G. Johannes "Critical Notes on Amos 2:7 and 8:4," *AJSL* 19 (1903), pp. 116-117. For a different interpretation of the meaning in Amos 5:11 (cf. 2:7), see, P.E. Dion, "Le message moral du prophète Amos s'inspirait - il du 'droit de l'alliance?'" *Sci Esprit* 27 (1975), pp. 5-34. Dion suggests that the opening line of 5:11 should read, "parce que vous dépouillez l'enfant du pauvre." One of the factors which has influenced this position is the parallel which Dion notes in the legend of King Keret. According to Dion, Keret condemns "Leux qui dépouillent l'enfant du pauvre." p. 25. Se also, H.H. Schmid, who suggests that צדיק in 2:6 is used in the "traditional juridical sense." *Gerechtigkeit*, p. 112. Also, Premnath, who says that 2:6b-8 has to do with a corrupt judicial system and in particular צדיק, "has a legal connotation: the 'righteous' one who is declared 'innocent' from the legal point of view." *Diss.*, pp. 139-140.

schism in the relationship between creditor and debtor. In these contexts also, the judgment of Yahweh is firmly expressed against those who oppress the poor.[107] It is precisely the prostitution of this gift of the land, by the rich landowners which is criticized.[108] The one element which is singled out here by Amos is "debt-slavery." Though this terminology is not used, the end result is the same. The poor peasant farmers are forced into business transactions with their wealthier counterparts and inevitably become indebted. While Amos does not specify the reasons, it is possible that indebtedness takes either the form of a loan or the incurring of debts, owed to merchants and graindealers who have used false scales and balances in order to cheat the poor. Another possibility is involvement in the web of rent-capitalism. As Coote notes, under rent capitalism rent is paid out to one or several owners of the various factors of production, and inevitably the cost of production escalates and thus places the peasant farmer in great debt, which in turn leads to serfdom and slavery.[109]

These are the two most likely possibilities, and it is conceivable that in certain situations the peasant farmer is involved with both. In any event the result is the same for the peasant farmer is sold, and so is the innocent person, because of debt. Amos makes it clear, both in 2:6 and 8:6 that it is the legal transaction between the two parties which brings this about. The handing over a "pair of sandals" or a "pair of shoes" is one tradition that indicates a le-

---

[107] Koch, who uses *derek* to mean "the unity of a person's conduct and the course of his life," says, "for [Amos'] *derek* anthropology, the ties between human beings and the God who confers salvation are inextricably linked with the economic freedom given by possession of one's own land. *Derek* on one's own land, given to the patriarchs by God, counts as the pre-condition which makes a successful and harmonious life possible." *The Prophets* I, pp. 45-46.

[108] This prostitution is most vividly expressed in Amos 2:8, where the items seized from peasant debtors become a part of their festivities within the cult. The last line does not refer to the seizure of land, but as, Coote observes, the wealthy are drinking wine from those who have been mulcted. He suggests that 'mulct' "means to seize patrimonial lands for prebendal estates through the oppressive use of interest and fines." *Amos among the Prophets*, p. 32.

[109] Coote, *Amos among the Prophets*, p. 29. This point is also pursued by Lang, who sees the peasant - landlord relationship in three possible ways. 1) patronage 2) partnership 3) exploitation. It is the third option which is exercised by the landowners. *Monotheism*, p. 118.

gal transaction. De Vaux points out that, "in the early days the transfer of property was verified by a symbolic action....One of the parties removed his sandal and gave it to the other. This action, performed before witnesses, signified the abandonment of a right."[110] The wealthy landowners use this as a means of selling the peasant farmers into slavery. In this manner, the peasant farmers are removed and the land becomes the property of the rich. The extremity of the situation as described by Amos, revolves around the state of the peasant farmer. Without the pressures of loans, and large debts to grain dealers, and rent capitalism, the peasant is still only peripherally within an acceptable economic position. However, by the time he is being sold for lack of payment and obligation to a legal transaction, he is not only a debtor but a slave. He is being sold into debt-slavery. (See, II Ki. 4:1-7) Not only is there public humiliation, but the most potent consequence is the separation of the members of the family. Since the family is incapable of purchasing him, he becomes the property of another wealthy owner. However, an even more cruel element in the "debt-slavery" cycle is that the peasant farmer can be sold abroad. When this occurs, the chance of being free again is remote.[111]

One final point will suffice here. Amos 8:5 combines several elements which express clearly the corruption of those with eco-

---

[110] De Vaux, *Ancient Israel*, p. 169. See also, Lang, who notes that, "the Hebrew word 'na'alayim' 'a pair of sandals' acquired the meaning of 'bond.' Applied to our passage of Amos: the poor man is being 'bought' [and sold] because of a bond or obligation." *Monotheism*, p. 125. Also, Harper, *Amos and Hosea*, p. 49. and Mays, *Amos*, p. 45. However, against this view is Erling Hammershaimb, *The Books of Amos*. trans. John Sturdy (Oxford: Blackwell), 1970. Hammershaimb notes that, "the creditors have been so hard-hearted that they have sold their debtors, because they were in arrears for as little as a pair of sandals." p. 47. Hammershaimb's understanding of the debtor's dilemma proves to be in the right direction but his reduction of "a pair of sandals" to mean "small sum" overlooks the transactional elements which is traditionally associated with this concept. It is not that Hammershaimb is ignorant of this idea, but he summarily dismisses it as improbable. See also, Kapelrud, *Central Ideas*, p. 64; Kipper, "A evolução...." p. 314 and Barstad, *The Religious Polemics*, p. 14. See Ruth 4:7; Ps. 60:10 [8] (108:10 [9]).
[111] See, Bernhard Lang, "Sklaven und Unfreie im Buch Amos (2:6, 8:6)," *VT* 31 (1981), pp. 482-486. See also, Koch, who notes that with the sale of the debtor into slavery, "the way of the poor is turned aside." (2:7) Koch suggests that this means, "his existence disappears." "Origin and effect..." p. 95.

nomic power. The lack of religious integrity is underlined by the grain dealers impatience with the period of the Sabbath and the New Moon. They are unable to wait for the end of Sabbath, a time for rest, when normal work is prohibited. Their question suggests that they are inconvenienced by the occurrence of the Sabbath and the New Moon. What is even more remarkable is the fact that the work which they are anxious about revolves around unscrupulous dealings in their grain trade. Not only do they not see fit to keep the holiness of the Sabbath, but their impatience points to the fact that they are willing to break the Sabbath laws for dishonest monetary gains.[112] The poor, who need the Sabbath to rest and survive another day, are viewed only as preys for the deceits of the grain dealers. Not only do the falsifying of the weights and measures aid in the corruption of the economic order,[113] but the incessant striving against the poor also utterly destroy any semblance of community between the two groups.[114]

5. Mic. 2:1-2

The words of Micah like his counterparts Amos and Isaiah, reflect strong criticism of those who have seized land and property

---

[112] See George Adam Smith, *The Book of the Twelve Prophets* I (London: Hodder and Stoughton). Smith observes that here, "Amos emphasizes that the Sabbath is threatened by the same worldliness and love of money which tramples on the helpless." p. 183. Also, Nolan P. Howington, "Toward an Ethical Understanding of Amos," *RE* 63 (1966) pp. 402-412. Howington notes that, "Actually they regarded religious institutions like the Sabbath with a degree of contempt, for they were bothersome interruptions of business." p. 406.
[113] See, Wolff, *Joel and Amos*, p. 327. See also, Kipper, who describes the perversion of weights and measures as "adultery." This term generally evokes sexual unfaithfulness, and in this instance it points clearly to foreign elements which are brought within an established relationship and which have negative implications and consequences. "A evolução...." p. 317.
[114] See, Walter Brueggemann, *Genesis*. INTERPRETATION (Atlanta: John Knox Press) 1982. Brueggemann insightfully notes, "The Sabbath is a sociological expression of *a new humanity* called by God. Sabbath is the end of grasping and therefore the end of exploitation. Sabbath is a day of revolutionary equality in society." p. 35.

from the poor.[115] There is a similarity between Mic. 2:2 and Isa. 5:8. The rich landowners are intent on seizing for themselves the land and property which are rightfully the personal *means* of livelihood for the poor.[116] Schmidt perceptively notes that, "when Micah criticized the economy based on large estates and the greed of the upper classes for houses and property, he seems to be giving concrete form to the tenth commandment."[117] While both Amos and Isaiah are critical of the unscrupulousness of the wealthy landowner, Micah is the only Eighth Century prophet who implies that this attitude is in contradiction to the Tenth Commandment.[118] What is evident here is that the wealthy landowners are breaching one of Israel's foundational elements. Hillers correctly observes that, "their actions constitute something more reprehensible than mere greed, for they are an assault on the basic structure of the people of God."[119]

In addition to his use of "covetousness," the reference to the landowners working "evil upon their beds" is also unique to Micah.

---

[115] See, Hans Walter Wolff, "Micah the Moreshite - The Prophet and His Background" in *Israelite Wisdom: Theological and Literary Essays in Honor of Samuel Terrien*. ed. John G. Gammie, et al. (Montana: Scholars Press), 1978, pp. 77-84. Wolff observes that, "it is striking that Micah never once calls his tormented compatriots poor (אביון), helpless (דל), or oppressed (עני), as is often done by Amos...and not infrequently by Isaiah...although Micah sees, just as those prophets, that they are being overpowered and punished to the point of bleeding." p. 81.
[116] Commenting on the use of עשק in Mic. 2:2, Mays says, "the contexts in which 'asaq appears...show that the verb specifically means taking something away from another through an advantage of position or power. For those who lost their property, the result involved more than simple economic impoverishment. In Israel's social order a man's identity and status in the community rested on his household or family, dwelling place, and land. His inheritance in his father's family was his 'portion' in the family. Lose it and he lost all the rights which were based on its possession; he had no 'place' in the community and had left only the life of a wage-labourer or a slave. His life passed into the hands of others." *Micah*, pp. 63-64. See also, von Rad, *Theol.* II, p. 150, note 5.
[117] Werner Schmidt, *Introduction to the Old Testament*, p. 223. See also, Hans Walter Wolff, *Confrontations with Prophets* (Philadelphia: Fortress Press), 1983, pp. 38-39.
[118] While Micah does not make this contradiction explicit, the word he uses to mean "covet" is חמד, which is the term used in Exod. 20:17.
[119] Hillers, *Micah*, p. 33.

When an individual retires to bed, it is generally assumed that he or she does so for rest, for sleep. However, those to whom Micah refers in 2:1 cannot spare the time for that, for even though their lives are full of oppressive acts, there is an insatiable appetite for more, hence the necessity of planning evil when they should be resting.[120] The description of "evil upon their beds" perhaps leans on the idea of the prostitution of oneself. While this is clearly not in reference to sexual immorality, nevertheless there is a sense of baseness, where the individual not only desecrates himself or herself, but also the idea of rest, which in Israel's tradition is conspicuously distinguished as a time to cease the routine work. As Wolff notes, "the crime of the officers and officials which Micah's *hôy* condemns begins, most significantly, with the secret dreams they cherish as they lie on their beds."[121]

However, the words of Micah do not appear to create any change in attitude by the rich landowners. Rather, the latter show indignation against Micah for preaching against the social and economic ills of the society. (2:6) There is the implication that Micah has overstepped the bounds of religious etiquette; that is, there are certain topics which must not be subjects for preaching. This is a classic example of self-righteousness and the feeling of standing securely (in their own eyes) under the pervasive protection of their theological presuppositions. There is, in these verses, a sense of incredulity on the part of Micah's audience. It is precisely because they see themselves as shrouded in holiness and in Yahweh's protection that social irresponsibility and oppression occur. They are simply unable to look at themselves with a discerning and critical eye. However, Micah is undaunted by the reaction

---

[120] It is useful to note the similarity here with Amos 8:5. While Amos is criticizing the breaking of the Sabbath laws only to cheat the poor, Micah is referring to the more mundane, though necessary, element of sleep. The common element in both *Amos* and *Micah* at this point is their criticism of those who oppress the poor, while they should be resting.

[121] Wolff, *Micah the Prophet*, p. 52. See, also, Allen, who notes that, "one's bed is the place in which to indulge in private thoughts and aspirations for which the bustle of daily life leaves little opportunity." *Joel, Obadiah, Jonah and Micah*, p. 287.

of the audience, and his movement from "those," "their," "they" in vv. 1-2, to "you" in v. 8, points to a dramatic confrontation.

E. Justice in the Gate: Isa. 5:23; Amos 5:12

Both Isaiah and Amos preach against the corruption of "justice in the gate." The judiciary is the one institution in the land which is meant to epitomize justice, and it is when this institution fails in its fundamental *raison d'être* that a society reaches abysmal depths of social malaise. When the judiciary fails to give attention to the state of the oppressed and conversely favors the wealthy and powerful, society is in a state of disarray.

The local ancient Israelite judicial system has become an occasion for the powerful in society to defend their own way of life by not allowing the poor to become a part of the judiciary. The privilege of serving as a judicial functionary "in the gate" comes with one's status in the community, and as long as the individual is economically depressed then the opportunity to serve in this capacity does not arise. Decision-making is being shaped by the power and wealth and not by the circumstances and evidence of the case. Thus the lack of משפט in the gate is seen to be closely tied to the economic unscrupulousness of the rich. What these powerful and rich judicial functionaries do, is thus not merely pronounce verdicts against the צדיקים but, rather, use the procedure as a means of trampling on the poor, linking this with their overall discrimination. Mays suggests that, "the old institution of the court in the gate is being undermined to make way for the economic exploitation of the weak."[122]

What is clear is that משפט becomes a commercial element, and the act of giving judgment takes on a meaning which is inherently alien to "justice in the gate." As Mays notes, "the courts were

---

[122] Mays, *Amos*, p. 94. See also, Ludwig Köhler, *Hebrew Man*. trans. Peter Ackroyd (London: SCM Press), 1956, who notes that, "the oral and public nature of its conduct of affairs presupposes that each assessor can speak what he thinks right, independently of others. But fear of those who have economic power and who can do real harm in the narrow common life of the village, makes men subservient and lacking in independence." p. 166.

not immune to the circumstances they were being used to create. As wealth grew and the difference between the rich and the rest became more pronounced, it happened that those who were rich could afford more justice than the others."[123] What in effect the prophets are criticizing is the entire judicial system, not only the external improprieties in the behavior, but the absence of צדק and the absence of that משפט which unites the judicial functionaries with Yahweh. Accordingly, it is the fundamentals of executing משפט which need changing. The presence of evil and the absence of good is reflected in the monopolizing of the judicial role by the powerful, and the corresponding oppression of the poor in order to exclude them from being an integral part of the community.

1. Isa. 5:23

The term שחד which occurs in Isa. 5:23 is generally rendered as "bribe" in the Old Testament, and this is often interpreted in a narrow sense. Davies, for example, believes that שחד is generally used to refer to any sum of money which is given to a judge, with the sole intent or influencing the decision particularly in favor of the briber.[124] The use of שחד in this sense presupposes that the subject is always a briber, one who is guilty and one who seeks acquittal by the judge. There is no doubt that there are occurrences of שחד which have a forensic overtone and others which refer specifically to judicial functionaries and to parties involved in a lawsuit. However, this is only one use, and to reduce entirely the presence of שחד in the Old Testament to a forensic use, is an oversimplified conclusion. This is not the place for a detailed study of שחד in the Old Testament. However, a brief résumé of its use in the Eighth Century prophets, will give some indication of its varied use while also indicating that there is in fact only one instance in Isaiah where there is a clear reference to injustice "in the gate." There are four occurrences of שחד in the Eighth Century prophets,

---

[123] Mays, "Justice...." p. 13.
[124] Davies, *Prophecy and Ethics*, pp. 108-109.

Isa. 1:23; 5:23; 33:15 and Mic. 3:11. In Isa. 1:23, the prophet rebukes the people and says:

> Your princes are rebels and companions of thieves.
> Everyone loves a bribe (שחד) and runs after gifts.
> They do not defend the orphan,
> and the widow's cause does not come before them.

שחד in this context does not have a forensic overtone, for it does not refer to a bribe taken by a judicial functionary. Rather, as Isaiah says, "everyone" is set up for hire, the primary motivation being monetary. With this incentive and insatiable appetite for wealth, there is no time for, or interest in, the welfare of those for whom they are particularly responsible. In this sense, it is not the judicial functionaries who are singled out for criticism, it is everyone in power, for they are willing to carry out their respective functions for a שחד.

In Isa. 5:23, שחד is used within the context of a series of "woe" oracles. "[Woe to those] who acquit (צדק) the guilty for a bribe (שחד) and deprive the innocent (צדיקים)[125] of their rights! (צדקה)." This "woe" is clearly pointed against those who are responsible for the administration of משפט and fail in their responsibility; in this instance שחד is used in a legal sense. Here, it is the judicial functionaries who are being criticized, for they are the ones who accept monetary bribes from the rich and, by implication, from the guilty. Here, the צדיק is referred to as "innocent." In this context, the acceptance of a שחד creates an ironic situation. Not only is the guilty party in the wrong, but in accepting a שחד, the judicial functionary declares this person to be innocent, a צדיק. Thus, even though the context does not specify that the true צדיק is declared guilty, nevertheless the implication is apparent. Not only is the guilty party declared צדיק (by being acquitted, which in this context means the declaration of being "in the right,") but the true צדיק is thereby further deprived and carries the label of "guilty." Clearly שחד in this

---

[125] There is a textual question involved here. צדיקים is plural but ממנו is singular. There are some manuscripts and versional support for reading צדיק. See, BHK and BHS.

Chapter VI   295

sense is forensic and is different from its use in Isa. 1:23. The third use of שחד in Isaiah occurs in 33:15.

> Those who walks righteously (צדק) and speaks uprightly,
> who despise the gain of oppression,
> who wave away a bribe (שחד), instead of accepting it,
> who stop their ears from hearing of bloodshed,
> and shut their eyes from looking on evil.

These words are spoken within a clearly defined context. Clements notes that the unit 33:14-16 may be classified as a "Torah-liturgy."[126] This classification would make it highly unlikely that שחד in this context refers to the acceptance of money by a judge. The notions of "hearing of bloodshed" or "looking upon evil" are not in regard to the ignoring of acts of this nature, but rather they refer to the refusal to participate in any such acts. This use of שחד probably relates closely to the occurrence of שחד in Ps. 26:10. In this instance, the psalmist declares great love for the temple and asks not to be swept away with bloodthirsty humans, humans with evil devices, and humans with bribes. The imagery here is similar to Isa. 33:15.

The fourth occurrence of שחד in the Eighth Century prophets is in Mic. 3:11.

> Its rulers give judgment for a bribe, (שחד) [127]

---

[126] Clements, *Isaiah 1-39*, p. 266. Clements notes also that this passage may be an exilic redaction. This, however, does not interfere with the question at hand.

[127] The first line of Mic. 3:11...ישפטו ראשיה בשחד is generally translated, "Its rulers give judgment for a bribe." This is the translation which is found in the NRSV and many scholars follow similarly. Leslie C. Allen, translates it as, "The city heads may be bribed to give a verdict." *Joel, Obadiah, Jonah and Micah*, p. 316. Mays, translates it as, "The Chiefs render decisions for a bribe." *Micah*, p. 86. Ralph L. Smith, *Micah - Malachi*. WBC (Waco, Texas: Word Books) 1984, translates it as "Her heads judge for a bribe." p. 34. Also, Wolff, translates it, "Her heads give judgment for a bribe." *Micah*, p. 90.

Mays, Smith and Wolff give translations which are based closely on the Hebrew, but Allen's rendering is much more of an interpretation than a translation. The grammatical structure does not allow for Allen's translation. What is common though, among these scholars, is the view that this sentence

its priests teach for a price,
its prophets give oracles for money;
yet they lean upon the LORD and say,
"Surely the LORD is with us!
No harm shall come upon us."

In this occurrence, שחד is an element which epitomizes the rule of the leaders. That is to say, whatever acts or decisions are made, they are made entirely for reasons of a שחד. There is a clear indication that at the heart of the rule of the leaders there is corruption. Those responsible for the welfare of the people are concerned more with receiving a שחד expressly with the intent of overlooking perversion, grievances, oppression, injustices, all for a price, monetary or otherwise.[128]

Two observations may be made at this point. First, it is clear, that at least in the Eighth Century prophets, שחד is not used exclusively within a judicial context, as Davies contends. Second, Isa. 5:23 speaks unequivocally of injustice in a judicial context. While this is the only clear example of a critique of injustice in Isaiah, it is, nevertheless, an essential part of Isaiah's overall social critique. Isaiah's critique of the judicial procedure focuses primarily on the acceptance of a monetary שחד, at the expense of impartiality.

2. Amos 5:12

For I know how many are your transgressions,
and how great are your sins -

---

must be characterized as judicial. Thus, שחד is to be understood in reference to "verdict" (Allen), "decision" (Mays), "judge" (Smith), "judgment" (Wolff). However, there is no concrete indication that the context merits a judicial overtone. In the earlier discussion of the root שפט, it was concluded that the general meaning may be taken to be "rule" rather than "judge." "Rule" in this instance would be a better choice as it includes the judicial sphere and corresponds with the presence of ראשיה.

[128] With a different perspective, see, Yaakov Hocherman, "Does the Concept of Bribery have a Positive side?" *Beth Mikra* 36 (1990-91), p. 220.

Chapter VI   297

you who afflict the righteous (צדיק), who take a bribe (שׁחד), and push aside the needy in the gate.

This is the only instance in Amos in which the prophet speaks out against bribery "in the gate." This criticism of bribery in the judiciary must be related to Amos's admonition in 5:15, where he says, "establish justice in the gate" and to his more general critique in 5:7, where משׁפט is subverted.[129]

While both Amos and Isaiah are critical of the judicial procedure "in the gate," and both speak against bribery there, their primary interests are not identical. While the bribery of which Isaiah speaks is שׁחד, Amos speaks of כפר. כפר in the Old Testament generally means "ransom,"[130] though as Wolff points out, כפר means literally, "'that which is to cover up something' hence perhaps 'hush-money.'"[131] In addition to this, Davies suggests, "the purpose of the payment of kōper was to restore equilibrium between two parties which had been disturbed by the wrongful act of one of them. The punishment was assessed in monetary terms, and the amount of damages awarded would no doubt have been related quantitatively to the extend of the loss."[132] It is clear from Amos's criticism of the judicial procedure that the manner in which כפר was used "in the gate" was unsatisfactory. Davies speculates that perhaps, "Amos' condemnation of the legal assemblies for their acceptance of kōper was based on the fact that these authorities were now allowing more serious offenses (such as murder) to be expiated by the payment of money instead of ensuring that the proper penalty for such offenses be duly carried."[133] This view of Davies misses an essential element in the understanding

---

[129] See, Wolff, who notes that, the statement in 5:12b "is an illustration of the general reproach in v.7." *Joel and Amos*, p. 248.
[130] See, Harper, who notes that, "Ordinarily כפר means *ransom*, the price paid for life by wealthy criminals...." *Amos and Hosea*, p. 122.
[131] Wolff, *Joel and Amos*, p. 248.
[132] Davies, *Prophecy and Ethics*, p. 109. Whether or not Davies' contention that "monetary terms" is essential for an understanding of כפר is dubious. However, his main point regarding the use of כפר as an element of restoration is not arguable.
[133] Ibid., p. 109.

of כפר. It is true, that the payment of a ransom in lieu of the death penalty is one element, and certainly fits the general meaning of כפר. However, in this instance, Amos is not only employing the general meaning of "ransom" but also the literal meaning, "cover." Thus the criticism of the judicial functionaries is to be understood at two levels. The criticism in Amos 5:12 includes the acceptance of a כפר by the judicial functionaries in order that they might overlook the seriousness of the crimes against the צדיקים and simply settle for a ransom by the guilty. This understanding takes into account both the literal and the derived meanings of כפר.

The criticism of the judicial system in the Eighth Century prophets includes "bribery" of two sorts. While there is little doubt that both Isaiah and Amos are strongly opposed to the corruption of משפט "in the gate," they see this corruption at different levels. Isaiah suggests that שחד is used in the judicial system as a means of showing partiality in the executing of משפט, while Amos indicates the כפר in the judicial system is being used instead of the respective penalty to which the guilty party is sentenced.

F. Corrupt Rulers and Leaders: Isa. 1:23; 10:1-2; Mic. 3:1-3, 9-11

The discussion in Chapter I of the use of שפט in the Old Testament concludes that the subjects most often associated with this term are rulers and leaders, inclusive of judicial functionaries. It is clear that these are the people who are the most powerful and also who are in a position to care for the people, particularly the poor. When there is corruption of משפט at this level, then those who suffer most are the poor. In the Old Testament, it is not so much a question of the abstract "poverty and oppression" as it is of the "poor and oppressed;" that is, there is a sense of the particular rather than the universal. Augustin George observes that, "in the biblical mind, the poor person is less one who is indigent and more one who is oppressed...it is a social idea."[134] This oppression is in

---

[134] Augustin George, "Poverty in the Old Testament" in *Gospel Poverty: Essays in Biblical Theology* (Chicago: Franciscan Herald Press), 1977, p. 6.

Chapter VI   299

great measure due to the corruption and unscrupulousness of the leaders and rulers.

1. Isa. 1:23; 10:1-2

The leaders in Israel as Isaiah describes them are caught up in the corruption of the society and are responsible for the oppression of the poor. They are perceived to be the ones from whom oppressive decisions and actions come. As was pointed out earlier, the leaders (Isa. 1:23) associate themselves with the basest elements of society, the thieves and rebels, and moreover they accept שחד. Because of this, those for whom they are particularly responsible become the victims of their oppression.

This is clearly evident in Isa. 10:1-2. In this instance, it is the leaders who pronounce decrees which serve to oppress the poor and powerless. The fact that these officials do not consider the moral and ethical effect of the decrees is clear, but the decrees are not necessarily illegal in a strictly legalistic sense.[135] This is particularly important precisely because it indicates that the welfare of the powerless is not foremost in their minds when the decrees are given. The decrees may not be illegal, but they certainly miss the spirit of the covenant relationship. In essence, the poor and powerless find themselves in an impossible situation where they become the periphery of an ever-increasing circle. In order to be a part of the legal assembly they need to have both power and financial recognition within the society. Because of the iniquitous decrees, the poor are relieved of whatever ownings they might have. As such, they not only lose their source of livelihood, but also, their chances of joining the legal assembly recede still further. Hence, the passing of iniquitous decrees reduce the poor and powerless to persons of no importance.

In both 1:23 and 10:2 the two groups who are singled out as powerless are the "orphans" and the "widows."[136] It is perhaps the

---

[135] See Clements, *Isaiah 1-39*, p. 61.
[136] Isaiah is the only Eighth Century prophet who shows specific concern for the יתום and the אלמנה. While the question of the oppression of the poor is clearly a hallmark of all the Eighth Century prophets, nevertheless it is only

specifying of these two groups which demonstrates the destructive force of these decrees, for these are two groups who have none to care for them and depend on the community led by responsible leaders. Though Isaiah speaks of the "fatherless" and the "widows," it is the plight of the latter that is most significant, for the "orphans" are in fact dependent on the "widows." Generally, in ancient Israel, the widow possessed no property of her own. Even though there is a law which gives some protection to the widow through the possibility of marriage to the brother-in-law (Deut. 25:5-10), nevertheless this arrangement is far from satisfactory, for it is still a situation in which the widow has no control over her own destiny. As a wife, her power, her ownership of property, her survival all depend on her husband and when he dies, then she is dependent on a ruler who often proves to be unreliable. The position of the widow thus becomes dependent on charity. She is a figure whose survival depends entirely on the benevolence of those in power. The critique of Isaiah, placing the widow in the context of the leaders as the object of the latter's corruption, shows the extent of that corruption. The harsh criticism of the rulers is best expressed in 28:14f where "scoffers" is the term used to designate those who rule the people. The fact that they show no concern for the poor and powerless is demonstrated in terms of the rejection of Yahweh's covenant for a covenant with Sheol.

2. Mic. 3:1-3, 9-11

Both 3:1 and 3:9 indicate clearly that Micah concentrates his remarks against the rulers of Israel. There appears to be a consensus regarding the meaning of ראש and קצין, suggesting that in these contexts, they both refer to judicial functionaries.[137] There

---

Isaiah who refers to the "widow and orphan." The word יתום does appear in Hos. 14:4 [3] but its use there is not germane to this discussion.
[137] See Hillers, who translates קצין as "judges" thus making his interpretation self-evident, *Micah*, p. 42. The translation of קצין as "judges" is unsatisfactory for in fact, there is no explicit idea of judicial activity in *Micah*. Also, Mays, who says that, "the leaders of Israel preside over an administration of injustice in the courts for which they are responsible." *Micah*, p. 77. Cf. Allen,

is no reason why these terms should have a judicial overtone, for they are not associated primarily with the judiciary. It is true that the ראש and קצין may include the judicial function in their role, but at best it can be only one element in their overall responsibility. The contexts clearly allude to leaders of various sorts, and the point of discussion here involves the general corruption and perversion of משפט. The one element which is in part used to support the theory that these contexts are forensic is the presence of משפט. Some scholars assume that the call for משפט by Micah is a call for proper judgment in the legal order.138 However, for these rulers to "know משפט" is not a reference to their knowledge of the law, but rather it refers to their responsibility to know what is essential for a right and proper relationship among Israelites. Inherent in the phrase לדעת את-המשפט is the idea that it is imperative for the rulers to be cognizant of this and live accordingly, particularly since they are the ones to whom the nation and, specifically, the poor look to for משפט.

The description of the perversion in 3:1-3 and 3:9-11 is indicative of the extent of the rulers' sin.139 While the words of Micah here can hardly be taken literally, nevertheless the imagery of extreme suffering and pain is quite vivid. The irony here is startling, for those who were once appointed with the responsibility to care for the powerless have themselves become subjects of corruption.

It is clear that the care of the powerless is not priority for the rulers, for, as 3:11 points out, everything is for sale, even those

---

Joel, Obadiah, Jonah and Micah, p. 305; Davies, *Prophecy and Ethics*, p. 99 and Hammershaimb, "Some Leading Ideas...." p. 33.
138 See, e.g. Wolff, who says that משפט in 3:1 refers to binding legal order. *Micah the Prophet*, p. 67. Also, Mays, who says that "to know משפט" means an acquaintance with the legal traditions. *Micah*, p. 70, and Hammershaimb, who says that "to know משפט" means "to know the law." "Some Leading Ideas...." p. 33. See also, Premnath, who notes that, "The crime of the leaders was the rejection of מִשְׁפָּט i.e., the established values and norms safeguarding the rights and interests of the innocent in the legal context." *Diss.*, p. 196.
139 Kipper, "A evolução...." p. 333. See also, Wolff, who notes that, "The people who are supposed to see that justice is done enjoy life at the expense of the ill-treated. This is the cannibalism of prosperity, and it has spread in Jerusalem to an unheard-of extent." *Confrontations*, p. 41.

things which were once thought to be sacrosanct. As Hillers notes, "judges...priests, and prophets sit in Jerusalem and sell their wares; justice, religious teaching and the inspired word of God are all for sale."[140] Self-interest has replaced covenantal responsibilities, and personal concerns have taken the place of societal demands. Even the material structure of Jerusalem, with its reflections of affluence, is at the expense of the poor. These external niceties have shrouded the reality of stark injustices which are prevalent; Israel is not unlike a tomb, concealing by its external brightness and propriety, the rottenness which it covers. Contrary to what the leaders may think, all is not well in Israel.

G. The "Day of Yahweh" and the Social Critique

The use of the "Day of Yahweh" by Amos and Isaiah serves further as a means of inveighing against the lifestyle of those who live opulent lives. While it is generally accepted among scholars that the concept of the "Day of Yahweh" was known in the Eighth Century, what is still in a state of dispute is the nature of this day and the expectations associated with it. There are four possible explanations of the origin of the "Day of Yahweh" which have been proposed by scholars, and the manner in which it is used in the Eighth Century prophets.

First, there is the view that this concept is associated entirely with the tradition of holy wars in Ancient Israel, in which Yahweh personally destroys the enemy of Israel.[141] Second, and

---

[140] Hillers, *Micah*, p. 44. However, as Mays, notes, "it is not necessary to suppose that these civic and religious leaders were always openly and crudely corrupt. In a culture fascinated by wealth and its acquisition, the morality of good business has a compelling power to influence decisions and attitudes in subtle and indirect ways." *Micah*, p. 89. In some ways, it is the subtlety of the corruption that is so devastating, for the powerless continue to place their confidence in these leaders, ignorant of the latter's self-interest.

[141] See, Gerhard von Rad, "The Origin of the concept of the Day of Yahweh," *JSS* 4 (1959), pp. 97-108. Von Rad argues that, "...the Day of Yahweh encompasses a pure event of war, the rise of Yahweh against his enemies, his battle and his victory." p. 103. In supporting this view, von Rad suggests that the "Day of Yahweh" is used by Amos, only in a casual manner and in fact Amos could have used any other traditional element and reverse or change the accustomed association. See also, Simon Cohen, "The Political Background of

perhaps the most commonly held view, is that the "Day of Yahweh" is associated with Israel's cult, with the Autumn festival. This view holds that the "Day of Yahweh" is traditionally a festal occasion and is so used by the prophets. Regarding its use in Amos 5:18ff, Kapelrud notes that, "After having mentioned the Day of Yahweh Amos goes immediately over to speak of cultic feasts, assemblies, burnt offerings, cereal offerings and peace offerings. ...The Day of Yahweh is mentioned in the same passage, which makes it evident that this day was also a cultic event."[142] Third, there is the view that the "Day of Yahweh" is an eschatological event. The proponents here suggest that the judgment which is spoken of by the prophets is one which will be executed in the "end-time." Traditionally, this view suggests that the "Day of Yahweh" is indeed associated with the epiphany of Yahweh in the Autumn festival, but in an eschatological perspective.[143] The fourth position has its main proponent in Fensham. He notes that the "Day of Yahweh" prophecies do refer to "holy-war" in some instances. (e.g. Jer. 46:10; Zeph. 1:16) However, he suggests that this cannot be the sole referent to the "Day of Yahweh" precisely because in the majority of cases, the prophecy is against Israel.

---

the Words of Amos," *HUCA* 36 (1965), pp. 153-160, especially p. 157. Also Waldemar Janzen, *Mourning Cry and Woe Oracle*. BZAW 125 (Berlin: Walter de Gruyter), 1972, pp. 49f. For an extensive critique of von Rad's view, see, Meir Weiss "The Origin of the 'Day of the Lord' Reconsidered," *HUCA* 37 (1966), pp. 29-72.

[142] Kapelrud, *Central Ideas*, p. 71. Also, Lindbolm, *Prophecy in Ancient Israel*, p. 318; Henry McKeating, *Amos, Hosea and Micah*. CBC (Cambridge: University Press), 1971, p. 46; and Mowinckel, *The Psalms in Israel's Worship*, pp. 119ff.

[143] See, John Gray, "The Day of Yahweh in Cultic Experience and Eschatological Prospect," *SEÅ* 39 (1974), p. 5-27. Gray, who rejects von Rad's hypothesis as a viable option, points to the use of this concept in the New Testament as a way of confirming his position. pp. 35-37. See also, H. Gressmann, *Der Ursprung der israelitisch - jüdischen Eschatologie*, Göttingen, 1905, p. 147, and, John D.W. Watts, *Vision and Prophecy in Amos* (Leiden: E.J. Brill), 1958, pp. 69ff. Against this view, see Kapelrud, who argues that, "A purely eschatological view of the Day of Yahweh in this early time cannot be held." *Central Ideas*, p. 72, and, C. van Leeuwen, "The Prophecy of the *Yom YHWH* in Amos 5:18-20," *OTS* 19 (1974), pp. 113-134. Van Leeuwen notes that, "The *Yōm Yhwh* was not originally eschatological. Even in the prophetic texts historical events as the fall of Jerusalem are retrospectively described as a *Day of the wrath of Yhwh*." p. 123.

Thus, he argues, the "Day of Yahweh" is both a "day of battle" and a "day of judgment."[144]

This fourth position appears to be the most likely and suitable for an understanding of the use of the "Day of Yahweh" in the Eighth Century prophets. Not only is there an implication of war and destruction as several passages in Isaiah would attest[145] but also a day of judgment (opposed to a day of festival); the latter view explains the words of Amos.[146] In Isaiah's case, Israel desires Yahweh's presence against the foreign nations, and in this instance von Rad's thesis that the "Day of Yahweh" is in reference to "holy-war" might have some legitimacy. There is no evidence that the "Day of Yahweh" in Isaiah refers to a festival occasion. Instead of aligning himself with Israel, Yahweh will reverse this expectation and rather use the occasion to punish Israel. Instead of defeating the enemy, Isaiah says, "Your men shall fall by the sword and your warriors in battle." (3:25)

Amos, on the other hand clearly uses the expectations associated with the festal occasion as a point of departure for his attack. He is the only prophet who combines the use of הוי with the "Day of Yahweh." This adds to his words a strong element of judgment. As Janzen notes, "Amos is fully conscious of the mourning function of *hôy* but employs it in anticipation of that particular mourning and wailing which will be called for by the Day of the Lord."[147] Amos's words regarding the "Day of Yahweh" while they are clearly pronounced in 5:18-20, are not separate and distinct from the larger context of his critique of the cult. There is a logical connection between 5:18-20 and 5:21-24.[148] This connec-

---

[144] See, F.C. Fensham, "A possible origin of the concept of the 'Day of the Lord'" in *Essays in OTWSA*, 1966, Potchefstroom, 1967, pp. 90-97; also, Van Leeuwen, "The Prophecy of the *Yōm YHWH*...." p. 125.
[145] See, e.g., Isa. 13:6, 9; 34:8.
[146] See, e.g. Amos 5:18-20; 8:3,9.
[147] Janzen, *Mourning Cry*, p. 49. It is interesting, that while 8:9-10 does not begin with הוי, nevertheless Amos makes it clear that the feasts will be mourning, which is precisely the intent of הוי in 5:18.
[148] See Hammershaimb, *Amos*, p. 80. Hammershaimb suggests that the unit is 5:18-27.

tion between the "Day of Yahweh" and cultic practice is also underlined clearly in 8:9-10.

In both of these instances there is the dramatic picture of the effect of the "Day of Yahweh," for the "Day of Yahweh" will not bring light, but rather darkness. Amos here is not alluding to a physical phenomenon when he speaks of the concept of darkness. Weiss notes that, "Amos himself gives us an idea of what he took this darkness to be by the simile 'As if a man did flee from a lion.'...Here a disaster is depicted from which there is no escape. From a methodological point of view one must assume, at least to begin with, that the simile constitutes an organic element in this prophecy. Now this can be so only if "darkness" is recognized as the common stereotyped metaphor it has proved to be, denoting distress and disaster."[149] That is to say, the "light-darkness" imagery is not in reference to eclipses; it is certain that Amos is not suggesting an eclipse will coincide with the "Day of Yahweh." An eclipse occurs naturally, but it is the unnatural events of the "Day of Yahweh" which are referred to here.

What is clear from the use of the "Day of Yahweh" in both Amos and Isaiah is the fact that the people have traditionally associated something inherently positive with the "Day of Yahweh." It is the occasion which serves to reaffirm Yahweh's relationship with Israel. Donald Williams suggests that the primary purpose of the "Day of Yahweh" is "to foster the covenantal relationship between Yahweh and Israel, a covenant which offered Yahweh's protection to his chosen people and a guarantee of peace and security upon the land."[150] These prophets speak of the "Day of Yahweh" in a way which points clearly to the fact that Israel has broken the covenant relationship and thus the expectations associated with this "day" are reversed.[151]

---
[149] Weiss, "The Origin...." p. 38.
[150] Donald Williams, "The Theology of Amos." p. 397.
[151] See, H. Wheeler Robinson, *Inspiration and Revelation in the Old Testament* (Oxford: Clarendon Press), 1946. Robinson notes that, "From the prophetic point of view it is immaterial whether the divine act be wrought through physical phenomena, such as earthquake and storm, or through human agency...or through some mysterious means beyond man's knowledge and previous range of experience. The characteristic feature of the day is that

This entire chapter has dealt in detail with the question of the prophetic critique and, in doing so, has examined the different contexts in which social justice is absent. It has, I hope, become clear from the discussion that the social critique of the prophets involve all of Israel's life and not only the so-called secular aspects. Both the cultic and the economic elements are inseparably intertwined. Thus, the nature of this cultic activity is not only a source of social injustice, but serves, in a pivotal way, to express the brokenness in Israelite society. In the cultic practices, it is evident that the cult has become an avenue for satisfying the religious whims of the upper classes and not an occasion for the renewal of faith in Yahweh's covenant relationship. All of the Eighth Century prophets see this as the major flaw in Israel's behavior. The cult is seen alongside the daily social and economic activities of the people and the influence of one on the other becomes commonplace. Once צדק between Yahweh and Israel disappears, then everything in Israel is affected. Israel's very existence is grounded in Yahweh, thus the absence of צדק adversely affects משפט in all areas of Israel's life. The discussion of the various contexts where injustice is present attests this. Thus, Mays' belief that most of the occurrences of משפט in the Eighth Century prophets refer to social injustice in the judicial area, is inadequate. It is clearly more than the judiciary which is in question here.

The unbridled affluence of the upper classes and the rich landowners is in sharp contrast to the conditions of those who are struggling to survive. The land, the quintessential expression of Yahweh's promise to Israel, the source of livelihood for all families, is being usurped by those with economic ambition. It is perhaps this situation which is most appalling in the eyes of the prophets, for there is a clear expression of Yahweh's relationship with Israel, and of the relationship amongst Israelites. From the leaders, who are elected to serve and protect the people and who

---

God acts, and that he is thereby decisively revealed as the God of effective action, the living God, the God who will be that which He will be, in deed and not simply in word....Moreover, such action is from without, transcendent and not immanent, though God many act from within either Nature or man in the achievement of His purpose." p. 145.

are ultimately responsible for the welfare of the poor and powerless and the upholding of משפט, to the local members of the community who sit in the gate, corruption is rampant. Every phase of life is touched by injustice, and the question of personal affluence at the expense of the other person is dominant. Indeed, Israel has changed from what is typically Israelite to a society which appears to contain no semblance of relational values. Perhaps it is as Herrmann suggests, "In terms of the conditions obtaining in the early period, the old system could be termed genuinely Israelite, whereas the new approach was essentially an economic one. It was not just concerned with the tilling of Yahweh's land; it also set out to create a way of tending it which furthered the well-being of the court and the apparatus of the state."[152] Greed and the new economic order have taken the place of משפט, and the poor and powerless have become pawns, being sold and traded as items. Yet in all of this, many merchants, wealthy landowners and the upper classes do not perceive themselves to be in conflict with Yahweh, for offerings and worship continue to flow in excess.

---

[152] Herrmann, *A History of Israel*, p. 236.

Conclusion

The investigation undertaken by this study leads to several conclusions, based primarily on the function of צדק, משפט and the aspects of social injustice in the Eighth Century prophets. It has become clear from this examination that in order to trace the development in meaning and the nuances of צדק and משפט in the Old Testament, these concepts must be studied and understood in the wider context of the Ancient Near East. While this does not determine the primary way in which the terms are used in the Old Testament, it does give a vital background against which the Old Testament usage might be clearly seen.

The Ancient Near Eastern use of ṣdq indicates that its primary use is forensic, while the examples in which ṣdq is associated with deity suggests also a religious use, with it also being used, on occasion, in an ethical sense. Perhaps even more important that these three aspects is the fact that ṣdq is used in many instances in "relationship" contexts in the Ancient Near East. This point serves as a major transition in the study of this term as "relationship" oriented, in the Old Testament. The importance and relevance of the background study of this term are seen in the similarity of uses which are found in the Old Testament. This similarity must, however, be kept in perspective, as the Old Testament introduces elements which are both distinct from those current in the Ancient Near East and unique to the Old Testament. In this regard, the presence of Yahweh, the election of Israel and Yahweh's covenant relationship with Israel are all new elements which shape the meaning of צדק in the Old Testament.

As in the case of ṣdq, an examinations of špṭ in the Ancient Near Eastern context establishes its fundamental meaning there, and this in turn presents an essential orientation for the study of משפט in the Old Testament. What is evident from such an examination is its contextual relation with authority. While there are many occurrences of špṭ which have forensic overtones, it can hardly be said that it is fundamentally a judicial term. Moreover, the examination of שפט in the Old Testament suggests that even with the different contexts and the different cultural and religious milieu, its Israelite usage remains similar to its use in the Ancient Near East. It is a concept which has its primary orientation in authority. Additionally, שפט in the Old Testament incorporates one other element in its general meaning, which is not apparent in the Ancient Near Eastern use, namely its use, as a term of relationship.

The connection between ṣdq and špṭ in the Ancient Near East and צדק and משפט in the Old Testament is not merely a nominal, but a substantial one.

The discussion of צדק and משפט in the Old Testament reveals that both of these terms are based fundamentally within the confines of "relationship." This in effect, departs from the commonly held views concerning these concepts. In the case of צדק it refutes the views of Diestel, Kautzsch, Nötscher, Fahlgren,[1] Snaith and Jacob, among others, who argue that צדק functions primarily as a norm. The study of משפט has made it clear that this concept is not primarily a forensic one, though this is certainly an element in its use, but that, like צדק, it is a term of "relationship." In this respect, the examination of משפט in this thesis also departs from the consensus regarding its meaning. In the course of this study, we have seen that משפט can be used in "forensic," "ethical" and "religious" contexts, but we have also seen that משפט can be understood as "relationship." Thus, Yahweh's involvement with Israel, even if punitive in terms of judgment, may be regarded as an element of his relationship with Israel.

It is clear that the idea of "relationship" in terms of צדק and משפט, is fundamental to a correct understanding of the relationship between Yahweh and Israel on the one hand, and between members of the Israelite community on the other.

The essence of this understanding of relationship is seen in the use of צדק and משפט in the Eighth Century prophets. It is the perversion of such relationship that is attested by the many ex-

---

[1] It must be noted here that Fahlgren attempts to incorporate the idea of "relationship" within a norm.

Conclusion

pressions of injustice in the Eighth Century. The fundamental factor in this regard is the corruption of Israel's cult. It is clear that this corrupt cult and all that it implies cannot be divorced from the elements and agents of injustice in society, for cult epitomizes Israel's relationship with Yahweh. Whether it is religious, as in the cult; economic, as in the monetary and latifundia economy; social, as in the judicial system, every aspect by its very nature, affects the existing relationships.

Outside of the linguistic study of צדק and משפט, the use of these concepts within the gamut of Israel's life in the Eighth Century confirms their fundamental function as terms of relationship. The fact that צדק and משפט are distinguished in terms of priority and function by the Eighth Century prophets indicates the prophets' interest in צדק and משפט respectively for the restoration of the people's broken relationship with Yahweh and with each other. It can be concluded from this study that צדק and משפט are not only primarily terms of relationship but that they are so used by the Eighth Century prophets in the latter's preaching against the many expressions of social injustice. The detailed study of the many passages from these prophets shows conclusively the indelible connections between the religious, the economic and the social aspects of Israel's life, all of which belong ideally together and can so belong only if they are firmly based on a true application of צדק and משפט.

Finally, while this study has focused on a subject which may be classified broadly as theological, the conclusions provide certain implications which are not only theological, but also socio-economic and theo-political. The understanding of the connection between cultic, economic and social expectations as expressed by this study will, I hope, assist in the use of the Old Testament as a whole, and the message of the Eighth Century prophets in particular, as a starting point for the relating of contemporary questions to the biblical message. In this regard, I believe that the results of this study could have practical implications for a theological appraisal of the structure and function of society especially in the "third world."

Bibliography

Books

Achtemeier, Elizabeth R. "The Gospel of Righteousness. A Study of the Meaning of *ṣdq* and its derivatives in the Old Testament." Ph.D. dissertation, University of Columbia, 1959.

Allen, Leslie C. *The Books of Joel, Obadiah, Jonah and Micah.* NICOT. Grand Rapids, Michigan: W.B. Eerdmans Publishing Company, 1976.

Anderson, Bernhard W. *The Eighth Century Prophets.* Philadelphia: Fortress Press, 1978.

Barr, James. *The Semantics of Biblical Language.* Trinity Press International, 1991.

Barstad, Hans M. *The Religious Polemics of Amos.* SVT. 34 Leiden: E.J. Brill, 1984.

Berkovits, Eliezer. *Man and God.* Detroit: Wayne State University Press, 1969.

Birot, Maurice. *Archives Royales de Mari.* Volume XIV. Paris: Libraire Orientaliste Paul Geuthner, S.A., 1974.

Boecker, Hans Jochen. *Law and the Administration of Justice in the Old Testament and the Ancient East.* Trans. Jeremy Moiser. Minneapolis: Augsburg Publishing House, 1980.

Boyer, Georges. *Archives Royales de Mari.* Volume VIII. Paris: Imprimerie Nationale, 1958.

Bright, John. *Covenant and Promise.* London: SCM Press, 1977.

Brown, Francis; S.R. Driver, and Charles A. Briggs. *A Hebrew and English Lexicon of the Old Testament.* Oxford: Clarendon Press, 1906.

Brueggemann, Walter. *Genesis.* INTERPRETATION. Atlanta: John Knox Press, 1982.

_____. *First and Second Samuel.* INTERPRETATION. Louisville: Westminster/John Knox Press, 1990.

Brunner, Emil. *Justice and the Social Order.* Trans. Mary Hottinger. London: Lutterworth Press, 1945.

Buber, Martin. The *Prophetic Faith*. New York: Harper and Row, 1949.
Buss, Martin J. *The Prophetic Word of Hosea*. BZAW III. Berlin: Alfred Topelmann, 1969.
Carpenter, S.C. *Politics and Society in the Old Testament*. London: Williams and Norgate, 1931.
Carroll, Mark Daniel R. *Contexts for Amos*. JSOTS. Sheffield: Sheffield Academic Press, 1992
Clements, Ronald E. *Isaiah 1-39*. NCBC. London: Marshall, Morgan and Scott, 1980.
_____. *Old Testament Theology*. London: Marshall, Morgan and Scott, 1978.
_____. *Prophecy and Covenant*. SBT. London: SCM Press, 1965.
Cooke, G.A. *A Text-book of North-Semitic Inscriptions*. Oxford: Clarendon Press, 1903.
Coote, Robert B. *Amos Among the Prophets*. Philadelphia: Fortress Press, 1981.
Corpus Inscriptionum Semiticarum. Tomus I. Parisiis: E Reipublicae Typographeo, 1881.
Cremer, Hermann. *Biblico-theological Lexicon of New Testament Greek*. Trans. D.W. Simon and William Urwick. Edinburgh: T and T Clark, 1872.
_____. *Biblisch-theologisches Wörterbuch der neutestamentlichen Gräcität*. Gotha, 1893[8].
Crenshaw, James L. *Hymnic Affirmation of Divine Justice: The Doxologies of Amos and Related Texts in the Old Testament*. SBL Dissertation Series 24. Missoula: Scholars Press, 1975.
Cripps, Richard S. *A Critical and Exegetical Commentary on the Book of Amos*. London: SPCK, 1960.
Davidson, Robert. *The Old Testament*. London: Hodder and Stoughton, 1964.
Davies, Eryl. W. *Prophecy and Ethics: Isaiah and the Ethical Traditions of Israel*. JSOTS 16. Sheffield: JSOT Press, 1981.
Dearman, John Andrew, *Property Rights in the Eighth-Century*. SBL Dissertation Series 106. Atlanta: Scholars Press, 1988.
Delcor, Maurice. *Le livre de Daniel*. Paris: Libraire Lecoffre, 1971.

Dietrich, W. *Jesaja und die Politik: Beiträge zur evangelischen theologie.* 74. Munich, 1976.
Dodd, G.H. *The Bible and the Greeks.* London: Hodder and Stoughton, 1935.
Dossin, Georges. *Archives Royales de Mari.* Volume I. Paris: Imprimerie Nationale, 1950.
Driver, G.R. and John C Miles. *The Babylonian Laws.* Oxford: Clarendon Press, 1955.
Duhm, B. *Das Buch Jesaja.* Göttingen: Vandenhoeck and Ruprecht, 1892.
Eichrodt, Walther. *Theology of the Old Testament.* Volume I. Trans. J.A. Baker. London: SCM Press, 1961.
Eissfeldt, Otto. *The Old Testament.* Trans. Peter Ackroyd. Oxford: Basil Blackwell, 1965.
Engnell, Ivan. *Studies in Divine Kingship in the Ancient Near East.* Oxford: Basil Blackwell, 1967.
Fahlgren, K.HJ. *Ṣᵉdāḳā, nahestehende und entgegengesetzte Begriffe im Alten Testament.* Uppsala: Almquist and Wiksells Boktryckeri-A-B, 1932.
Fensham, Frank Charles. "The Mišpaṭim in the Covenant Code." Ph.D. dissertation, Johns Hopkins University, 1960.
Galling, Kurt. *Biblisches Reallexikon.* Tübingen: J.C.B. Mohr (Paul Siebeck), 1977.
Gardner, E. Clinton. *Biblical Faith and Social Ethics.* New York: Harper and Brothers, 1960.
Gelb, Ignace J.; Benno Landsberger and A. Leo Oppenheim. eds. *The Assyrian Dictionary.* Volume 16. Chicago: Oriental Institute, 1962.
de Geus, C.H.J. *The Tribes of Israel.* Amsterdam: Van Gorcum, Assen, 1976.
Gibson, John C.L. *Canaanite Myths and Legends.* Edinburgh: T and T Clark, 1977.
_____. *Textbook of Syrian Semitic Inscriptions.* Volume III. Oxford: Clarendon Press, 1982.
Glueck, Nelson. *Ḥesed in the Bible.* Trans. Alfred Gottschalk. Cincinnati: Hebrew Union College Press, 1967.

Gordon, Cyrus H. *Ugaritic Literature*. Roma: Pontificum Institutum Biblicum, 1949.
_____. *Ugaritic Textbook*. Roma: Pontificum Institutum Biblicum, 1975.
Gottwald, Norman K. *A Light to the Nations*. New York: Harper and Row, 1959.
_____. The *Tribes of Yahweh*. Maryknoll, New York: Orbis Books, 1979.
Gray, George Buchanan. *The Book of Isaiah* 1-39. ICC. Edinburgh: T and T Clark, 1912.
Gray, John. *I and II Kings*. OTL. London: SCM Press, 1964.
_____. *The Legacy of Canaan*. SVT 5. Leiden: E.J. Brill, 1965.
Gressmann, H. *Der Ursprung der israelitisch-jüdischen Eschatologie*. Göttingen, 1905.
Gutierrez, Riocerezo C. *La justicia social en los Profetas del siglo VIII: Amos, Oseas, Isaias y Miqueas*. Fribourg, 1970.
Hammershaimb, Erling. *The Book of Amos*. Trans. John Sturdy. Oxford: Blackwell, 1970.
Harper, William Rainer. *A Critical and Exegetical Commentary on Amos and Hosea*. ICC. Edinburgh: T and T Clark, 1905.
Harris, Z. *A Grammar of the Phoenician Language*. New Haven: American Oriental Series, 8, 1936.
Hartmann, Louis F. and Alexander A. DiLella. *The Book of Daniel*. AB. New York: Doubleday and Co., 1978.
Hatch, Edwin and Henry A. Redpath. *A Concordance to the Septuagint*. Volumes I & II. Austria: Akademische Druck - U. Verlagsanstalt, 1975.
Hayes, John H. *Amos: The Eighth Century Prophet*. Nashville: Abingdon Press, 1988.
Herrmann, Siegfried. *A History of Israel in Old Testament Times*. Trans. John Bowden. London: SCM Press, 1981.
Hertzberg, H.W. *I & II Samuel*. OTL. London: SCM Press, 1964.
Heschel, Abraham J. *The Prophets*. New York: Harper and Row, 1962.
Hill, David. *Greek Words and Hebrew Meanings*. SNTSMS. Cambridge: Cambridge University Press, 1967.

Hillers, Delbert R. *Micah.* HERMENEIA. Philadelphia: Fortress Press, 1984.
ibn-Manzur, and Muhammad ibn Mukarram al-Masii. *Lisan al 'Arab.* Volumes 11-12. Bulaq, 1303-7.
Jacob, Edmond. *Theology of the Old Testament.* Trans. Arthur W. Heathcote and Philip J. Allcock. New York: Harper and Brothers, 1958.
Janzen, Waldemar. *Mourning Cry and Woe Oracle.* BZAW 125. Berlin: Walter de Gruyter, 1972.
Jean, Charles F. *Archives Royales de Mari.* Volume II. Paris: Imprimerie Nationale, 1950.
Jean, Charles F. and Jacob Hoftijzer. *Dictionnaire des Inscriptions Sémitiques de L'Ouest.* Leiden: E.J. Brill, 1965.
Jones, Gwilym H. *I & II Kings.* Volumes I & II. NCBC. London: Marshall, Morgan and Scott, 1984.
Kaiser, Otto. *Isaiah 1-12.* OTL. London: SCM Press, 1983.
_____. *Isaiah 13-39.* OTL. London: SCM Press, 1974.
Kapelrud, Arvid S. *Central Ideas in Amos.* Oslo: Universitetsforlaget, 1961.
Kautzsch, Emil Friedrich. *Ueber die Derivate des Stammes* צדק *im alttestamentlichen Sprachgebrauch.* Tübingen, 1881.
Kinet, Dirk, ed. *Der aufhaltbare Untergang; Hosea-Joël-Amos-Micha.* Stuttgart: Katholisches Bibelwerk GmbH. Verlag, 1981.
King, Philip J. *Amos, Hosea, Micah: An Archaelogical Commentary.* Philadelphia: The Westminster Press, 1988.
Knudtzon, J.A. *Die El-Amarna-Tafeln.* Leipzig: J.C. Hinrichs' sche Buchhandlung, 1910.
Koch, Klaus. *The Prophets.* Volume I & II Trans. Margaret Kohl. London: SCM Press, 1982.
_____. "Ṣdq im Alten Testament - Eine traditiongeschichtliche Untersuchung." Ph.D. dissertation, University of Heidelberg, 1953.
Köhler, Ludwig. *Hebrew Man.* Trans. Peter Ackroyd. London: SCM Press, 1956.
Kuhl, Curt. *The Prophets of Israel.* Trans. Rudolf J. Ehrlich and J. P. Smith. Edinburgh: Oliver and Boyd, 1960.

Lambert, W.G. *Babylonian Wisdom Literature.* Oxford: Clarendon Press, 1960.
Lang, Bernhard. *Monotheism and the Prophetic Minority.* SWBAS. Sheffield: The Almond Press, 1983.
Lindblom, J. *Prophecy in Ancient Israel.* Oxford: Basil Blackwell, 1963.
McAvoy, H.W. "A Study of the Root *špṭ* with Special Reference to the Psalter." Ph.D. dissertation, University of Edinburgh, 1973.
McKeating, Henry. *Amos, Hosea and Micah.* CBC. Cambridge: Cambridge University Press, 1971.
Mandelkern, Solomon. *Veteris Testamenti Concordantiae.* Lipsiae: Veit et Comp, 1900.
Mariottini, Claudemiro Francisco. "The Problem of Social Oppression in the Eighth Century Prophets." Ph.D. dissertation, Southern Baptist Theological Seminary, 1983.
Martin, James D. *The Book of Judges.* CBC. Cambridge: Cambridge University Press, 1975.
Martin Achard, R. *Amos: L'homme, le message, l'influence.* Geneva: Labor et Fides, 1984.
Mayes, A.D.H. *Israel in the Period of the Judges.* SBT 29. London: SCM Press, 1974.
Mays, James Luther. *Amos.* OTL. Philadelphia: The Westminster Press, 1969.
_____. *Hosea.* OTL. Philadelphia: The Westminster Press, 1969.
_____. *Micah.* OTL. Philadelphia: The Westminster Press, 1976.
Miller, Patrick D., Jr. *Sin and Judgment in the Prophets.* SBLMS 27. California: Scholars Press, 1982.
Mowinckel, Sigmund. *The Psalms in Israel's Worship.* Trans. D.R. AP-Thomas. Oxford: Basil Blackwell, 1962.
Muilenburg, James. *The Way of Israel.* London: Routledge and Kegan Paul, 1961.
Neher, André. *Amos: Contribution à l'étude du prophétisme.* Paris: Libraire Philosophique J. Vrin, 1950.
Noth, Martin. *The Deuteronomistic History.* JSOTS 15. Sheffield: JSOT Press, 1981.

_____. *The History of Israel.* Trans. Stanley Godman. London: Adam and Charles Black, 1958.

Nötscher, F. *Die Gerechtigkeit Gottes bei den vorexilischen Propheten.* Münster, 1915.

van Oyen, Hendrik. *Ethik des Alten Testaments.* Gesambherstellung: Claussen and Bosse, Leck, 1967.

Paul, Shalom S. *Studies in the book of the Covenant in light of Cuneiform and Biblical law.* SVT 18. Leiden: E.J. Brill, 1970.

_____. *Amos.* HERMENEIA. Minneapolis: Fortress Press, 1991.

Pedersen, Johannes. *Israel: Its Life and Culture.* Volumes I-II. London: Oxford University Press, 1926.

Premnath, Devadasan Nithya. "The Process of Latifundialization mirrored in the Oracles pertaining to 8th Century B.C.E. in the Books of Amos, Hosea, Isaiah and Micah." Th.D. dissertation, Graduate Theological Union, 1984.

Pritchard, James, ed. *Ancient Near Eastern Texts Relating to the Old Testament.* Princeton: Princeton University Press, 1969.

Quell, Gottfried, and Gottlob Schrenk. *Righteousness.* Trans. from Gerhard Kittel's *Theologisches Wörterbuch zum Neuen Testament.* London: Adam and Charles Black, 1951.

von Rad, Gerhard. *The Message of the Prophets.* Trans. D.M.G. Stalker. London: SCM Press, 1968.

_____. *Old Testament Theology.* Volumes I & II. Trans. D.M.G. Stalker. Edinburgh: Oliver and Boyd, 1965.

Ringgren, Helmer. *Israelite Religion.* Trans. David Green. London: SPCK, 1966.

Robinson, H. Wheeler. *Inspiration and Revelation in the Old Testament.* Oxford: Clarendon Press, 1946.

Rosenberg, M.S. "The Stem *Špṭ*: An Investigation of Biblical and Extra-Biblical Sources." Ph.D. dissertation, University of Pennsylvania, 1963.

Routtenberg, Hyman J. *Amos of Tekoa.* New York: Vantage Press, 1971.

Rowley, H.H. *The Rediscovery of the Old Testament.* London: James Clarke and Company, 1945.

_____. *The Unity of the Bible.* London: Carey Kinsgate Press, 1953.

Ruble, Randall T. "A study of root ṢDK in the Psalter." Ph.D. dissertation, University of Edinburgh, 1964.
Sawyer, J.F.A. *Semantic in Biblical Research.* London: SCM Press, 1972.
Schmid, Hans Heinrich. *Gerechtigkeit als Weltordnung.* BHTh 40. Tübingen: J.C.B. Mohr (Paul Siebeck), 1968.
Schmidt, Werner H. *Das Königtum der Götter in Ugarit und Israel.* BZAW 80. Berlin: Verlag Alfred Topelmann, 1961.
_____. *Introduction to the Old Testament.* Trans. Matthew J. O'Connell. London: SCM Press, 1984.
Schrey, Heinz-Horst; Hans Hermann Walz and W. A. Whitehouse, *The Biblical Doctrine of Justice and Law.* London: SCM Press, 1955.
Skinner, John. *Prophecy and Religion.* Cambridge: Cambridge University Press, 1922.
Smend, Rudolf. *Yahweh War and Tribal Confederation.* trans. Max Gray Rogers. Nashville: Abingdon Press, 1970.
Smith, George Adam. *The Book of the Twelve Prophets.* Volume I. London: Hodder and Stoughton, 1929.
Smith, Ralph L. *Micah-Malachi.* WBC. Waco, Texas: Word Books, 1984.
Smith, Gary V. *Amos: A Commentary.* Grand Rapids, Michigan: Zondervan, 1989.
Snaith, Norman H. *The Distinctive Ideas of the Old Testament.* London: The Epsworth Press, 1944.
Soggin, J. Alberto. *Judges.* OTL. London: SCM Press, 1981.
_____. *The Prophet Amos.* London: SCM Press, 1987.
Sperber, Alexander, ed. *The Bible in Aramaic.* 4 vols. Leiden: E.J. Brill, 1959. Volume I: *The Pentateuch According to TARGUM ONKELOS.*
_____. *The Bible in Aramaic.* 4 vols. Leiden: E.J. Brill, 1962. Volume III: *The Latter Prophets According to TARGUM JONATHAN.*
de Vaux, Roland. *Ancient Israel: Its Life and Institutions.* Trans. John McHugh. London: Darton, Longman and Todd, 1961.
Vriezen, Th.C. *An Outline of Old Testament Theology.* Oxford: Basil Blackwell, 1966.

Ward, James M. *Amos and Isaiah.* Nashville: Abingdon Press, 1969.
_____. *Hosea.* New York: Harper and Row, 1966.
_____. *Thus Says the Lord.* Nashville: Abingdon Press, 1991.
Watts, John D.W. *Vision and Prophecy in Amos.* Leiden: E.J. Brill, 1958.
Wellhausen, Julius. *Prolegomena to the History of Ancient Israel.* New York: The Meridian Library, 1957.
Weinfeld, Moshe. *Justice and Righteousness in Israel and the Nations: Equality and Freedom in Ancient Israel in Light of Social Justice in the Ancient Near East.* Jerusalem: The Magnes Press, 1985. (Hebrew)
Whitaker, Richard E. *A Concordance of the Ugaritic Literature.* Massachusetts: Harvard University Press, 1972.
Whitelam, Keith W. *The Just King.* JSOTS. Sheffield: JSOT Press, 1979.
Whitley, C.F. *The Prophetic Achievement.* London: A.R. Mowbray, 1963.
Wigley, A.L. *Amos and Social Righteousness.* London: Christian Endeavour Union, 1947.
Wildberger, Hans. *Isaiah 1-12.* Minneapolis: Augsburg Fortress Press, 1991.
_____. *Jesaja 13-27.* Volume II. Biblischer Kommentar Altes Testament. Neukirchener Verlag, 1972.
_____. *Jesaja 28-39.* Volume III. Biblischer Kommentar Altes Testament. Neukirchener Verlag, 1982.
Wolff, Hans Walter. *Amos the Prophet.* Trans. Foster R. McCurley. Philadelphia: Fortress Press, 1973.
_____. *Confrontations with Prophets.* Philadelphia: Fortress Press, 1983.
_____. *Hosea.* HERMENEIA. Trans. Gary Stansell. Philadelphia: Fortress Press, 1974.
_____. *Joel and Amos.* HERMENEIA. Trans. Waldemar Janzen; S. Dean McBride, Jr. and Charles A. Muenchow. Philadelphia: Fortress Press, 1977.
_____. *Micah the Prophet.* Trans. Ralph D. Gehrke. Philadelphia: Fortress Press, 1981.

_____. *Micah*. Minneapolis: Augsburg Fortress Press, 1990.
_____. *The Old Testament: A Guide to its Writings*. Trans. Keith Crim. Philadelphia: Fortress Press, 1973.
_____. *Die Stunde des Amos*. München: Chr. Kaiser Verlag, 1979.
Zeitlin, Irving M. *Ancient Judaism*. Cambridge: Polity Press, 1984.
Ziesler, J.A. *The Meaning of Righteousness in Paul*. Cambridge: Cambridge University Press, 1972.

Articles

Achtemeier, Elizabeth R. "Righteousness in the Old Testament." In *The Interpreters Dictionary of the Bible*. Volume 4. ed. George Buttrick. Nashville: Abingdon Press, 1962, pp. 80-85.
Albrektson, Bertil. "Prophecy and Politics in the Old Testament." In *The Myth of the State*. ed. Haralds Biezais. Stockholm: Almquist and Wiksell, 1972. pp. 45-56.
Albright, W.F. "The Phoenician Inscriptions of the Tenth Century B.C. from Byblus," *Journal of the American Oriental Society* 67 (1947), 153-160.
Alger, B. "The Theology and Social Ethic of Amos," *Scripture* 17 (1965), 109-116; 318-328.
Allen, Leslie C. "Amos, Prophet of Solidarity," *Vox Evangelica* 6 (1969), 42-53.
Alt, A. "Der Anteil Des Königtums an der sozialen Entwicklung in den Reichen Israel und Juda." In *Grundfragen der Geschichte des Volkes Israel*. München, 1979, pp. 348-372.
Anderson, George W. "A Study of Micah 6:1-8," *Scottish Journal of Theology*, 4 (1951), 191-197.
_____. "Israel: Amphictyony: 'AM; Kahal; Edah." In *Translating and Understanding the Old Testament*. Nashville: Abingdon Press, 1970. pp. 135-151.
Bailey, Joseph G. "Amos: Preacher of Social Reform," *The Bible Today* 19 (1981), 306-313.
Bardtke, H. "Die Latifundien in Juda während der Zweiten Häfte des achten Jahrhunderts V. Chr. (zum Verständnis von Jes.

5:8-10)." In *Hommages à André Dupont-Sommer*. Paris: Libraire d'Amerique et d'Orient, 1971, pp. 235-257.

Barton, John. "Ethics in Isaiah of Jerusalem," *Journal of Theological Studies* (1981), 1-18.

Batten, L.W. "The Use of מִשְׁפָּט," *Journal of Biblical Literature* XI (1892), 206-210.

Bazak, Jacob. "The Meaning of the Term 'Justice and Righteousness' (משפט וצדקה) in the Bible," *The Jewish Law Annual* VIII, 5-13.

Beek, M.A. "The Religious Background of Amos II 6-8," *Oudtestamentische Studiën* V (1948), 132-139.

Berkovits, Eliezer. "The Biblical Meaning of Justice," *Judaism* 18 (1969), 188-209.

Beuken, W.A.M. "*Mišpaṭ*. The First Servant Song and its Context," *Vetus Testamentum* 22 (1972), 1-30.

Bewer, Julius. "Critical Notes on Amos 2:7 and 8:4," *American Journal of Semitic Languages and Literature* 19 (1903), 116-117.

Bianchi, H. "Tsedeka-Justice," *Bijdragen. Tijdschrift voor Philosophie en Theologie* 34 (1973), 306-318.

Booth, Osborne. "The Semantic Development of the Term מִשְׁפָּט in the OT," *Journal of Biblical Literature* LXI (1942), 105-110.

Botterweck, G. Johannes "אביון." In *Theological Dictionary of the Old Testament*. Volume I. ed. G. Johannes Botterweck and Helmer Ringgren. Trans. John T. Willis. Grand Rapids, Michigan: W.B. Eerdmans Publishing Company, 1974. pp. 27-41.

_____. "Sie verkaufen den Unschuldigen um Geld: zur sozialen Kritik des Propheten Amos," *Bibel und Leben* 12 (1971), 215-231.

Brueggemann, W. "Amos IV: 4-13 and Israel's Covenant Worship," *Vetus Testamentum* 15 (1965), 1-15.

Buchsel, Friedrich. "κρίνω: Linguistic." In *Theological Dictionary of the New Testament*. Volume III. ed. Gerhard Kittel. Trans. Geoffrey W. Bromiley. Grand Rapids, Michigan: W.B. Eerdmans Publishing Company, 1965. pp. 922-923.

Candelaria, Michael. "Justice: Extrapolations from the Concept *Mishpat* in the Book of Micah," *APUNTES* 3 (Winter 1983), 75-82.

Casalis, G. "Du texte au Sermon: Amos 8," *Études Théologiques et Religieuses* 46 (1971), 113-124.

Cazelles, H. "A Propos de quelques textes difficiles relatifs à la justice de Dieu dans L'Ancien Testament," *Revue Biblique* 58 (1951), 169-188.

Clements, Ronald E. "Temple and Land: A Significant Aspect of Israel's Worship," *Transactions of Glasgow University Oriental Society* 19 (1961-62), 16-28.

Cohen, Martin A. "The Prophets as Revolutionaries," *Biblical Archeology Review* 5 (3, 1979), 12-19.

Cohen, Simon. "The Political Background of the Words of Amos," *Hebrew Union College Annual* 36 (1965), 153-160.

Compstom, H.F.B. "Ladies' Finery in Isaiah 3:18:23," *Church Quarterly Review* 103 (1926-27), 316-330.

Cox, D. "Inspired Radicals: The Prophets of the Eighth Century," *Studii Biblici Franciscani Liber Annuus* 25 (1975), 90-103.

_____. "Ṣedaqa and Mišpat: The Concept of Righteousness in Later Wisdom," *Studii Biblici Franciscani Liber Annuus* 27 (1977), 33-50.

Craghan, John F. "The Prophet Amos in Recent Literature," *Biblical Theological Bulletin* 2 (1972), 242-261.

Crusemann, Frank. "Kritik an Amos im deuteronomistischen Geschichtswerk." In *Probleme biblischer Theologie.* ed. Hans Walter Wolff. München: Chr. Kaiser Verlag, 1971, pp. 37-51.

_____. "Jahwes Gerechtigkeit [ṣᵉdaqa/ṣaddāq] im Alten Testament," *Evangelische Theologie* 36 (1976), pp. 427-450.

Dahood, M. "To Pawn One's Garment," *Biblica* 42 (1961), 359-366.

Davies, G. Henton. "The Yahwistic Tradition in the Eighth Century Prophets." In *Studies in Old Testament Prophecy.* ed. H.H. Rowley. Edinburgh: T and T Clark, 1950, pp. 37-51.

Dearman, J. Andrew. "Hebrew Prophecy and Social Criticism: Some Observations for Perspective," *Perspectives in Religious Studies* 9 (Summer 1982), 131-143.

Descamps, A. "Justice et Justification," *Supplément Dictionnaire de la Bible* 6 (1949), column 1418.
Diestel, Ludwig. "Die Idee der Gerechtigkeit, vorzüglich im Alten Testament, biblisch-theologish dargestellt," *Jahrbücher für Deutsche Theologie* 5 (1860), 173-253.
Dion, P.E. "Le message moral du prophète Amos s'inspirait-il du 'droit de l'alliance,'" *Science et Esprit* 27 (1975), 5-34.
Donner, H. "Die soziale Botschaft der Propheten im Lichte der Gesellschaftsordnung in Israel," *Oriens Antiquus* 2 (1963), 229-245.
Dossin, Georges. "L'Inscription De Fondation de Iaḫdun-lim, Roi de Mari," *Syria* 32 (1955), 1-28.
Driver, G.R. "Difficult Words in the Hebrew Prophets." In *Studies in Old Testament Prophecy*. ed. H.H. Rowley. Edinburgh: T and T Clark, 1950, pp. 52-72.
_____. "Linguistic and Textual Problems: Isaiah I-XXXIX," *Journal of Theological Studies* 38 (1937), 36-50.
Elliger, K. "Prophet und Politik," *Zeitschrift für die Alttestamentliche Wissenschaft* 53 (1935), 3-22.
Engnell, Ivan. "Prophets and Prophetism in the Old Testament," In *Critical Essays on the Old Testament*. Trans. John T. Willis. London: SPCK, 1970, pp. 123-179.
Eybers, I.H. "The Stem S-P-T in the Psalms," *Die Ou Testamentiese Werkgemeenskap in Suid-Afrika* (1963), 58-63.
Fabry, H.J. "דַּל." In *Theological Dictionary of the Old Testament*. Volume III. ed. G. Johannes Botterweck and Helmer Ringgren. Trans. John T. Willis; Geoffrey W. Bromiley and David E. Green. Grand Rapids, Michigan: W.B. Eerdmans Publishing Company, 1978, pp. 208-230.
Fendler, Marlene. "Zur Sozialkritik des Amos. Versuch einer wirtschafts- und sozial-geschichtlichen Interpretation alttestamentlicher Texte," *Evangelische Theologie* 33 (1973), 32-53.
Fensham, Frank Charles. "The Judges and Ancient Israelite Jurisprudence," *Die Ou Testamentiese Werkgemeenskap in Suid-Afrika* (1959), 15-22.

_____. "Widow, Orphan and the Poor in Ancient Near Eastern Legal and Wisdom Literature," *Journal of Near Eastern Studies* 21 (1962), 129-139.

_____. "A possible origin of the concept of the Day of the Lord," *Essays in Die Ou Testamentiese Werkgemeenskap in Suid Afrika* (1966-1967), 90-97.

Ferguson, Henry. "The Verb שפט," *Journal of Biblical Literature* (1888), 130-136.

Fichtner, Johannes. "Jesaja unter den Weisen," *Theologische Literaturzeitung* 79 (1949), 75-80.

Fuchs, H. "Das alttestamentliche Begriffsverhältnis von Gerechtigkeit (*ṣedeq*) und Gnade (*Chesed*) in Profetie und Dichtung," *Christentum und Wissenschaft* 3 (1927), 101-118.

Gamoran, Hillel. "The Biblical Law against Loans on Interest," *Journal of Near Eastern Study* 30 (1971), 127-134.

George, Augustin. "Poverty in the Old Testament." In *Gospel Poverty. Essays in Biblical Theology*. Trans. Michael D. Guinan. Chicago: Franciscan Herald Press, 1977, pp. 3-24.

Gerstenberger, Erhard. "The Woe-Oracles of the Prophets," *Journal of Biblical Literature* 81 (1962), 249-263.

Ginsberg, H.L. "The North-Canaanite Myth of Anath and Aqhat," *Bulletin of American Society of Oriental Research* 97 (February 1945), 3-10.

Gossai, Hemchand. "*Ṣaddîq* in Theological, Forensic and Economic Perspectives," *Svensk Exegetisk Årsbok* 53 (1988), 7-13.

Graesser, Carl. "Righteousness, Human and Divine," *Currents in Theology and Mission* 10 (1983), 134-141.

Graham, William Creighton. "Notes on the Interpretation of Isaiah 5:1-14," *American Journal of Semitic Languages* 45 (1928-29), 167-178.

Gray, John. "The Day of Yahweh in Cultic Experience and Eschatological Prospect," *Svensk Exegetisk Årsbok* 39 (1974), 5-37.

_____. "The Goren at the City Gate And The Royal Office in the Ugaritic Text 'Aqht," *Palestine Exploration Quarterly* (1953), 118-123.

Grether, Oskar. "Die Bezeichnung 'Richter' für die charismatischen Helden der vorstaatlichen Zeit," *Zeitschrift für die Alttestamentliche Wissenschaft* 57 (1939), 110-121.
Hammershaimb, Erling. "Some Leading Ideas in the Book of Micah." In *Some Aspects of Old Testament Prophecy from Isaiah to Malachi*. København: Rosenkilde og Bagger, 1966, pp. 29-50.
_____. "On the Ethics of the Old Testament Prophets," *Supplements to Vetus Testamentum* 7 (1959), 75-101.
Hanson, Paul D. "The Theological Significance of Contradiction within the Book of the Covenant." In *Canon and Authority*. eds. George W. Coats and Burke O. Long. Philadelphia: Fortress Press, 1977, pp. 110-131.
Henrey, K.H. "Land Tenure in the Old Testament," *Palestine Exploration Quarterly* 86 (1954), 5-15.
Herntrich, Volkmar. "κρίνω: The OT term מִשְׁפָּט." In *Theological Dictionary of the New Testament*. Volume III. ed. Gerhard Kittel. Trans. Geoffrey W. Bromiley. Grand Rapids, Michigan: W.B. Eerdmans Publishing Company, 1965, pp. 923-933.
Hertzberg. H.W. "Die Entwicklung des Begriffes מִשְׁפָּט im AT," *Zeitschrift für die Alttestamentliche Wissenschaft* 40 (1922), 256-287.
_____. "Die Entwicklung des Begriffes מִשְׁפָּט im AT," *Zeitschrift für die Alttestamentliche Wissenschaft* 41 (1923), 16-76.
Heuser, Alan J. "The 'Minor Judges' - A Re-evaluation," *Journal of Biblical Literature* 94 (1975), 190-200.
Hocherman, Yaakov. "Does the Concept of Bribery Have a Positive Side?" *Beth Mikra* 36 (1990-91), 220-222.
Hoffman, Yair. "The Day of the Lord as a Concept and a term in Prophetic Literature," *Zeitschrift für die Alttestamentliche Wissenschaft* 93 (1981) 37-50.
Holm-Nielsen, Svend. "Die Sozialkritik der Propheten." In *Denkender Glaube*. ed. Otto Kaiser. Berlin: Walter de Gruyter, 1976, pp. 7-23.
Honeycutt, R.L. "Amos and Contemporary Issues," *Review and Expositor* 63 (1966), 441-457.

Howington, N.P. "Toward an ethical understanding of Amos," Review and Expositor 63 (1966), 405-412.

Huey, F.B. "The Ethical Teaching of Amos, its Content and Relevance," Southwestern Journal of Theology 9 (1966), 57-67.

Hyatt, J. Philip. "The Prophetic Criticism of Israelite Worship." In Interpreting the Prophetic Tradition. LBS. ed. by Harry M. Orlinsky. Cincinnati: The Hebrew Union College Press, 1969, pp. 201-224.

_____. "The Translation and Meaning of Amos 5:23-24," Zeitschrift für die Alttestamentliche Wissenschaft 67-68 (1955-1956), 17-24.

Ishida, T. "The Leaders of the Tribal Leagues 'Israel' in the Pre-Monarchic Period," Revue Biblique 81 (1973), 514-530.

Jacob, Edmond. "The Biblical Prophets: Revolutionaries or Conservatives," Interpretation 19 (January 1965), 47-55.

Jepsen, Alfred. "צדק und צדקה im Alten Testament." In Gottes Wort und Gottes Land. ed. Henning Graf Reventlow. Göttingen: Vandenhoeck and Ruprecht, 1965, pp. 78-89.

Johnson, Bo. "Der Bedentungs unterscheid Zwischen $ṣādaq$ und $ṣedaqa$," Annual of Swedish Theological Institute 11 (1977-78), 31-39.

Johnstone, W. "Old Testament Expressions in Property Holding," Ugaritica 6 (1969), 308-317.

Justeson, J.P. "On the meaning of ṢADAQ," Andrews University Seminary Studies 2 (1964), 53-61.

Kapelrud, Arvid S. "New Ideas in Amos," Supplements to Vetus Testamentum 15 (1966), 193-206.

_____. "The Role of the Cult in Old Israel." In The Bible in Modern Scholarship. ed. J. Philip Hyatt. Nashville: Abingdon Press, 1965, pp. 44-56.

Kelley, P.H. "Contemporary Study of Amos and Prophetism," Review and Expositor 63 (1966), 375-385.

Kelly, J. "The Biblical Meaning of Poverty and Riches," The Bible Today 33 (1967), 2282-91.

Kendall, Daniel. "The use of Mišpaṭ in Isaiah 59," Zeitschrift für die Alttestamentliche Wissenschaft 96 (1984), 391-404.

Kipper, P.J. Balduino. "A evolução econômico-social em Israel e a pregação das profetas," *Revista de Cultura Biblica* 20 (1977), 309-351.

Koch, Klaus. "Die Entstehung der sozialen Kritik bei den Profeten." In *Probleme biblischer Theologie.* ed. Hans Walter Wolff. München: Chr. Kaiser Verlag, 1971, pp. 236-257.

_____. "Origin and Effect of Social Critique of the Pre-exilic Prophets," *Bangalore Theological Forum* 11 (1979), 91-108.

Kraus, H.J. "Die Prophetische Botschaft gegen das soziale Unrecht Israels," *Evangelische Theologie* 15 (1955), 295-307.

Kuyper, Lester J. "Righteousness and Salvation," *Scottish Journal of Theology* 30 (1977), 233-252.

Labuschagne, C.J. "Amos' conception of God and the popular theology of his time." In *Studies on the Books of Hosea and Amos, 7th and 8th congresses of Die O.T. Werkgemeenskap in Suid-Afrika, 1964-65.* Potchefstroom: Rege-Pers Beperk, 1965, pp. 122-133.

Lang, Bernhard. "The Social Organization of Peasant Poverty in Biblical Israel," *Journal for the Study of the Old Testament*, 24 (1982), 47-63.

_____. "Sklaven und Unfreie im Buch Amos (ii 6, viii 6)," *Vetus Testamentum* 31 (1981), 482-486.

van Leeuwen, C. "The Prophecy of the Yōm YHWH in Amos 5:18-20," *Oudtestamentische Studiën* 19 (1974), 113-134.

Long, B.O. "Social Dimensions of Prophetic Conflict," *Semeia* 21 (1982), 31-53.

Loretz, O. "Die Prophetische Kritik des Rentenkapitalismus: Grundlagen - Probleme des Propheten Forschung," *Ugarit - Forschungen* 7 (1975), 271-278.

Lucal, J.A. "God of Justice - the Prophets as Social Reformers," *The Bible Today* 32 (1967), 2221-2228.

McGrath, A.E. "Justice and Justification: Semantic and Juristic Aspects of the Christian Doctrine of Justification," *Scottish Journal of Theology* 35 (1982), 403-418.

McKane, William. "Prophecy and the Prophetic Literature." In *Tradition and Interpretation.* ed. G.W. Anderson. Oxford: Clarendon Press, 1979, pp. 163-188.

_____. "Prophet and Institution," *Zeitschrift für die Alttestamentliche Wissenschaft* 94 (1982), 251-266.

McKay, J.W. "Exodus XXVIII 1-3, 6-8. A Decalogue for the Administration of Justice in the City Gate," *Vetus Testamentum* 21 (1971), 311-325.

McKenzie, D.A. "The Judge of Israel," *Vetus Testamentum* 17 (1967), 118-121.

_____. "Judicial Procedure at the Town Gate," *Vetus Testamentum* 14 (1964), 100-104.

Malamat, A. "Aspects of Tribal Societies in Mari and Israel," *Rencontre Assyriologique Internationale* 15 (1966), 129-138.

_____. "The Period of the Judges." In *The World History of the Jewish People*. Volume III. ed. Benjamin Mazar. London: W.H. Allen, 1971, pp. 129-163.

Maloney, Robert P. "Usury and Restrictions on Interest-taking in the Ancient Near East," *Catholic Biblical Quarterly* 36 (1974), 1-20.

Marzal, A. "The Provincial Governor of Mari: His title and appointment," *Journal of Near Eastern Study* 30 (1971), 186-219.

Mays, James Luther. "Justice: Perspectives from the Prophetic Tradition," *Interpretation* 37 (1983), 5-17.

_____. "The Theological Purpose of the book of Micah." In *Beiträge zur Alttestamentlichen Theologie*. eds. Herber Donner; Robert Hanhart and Rudolf Smend. Göttingen: Vandenhoeck and Ruprecht, 1977, pp. 276-287.

_____. "Words about the Words of Amos," *Interpretation* 13 (1959), 259-272.

Mogensen, Bent. "Ṣedaqa in the Scandinavian and German Research traditions." In *The Productions of Time: Tradition History in Old Testament Scholarship*. eds. Knud Jeppesen and Benedikt Otzen. Sheffield: The Almond Press, 1984, pp. 67-80.

Morgenstern, Julian. "Amos Studies IV," *Hebrew Union College Annual* 32 (1961), 295-350.

Morris, Leon. "Judgement and Custom," *Australian Biblical Review* 7 (December 1959), 72-74.

Neubauer, Karl Wilhelm. "Erwägungen zu Amos 5:4-15," *Zeitschrift für die Alttestamentliche Wissenschaft* 78 (1966), 292-316.

Neufeld, Edward. "The Emergence of Royal-Urban Society in Ancient Israel," *Hebrew Union College Annual* 31 (1960), 31-54.

_____. "The Prohibitions against Loans at Interest in Ancient Hebrew laws," *Hebrew Union College Annual* 26 (1955), 355-412.

Orlinsky, Harry M. "The Tribal System of Israel and Related Groups in the Period of the Judges." In *Studies and Essays in Honor of Abraham A. Neuman*. eds. Meir Ben-Horin; Bernhard D. Weinryb and Solomon Zeitlin. Leiden: E.J. Brill, 1962, pp. 375-387.

Patterson, Richard D. "The Widow, the Orphan and the Poor in the Old Testament and the Extra-Biblical Literature," *Bibliotheca Sacra* 130 (1973), 223-234.

Pidoux, G. "Judgement: O.T." In *Vocabulary of the Bible*. ed. J.J. von Allmen. London: Lutterworth Press, 1958, pp. 209-211.

van der Ploeg, J. "ṢĀPAṬ et MIŠPĀṬ," *Oudtestamentische Studiën* II (1943), 144-155.

Porteous, Norman W. "The Basis of the Ethical Teaching of the Prophets." In *Studies in Old Testament Prophecy*. ed. H.H. Rowley. Edinburgh: T and T Clark, 1950, pp. 143-156.

_____. "The Care of the Poor in the Old Testament." In *Living the Mystery*. Oxford: Basil Blackwell, 1967, pp. 143-156.

Procksch, O. "Die hebräische Wurzel der Theologie," *Christentum und Wissenschaft* 2 (1926), 451-461.

von Rad, Gerhard. "The Origin of the Concept of the Day of Yahweh," *Journal of Semitic Studies* 4 (1959), 97-108.

_____. "'Righteousness' and 'Life' in the Cultic Language of the Psalms." In *The Problem Of The Hexateuch And Other Essays*. Edinburgh: Oliver And Boyd, 1966, pp. 243-266.

Ramsey, Paul. "Elements of a Biblical Political Theory," *The Journal of Religion* 29 (1949), 258-283.

Reventlow, Henning Graf. "Righteousness as Order of the World: Some Remarks toward a Programme." In *Justice and Righteousness: Biblical Themes and their Influence*. eds. Henning

Graf Reventlow and Yair Hoffmann. JSOTS 137. Sheffield: Sheffield Academic Press, 1992, pp. 163-172.

Richter, Wolfgang. " Zu Den 'Richern Israels,'" *Zeitschrift für die Alttestamentliche Wissenschaft* 77 (1965), 40-71.

Rooy, Sidney. "Righteousness and Justice," *Evangelical Review of Theology* 6 (1982), 260-274.

Rosenberg, M.S. "The Sofeṭim in the Bible," *Eretz-Israel* (1975), 77-86.

Rosenthal, Franz. "SEDAKA, CHARITY," *Hebrew Union College Annual* 23, (Part 1, 1950-51), 411-430.

Rowley, H.H. "The Nature of Prophecy in the Light of Recent Study," *Harvard Theological Review* 38 (1945), 1-38.

Safren, Jonathan D. "New Evidence for the Title of the Provincial Governor at Mari," *Hebrew Union College Annual* 50 (1979), 1-15.

Scaria, K.J. "Social Justice in the O.T.," *Bible Bhashyam* 4 (1978), 163-192.

Seilhamer, Frank H. "The role of Covenant in the Mission and Message of Amos." In *A Light Unto my Path: Old Testament Studies in Honor of Jacob M. Myers.* eds. Howard N. Bream; Ralph D. Heim and Carey A. Moore. Philadelphia: Temple University Press, 1974, pp. 435-452.

Skinner, John. "Righteousness in the Old Testament." In *A Dictionary of the Bible.* Volume IV. ed. J. Hastings. Edinburgh: T and T Clark, 1900, pp. 272-281.

Smith, H.P. "צדק and its derivatives," *The Presbyterian Review* 3 (1882), 165-168.

Smith, Ralph L. "The Theological Implications of the Prophecy of Amos," *Southwestern Journal of Theology* 9 (1966), 49-56.

Stein, S. "The Law on Interest in the Old Testament," *Journal of Theological Studies* 4 (Part II, October 1953), 161-170.

Swetnam, J. "Some Observations of the Background of צדיק in Jeremias 23.5a," *Biblica* 46 (1965), 29-40.

Thompson, H.C. "*Shopheṭ* and *Mishpaṭ* in the Book of Judges," *Transactions of Glasgow University Oriental Society* 19 (1961-62), 74-85.

Varro, R. "Amos: les justes, les pauvres et le prophète," *Masses Ouvrière* 297 (1973), 24-37.
Vesco, Jean Luc. "Amos de Teqoa, défenseur de l'homme," *Revue Biblique* 87 (1980), 481-513.
von Waldow, H. Eberhard. "Social Responsibility and Social Structure in Early Israel," *Catholic Biblical Quarterly* 32 (1970), 182-204.
Wanke, G. "Zu Grundlagen und Absicht prophetischer Sozialkritik," *Kerygma und Dogma* 18 (1972), 2-17.
Warner, Sean. "The Period of the Judges Within the Structure of Early Israel," *Hebrew Union College Annual* 47 (1976), 57-79.
Waterman, Leroy. "The Ethical Clarity of the Prophets," *Journal of Biblical Literature* 64 (1945), 297-308.
Watson, P. "Form criticism and an exegesis of Micah 6:1-8," *Restoration Quarterly* 7 (1963), 62-72.
Watts, John D.W. "A Critical analysis of Amos 4:1ff." In *Book of Seminar Papers* II. SBL. ed. Lane C. McGaughy. Society of Biblical Literature, 1972, pp. 489-500.
_____. "Note on the Text of Amos 5:7," *Vetus Testamentum* 4 (1954), 215-216.
Weinfeld, Moshe. "Judge and Officer in Ancient Israel and in the Ancient Near East," *Israel Oriental Studies* 7 (1977), 65-88.
_____. "'Justice and Righteousness' in Ancient Israel against the Background of 'Social Reforms' in the Ancient Near East" In *Mesopotamien und Seine Nachbarn*. eds. Hans-Jörg Nissen and Johannes Renger. Berlin: Dietrich Reimer Verlag, 1982, pp. 491-520.
_____. "'Justice and Righteousness'----משפט וצדקה---The Expression and its Meaning." In *Justice and Righteousness: Biblical Themes and their Influence*. eds. Henning Graf Reventlow and Yair Hoffmann. JSOTS 137. Sheffield: Sheffield Academic Press, 1992, pp. 228-246.
Weiss, Meir. "The Origin of the 'Day of the Lord' reconsidered," *Hebrew Union College Annual* 37 (1966), 29-72.
Williams, Donald L. "The Theology of Amos," *Review and Expositor* 63 (1966), 393-403.

Williams, James G. "The Alas-Oracles of the Eighth Century Prophets," *Hebrew Union College Annual* 38 (1967), 75-92.
_____. "The Social Location of Israelite Prophecy," *Journal of the American Academy of Religion* 37 (1969), 153-165.
Willis, John T. "Fundamental Issues in Contemporary Micah Studies," *Restoration Quarterly* 13 (1970), 77-90.
_____. "Micah 2:6-8 and the 'People of God' in Micah," *Biblische Zeitschrift* 14 (1970), 72-87.
_____. "Review of Th. Lescow, Micha 6, 6-8," *Vetus Testamentum* 18 (1968), 273-278.
Wolff, Hans Walter. "Micah the Moreshite - The Prophet and His Background." In *Israelite Wisdom: Theological and Literary Essays in Honor of Samuel Terrien.* eds. John G. Gammie; Walter A. Brueggemann; W. Lee Humphreys and James M. Ward. Montana: Scholars Press, 1978, pp. 77-84.
Yee, Gale A. "A Form-Critical Study of Isaiah 5:1-7 as a Song and a Juridical Parable," *Catholic Biblical Quarterly* 43 (1981), 30-40.
Zerfass, R. "Es ist dir gesagt, Mensch, was du tun sollst" (Mic 6:8), *Bibel und Kirche* 25 (1970), 109-110.
Zimmerli, Walter. "Das Gottesrecht bei den Propheten Amos, Hosea und Jesaja." In *Werden und Wirken des Alten Testaments.* eds. Rainer Albertz; Hans-Peter Müller; Hans Walter Wolff and Walther Zimmerli. Göttingen: Vandenhoeck and Ruprecht, 1980, pp. 216-235.

Index of Biblical References

Genesis

4:1	192
6:9	26
7:1	26
12:1-4	188
14:18	16
15:6	26, 64
15:18	188
16	187
16:5	187, 189,
18:20	26
18:23ff	86
18:23	26
18:24	26
18:25	26, 141
18:28	26
19:19	20
20:4	26, 84 n.151
20:5	20
20:13	20
21:23	20
23	275 n.81
23:10	97
23:20	285 n.101
24:49	20
30:6	116
30:33	25 n. 43, 26, 60
32:11	20
34:20	97
38:1-26	51
38:26	26, 31, 62
40:13	179, 142
44:16	26

Exodus

2	138
2:14	138
6:5	188
6:6	188
9:27	27
15:13	20
15:25	142, 147 n.9
20:17	290 n.118
21-23	143 n.3
21:1	142, 179
21:9	142, 143
21:31	142
22-23	232
22:24	281 n.88, 282
22:25	249
23:5	87
23:6	117, 143
23:7	27, 28, 66 n.115, 86
23:8	27, 66 n.115, 86
24:1	123 n.119
24:3	142
26:30	143
28:15	142
28:29	142
28:30	142
34:7	20
25:17	97
40:8	97

Leviticus

3	260 n.41
5:10	143
8:19	191

8:30 191
8:31 191
9:16 .... 143, 191
18:4 .... 143, 191
18:5 143
18:5-6 179
18:26 143
18:36 191
19:15 ..... 27, 67 n.117,
.... 72 n.129, 144, 183,
.... 201, 202, 210
19:35 ...... 50 n.77, 144
19:36 ... 27-28, 29 n.47
.... 50 n.77, 69 n.123
19:37 143
20:22 143
24:22 144
25:18 ....143, 179
25:23 278
25:35-38 281 n.88, 282
25:39-40 280
26:15 143
26:43 143
25:46 143

Numbers

9:3 144
9:14 144
15:16 144
15:24 144
27:5 144
27:11 ...... 144, 147 n.9
27:21 ....117, 145
29:6 144
29:18 144
29:21 144
29:24 144
29:27 144
29:30 144
29:33 144

29:37 144
35:12 ...... 145, 147 n.9
35:16-23 145
35:24 144
35:29 ...... 144, 147 n.9
36:13 144

Deuteronomy

1:16 29
1:16-18 181
1:17 ......117, 146, 181,
...............................182
4:1 145
4:5 ....145, 179
4:8 .... 29, 145, 202
4:14 145
4:45 145
5:1 145
5:2 145
6:1 145
6:20 145
6:25 23 n.41, 77 n.139
7:11 145
8:11 ....145, 179
9:4-6 28
10:18 .... 99 n.38
11:1 145
11:32 145
12:1 145
16:18 ... 67 n.117, 146,
...............................202
16:18-20 28
16:19 ...... 87, 146, 202
17:8 146
17:9 ....117, 146
17:11 ....117, 146
18:3 180
19:6 147
21:17 147,180
21:22 147

Index

23:20 283
23:20-21 281 n.88, 282
24:6 249
24:10-17 280
24:13 .... 23 n.41
24:13 29
24:17 146
25:1 ......29, 66, 67, 87,
...................147, 202
25:5-10 300
25:15 .... 29, 29 n.47,
.... 69 n.123
26:16 145
26:17 145
27:19 146
27:25 87
30:16 145
32:4 29, 85 n.154,146,
.... 202
32:14 .... 273 n.76
32:36 116
32:41 147
33:10 145
33:19 29
33:21 ...... 29, 146, 202

Joshua

6:15 147
10:1 16
20:6 147
24:14 20
24:25 147

Judges

2:11 121
2:16 .... 121, 127 n.133
2:16-18 .... 121 n.113
2:18 .... 121, 127 n.133
3:9 ..... 121, 127 n.133,
.... 128 n.135
3:15 ..... 121, 128 n.135
4:5 148
5:11 ..... 25 n.43, 29, 53
6:35 .... 128 n.135
8:14 122
8:16 122
9:55 .... 285 n.101
10:1 ..... 121, 126 n.129
10:3 ..... 121, 126 n.129
11:1-11 121
12:3 .... 128 n.135
13:12 ..... 148, 179, 180
18:7 180
18:12 148
19:28 .... 285 n.101

Ruth

4:7 .... 288 n.110
4:11 .... 97 n.29

I Samuel

2:10 .... 115 n.98
2:13 .... 148, 180
2:20 .... 285 n.101
4:18 .... 128 n.134
7:6 21
8:3 149
8:4 123
8:5ff 134
8:5 133
8:5-6 132
8:9 .... 148, 180
8:11 148
8:20 134
9 185
9:16 185
9:17 185
10:26 148

12:1-5	135
12:2	135
12:5	135
12:7	25 n.43, 30
24:16	116, 125
24:18	30, 31, 84 n.151
26:23	30, 79
27:5	285 n.101
27:11	148
29:4	285 n.101
30:25	149

II Samuel

3:17	123
4:11	31
5:2	137 n.159
5:3	123
7	136
7:11	137
8:13	202
8:14	202
8:15	25 n.43, 30, 149, 202, 203, 209
15:1-4	136
15:2	136, 149
15:4	30, 68 n.119, 149, 202, 203
15:6	149
16:8	161 n.26
18:19	125
19:29	31, 78 n.141
19:40	285 n.101
22:21	31
22:23	149
22:25	31
23:3	30

I Kings

2:3	150
2:32	31
3:6	31
3:9	139
3:11	150
3:28	150
5:8	151
6:12	150
6:38	151, 190
7:7	150
8:45	150, 175
8:49	150, 175
8:58	150
8:59	150
8:32	31, 47, 87
9:4	150
10:9	31, 47, 68 n.119, 151, 175, 203, 209
11:33	150
18:28	151
20:40	151
21:1-16	283 n.94
22:10	97

II Kings

1:7	152, 180
1:8	152
4:1-7	288
10:9	32, 66
11:14	152, 179
15:1-5	136
17:26	151, 185, 192
17:27	151, 151
17:34	151
17:37	151
17:40	151
21:10ff	80
25:6	152

I Chronicles

6:17 174
11:2 .... 137 n.159
15:13 174
16:8-22 174
16:12 174
16:14 174
16:15 174
17:6 .... 137 n.159
18:14 ...... 47, 174, 209
23:31 174
24:19 174
28:7 174
29:17 20

II Chronicles

1:2 .... 138 n.161
4:7 175
4:20 175
6:23 47
6:35 175
6:39 175
7:17 174
8:14 174
9:8 .. 47, 68 n.119, 175
12:6 .... 47, 175
19:8 175
19:10 174
30:16 175
33:8 .... 174, 175
35:13 .... 174, 175

Ezra

3:4 173
7:10 .... 147 n.9, 173
7:25 132
9:15 .... 46, 85 n.154

Nehemiah

1:17 172
2:20 47
8:18 172
9:8 .... 47, 85 n.154
9:13 172
9:29 172
9:33 47
10:1 172
10:30 172

Esther

1:1 .... 115 n.98
1:22 .... 115 n.98
9:2 .... 115 n.98
9:28 .... 115 n.98

Job

4:7 43
4:17 22
6:29 44
8:3 .. 43, 82 n.148, 168,
.... 184, 208
9:2 43
9:15 43
9:19 168
9:20 43
9:20ff 82 n.149
9:23 21
9:24 .... 123 n.119
9:32 .... 169, 183
10:15 43
11:2 43
12:4 43
12:17 .... 123 n.119
13:18 ...... 44, 82 n.149,
.... 169, 183, 208
14:3 .... 169, 183

15:14 43
17:8 21
17:9 .... 22, 43
19:7 168
22:3 .... 22, 43
22:4 169
22:7-9 .... 99 n.38
22:19 ...... 43, 86 n.158
23:4 .... 169, 183, 43
27:2 168
27:5 43
27:6 43
27:17 ...... 43, 86 n.158
29:12-13 .... 99 n.38
29:14 42, 44, 169, 208
31:6 44
31:13 169
31:16-17 .... 99 n.38
32:1 43
32:2 43
32:9 169
33:12 43
33:26 .... 25 n.43, 44
33:32 44
34:4 168
34:5 .... 43, 82 n.149,
................168, 208
34:6 168
34:12 168
34:17 ..... 43, 82 n.148,
.... 168
34:23 169
35:2 .... 43, 169, 208
35:7 43
35:8 43
36:3 .... 43, 82 n.148
36:7 .... 168, 43
36:17 168
37:23 ..... 43, 82 n.148,
.... 168, 184, 208
40:8 ...... 82 n.148, 169

Psalms

1.................... 79
1............... 85 n.152
1:5 .... 42, 166, 207
1:6 42
2................... 137
2:10 137
4:6 43
5:9 42
5:13 42
7............... 117 n.103
7:1 42
7:7 166
7:9 .... 42, 117, 139
7:10 42
7:12 ....42, 75, 85
7:18 42
9:4 .... 74 n.131
9:5 .... 42, 167, 206
9:8 166
9:9 42
9:17 166
10:5 166
11:3 42
11:7 .... 42, 85
14:5 .... 42, 85
15:2 42
15:5 .... 87, 283 n.93
16:1 79
17:2 167
17:7 .... 128 n.135
17:55 42
18:21 42
18:23 166
18:25 42
19:10 ..... 42, 166, 206
22:9 79
22:12 .... 273 n.76
22:32 42
23:3 43

24:5	42
24:8	23 n.41
25:9	167
26:1	79
26:1-7	85
26:10	295
31:2	42
31:19	42
32:11	42
33:1	42
33:5	23 n.41, 43, 167, 206
34:16	42, 85
34:20	42
34:22	42
35:24	42
35:27	42
35:28	42
36:6	74-75
36:7	42, 167
36:11	42
37	85 n.152
37:6	42, 155 n.21b, 167, 206
37:12	42
37:16	42
37:17	42
37:25	42
37:28	42, 167
37:29	42
37:30	42, 167, 207
37:39	42
38:21	20
40:10	25 n.43, 42
40:11	42
42	42
45:5	42
45:8	43
48:11	42
48:12	166
50:6	42, 74 n.131
51:1	43 n.66
51:6	42
51:16	42
51:21	43
52:3	25 n.43
52:8	42
55:23	42, 85
58	85 n.152
58:2	43
58:11	42, 79
58:12	42
60:10	288 n.110
64:11	42
65:6	42
68:4	42
69:28	43
69:29	42
71:2	42
71:15	42
71:16	42
71:19	42
71:24	25 n.43, 42
72:1	30, 42, 207
72:1-2	167
72:2	42, 168 n.31, 207
72:3	42, 76
72:7	42
73	79, 85 n.152
76:10	166
78:72	137 n.159
81:5	166
82:2-4	99 n.38
82:3	42
85:11	42
85:12	42
85:14	42
88:13	42
89:15	43, 76, 206
89:17	42
89:28-37	58 n.100
89:31	166

92:13	42
94:15	42, 167, 207
94:21	42
96:13	42, 74 n.131, 130
97:2	43, 167, 206
97:8	166
97:11	42
97:12	42
98:2	42
98:9	42
99:4	42, 74 n.131, 167, 206
101:1	167
103:6	23 n.41, 42, 167, 206
103:17	42
105:1-15	174
105:5	168, 168 n.31, 174
105:7	168, 168 n.31, 174
105:8	168
106:3	42, 43, 168, 207
106:31	42
111:3	42
111:7	167
112:3	42
112:4	42
112:5	42
112:6	42
112:9	42
116:5	42
118:15	42
118:19	43
118:20	42
119:7	42, 166, 206
119:13	166, 168
119:20	166
119:30	166
119:32	167
119:39	166
119:40	42
119:43	166
119:52	166
119:62	42, 166, 206
119:75	42, 166, 206
119:84	166
119:91	167
119:102	166
119:106	42, 166, 206
119:108	166
119:121	42, 208
119:123	42
119:137	42, 166, 206
119:138	42
119:142	42
119:144	42
119:149	167
119:156	167
119:160	42, 116, 206
119:164	42, 166, 206
119:172	42
119:175	166
122:5	166
125:3	42
129:4	42
140:13	167
140:14	42
141:5	42
142:8	42
143:1	42
143:2	42, 166, 167
143:11	42, 75
145:7	42
145:17	42
146:7	168
146:8	42
147:19	166
147:20	166
148:11	138 n.161
149:9	166

Proverbs

1:3 .... 44, 171, 208
1:22 .... 20, 21
2:8 149
2:9 .... 44, 169
2:20 45
3:32 21
3:33 .... 44, 86 n.156
4:18 45
8:8 45
8:15 44
8:16 ...... 44, 138 n.163
8:18 .... 25 n.43, 44
8:20 .... 44, 171
9:9 44
10:2 45
10:3 .. 44, 86, 86 n.156
10:4 233
10:6 44
10:7 44
10:11 44
10:12 .... 115 n.98
10:16 44
10:20 44
10:24 44
10:25 44
10:28 44
10:31 44
10:32 44
11:3 21
11:5 44
11:6 44
11:8 44
11:9 44
11:18 44
11:19 44
11:30 44
12:3 44
12:5 .... 44, 170, 208

12:7 44
12:10 44
12:12 .... 22, 44
12:13 44
12:17 45
12:21 44
12:26 44
12:28 44
13:5 44
13:6 44
13:9 44
13:21 44
13:22 45
13:23 171
13:25 44
14:9 21
14:19 44
14:32 44
14:34 44
15:6 44
15:9 44
15:28 44
15:29 .... 44, 86 n.156
16:8 . 45, 171, 208, 210
16:10 .... 170, 171
16:11 ...... 29 n.47, 169,
.... 170
16:12 .... 44, 68
16:13 44
16:31 44
16:33 ..... 169, 170, 183
17:14 20
17:15 .... 44, 86 n.156
17:23 170
17:26 44
18:5 44
18:5-7 .... 66 n.115
18:10 .... 44, 86 n.156
18:17 45
18:19 .... 115 n.98
19:28 170

20:7 44
21:2 21
21:3 .... 44, 169, 170
21:7 171
21:12 44
21:15 ...... 44, 170, 209
21:16 21
21:18 .... 21, 44
21:19 .... 115 n.98
21:21 44
21:26 44
21:28 20
22:22 ...... 97 n.29, 233
23:24 44
23:29 .... 115 n.98
24:15 44
24:16 44
24:23 170
24:24 44
25:5 44
25:26 44
26:21 .... 115 n.98
28:1 44
28:5 171
28:12 44
28:18 21
28:28 44
29:2 44
29:4 .... 170, 171
29:6 44
29:7 44
29:16 44
29:26 ....169, 170
29:27 44
31:9 .... 115, 186

Ecclesiastes

3:16 45, 172, 209, 210
3:17 45
5:7 .... 172, 209

5:8 .... 45, 186
7:14 .... 86 n.157
7:15 45
7:16 45
7:20 45
8:5 171
8:6 171
8:14 .... 45, 86 n.156
9:1 .... 45, 86 n.156
9:2 .... 45, 86 n.157
11:9 171
12:14 ....171, 172

Isaiah

1:2ff..................... 262
1:10-17 . 254, 260, 266
1:11-15 254
1:13-17 250
1:16-17 ....254, 257
1:17 .... 21, 71 n.126,
.... 99 n.38, 153, 257
1:21 .... 33, 71 n.126,
.... 153, 219, 243, 253,
.... 256 n.31
1:23 ......294, 295, 298,
.............................299
1:26 33
1:27 . 23 n.41, 33, 152,
.... 243
2:1-4 .... 189, 190
2:4 189
3:2-4 .... 123 n.119
3:10 33
3:12 ....281, 284
3:12-15 .... 273 n.75,
......................275, 282
3:13 ...... 115, 116, 272
3:13-15 284
3:14 ... 116 n.102, 152,
.... 153, 154, 183

Index

3:14-15 272
3:14ff 71 n.126
3:16-17 .... 272 n.73
3:18-23 272
3:18-24 271
3:24 274
4:4 152
5:1 153
5:1-7 251
5:1-14 .... 254 n.26
5:2 252
5:4 253
5:5-6 253
5:6 253
5:7 .. 33,71 n.126, 153,
.... 219, 244, 252, 253,
..... 254 n.26, 256 n.31
5:8 . 208 n.4, 244, 275,
..... 280, 282, 285, 290
5:8-9 .... 254 n.26
5:10-12 244
5:16 64, 74 n.131, 152
5:22 .... 208 n.4
5:23 .... 33, 66 n.115,
67 n.117, 71 n.127, 87,
..... 271, 292, 293, 294
6 .... 266, 267
9:6 .... 22, 33, 152
9:6-7 270
9:7 30
10:1 ....152, 285
10:1-2 .... 208 n.4, 298,
.... 299
10:1-4 286
10:1ff 71 n.126
10:2 .... 99 n.38, 152
10:22 32
11:1-4 270
11:4 .... 22, 32
11:4-5 .... 67 n.117
11:5 76

11:15 33
13:6 .... 304 n.145
13:9 .... 304 n.145
16:5.33, 152, 186, 270
24:5 125
24:16 .... 85 n.154
26:2 33
26:7 33
26:8 154
26:9 .... 32, 152
26:10 33
26:28 179
28:6 .... 152, 153
28:14 218
28:15 125
28:17 .... 33, 152, 217
28:26 152
29:21.33, 66 n.115, 87
30:18 152
32:1 .... 33, 154, 270
32:7 152
32:16 154
32:16-17 270
32:17 33
33 .... 33 n.53
33:5 .... 32, 152
33:8 125
33:14-16 295
33:15 33
33:15 .... 294, 295
33:22 .... 138 n.161
34:5 152
34:8 .... 304 n.145
38:29 20
39:8 20
40-55 77
40:2 78
40:14 156
40:27 156
41;1 156
41:2 34

41:10 34
41:10 .... 75 n.134
41:21-29 156
41:26 .... 22, 34
42:1 154
42:3 154
42:4 154
42:6 .... 34, 75 n.134
42:21 34
43:9 34
34:10 78
43:26 .... 34, 75
44:28 .... 137 n.159
45:8 34
45:13 ...... 34, 75 n.134
45:15 .... 128 n.135
45:19 34
45:19-21 75
45:21 ...... 34, 85 n.154
45:23 34
45:24 34
45:25 34
46:12 .... 23 n.38, 34
46:13 . 23, 34,78 n.140
48:1 34
48:18 34
49............................ 77
49:4 ..... 78 n.142, 154,
.... 155
49:8 77
50:8 .... 34, 78 n.142,
.... 156, 203
51:1 34
51:4 .... 155 n.21b, 156
51:5 .... 34, 78 n.140
51:6 34
51:7 34
51:8 34
52:10 .... 78 n.140
53:7 155
53:8 154

54:14 34
54:17 ..... 34, 154, 155,
.... 203
56:1 .. 22, 34, 157, 203
57:1 34
57:12 34
58:2 .... 34, 156, 203
58:8 34
59:4 34
59:8 155
59:9 .... 34, 155, 204
59:11 155
59:14 ...... 34, 155, 204
59:15 155
59:16 .... 23 n.41, 34
59:17 34
60:17 34
60:21 34
61:3 34
61:8 156
61:10 .... 22, 34
61:11 34
62:1 34
62:2 34
63:1 34
64:4 34
64:5 34

Jeremiah

1:16 157
3:11 .... 35, 36 n.57
3:12 35
3:15 .... 137 n.159
4:1 .... 36 n.57
4:22 5 n.43, 35, 158, 205
4:12 157
5:1 159
5:4 157
5:5 157
5:28 159

7:5 158
8:7 157
9:22 204
9:23 .... 35, 158, 204
10:24 ...... 145 n.6, 159
11:20 35, 74 n.131, 76
12:1 35, 85 n.154, 204
12:1ff 80
17:11 158
20:12 36
21:12 159
22:1 193
22:3 36, 71 n.126, 158,
.... 185, 193, 204
22:5 194
22:8-9 194
22:13 ... 71 n.126, 158,
.... 205
22:15 .... 71 n.126, 158
22:15-16 205
22:16 116
23:1ff 71 n.126
23:4 .... 137 n.159
23:5 35, 158, 204, 205
23:6 .... 35, 205
26:11 .... 158, 161 n.26
26:16 .... 158, 159
30:11 159
30:18 .... 159, 190
31:23 35
31:29 80
32:7 159
32:8 159
33:15 ..... 35, 158, 204,
.... 205
33:16 35
39:5 157
46:10 303
46:28 ...... 145 n.6, 159
48:21 157
49:12 160

50:7 35
51 61
51:9 157
51:10 ... 25 n.43, 35, 61
52:9 157

Lamentations

1:18 45
3:35 172
3:59 172
4:13 45

Ezekiel

3:20 .... 36, 81
3:21 36
5:6 160
5:7 160
5:8 160
7:23 161
7:27 160
11:12 .... 160, 178
11:20 160
13:22 .... 38, 81
14:14 .... 37, 81 n.147
14:20 .... 37, 81 n.147
16 60
16:38 160
16:51 37,81
16:51-52 60
16:52 37,81
18:5 .... 36, 161, 205
18:5-9 .... 36 n.59
18:8 161
18:9 .... 37, 160, 205
18:17 160
18:19 ...... 37, 81 n.147,
.... 161, 205
18:20 .... 37, 81
18:21 37

18:22 37
18:24 .... 36, 81
18:26 36
18:27 ...... 37, 161, 205
20:11 160
20:13 160
20:16 160
20:18 160
20:19 160
20:21 160
20:24 160
20:25 160
21:8 37
21:9 37
21:32 161
22:12 .... 283 n.93
22:29 161
23:24 160
23:45 37, 81, 160, 205
33:12 36
33:13 36
33:14 37
33:16 ...... 37, 161, 205
33:18 36
33:19 37
34:16 161
36:27 160
37:24 160
39:18 .... 273 n.76
39:21 160
42:1 190
42:11 162
44:24 194
45:9 37
45:9 81
45:9 162
45:9 205
45:10 .... 29 n.47, 37,
.... 69 n.123, 81

Daniel

4:24 .... 23 n.39
6:23 21
8:12 20
8:14 .... 46, 61
9:4 85 n.154, 172, 196
9:5 ....172, 196
9:7 .... 46, 196
9:8 196
9:9 196
9:11 196
9:13 20
9:14 46
9:16 .... 23 n.41, 46
9:18 46
9:24 46
12:3 46

Hosea

2:20 125
2:21 .... 38, 162, 244
5:1 162
5:11 162
6:4-6 .... 269 n.66
6:5 ....117, 162
6:6 ....257, 258
6:7 74 n.130, 125, 162
7............................ 137
7:3 137
7:5 137
7:7 ...... 123 n.119, 137
8:1 .... 74 n.130, 125
9:1 236
9:10 230
10:1 76
10:4 125
10:4 162
10:12 38
10:12 .... 71 n.126

Index

11:1	230
12:2	125
12:7	163
12:10	230
13:4	230
13:5	230
13:10	138 n.163
14:4	300 n.137
14:10	38

Joel

2:20	39
2:23	39, 51
2:26-27	39

Amos

1-2	74 n.132
1:9	125
2:3	138 n.163
2:6	39, 87, 88, 89, 287, 288 n.111
2:6-7	70, 275
2:6-8	286
2:8	246, 249. 275, 287 n.108
2:9-11	230
2:11-12	226
3:1-2	230
3:13-15	250
3:14-15	271, 274
3:25	304
4:1	271
4:1ff	273
4:2f	274
4:4	248
4:4-5	258, 259, 260
4:4-13	260 n.40
4:4f	246
5:4-5	258, 259, 260
5:5	246
5:7	39, 71 n.126, 163, 213, 214, 216, 261, 297
5:10	97 n.29
5:11	271, 274, 275, 286
5:12	39, 87, 88, 89, 97 n.29, 271, 292, 296, 298
5:14	97 n.29
5:15	71 n.126, 163, 297
5:18	208 n.4
5:18-20	304, 304 n.145
5:18ff	77 n.138, 303
5:21-23	248, 266
5:21-24	244, 250, 258, 260, 261, 265, 271, 304
5:21ff	246
5:22	260 n.41, 266
5:23-24	244 n.4, 246, 247, 247 n.9
5:24	39, 71 n.126, 163, 214, 261, 261 n.43, 266
5:25	74 n.130, 265
5:27	246
6:1	208 n.4
6:4	208 n.4, 271
6:4-6	274
6:6-11	226
6:12	39, 71 n.126, 163, 214, 216, 217, 261
7:10	229
7:10-13	227
8:2	236
8:3	264
8:3	304 n.146
8:4-6	275, 286

8:5 .... 69 n.123, 288,
.... 291 n.120
8:6 89, 287, 288 n.111
8:9 .... 304 n.146
8:9-10 . 304 n.147, 305
8:10 ....246, 248
9:7 230

Micah

2:1-2 ..... 275, 289, 292
2:1ff 71 n.126, 245
2:2 290
2:6 291
2:8 292
2:8ff 71 n.126
3:1 ....163, 164
3:1-3 .... 71 n.126, 298,
......................300, 301
3:1ff 245
3:8 164
3:9 .... 163, 164, 245
3:9-11 ... 298, 300, 301
3:9ff 71 n.126
3:11 ...... 245, 294, 295
3:12 236
4:1-3 ....
5:4 .... 137 n.159
6:1-5 261
6:1-8 261
6:3-5 .... 262, 263
6:5 40
6:6-7 ..... 262, 263, 265
6:6-8 .... 245, 250
6:8 ....164, 263
7:3 .... 123 n.119,
.... 138 n.163
7:8-20 .... 40 n.64
7:9 .... 21, 40, 164, 244
7:14 .... 273 n.76

Nahum

3:1 .... 161 n.26

Habakkuk

1:4 77 n.139, 164, 206
1:7 164
1:12 164
1:13 .... 40, 77 n.139
1:14 40
2:4 ....

Zephaniah

1:16 303
2:3 .... 41, 165
3 195
3:3 .... 123 n.119,
.... 138 n.163
3:5 .... 41, 85 n.154,
... 155 n.21b, 165, 195
3:8 ....165, 195
3:15 165

Zechariah

3:7 .... 115 n.98
7:9 165
8:8 41
8:16 165
9:9 41

Malachi

2:17 165
3:3 41
3:5 166
3:18 41
3:20 42
3:22 166

Tobit

4:10 .... 23 n.40
7:9 .... 23 n.40

Sirach

3:30 .... 23 n.40
7:10 .... 23 n.40
29:12 .... 23 n.40

Matthew

21:5 .... 41 n.65

John

12:14-15 .... 41 n.65

www.ingramcontent.com/pod-product-compliance
Lightning Source LLC
Chambersburg PA
CBHW061423300426
44114CB00014B/1514